# Database Design and SQL for DB2

## James Cooper

MC PRESS

MC Press Online, LLC
Boise, ID 83703

**Database Design and SQL for DB2**
James Cooper

First Edition
First Printing—March 2013

MC Press offers excellent discounts on this book when ordered in quantity for bulk purchases or special sales, which may include custom covers and content particular to your business, training goals, marketing focus, and branding interest.

*Corporate Offices:* MC Press Online, LLC, 3695 W. Quail Heights Court, Boise, ID 83703-3861 USA
*Sales and Customer Service:* (208) 629-7275 ext. 500; service@mcpressonline.com
*Permissions and Special Orders:* mcbooks@mcpressonline.com

Additional material related to this book, including exercises, assignments, case studies, and instructor materials, can be found on the companion website: *www.jcooperbooks.com*.

ISBN: 978-1-58347-357-3

*To*

*My wife Liane*

*and daughters Lisa and Amy*

# ACKNOWLEDGMENTS

Books do not get published without the help of many people. Without the aid of the following individuals, this edition would not have been possible.

My special thanks to Katie Tipton at MC Press Online for her exceptional editing and layout of the manuscript. In addition, a special thank you goes to Jeff Phillips, Marketing Director, and Dan DiPinto, Graphic Designer, for the cover design.

A special word of thanks to those members of the IBM i college and business community who showed their support and encouragement for writing a Database Design and SQL book. Many thanks also to the following people for their many helpful suggestions and contributions: Herb Kronholm, Mid-State Technical College; Brian Lord, Delaware Technical and Community College; Ted Tucker, Metropolitan Community College; and Saad Yousuf, Gateway Technical College.

A special thank you also goes to several individuals who with their invaluable knowledge have provided support over the years and have always been there to respond quickly with comments, solutions, and advice to my many questions: Jon Paris and Susan Gantner, Partner400; Niels Lissburg, Chief Software Architect, System & Method International; and Kent Milligan, Senior DB2 Consultant, IBM.

# CONTENTS At a Glance

# CONTENTS

# INTRODUCTION

Structured Query Language (SQL) is the standard language used with relational database management systems. Some common relational DBMSs that use SQL include DB2, Microsoft SQL Server, MySQL, and Oracle.

SQL can be used to perform tasks such as updating data in a database or retrieving data from a database. Although database systems use SQL, most of them also have their own additional proprietary extensions that are usually used only on their system. This book focuses on SQL for DB2. However, the standard SQL commands can be used across all SQL implementations to accomplish everything that needs to done with a database.

This book provides that understanding to students and practicing developers. Once you master the topics covered in *Database Design and SQL for DB2*, you will be able to design and create *professional-level* databases for real applications. A professional developer requires skills in several areas, including modeling the system, designing the system implementation, and implementing the system's database and software. In other words, you need to understand a system from the user's point of view, design a suitable system conceptually, and then implement it. You cannot neglect any of these areas and expect much success. That is why this book gives developers extensive advice on database *design* as well as *programming*.

## INTENDED AUDIENCE

This book is intended for readers with no previous database design or SQL experience as well as for professionals with background in the computing field. It has been specially designed for use in two- and four-year college and university courses on database design and SQL. It also works well for developers and can serve in place of IBM's database-related manuals. All the essential SQL and related DB2 topics are covered from an introductory to an advanced level.

## COMPANION WEBSITE

The companion website for this book is *www.jcooperbooks.com*. At this site, you will find many things that enhance the material in the book, including additional end-of-chapter exercises, assignments, and case studies. The companion website is updated continuously, so please check back often to see what is new.

## INSTRUCTORS

On the companion website, instructors will find end-of-chapter material for each chapter in the book. In addition, you will find Microsoft® PowerPoint® slides, assignments, projects, tests, and other material that can be used to enhance your course. Some material will require a user ID and password to access the content.

## STUDENTS

On the companion website, students will find the data files used in the book. In addition, the site provides links to important websites and numerous examples of RPG web applications.

## CONTRIBUTORS

Everyone has an opportunity to contribute to the companion website. If you wish to contribute presentation slides, tests, assignments, RPG web applications, or other material that would enhance the teaching and learning experience, locate the contributor section on the companion website and follow the instructions.

This book will be updated regularly so students and professionals are offered the most modern and up-to-date material on database design and SQL. Your comments and suggestions are welcome. Jim Cooper can be reached via e-mail at *Jim.Cooper@LambtonCollege.ca*.

# CHAPTER 1

## DATABASE CONCEPTS

## CHAPTER OBJECTIVES

Upon completion of this chapter, you should be able to:

- Define database and database management system
- Describe the steps for the database development process
- Explain the purpose of conceptual, logical, and physical database design
- Explain the relational database model

## INTRODUCTION TO DATABASE AND DATABASE MANAGEMENT SYSTEM

A **database management system** (**DBMS**) is a set of software programs that control the organization, storage, and retrieval of data in a database. A **database** is an organized collection of related tables that can be joined to provide information to users. Common relational database management systems that include Structured Query Language (SQL) are IBM® DB2®, Microsoft SQL Server®, MySQL, Oracle®, Sybase, and others.

A DBMS is a software system that uses a standard method of cataloging, retrieving, and running queries on data. The DBMS manages incoming data, organizes it, and provides ways for the data to be modified or extracted by users or other programs.

A DBMS lets users create and access data in a database. The DBMS manages database requests so users and programs do not have to understand where the data are physically located on disk or who else may be accessing the data. In handling database requests, the DBMS ensures the integrity of the data; that is, it makes sure the data are available and are organized as intended. In addition, the DBMS provides security by ensuring that only those users and programs with access privileges can access the data.

## RELATIONAL DATABASE MODEL

The foundation of most commercial database management systems today is the **relational database model**, which was first introduced in the paper "A Relational Model of Data for Large Shared Data Banks," published by Edgar Codd in 1970 [*Communications of the ACM* 13 (6): 377–387]. Since the publication of this paper, the relational model has been developed extensively into common relational database management systems such as DB2, Microsoft SQL Server, MySQL, Oracle, and others. In addition to relational databases, there are also hierarchical, network, and object-oriented databases.

## THE DB2 DATABASE

**DB2** refers to an entire family of IBM databases:

- DB2 for i
- DB2 for z/OS
- DB2 for Linux, UNIX and Windows (also referred to as DB2 LUW)

This book uses the IBM database management system DB2 for i, which is referred to simply as "DB2" throughout the book.

**DB2 for i** is an integrated part of IBM i, the operating system that runs IBM's System i® hardware platform. DB2 is not purchased as a separate software product, and any application can take advantage of its features. DB2 provides a DBMS that all computer programs use to access data stored in DB2 databases.

As mentioned, a database is an organized collection of related tables that can be joined to provide information to users. In the DB2 database approach, tables are defined independently of any applications that use them. Data remains in independent, simple, linear tables, but indexes are created that indicate how the rows of the different tables relate to each other in the sense of the join concept. These indexes can be created before any queries are run, or they can be created at run time as the join query is executed.

## DATABASE TERMINOLOGY

There are two groups of terms used interchangeably when discussing databases. The reason there are two sets of terms is that before the use of SQL, people used traditional system terms. With SQL, a new set of terms more representative of a typical spreadsheet type of relational table became more common. Thus, the non-SQL world sometimes uses different terms than the SQL world uses. The table in Figure 1-1 shows the relationship between the SQL relational database terms and the non-SQL terms.

| SQL term | Non-SQL term |
|---|---|
| *Schema.* A logical grouping consisting of a library, a journal, a journal receiver, an SQL catalog, and optionally a data dictionary. A schema groups related objects and lets the objects be found by name. | *Library.* Groups related objects and allows the objects to be found by name. |
| *Table.* A set of columns and rows. | *Physical file.* A set of records. |
| *Row.* The horizontal part of a table containing a set of columns. | *Record.* A set of fields. |
| *Column.* The vertical part of a table of one data type. | *Field.* One or more characters of related information of one data type. |
| *View.* A subset of columns and rows of one or more tables. | *Logical file.* A subset of fields and records of one or more physical files. |
| *Package.* An object type that is used to run SQL statements. | *SQL package.* An object type that is used to run SQL statements. |

FIGURE 1-1    Relationships between SQL terms and non-SQL terms

## THE IMPORTANCE OF DATABASE DESIGN

Database design is an important stage of a development project that should precede the coding and creation of a database. Before creating database tables, one should know exactly *what* kinds of tables need to be created. Consider how meaningless it would be to create a customer table before knowing what customer data a company needed to have. For example, some companies might need to know their customers' occupations, while others might not care what their customers do for a living. The general requirement for database tables, of course, is to store data that the organization needs so the data can be used effectively. Determining exactly what those needs are and how best to implement a database that meets the requirements clearly should happen *before* coding begins.

Determining business requirements and documenting them, including both data and processes that use data, are tasks often collectively referred to as "modeling" because the result of the effort is a model, usually in diagrams, of the way the business works and the data it uses. The part of this effort that concentrates on the organization's data requirements is called **database design**.

Once a data model is completed, there is a specification of what data needs to be stored and at least some of the ways in which the data is used. For example, the data model for a particular company might specify that the company needs to keep track of customers, including their names, shipping and billing addresses, telephone and fax numbers, and credit ratings. This data model might also document that the company needs complete customer lists, in order by the customers' names. From this model or specification, one can then decide which data should be stored in database tables. A data model says *what* the organization needs, not *how* a system will be implemented to address those needs.

A system to provide for storing, updating, and retrieving the data specified in a particular data model might be implemented in any number of ways. The task of deciding how to implement a system for a particular data model is called physical database design or database design. The term "database design" is often used as an abbreviated way to refer to both the logical data modeling and the physical database design processes.

A database model identifies what data are to be stored in a database, how the data will be used, and how the tables in the database are related to each other. A database model that is well designed reduces the need for changes. The final development step, or actual **database implementation**, is the coding and creation of the database tables according to the database design specification.

## DATABASE DEVELOPMENT PROCESS

As mentioned, a database is an organized collection of related tables that can be joined to provide information to users. The collection of related tables that comprise a database can be quite complex to develop. Because of this, it is important that a set of steps be followed in the development of a database so users can retrieve the necessary information when needed and in a timely way. The process of doing database design generally consists of a number of steps that are carried out by a systems analyst or database designer. Not all of these steps are necessary in all cases. Logically, the steps flow sequentially; however, in practice it is common to skip around as knowledge about the system being developed is gathered. The database design process may include the following steps:

1. Database planning
2. Requirements analysis—Focused on the requirements that need to be represented in the system
3. Database design—The conceptual and logical database design
4. Physical database design
5. DBMS selection—Based on hardware and operating system
6. Database implementation—Creating the database
7. Testing and evaluation—Testing and evaluating the database to determine whether all user requirements have been met

8. Database deployment—Placing the database into production
9. Database maintenance—Maintaining the database system according to user needs

The primary purpose of this book is to focus on the design and implementation of databases. For that reason, this book focuses on database design and database implementation.

## DATABASE PLANNING

The database planning phase begins when a customer submits a request for the development of an information system project. It consists of a set of tasks or activities that decide both the resources required in the database development and the time limits of different activities. During the planning phase, four major activities are performed:

- Review and approve the database project request.
- Prioritize the database project request.
- Allocate resources such as money, people, and tools.
- Arrange a development team to develop the database project.

Database planning should also include the development of standards that govern how data will be collected, how the format should be specified, and what documentation will be needed.

Before embarking on a major data modeling project, the developer should get two things in order: naming conventions and how to store the gathered information. Many business applications involve hundreds of variable names, and keeping them organized in data modeling can be difficult. Establish abbreviation and naming standards for data model objects such as tables, columns, relationships, domains, and programs. Most important, make sure names are consistent and express clearly what an item represents or stores.

Following the naming standard, one table should be created for valid abbreviations that can be used to form names, and another table should be created for valid names. In other words, before starting to generate names, know how they are going to be formed. It may be necessary to record a lot of information about names, including synonyms, preferred usage, a description, and short, standard, and long variations.

Once naming standards have been established and a place to track the names has been settled on, the next step is to create a **data dictionary**. A data dictionary is not one thing. It is many things: all the containers used to hold everything that is recorded during the modeling process. A typical project might have some word-processing documents that contain descriptions of business rules or processes, a database table that contains table and column names and brief descriptions, and some entity relationship diagrams. Together, all these records of the data model make up the data dictionary.

It is good practice to establish naming standards and tables before creating too many other computer-based data dictionary objects, such as documents and files, because as the data model progresses, it is important for the dictionary objects as well as the business objects to follow a rational naming standard.

## REQUIREMENTS ANALYSIS

The first step in developing an information system is the requirements analysis usually conducted by a systems analysis. The purpose of the **requirements analysis** is to gather the business requirements so they can be used in the development of a data model. This step involves gathering information about processes, entities (categories of data), and organizational units. After this information is collected, it is used in the database design step. The diagrams produced should show the processes and data that exist as well as the relationships between business processes and data.

Data modeling goes together with systems analysis, and the two occur together as a development project proceeds. Systems analysis includes discovering such aspects as how orders are entered and fulfilled and how customer credit limits are calculated. Obviously, the description of a process requires referring to the data model to identify where some of the values used in calculations come from and where user input and the results of calculations are stored. The data model may also refer to process definitions for actions that are triggered when some change occurs in the database.

During the requirements analysis phase, the requirements and expectations of the users are collected and analyzed. The collected requirements help to understand what the new system will accomplish. The goal of this phase is essentially to understand how the company works, discover what problems and limitations users have, understand what the company wishes to accomplish, and define the scope and boundaries of the project. The scope and boundaries are essential to make sure the database is created exactly as specified.

Much of the information is developed from interviewing end users or reading procedure manuals, forms, and other sources that explain how the business works. Thus, when talking to an end user or reading a procedure manual, the developer may learn things that are covered in several of the later steps of the process. The first conversation may provide enough information to enable the development of a broad overview of the most important entities and their interrelationships, with details being filled in through further conversations and reading documents.

In most cases, a person who is doing the design of a database is a person with expertise in the area of database design rather than expertise in the area within the company from which the data to be stored is drawn (e.g., financial, manufacturing, transportation). Therefore, the data to be stored in the database must be determined in cooperation with the people who have expertise in that area and are aware of what data must be stored within the system. This process is one that is generally considered part of requirements analysis, and it requires skill on the part of the analyst to obtain the needed information from those with the knowledge. This is because the individuals with the necessary knowledge frequently cannot express clearly what their system requirements for the database are because they are unaccustomed to thinking in terms of the data elements that must be stored.

## DATABASE DESIGN

With a good idea of what the organization needs to keep track of and how that data is used, the next step is to decide how best to implement a system to support the organization's requirements. Suppose the business has customers; is it obvious that a customer database table is required? What if the business has fairly independent divisions in different regions of the country? Should there be a single customer table at the home office, or should there be separate tables in each regional office? Questions such as these are answered in the database design stage, which follows the data requirements analysis stage.

After all the requirements have been gathered for a proposed database, they must be modeled. Database design is the process of producing a detailed data model of the database that will meet end-user requirements. Models are created to visually represent the proposed database so that business requirements can easily be associated with database objects to ensure that all requirements have been completely and accurately gathered. Different types of diagrams are typically produced to illustrate the business processes, rules, entities, and organizational units that have been identified. The actual model is frequently called an **entity relationship model (ERM)** because it depicts data in terms of the entities and relationships described in the data. An entity relationship model is an abstract conceptual representation of structured data. Basically, data modeling serves as a link between business needs and system requirements.

Designers create an abstract data model that attempts to model real-world objects by creating a conceptual design. Designers must consider end-user views; define entities, attributes, and relationships; and identify processes and access requirements. The conceptual design is then translated into the logical design, which is DBMS-dependent. Database design includes three design steps:

1. Conceptual database design
2. Logical database design
3. Physical database design

The significance of this approach is that it allows the three perspectives to be relatively independent of each other. Storage technology can change without affecting either the conceptual or the logical model. The table/column structure can change without (necessarily) affecting the conceptual model. In each case, of course, the structures must remain consistent with the other model. The table/column structure may be different from a direct translation of the entity classes and attributes, but it must ultimately carry out the objectives of the conceptual entity class structure. Early phases of many software development projects emphasize the design of a conceptual data model. Such a design can be detailed into a logical data model. In later stages, this model may be translated into a physical data model.

## CONCEPTUAL DATABASE DESIGN

**Conceptual database design** is the process of constructing a data model from the information collected in the requirements analysis phase. The **conceptual model** is a representation of an organization's data, organized in terms of entities, attributes, and relationships; it is independent of any particular DBMS. This phase is independent of physical considerations and involves constructing an ER model and checking the model for redundancy.

## ER MODEL

A pictorial representation of the real-world problem in terms of entities, attributes, and relations between the entities is referred as an entity relationship diagram (ERD). An ERD includes:

- *Entities:* An entity is a class of distinct identifiable objects or concepts.
- *Attributes:* Attributes are properties or characteristics of entities.
- *Relations:* Relations are associations between or among entities.

## LOGICAL DATABASE DESIGN

**Logical database design** consists of converting the entity relationship diagram from the conceptual model into tables or relational schemas in normal forms using a technique called normalization.

Once the relationships and dependencies amongst the various pieces of information have been determined in the conceptual model, it is possible to arrange the data into a logical structure, which can then be mapped into the storage objects supported by the database management system. In the case of relational databases, the storage objects are tables that store data in rows and columns.

Each table may represent an implementation of either a logical object or a relationship joining one or more instances of one or more logical objects. Relationships between tables may then be stored as links connecting child tables with parents. Because complex logical relationships are themselves tables, they will probably have links to more than one parent.

The logical data model contains all the needed logical and physical design choices and physical storage parameters needed to generate a design in a data definition language, which can then be used to create a database. A fully attributed data model contains detailed attributes for each entity.

### NORMALIZATION OF TABLES

Normalization is used to check the entity relationship model and help eliminate redundancy and other anomalies in the database. Some splitting and even recombination of entity types may result from normalization, and the entity relationship model will have to be updated accordingly. The entity relationship model and the table definitions resulting from normalization should be consistent.

## PHYSICAL DATABASE DESIGN

**Physical database design** consists of creating tables in the selected DBMS according to the requirements that were established during logical modeling. Conceptual and logical modeling mainly involves gathering the requirements of the business, with the latter part of logical modeling directed toward the goals and requirements of the database. Physical modeling deals with the conversion of the logical, or business, model into a relational database model. When physical modeling occurs, objects are being defined at the schema level. A schema is a group of related objects in a database. A database design effort is normally associated with one schema.

During physical modeling, objects such as tables and columns are created based on entities and attributes that were defined during the conceptual and logical design phases of database design. Constraints are also defined, including primary keys, foreign keys, other unique keys, and check constraints. Views can be created from database tables to summarize data or to simply provide the user with another perspective of certain data. Other objects, such as indexes, can also be defined during physical modeling. Physical modeling is when all the pieces come together to complete the process of defining a database for a business.

Physical modeling is database-software–specific, meaning that the objects defined during physical modeling can vary depending on the relational database software being used. For example, most relational database systems have variations in the way data types are represented and the way data is stored, although basic data types are conceptually the same among different implementations. In addition, some database systems have objects that are not available in other database systems.

Physical database design is the process that weighs the alternative implementation possibilities and carefully lays out exactly how tables and other elements of the system will be implemented. For the database implementation, the most important tangible result of the design is a set of table layouts, including detailed column specifications. Other important elements of the database design are specific end-user views of the data and various integrity constraints that must be enforced. The database design details how these elements will be implemented with a particular database system.

The physical design of the database specifies the physical configuration by which data are stored on the storage media. This step involves describing the base relations, file organizations, and index design used to achieve efficient access to the data, as well as any associated integrity constraints and security measures.

## DATA MODEL VS. PHYSICAL DESIGN

The logical data model and the physical database design are quite different in their objectives, goals, and content. The table shown in Figure 1-2 provides a comparison between logical data modeling and physical database design.

| Logical data modeling | Physical database design |
|---|---|
| Includes entities, attributes, and relationships | Includes tables, columns, keys, data types, validation rules, database triggers, stored procedures, and access constraints |
| Uses business names for attributes | Uses abbreviated column names that are limited by the DBMS being used |
| Is independent of the technology that will be used to implement the database | Defines primary keys and indexes for fast data access |
| Is normalized to at least third normal form | May be denormalized to meet performance requirements |

FIGURE 1-2    Differences between logical data modeling and physical database design

## DBMS SELECTION

In many situations, the DBMS selection phase is a formality. The reason for this is many companies have already determined and implemented the hardware and a DBMS, and all future information systems are developed for their specific DBMS. Once a company determines the DBMS and the hardware on which it is going to run, the expense and person-hours required to change systems prohibits such a change.

However, there are situations in which this phase applies. Consider a company that decides to implement a new database structure and also decides to change hardware vendors and thus the DBMS. In this phase, an appropriate DBMS is selected to support the information system.

A number of factors are involved in DBMS selection, including technical and economic factors. The technical factors concern the suitability of the DBMS for information systems. The following technical factors are considered:

- Type of DBMS (e.g., relational, object-oriented)
- Storage structure and access methods that the DBMS supports
- Available user and programmer interfaces
- Type of query languages
- Development and other tools

## DATABASE IMPLEMENTATION

After the design phase and selection of a suitable DBMS, the database system is implemented. The purpose of the implementation phase is to construct and install the information system according to the plan and design as described in previous phases. In this phase, the DBMS software is installed, the database (or databases) is produced, and the tables are populated with data. This phase also requires that the database performance is evaluated, security standards are set up, backup and recovery procedures are put in place, and data integrity is enforced. Finally, the database administrator must ensure that company standards are being followed by implementing and enforcing them in the database.

## TESTING AND EVALUATION

The testing and evaluation phase requires that the database is tested again for performance. It is tested during implementation; however, in this phase it is tested again and fine-tuned. Testing also requires that the administrator test integrity, security, and multi-user load.

## DATABASE MAINTENANCE

Once the database system is implemented, the maintenance phase of the database system begins. **Database maintenance** is the process of monitoring and maintaining the database system. Maintenance includes activities such as adding new columns to tables, changing the size of existing columns, adding new tables, adding new constraints, adding views, and so on. As the database system requirements change, it becomes necessary to add new tables or remove existing tables and to reorganize some tables by changing primary access methods or by dropping old indexes and constructing new ones. Some queries or transactions may be rewritten for better performance. Database tuning or reorganization continues throughout the life of the database and while the requirements continue to change.

## OPERATION

Essentially at this point, the database is fully functional. Users are allowed to fully use the system and report any issues. Any problems are resolved according to severity.

# END-OF-CHAPTER

## CHAPTER SUMMARY

1.  A database management system (DBMS):

    a.  Is a set of software programs that controls the organization, storage, and retrieval of data in a database

    b.  Uses a standard method of cataloging, retrieving, and running queries on data

    c.  Manages incoming data, organizes it, and provides ways for the data to be modified or extracted by users or other programs

2.  A database is an organized collection of related tables that can be joined to provide information to users.

3.  SQL has its own set of database terminology:

| SQL terms |
|---|
| *Schema.* A logical grouping consisting of a library, a journal, a journal receiver, an SQL catalog, and optionally a data dictionary. A schema groups related objects and lets the objects be found by name. |
| *Table.* A set of columns and rows. |
| *Row.* The horizontal part of a table containing a set of columns. |
| *Column.* The vertical part of a table of one data type. |
| *View.* A subset of columns and rows of one or more tables. |
| *Package.* An object type that is used to run SQL statements. |

4.  Before implementing database tables, the developer needs to know what the tables should contain and how they are related. This information is developed by three processes that should occur before implementation:

    a.  Conceptual database design

    b.  Logical database design

    c.  Physical database design

5.  Conceptual database design:

    a.  Is the process of constructing a data model from the information collected in the requirements analysis phase

    b.  Is a representation of an organization's data, organized in terms of entities, attributes, and relationships

    c.  Is independent of any particular database management system

    d.  Involves constructing an ER model and checking the model for redundancy

6. Logical database design:

    a. Consists of converting the entity relationship diagram from the conceptual model into tables or relational schemas
    b. Uses normal forms using a technique called normalization

7. Physical database design:

    a. Evaluates the anticipated volume of data, types of access, and available hardware, software, and personnel to decide the most effective way to implement the capabilities specified in the data model
    b. Results in a specification for the database tables, columns, and other related items
    c. Provides a design specification that is used as the basis for coding SQL and creating the actual tables

## KEY TERMS

| | |
|---|---|
| column | entity relationship model |
| conceptual database design |   (ERM) |
| conceptual model | logical database design |
| data dictionary | package |
| database | physical database design |
| database design | relational database model |
| database implementation | requirements analysis |
| database maintenance | row |
| database management system | schema |
|   (DBMS) | table |
| DB2 | view |
| DB2 for i | |

# CHAPTER 2

## CONCEPTUAL DESIGN USING ER DIAGRAMS

### CHAPTER OBJECTIVES

Upon completion of this chapter, you should be able to

- Explain conceptual data modeling
- Explain what entity relationship diagrams (ERDs) are
- Identify and explain the steps for developing an ERD
- Demonstrate the use of ERDs

### INTRODUCTION TO DATABASE DESIGN

Many steps that occur during the database design stage of a development project require some form of documentation to specify the data that the organization requires and how it is structured. Often, this documentation is reviewed by the person creating the data model, the end user, and the person responsible for the physical database design. The data model must be clear and comprehensible.

A **conceptual data model** represents the data used in an organization and the relationships between the data. A conceptual data model specifies the following items of interest to the organization:

- Entities (people, places, things, or concepts about which information must be recorded, such as customers or employees)
- Events (such as placing an order, approving a loan)
- Attributes for entities, events, and relationships (such as customers' names, dates on which orders were placed)
- Relationships among entities and events (for example, a customer places an order, a loan officer approves a loan)
- Business rules or policies (for example, a borrower must have an adjusted gross income of at least half his or her total outstanding debt)

Many of an organization's rules are already documented in policy manuals, operating guides, or other documents. These documents can be referenced in a data model without documenting every detail. If the requirement exists to track some piece of data, it is wise to clearly identify this requirement in the data model *before* coding begins.

In effect, a data model serves as a contract between the end users and the designers. As with any contract, both parties should have no question about its meaning. The data model, as a contract, specifies the *minimum* requirements for the database design. With that perspective, it is apparent that the person(s) producing the data model cannot take for granted that the person(s) doing the database design will put anything in the final design unless the data model clearly calls for it.

Database modeling is usually a two-step process. The first step is the development of a conceptual data model using an entity relationship diagram. An **entity relationship diagram** (**ERD**) is a graphical representation of the proposed database. There are four goals of ER diagrams:

- Capture all required information.
- Ensure data appears only once in the database design.
- Do not include in the data model any data that is derived from other data that is already in the data model.
- Arrange data in the data model in a logical manner.

The second step is logical data modeling, which uses a process called normalization that helps evaluate the entity relationship diagram for alternative designs. Chapter 3 discusses the normalization process.

Entity relationship diagrams are a data modeling technique that can improve the clarity and comprehensibility of a data model. An ERD is a diagram model used to organize the data in a project into entities and attributes and to define the relationships between the entities. An ERD is often used as a way to visualize a relational database. Each entity in the diagram represents a table in the relational database. The entities are connected with lines that represent the relationship between the two entities.

## DEVELOPING ENTITY RELATIONSHIP DIAGRAMS

Figure 2-1 shows a simple entity relationship diagram. This chapter examines the steps required to create such diagrams.

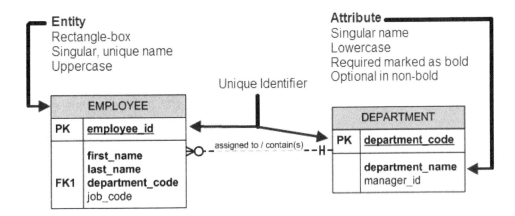

Each employee must be assigned to one and only one department.
Each department may contain zero to many employees.

FIGURE 2-1          Example of an entity relationship diagram (ERD)

After the business rules have been determined from the requirements analysis phase, database design can begin. The first step in database design in the conceptual model is where an entity relationship diagram is developed. Figure 2-2 provides a guideline for developing an ERD.

## ERD CASE STUDY

The BDE Consulting Company wants a database system to maintain employee projects. This employee project system will capture data about departments, employees, jobs, and projects. The following business rules apply:

- Each employee may be assigned to one and only one department. Some employees may not be assigned to any department. The employee data is stored in the employee entity.
- Each department could have many employees assigned to it. Some departments, however, may not have any employees assigned to them. The department data is stored in the department entity.
- Each employee may have one and only one job title. Under certain circumstances, some employees many not be assigned a job title.
- Each job title may be assigned to many employees. Some jobs titles, however, may not be assigned to any employees. The job data is stored in the job entity.

| Step | Title | Description |
|------|-------|-------------|
| 1 | Create Entities | Identify the people, places, or events about which the end users want to store data. |
| 2 | Define Attributes | Define the attributes that are essential to the system under development. For each attribute, match it with exactly one entity that it describes. |
| 3 | Identify Unique Identifier | Identify the data attribute(s) that uniquely identify one and only one occurrence of each entity. Eliminate many-to-many relationships, and include a unique identifier (UID) and foreign keys in each entity. |
| 4 | Define Relationships | Find the natural associations between pairs of entities using a relationship matrix. Arrange entities in rectangles, and join those entities with a line. |
| 5 | Determine Optionality and Cardinality | Determine the number of occurrences of one entity for a single occurrence of the related entity. |
| 6 | Name Relationships | Name each relationship between entities. |
| 7 | Eliminate Many-to-Many Relationships | Many-to-many relationships cannot be implemented into database tables because each row will need an indefinite number of attributes to maintain the many-to-many relationship. Many-to-many relationships must be converted to one-to-many relationships using associative entities. |
| 8 | Determine Data Types | Identify the data types and sizes of each attribute. |

FIGURE 2-2    Steps to develop an entity relationship diagram

- Each employee may be assigned to many projects. Sometimes, however, an employee may be off work and is not assigned to any projects.
- Each project must be assigned to at least one employee. Some projects may have several employees assigned to them. The project data is stored in the project entity.

The requirements analysis has determined that the following data is to be stored. For employees, store the employee identification, first name, last name, Social Security number, hire date, department code, and job identification. For departments, store the department code and the department name. For jobs, store the job identification, job title, minimum salary, and maximum salary. For projects, store the project identification, project title, and projected completion date.

## STEP 1: IDENTIFY ENTITIES

Study the system request to identify entities for which the company wishes to store data. This study is sometimes referred to as the entity discovery. An **entity** is something of significance to the business about which data must be stored and retrieved. An entity is named as a singular noun, such as EMPLOYEE, DEPARTMENT, JOB, PROJECT, and so on.

An entity has multiple instances. That is, an **entity instance** is a single occurrence of an entity. For example, in an EMPLOYEE entity, each employee would be an instance within the EMPLOYEE entity. The entity DEPARTMENT could have instances of engineering, planning, accounting, IT, and so on. Entities also have attributes. For example, the attributes of the EMPLOYEE entity might include employee_id, first_name, middle_initial, last_name, hire_date, and so on. The attributes of the DEPARTMENT entity might include department_code and department_name.

Determine who in the business best knows what needs to be implemented. Usually that is the end users, the people who carry out or manage the day-to-day operations of the organization. It might also be necessary to work with top-level administrators, especially if the system is ultimately to implement new ways of doing business. While speaking to end users, also collect manuals, documents, sample computer report listings, sample screen shots, and anything else that will help document the data the organization uses. Take care to make clear, written notes when talking with an end user. Record a precise description of the various objects, events, relationships, and processes that individual users or departments are concerned with. Keep the notes and collected materials well organized. This may sound like obvious advice, but keeping project material well organized is crucial to successful data modeling.

An object, such as a customer, and an event, such as placing an order, are two types of entities, or things about which facts should be recorded; these objects and events can be represented as entities. Complex objects and events may be represented by a group of entities, so there is not necessarily only one entity per object.

When an entity is discovered, be sure to enter it in the data dictionary. Here are some of the things to record about an entity:

- The official name for the entity as a singular noun, as used in the rest of the data model (e.g., EMPLOYEE)
- Synonyms, or other names for the entity that end users use or that appear on such things as forms and screens (e.g., WORKER)
- A short textual description (e.g., "Someone working for the organization under an Employment Contract or recognized as an employee for purposes of tax reporting")
- Approximate or estimated yearly volumes (e.g., "Approximately 50 new employees are hired each year; approximately 40 employees leave employment")

This information can go into word-processing documents, spreadsheets, or database tables set up for the purpose.

The first step in developing a conceptual database model is to identify entities. An entity is a real-world item for which data is collected and stored. Entities are like nouns consisting of persons, places, or things, such as students, courses, rooms, and professors. Specific examples of an entity are called instances.

Each entity is represented by a rectangle within the ERD. An entity might be thought of as a container that holds all the instances of a particular thing in a system. Entities are equivalent to database tables in a relational database, with each row of the table representing an instance of that entity. The four entities in Figure 2-3 identify the entities in the Employee Projects system as EMPLOYEE, DEPARTMENT, JOB, and PROJECT.

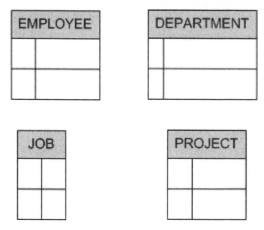

FIGURE 2-3     Example of entities for Employee Projects system

The best way to identify entities is to ask the system owners and users to identify things about which they would like to capture, store, and produce information. Another source for identifying entities is to study the forms, files, and reports generated by the current system. For example, a student registration form would refer to Student (a role) but also to Course (an event), Instructor (a role), Advisor (a role), Room (a location), and so on.

## STEP 2: IDENTIFY ATTRIBUTES

An **attribute** is a characteristic that identifies or describes an entity. Attributes are represented as columns in a database table. Attributes are single-valued. That is, each attribute can have only one value for each instance of the entity. For example, employee_id, first_name, last_name, and hire_date are attributes of the EMPLOYEE entity. Moreover, each attribute, such as `first_name` and `last_name`, can have only one value for each instance. Attribute names are listed inside an entity's rectangle as Figure 2-4 shows. Here, the `EMPLOYEE` entity contains the attributes `employee_id`, `first_name`, `last_name`, `soc_sec_no`, and `hire_date`.

```
┌─────────────────┐
│ EMPLOYEE        │
├─────────────────┤
│                 │
├─────────────────┤
│ employee_id     │
│ first_name      │
│ last_name       │
│ soc_sec_no      │
│ hire_date       │
└─────────────────┘
```

FIGURE 2-4     **Example of an entity with attributes**

## VOLATILE ATTRIBUTES

Attributes that change over time are called **volatile attributes**. For example, the attribute `age` would be a volatile attribute in the entity `EMPLOYEE` if the entity also contained the attribute `birth_date`. The attribute `age` would be considered a volatile attribute because it could be derivable from the `birth_date` attribute. Because `age` changes over time, it is considered volatile; `birth_date` is static and does not change.

Another example would be years of service. In the `EMPLOYEE` entity depicted in Figure 2-4, the `years_of_service` can be calculated using the `hire_date` attribute. Thus, `years_of_service` would be considered a volatile attribute that could be calculated when needed.

## REQUIRED AND OPTIONAL ATTRIBUTES

Each instance of an entity contains attributes that can hold a potential value. An attribute that must contain a value for each instance of the entity is called a **required** or **mandatory attribute**. For example, a `CUSTOMER` entity would contain a `customer_name` attribute that would be a required attribute. If an attribute is identified as required, it will appear as bold in the entity rectangle, as shown in Figure 2-5.

On the other hand, an attribute that may not have a value or is null is called an **optional attribute**. For example, in a `CUSTOMER` entity, the phone number and e-mail address attributes may not be required to have a value. In this situation, these attributes are considered to be optional attributes.

Notice that `employee_id`, `first_name`, `last_name`, and `soc_sec_no` in the EMPLOYEE entity are in bold, indicating that these attributes are required and must contain a value. Any remaining attributes, such as `hire_date`, are optional and can contain null values.

```
+--------------------+
|      EMPLOYEE      |
+--------------------+
|                    |
+--------------------+
|  employee_id       |
|  first_name        |
|  last_name         |
|  soc_sec_no        |
|  hire_date         |
+--------------------+
```

**FIGURE 2-5**    **Example of required and optional attributes**

## DOMAINS

Attributes have a domain. A **domain** defines two aspects of an attribute: its allowable values and the allowable operations on the attribute. By explicitly defining domains, guidelines can be established for ensuring that the implementation will not let invalid values be put into an attribute and will not improperly use the attribute in an operation. For example, with clear definitions of the domains of `hourly_wage` and `monthly_salary`, one can ensure that neither column ever contains negative values and that `hourly_wage` is not added to `monthly_salary` without conversion.

It normally is not necessary to explicitly define the entire set of allowable operations on a domain; such a definition would require the consideration of a very large number of cross-domain operations. Instead, define domains so that their allowable values and meaning are clear and so that the allowable operations can be inferred from the partial definition. Start by recording a concise, clear, verbal description of each domain, including its allowable values and constraints on operations. Once domains are defined, the appropriate domain name can be added to each attribute definition.

## TIME-DEPENDENT ATTRIBUTES

Identify which attributes are time-dependent. For example, if a part's cost must be known on different dates, cost is a **time-dependent attribute**.

## DEFAULT VALUES

Identify, for each attribute, whether there is a default value that should be used if no explicit value is supplied when a new instance is added.

## DOCUMENTING ATTRIBUTES

As various attributes that are important to the organization become known, identify them with at least the following information:

- The official name for the attribute (column), as used in the data model (e.g., `annual_salary`).
- A short textual description (e.g., "The annual gross pay before taxes for an employee").
- The source in the business process (e.g., "Defined in employee's Employment Contract").
- The allowable values for the attribute (e.g., `salary > 0`).
- Whether a value for the attribute is required or optional.
- The default value, if any, to be used for a new attribute.
- Whether the attribute is part of a unique identifier, candidate key, or foreign key.
- Whether the attribute is a direct or a derived attribute. Direct attributes cannot be derived from other attributes. For example, an employee's name is a direct attribute. An employee's number of months in service is a derived attribute because it can be calculated from the starting and ending dates in the employee's employment history. An employee's annual salary might be direct, or it might be derived, as in the case when there is also a monthly salary attribute from which the annual salary can be computed.

At this stage of the data model, do not worry about all the details of each attribute. Some items that at first are considered attributes might later turn out to be entities. For example, a product's color might first be mentioned by a salesperson as a simple (atomic) type of value, such as red, green, or blue. But someone in manufacturing might view color as an entity, with its own attributes, including chemical components or suppliers. With a data modeling technique that is based on the relational model, this kind of adjustment is straightforward; those tables that had `color` as a column now would have `color_id` as a foreign key referencing the unique identifier of the COLOR table.

An attribute is a characteristic common to all instances of an entity. In this step, identify and name all the attributes essential to the system. The best way to do this is to study the forms, files, and reports currently kept by the users of the system and to circle each data item on the paper copy. Cross out those that will not be transferred to the new system, extraneous items such as signatures, and constant information that is the same for all instances of the form, such as the company name and address. The remaining circled items should represent the attributes required. Always verify these items with your system users because forms and reports are sometimes out-of-date.

Figure 2-6 identifies the attributes for the DEPARTMENT, EMPLOYEE, JOB, and PROJECT entities.

| Entity | Attribute |
|---|---|
| DEPARTMENT | Department Code |
| | Department Name |
| EMPLOYEE | Employee Identification |
| | First Name |
| | Last Name |
| | Social Security Number |
| | Hire Date |
| JOB | Job Identification |
| | Job Title |
| | Minimum Salary |
| | Maximum Salary |
| PROJECT | Project Identification |
| | Project Title |
| | Projected Completion Date |

**FIGURE 2-6**      **Attributes associated with entities**

Each attribute must be matched with exactly one entity. Often, it seems as if an attribute should go with more than one entity (e.g., first_name). In that case, either add a modifier to the attribute name to make it unique—such as customer_name, employee_name, and so on—or determine which entity the attribute "best" describes. If attributes without corresponding entities remain left over, an entity and its corresponding relationships may have been missed. Identify these missed entities, and add them to the relationship matrix. The ERD in Figure 2-7 lists the attributes for each entity in the Employee Projects example.

| DEPARTMENT |
|---|
| |
| department_code<br>department_name |

| JOB |
|---|
| |
| job_id<br>job_title<br>min_salary<br>max_salary |

| EMPLOYEE |
|---|
| |
| employee_id<br>first_name<br>last_name<br>soc_sec_no<br>hire_date |

| PROJECT |
|---|
| |
| project_id<br>project_title<br>projected_date |

**FIGURE 2-7**  **Example of entities with attributes**

## STEP 3: IDENTIFY UNIQUE IDENTIFIER (UID)

Every entity must have a unique identifying attribute called a unique identifier. A **unique identifier (UID)** is a single attribute or a combination of attributes that uniquely identifies one and only one instance of an entity. That is, the UID must be unique for each instance of the entity. For example, if employee_id is the UID for the EMPLOYEE entity, each instance of the EMPLOYEE entity must have a unique value assigned to employee_id. Thus, each instance of the EMPLOYEE entity must be identified by a unique employee identification number. When two or more attributes are used as the unique identifier, this is called a **concatenated key**.

### CANDIDATE KEYS

During the entity discovery stage, it might be determined that there are several attributes that could be the unique identifier. For example, in an EMPLOYEE entity, the employee identification (employee_id), Social Security number (soc_sec_no), e-mail address (e_mail_address), and telephone number (phone_number) attributes could be used to uniquely identify an EMPLOYEE instance. When this occurs, each of the attributes that can serve as the unique identifier is known as a **candidate key**. For these situations, one candidate key should be selected to serve as the unique identifier.

Each candidate key must meet the following criteria:

- Candidate key values must be unique for each instance within the entity.
- Candidate key values must never be missing, incomplete, or NULL for an instance.
- Each candidate key must use no attributes other than those necessary to uniquely identify an instance of an entity.

A unique identifier should also meet the following criteria:

- It should be meaningless, other than as an identifier.
- A unique identifier value should never change.
- There should be no practical limit to the number of unique identifier values available.
- Only one unique identifier should be specified for each table.

Often, the best choice for a unique identifier is a large, meaningless, arbitrarily assigned, positive integer. This type of unique identifier may be something like an invoice number that is already part of the user's way of doing business, or a new attribute may have to be introduced that is automatically generated by the DBMS when no naturally occurring attributes meet the unique identifier criteria. System-generated unique identifiers avoid problems that can sometimes occur with natural identifiers. For instance, a Social Security number, which might seem like a good candidate key for employees, in practice may change, may be missing, or may violate other rules for unique identifiers. A better choice might be an arbitrary employee number that is assigned when a person is hired.

A unique identifier is one of the candidate keys that has been identified to uniquely identify each instance of an entity. In Figure 2-8, the unique identifier for the EMPLOYEE entity is employee_id. The unique identifier is always the first attribute to be listed. In addition, the unique identifier is underlined and identified by the letters PK (primary key). Unique identifiers become primary keys in the physical database. Also notice that employee_id is bold, indicating that it is a required attribute.

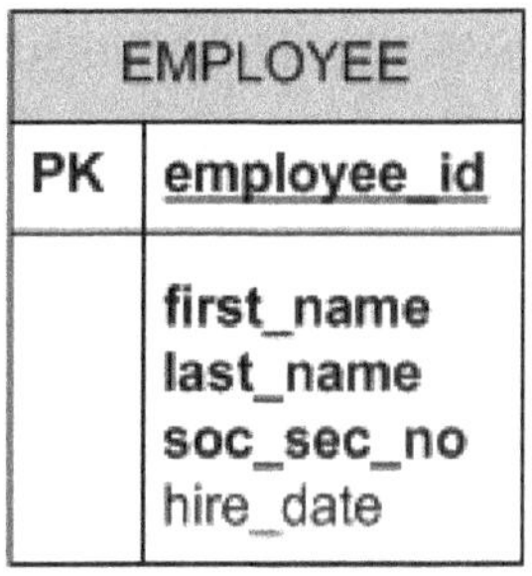

FIGURE 2-8    Example of an entity with a unique identifier (UID)

A unique identifier must exist for each entity so that the instances of that entity can be distinguished from one another. Usually, a single attribute is the unique identifier (e.g., `employee_id`).

The unique identifiers for the Employee Projects example are `department_code`, `employee_id`, `job_id`, and `project_id`, as shown in Figure 2-9.

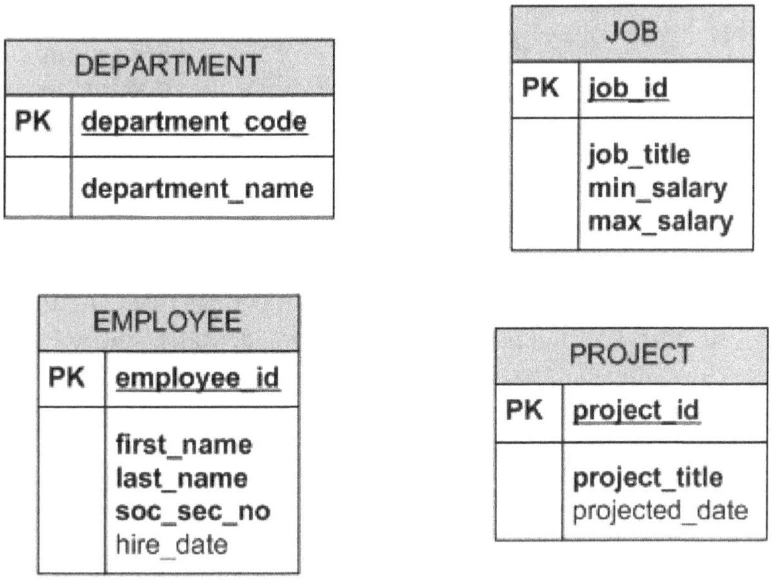

FIGURE 2-9    Example of entities with unique identifiers

## STEP 4: DETERMINE RELATIONSHIPS

A **relationship** is like a verb that shows some dependency or natural association between two entities; for example, a student takes courses, a course has students, a room is scheduled for classes, and a professor teaches courses. The nature of relationships in an ERD reveals a lot about the structure of an organization's data. Being able to identify the relationship between two entities or one entity twice makes it easier to understand the connection between different pieces of data. As Figure 2-10 shows, a relationship between two entities is represented by a line joining the two entities. Relationship lines indicate that each instance of an entity may have a relationship with instances of the connected entity, and vice versa. Thus, relationship lines express how entities are mutually related.

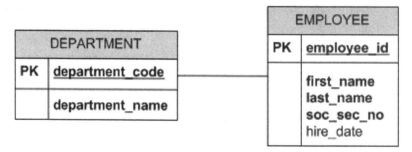

FIGURE 2-10     Example of a relationship between two entities

A relationship always has two perspectives. In this example, the relationship line indicates that the DEPARTMENT entity has some relation-ship with the EMPLOYEE entity. Likewise, the EMPLOYEE entity has some relationship with the DEPARTMENT entity. More specifically, there may be a relationship between a particular DEPARTMENT (an instance of the DEPARTMENT entity) and a particular employee (an instance of the EMPLOYEE entity). Likewise, there is a relationship between the EMPLOYEE entity and the DEPARTMENT entity in which the employee is assigned.

## STEP 5: DETERMINE OPTIONALITY AND CARDINALITY

For each relationship, its *cardinality* should be determined. There are three major categories of cardinality:

- One-to-one (e.g., each company-owned car may have a single designated parking space, and each parking space may have a single authorized company car assigned to it)
- One-to-many (e.g., one customer may have many orders, but each order has only one customer)

- Many-to-many (e.g., a supplier may supply many parts, and a part may be supplied by many suppliers)

In the relational model, a simple one-to-one or one-to-many relationship can be represented with a foreign key. A many-to-many relationship should be represented in a new table reflecting two or more one-to-many relationships. For example, a many-to-many relationship between parts and suppliers can be represented with a PART_SUPPLIER entity. The PART and SUPPLIER entities would then both have a one-to-many relationship with the PART_SUPPLIER entity.

It helps to identify more specifically what a relationship's cardinality is. In general, after the many-to-many relationships are split into one-to-many relationships, the following should be determined:

- For all "one" sides of the relationships, whether the "one" means "zero-or-one" or "exactly one," and
- For all "many" sides of the relationships, whether the "many" means "zero-or-more" or "one-or-more. "

If there are more specific cardinality rules (e.g., "there must be exactly five players on each team"), record these, too. The most important reasons to determine precise cardinality rules is to know whether one side of a relationship is optional or required and to know the maximum number, if any, of associated instances. One would not want to implement a basketball database that lets a user put six people on the court.

Symbols are placed at the ends of relationship lines to indicate the optionality and the cardinality of each relationship. **Optionality** expresses whether the relationship is optional or mandatory. **Cardinality** defines the number of occurrences of one entity for a single occurrence of the related entity. For example, an employee may be assigned to one department, many departments, or no department depending on the nature of his or her job.

Figure 2-11 indicates all the possible optionality and cardinality combinations. Two symbols are specified at the end of the relationship line where it joins an entity. The first, or outer, symbol is the optionality indicator. A circle ( O ) indicates that the relationship is optional; that is, the minimum number of relationships between each instance of the first entity and instances of the related entity is zero. Consider the circle as a zero, or think of a letter O for "optional." A stroke ( | ) indicates that the relationship is mandatory; the minimum number of relationships between each instance of the first entity and instances of the related entity is one.

The second, or inner, symbol indicates cardinality. A stroke (|) indicates that the maximum number of relationships is one. A "crow's foot" (<) indicates that many relationships can exist between instances of the related entities.

| ERD notation | Meaning |
|---|---|
| TableA — TableB | Each instance of TableA is related to a minimum of zero and a maximum of one instance of TableB. |
| TableA — TableB | Each instance of TableB is related to a minimum of one and a maximum of one instance of TableB. |
| TableA — TableB | Each instance of TableA is related to a minimum of zero and a maximum of many instances of TableB. |
| TableA — TableB | Each instance of TableB is related to a minimum of one and a maximum of many instances of TableB. |

**FIGURE 2-11**     **Possible combinations for optionality and cardinality**

In Figure 2-12, a department might not have any employees (*a minimum of zero*) and may have *a maximum of many* employees. In addition, each employee works in exactly one department. That is, an employee can work in *a minimum of one* department and *a maximum of one* department.

This ERD is a clear depiction of an important aspect of a business: The system under consideration deals with departments and employees. This ERD's clarity and simplicity illustrate why ERDs are a popular technique that business analysts use to describe a business model to end users.

The line representing the relationship in the diagram indicates two other important aspects of the business model: Each employee works in only one department, and a department may have zero, one, or many employees.

The two strokes on the line attached to the DEPARTMENT entity specify that each employee is associated with one department. The circle and crow's foot portion of the line attached to the EMPLOYEE entity specify that each department can have zero, one, or more employees.

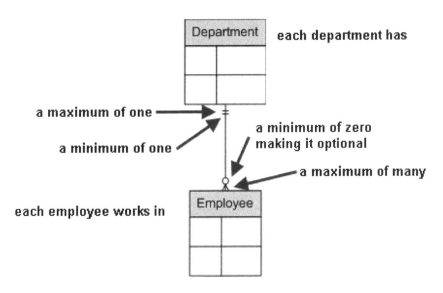

FIGURE 2-12    Example of optionality and cardinality

The diagram in Figure 2-13 shows an easy way to remember what the crow's foot means and on which end of the line it should be placed. As depicted, the crow's foot is shorthand for showing multiple instances of an entity.

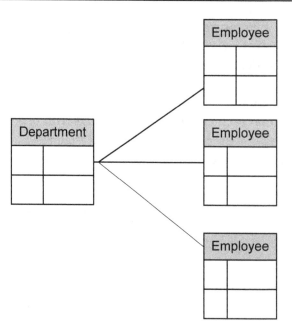

**FIGURE 2-13**     Crow's foot represents many instances of the EMPLOYEE entity

## FOREIGN KEYS

When a relationship exists between two entities, the unique identifier of one entity becomes a **foreign key** in the other entity. The purpose of the foreign key is to ensure referential integrity of the data by permitting only those values that are supposed to appear in the database. A relationship between two entities implies that one of them has one or more attributes that represent the foreign key values from the other entity. The ERD in Figure 2-14 shows that the EMPLOYEE entity specifies the foreign key `department_code` that associates each employee with a specific department.

The letters FK (foreign key) are placed beside foreign key attributes to indicate which relationship the attribute serves as a foreign key for and which attribute in the target entity the attribute is paired with. The foreign key designates the rows in the child (EMPLOYEE) entity that are associated with one row in the parent (DEPARTMENT) entity.

Consider the relationship between the DEPARTMENT and EMPLOYEE entities. Each department can contain zero, one, or many employees. Each employee must be assigned to one and only one department. For this relationship to exist, the child entity (many side) of the relationship

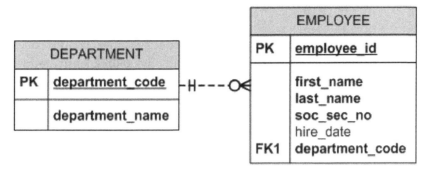

FIGURE 2-14    Example of an entity with a foreign key

must include the UID of the parent entity as a foreign key. For example, when the DEPARTMENT and EMPLOYEE entities are joined in a relationship, the UID, department_code, of the DEPARTMENT entity is included as a foreign key in the EMPLOYEE entity as shown in Figure 2-14. The foreign key department_code in the EMPLOYEE entity designates the row in the DEPARTMENT entity that the employee is assigned to.

Also indicate the nature of the relationship by specifying the **delete-update-insert rules** for the primary and foreign keys in each relationship. These rules define the specific way referential integrity will be enforced. This task involves two parts. First, determine the action to take if a unique identifier value in the target table is deleted or updated, potentially leaving orphan rows in the designating table that no longer reference an existing row in the target table. For example, specify what should or should not happen when a row is deleted from the CUSTOMER table and there are rows in the ORDER table that reference the deleted CUSTOMER row. In other words, how should the system handle an attempt to delete a customer who has outstanding orders? In this case, several possible actions can be taken:

- Reject the delete or update, and signal an error.
- Handle it with a custom procedure.
- Cascade the delete or update to all the related dependent tables.
- Set the related dependent foreign key column(s) to null or a default value, if allowed.

The end user's description of how the business operates is the basis for making this decision.

Next, determine the action to take if an insertion or update in the designating table creates an unmatched, non-null foreign key value in the designating table. For example, specify what should or should not happen when a row is inserted into the ORDER entity and there is no customer number in the CUSTOMER entity that matches the customer number in the new ORDER row (in other words, when an attempt is made to insert an order with no matching customer). Any of the following rules can be specified:

- Reject the insert or update, and signal an error.
- Handle it with a custom procedure.
- Create a default parent row in the target table, and give it the same unique identifier value as the new foreign key value.
- Reset the new or changed foreign key to null or to a default value, if allowed.

Note how the various rules can reflect different approaches to the structure of the organization's data and the way the organization operates. The delete-update-insert rules can be documented with the other information for the table that contains the foreign key to which the rules apply.

Consider the ERD in Figure 2-15 for the Employee Projects system and examine the optionality, cardinality, and foreign keys. If the diagram is read like a sentence, the entity is the subject, the relationship is the verb, and the cardinality after the relationship tells how many direct objects (second entity) there are.

From the description of the problem, we determine that:

- Each employee <u>may</u> *work for* zero or one department.
- Each department <u>may</u> *have* zero, one, or many employees.
- Each job <u>may</u> *be assigned to* zero, one, or many employees.
- Each employee <u>may</u> *be assigned* zero or one job title.
- Each employee <u>may</u> *work on* zero, one, or many projects.
- Each project <u>must</u> *be assigned to* one or more employees.

## Relationship Strength

Any time there is a relationship between entities, the unique identifier (primary key) of the parent entity appears as a foreign key attribute in the child entity. How that foreign key attribute is implemented into the child entity determines the strength of the relationship between the entities. There are two ways in which the relationship can be determined. These methods are discussed next.

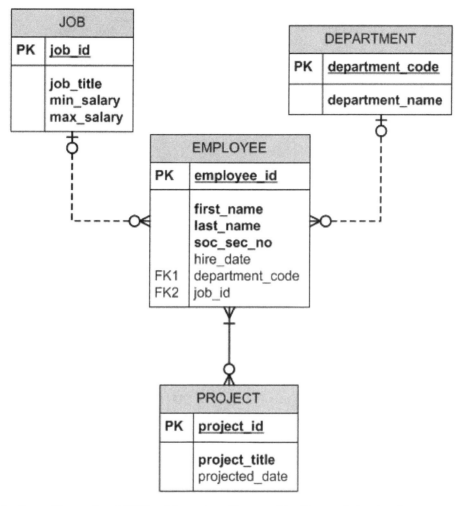

FIGURE 2-15    Example of ERD with optionality, cardinality, and foreign keys

### WEAK OR NON-IDENTIFYING ENTITY

A **weak** or **non-identifying relationship** exists between two entities when the unique identifier (primary key) of the parent entity is not a component of the unique identifier of the child entity. For example, Figure 2-16 represents a weak entity because the unique identifier department_code of the DEPARTMENT entity is not a component of the unique identifier of the EMPLOYEE entity. The crow's foot notation represents a non-identifying relationship as a dashed relationship line between the two entities.

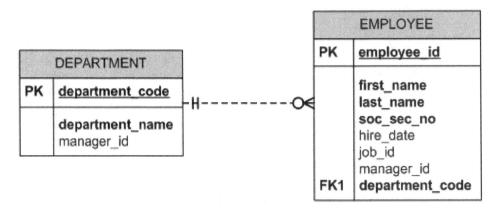

FIGURE 2-16        Example of a weak or non-identifying entity

STRONG OR IDENTIFYING ENTITY

When a **strong** or identifying relationship exists between two entities, the unique identifier (primary key) of the parent entity becomes a component of the unique identifier of the child entity. For example, in Figure 2-17, `department_code` is the unique identifier of the DEPARTMENT entity. In an identifying relationship, the `department_code` becomes part of the unique identifier of the EMPLOYEE entity. As a result, the `department_code` attribute in the EMPLOYEE entity is a unique identifier and foreign key. The crow's foot notation represents an identifying relationship as a solid relationship line between the two entities.

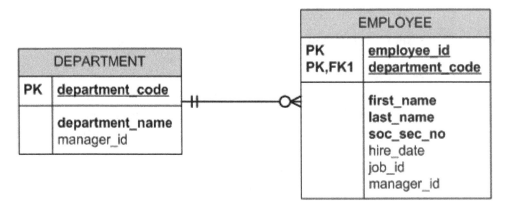

FIGURE 2-17        Example of a strong or identifying entity

## STEP 6: ELIMINATE MANY-TO-MANY RELATIONSHIPS

Because of their simplicity, unique identifiers (UIDs) consisting of just one attribute are preferable to UIDs with more than one attribute. However, there are two cases in which a composite unique identifier works satisfactorily in place of a single-column unique identifier. First, the unique identifier for an entity that represents a many-to-many relationship can be the combination of the foreign keys that designate the related entities. A foreign key is one or more attributes whose values for a particular instance match the unique identifier value of some other instance in the same or a different entity.

In Figure 2-18, there is a many-to-many relationship between EMPLOYEE and PROJECT. This many-to-many relationship is identified with crow's feet on both ends of the relationship line and is read as follows:

- Each employee <u>may</u> *work on* zero, one, or many projects.
- Each project <u>must</u> *be assigned to* one or more employees.

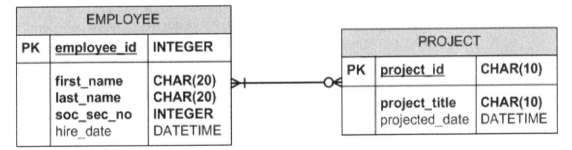

FIGURE 2-18    Example of many-to-many relationships

Many-to-many relationships add complexity and confusion to the model and to the application development process. Such relationships will be a problem later when the related entities are implemented into database tables because each row will need an indefinite number of attributes to maintain the many-to-many relationship.

The problem can be solved by separating the two entities in the many-to-many relationship and introducing a new entity, called an **associative** or **intersection entity**, for each many-to-many relationship as shown in Figure 2-19.

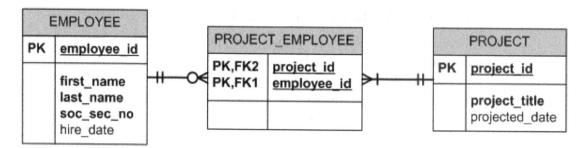

FIGURE 2-19    Example of an intersection or associative entity

This ERD is read as follows:

- Each employee <u>may</u> *work on* zero, one, or many projects.
- Each project <u>must be</u> *assigned to* one or more employees.

The name of the new intersection entity will be the hyphenation of the names of the two originating entities. In this example, the PROJECT_EMPLOYEE entity becomes the intersection entity. It will have a concatenated UID consisting of the UIDs from the PROJECT and EMPLOYEE entities. Thus, project_id and employee_id are concatenated together to form the UID of the PROJECT_EMPLOYEE intersection entity. The PROJECT_EMPLOYEE entity will have a one-to-many relationship with each of its parent entities as shown in the figure.

## USING ASSOCIATIVE ENTITIES FOR MULTIVALUED ATTRIBUTES

A composite unique identifier also works satisfactorily for tables whose sole purpose is to define multivalued attributes. For example, consider Figure 2-20, where there is a many-to-many relationship between the SUPPLIER and PART entities. This many-to-many relationship can be read as follows:

- Each supplier <u>may</u> *supply* zero, one, or many parts.
- Each part <u>may</u> *be supplied by* zero, one, or many suppliers.

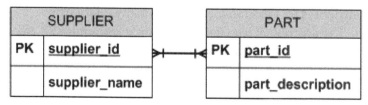

FIGURE 2-20    Example of many-to-many relationship

The way this ERD is drawn, a supplier may supply zero, one, or more parts, and a part may have zero, one, or more suppliers. There is no place on this diagram, however, to place the price that a specific supplier charges for a particular part. Because PART can have a different price for each supplier, it is considered a multivalued attribute.

In Figure 2-21, the many-to-many relationship is split into two one-to-many relationships, and a new SUPPLIER_PART entity is added to represent the association. This new entity provides a place to list the price attribute.

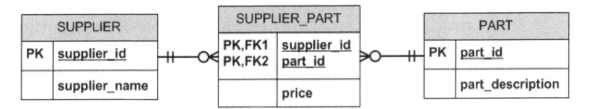

FIGURE 2-21     Associative entity

In this example, the SUPPLIER_PART intersection entity's unique identifier consists of the attributes supplier_id and part_id that represents the associated values of SUPPLIER and PART instances.

## STEP 7:  NAMED RELATIONSHIPS

A relationship can be labeled to define the relationship. In this case, one can infer that a department has employees, or that an employee works for a department. Figure 2-22 shows how this relationship could be labeled for clarification.

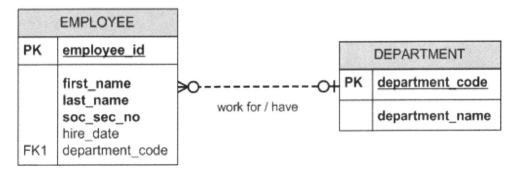

FIGURE 2-22     Identifying the entity relationships

The named relationships are read as follows:

- Each employee <u>may</u> *work for* zero or one department.
- Each department <u>may</u> *have* zero, one, or many employees.

The entity and relationship labels, together with the way the relationship line is drawn, provide the pieces for verbal descriptions of the data model.

## RELATIONSHIP MATRIX

Entities do not exist in isolation; they are interrelated. When a relationship is identified between two entities, document it and give it a name. Relationships should be named with verb phrases from parent to child.

A **relationship matrix** can be developed where entity relationships are listed down the left column and across the top, as shown Figure 2-23. An active verb can be filled in at the intersection of two entities that are related. Each row and column should have at least one relationship listed, unless the entity associated with that row or column does not interact with the rest of the system.

|  | Department | Employee | Job | Project |
|---|---|---|---|---|
| **Department** |  | have |  |  |
| **Employee** | work for |  | be assigned | work on |
| **Job** |  | be assigned to |  |  |
| **Project** |  | be assigned to |  |  |

FIGURE 2-23    Relationship matrix

Once the entity relationships are determined, they are applied to the entity relationship diagram. The result is the ERD shown in Figure 2-24.

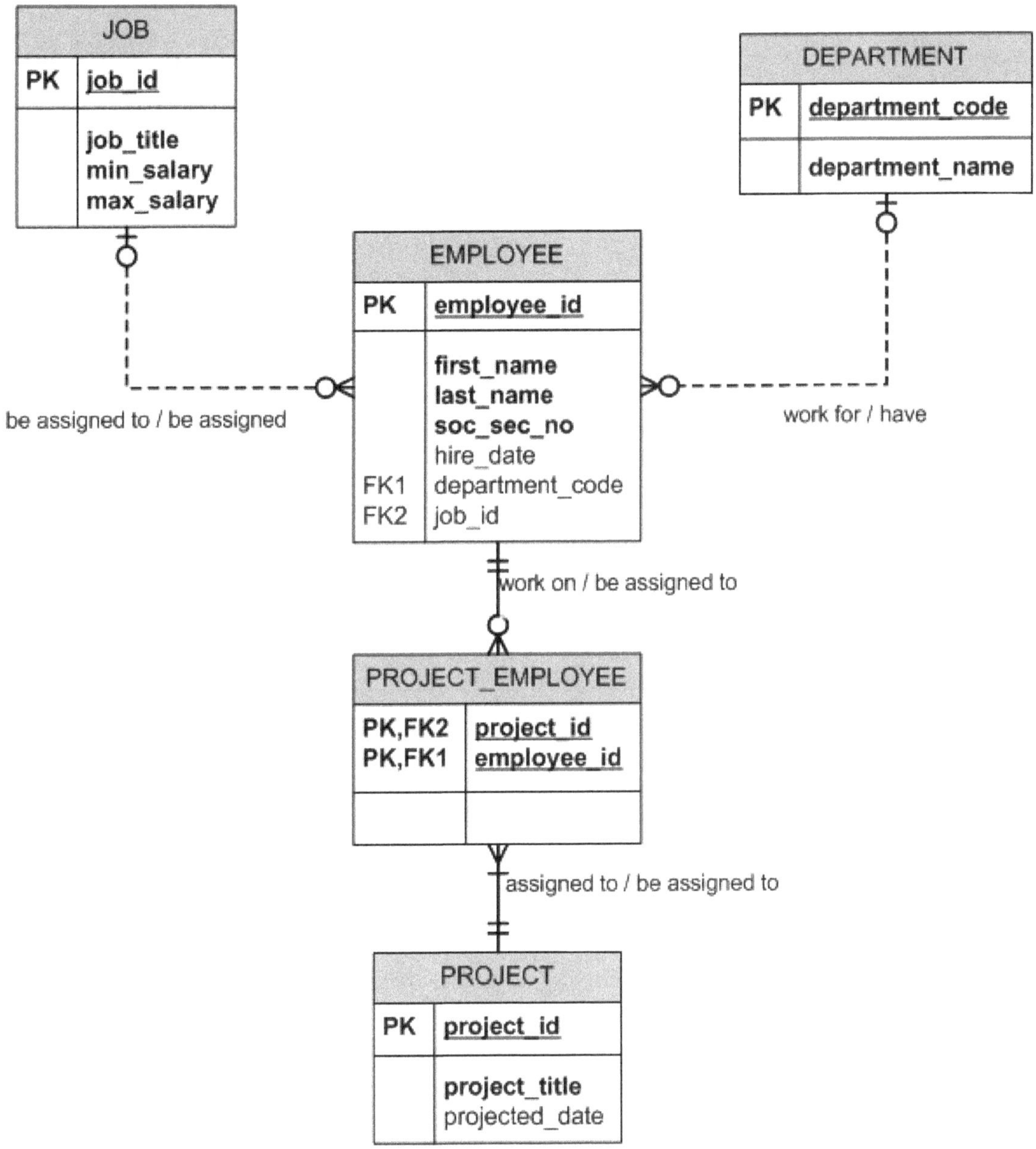

FIGURE 2-24     Example of entity relationship diagram with named relationships

The named relationships are read as follows:

- Each employee <u>may</u> *work for* zero or one department.
- Each department <u>may</u> *have* zero, one, or many employees.
- Each job <u>may</u> *be assigned to* zero, one, or many employees.
- Each employee <u>may</u> *be assigned* zero or one job title.
- Each employee <u>may</u> *work on* zero, one, or many projects.
- Each project <u>must</u> *be assigned to* one or more employees.

## STEP 8: DETERMINE DATA TYPES

Once the entities and attributes are included in the ERD, the data type and size can be determined and included. Every attribute must include a data type that specifies the type of data that will be stored as well as a size that indicates the maximum length of the data. UID and foreign keys that are defined across several entities must be defined with the same data types and size. Figure 2-25 identifies the most common data types used in entity relationship diagrams.

| Data type | Description |
|---|---|
| CHAR(length) | Character data |
| NUMERIC | Numeric data that can contain decimal places |
| INTEGER | Numeric data that is a whole number |
| DATE | Date |

**FIGURE 2-25**    **Common data types**

Figure 2-26 illustrates the completed entity relationship diagram. This ERD is read as follows:

- Each employee <u>may</u> *work for* zero or one department.
- Each department <u>may</u> *have* zero, one, or many employees.
- Each job <u>may</u> *be assigned to* zero, one, or many employees.
- Each employee <u>may</u> *be assigned* zero or one job title.
- Each employee <u>may</u> *work on* zero, one, or many projects.
- Each project <u>must</u> *be assigned to* one or more employees.

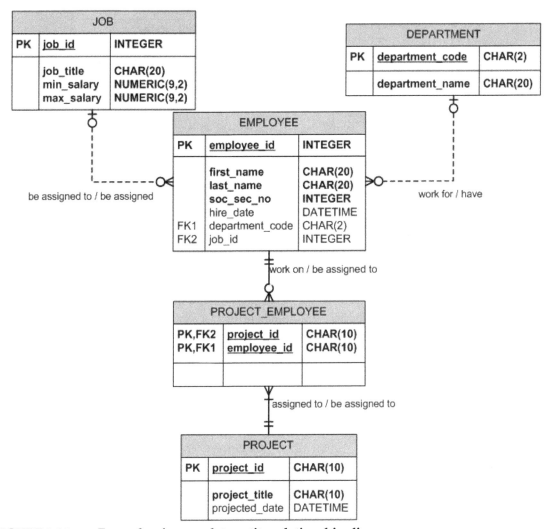

FIGURE 2-26    Example of a complete entity relationship diagram

## RECURSIVE RELATIONSHIP

A **recursive relationship** occurs when an entity has a relationship with itself. Let us consider a situation where, as in many companies, each employee, except the president, is supervised by one manager. This can be represented by the ERD in Figure 2-27.

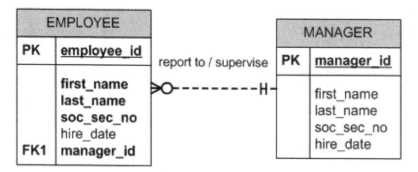

FIGURE 2-27    Example of an ERD between the EMPLOYEE and MANAGER entities

This ERD is read as follows:

- Each employee <u>must</u> *report to* one and only one manager.
- Each manager <u>may</u> *supervise* zero, one, or many employees.

The problem with this ERD is that each manager is also an employee. Creating the second MANAGER entity not only duplicates data from the EMPLOYEE entity, but it virtually guarantees that there will be mistakes and conflicts in the data. This problem can be fixed by eliminating the redundant entity and re-drawing the association line.

In the ERD in Figure 2-28, the MANAGER entity has been eliminated, and the relationship line has been changed so that the EMPLOYEE entity has a relationship with itself. There are three important points to be made here:

- Every employee has a manager, except for the president.
- Every manager is an employee.
- Not all employees are managers.

This ERD is read as follows:

- Each manager <u>may</u> *have* zero, one, or many employees.
- Each employee <u>must</u> *report to* one and only one manager.

## ENTITY SUBTYPES

As entities are identified, also identify **entity hierarchies**. For example, if some parts are produced on-site and others are purchased, both are subtypes of the PART entity. As another example, SALARY_EMPLOYEE and HOURLY_EMPLOYEE are subtypes of the EMPLOYEE entity. A **subtype** has all the attributes and integrity rules of its supertype.

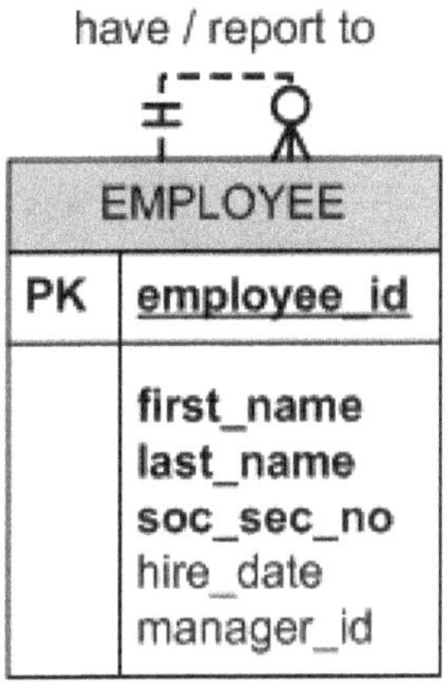

have / report to

FIGURE 2-28    Example of a recursive relationship

For example, the SALARY_EMPLOYEE and HOURLY_EMPLOYEE subtypes have all the attributes of the EMPLOYEE entity, such as employee_id, first_name, last_name, hire_date, department_code, and so on. In addition, the SALARY_EMPLOYEE subtype could include a salary attribute, while the HOURLY_EMPLOYEE subtype could include the hourly_rate attribute.

When two potential entities are encountered that seem very similar but not quite the same, ERD **entity subtypes** can be used to represent them. The example in Figure 2-29 shows an EMPLOYEE entity that has SALARY and HOURLY employee subtypes.

This diagram tells us that all salary people are employees and all hourly people are employees, and salary people and hourly people share some common attributes of the EMPLOYEE entity, such as hire_date and the department_code in which they work. Subtyping employees lets the ERD show that there are attributes of salary people that do not apply to hourly people, and vice versa.

The ERD can also depict relationships between other entities, such as the DEPARTMENT entity and an EMPLOYEE, SALARY_EMPLOYEE, or HOURLY_EMPLOYEE entity, depending on how the organization's data is structured. In the example, the two "Has" relationships are shown as exclusive relationships to the SALARY_EMPLOYEE and HOURLY_EMPLOYEE entities. The explicit depiction of subtypes gives a more precise view on the ERD of the underlying data model.

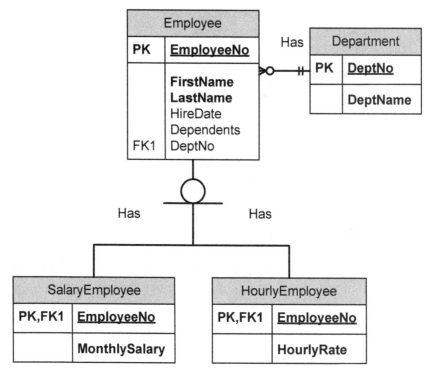

**FIGURE 2-29**    Example of entity subtypes

## END-OF-CHAPTER

### CHAPTER SUMMARY

1.  Basic entity relationship diagram (ERD) concepts:

    a.  Entity—Is like a noun consisting of persons, places, or things
    b.  Relationship—Is like a verb that shows some dependency between two or more entities
    c.  Optionality—Expresses whether the relationship is optional or mandatory
    d.  Cardinality—Defines the number of occurrences of one entity for a single occurrence of the related entity
    e.  Unique identifier—Uniquely identifies each row in an entity
    f.  Foreign key—Links the related rows between two entities
    g.  Attributes—Are like adjectives that describe an entity

2. ERD diagrams:

   a. Represent entities, relationships, and their attributes in pictorial form
   b. Use rectangles to represent entities
   c. Use lines to represent relationships
   d. List attributes in the rectangles with annotation to show required and optional values, identifier attributes, and referencing attributes
   e. Can show alternative types of relationships, including one-to-one, one-to-many, and many-to-many relationships
   f. Show whether one or more related instances are optional or required

3. To complete a data model, one normally works on several steps at the same time. Some steps may need to be repeated to refine the model.

4. The following steps are a guideline for developing an entity relationship diagram (ERD):

| Step | Title | Description |
|---|---|---|
| 1 | Create Entities | Identify the people, places, or events about which the end users want to store data. |
| 2 | Define Attributes | Define the attributes that are essential to the system under development. For each attribute, match it with exactly one entity that it describes. |
| 3 | Identify Unique Identifier | Identify the data attribute(s) that uniquely identify one and only one occurrence of each entity. Eliminate many-to-many relationships, and include a unique identifier (UID) and foreign keys in each entity. |
| 4 | Define Relationships | Find the natural associations between pairs of entities using a relationship matrix. Arrange entities in rectangles, and join those entities with a line. |
| 5 | Determine Optionality and Cardinality | Determine the number of occurrences of one entity for a single occurrence of the related entity. |
| 6 | Name Relationships | Name each relationship between entities. |
| 7 | Eliminate Many-to-Many Relationships | Many-to-many relationships cannot be implemented into database tables because each row will need an indefinite number of attributes to maintain the many-to-many relationship. Many-to-many relationships must be converted to one-to-many relationships using associative entities. |
| 8 | Determine Data Types | Identify the data types and sizes of each attribute. |

## KEY TERMS

| | |
|---|---|
| associative entity | intersection entity |
| attribute | mandatory attribute |
| candidate key | non-identifying relationship |
| cardinality | optional attribute |
| concatenated key | optionality |
| conceptual data model | recursive relationship |
| delete-update-insert rules | relationship |
| domain | relationship matrix |
| entity | required attribute |
| entity hierarchy | strong relationship |
| entity instance | subtype |
| entity relationship diagram (ERD) | time-dependent attribute |
| entity subtype | unique identifier (UID) |
| foreign key | volatile attribute |
| identifying relationship | weak relationship |

# CHAPTER 3
## NORMALIZATION

## CHAPTER OBJECTIVES

Upon completion of this chapter, you should be able to

- Explain the term normalization
- Explain the different normal forms
- Use 1NF, 2NF, and 3NF

## NORMALIZATION

In addition to entity relationship diagrams (ERD), normalization is a very valuable part of the database development process. **Normalization** is a series of steps used to evaluate and modify table structures to ensure that every non-key column in every table is directly dependent on the primary key. The results of normalization are reduced redundancies, fewer anomalies, and improved efficiencies. Normalization is another process toward a good database design. Normalization has two purposes:

- Eliminate redundant data; that is, eliminate the storing of the same data in more than one table
- Ensure that data within a table are related

Eliminating redundant data is achieved by splitting tables with redundant data into two or more tables without the redundancy.

## NORMAL FORMS

Normalization involves the process of applying rules called **normal forms** to table structures that produce a design that is free of data redundancy problems. The steps for normalization are called normal forms, abbreviated as NF. Several normal forms exist, with the most common being first normal form (1NF), second normal form (2NF), and third normal form (3NF). Each normal form addresses the potential for a particular type of redundancy, and a table is said to be in one of the normal forms if it satisfies the rules required by that form. The chart in Figure 3-1 identifies the normalization steps.

| Normal form (NF) | Description |
|---|---|
| First normal form (1NF) | • Two-dimensional table format.<br>• No repeating groups; each column can contain only one value.<br>• Primary key is identified. |
| Second normal form (2NF) | • 1NF.<br>• No partial dependencies; all non-key columns are fully dependent on the entire primary key. |
| Third normal form (3NF) | • 2NF.<br>• A non-key column cannot determine the value of another non-key column. Every non-key column must depend directly on the primary key. |
| Boyce-Codd normal form (BCNF) (sometimes referred to as 3.5NF) | • Every determinant in a table is a candidate key. If there is only one candidate key, 3NF and BCNF are the same. |

**FIGURE 3-1**    **Normal forms**

This book examines database normalization by focusing on the first three normal forms. Although additional normal forms exist, for most database designs obtaining a normalization of 3NF is adequate.

## REPRESENTING DATABASE TABLES

There are several ways to represent database tables during the normalization process. The two methods used in this book are the table form and relational schema.

### TABLE FORM

Figure 3.2 illustrates two tables in **table form**. Each table is defined as follows:

- Capitalize entity names.
- Bold and underline the primary key.
- Italicize foreign keys.

In addition, each table includes sample data that can help in the normalization process. With sample data, it can be easier to identify where repeating groups exist.

| dept id | dept_name |
|---------|-----------|
| 275 | Sales |
| 486 | Manufacturing |
| 694 | Information Systems |

**DEPARTMENT**

| emp id | first_name | last_name | dept_id |
|--------|------------|-----------|---------|
| 111 | Robert | Jackson | 486 |
| 222 | Betty | Rogers | 486 |
| 333 | Kumar | Patel | 275 |

**EMPLOYEE**

FIGURE 3-2    Representing tables in table form

## RELATIONAL SCHEMA

A **relational schema** is a text-based method to represent database tables. In this method, each table is identified by its name, followed by a list of the table's attributes in parentheses. A relational schema is defined as follows:

- Capitalize the entity name.
- Put attributes in parentheses.
- Bold and underline the primary key.
- Italicize foreign keys.

Figure 3-3 shows an example of a relational schema. In this example, there are two tables: DEPARTMENT and EMPLOYEE.

DEPARTMENT (**dept id**, dept_name)

EMPLOYEE(**emp id**, first_name, last_name, *dept_id*)

FIGURE 3-3    Relational schema

## FUNCTIONAL DEPENDENCY

A **functional dependency** occurs when one attribute in a table uniquely determines another attribute. This can be written product_id → prod_desc, which is the same as stating "prod_desc is functionally dependent upon product_id." The value of prod_desc cannot be determined without knowing the value of product_id.

Consider the INVENTORY table shown in Figure 3-4.

| whse_id | product_id | prod_desc | bin | qty | whse_address | city | state | zip |
|---------|-----------|-----------|-----|-----|--------------|------|-------|-----|
| 111 | 167 | Shovel | 15 | 10 | 1511 Central Ave | Detroit | MI | 48220 |
| 111 | 448 | Hammer | 88 | 26 | 1511 Central Ave | Detroit | MI | 48220 |
| 222 | 167 | Shovel | 24 | 20 | 6803 Alder St | Dallas | TX | 97335 |
| 222 | 302 | Rake | 21 | 18 | 6803 Alder St | Dallas | TX | 97335 |

INVENTORY

**FIGURE 3-4    INVENTORY table**

Based on this table, the functional dependencies can be determined as follows:

```
product_id → prod_desc
whse_id, product_id → bin, qty
whse_id → whse_address, city, state, zip
```

## FIRST NORMAL FORM (1NF)

A database table is in **first normal form (1NF)** when

- There are no repeating groups. All columns in the table contain a single value; that is, every intersection of a row and column in the table contains only one value.
- A primary key has been defined that uniquely identifies each row in the table.
- All columns in the table are dependent on the primary key.

Consider the INVENTORY data in Figure 3-5, where there are several repeating groups consisting of the whse_id (warehouse ID), bin (bin number), qty (quantity), and whse_address (warehouse address), city, state, and zip. Removing these repeating groups is the first rule of first normal form.

| product_id | prod_desc | whse_id | bin | qty | whse_address | city | state | zip |
|-----------|-----------|---------|-----|-----|--------------|------|-------|-----|
| 167 | Shovel | 111 | 150 | 19 | 1511 Central Ave. | Detroit | MI | 48220 |
|  |  | 222 | 244 | 26 | 6803 Alder St. | Dallas | TX | 97338 |
| 448 | Hammer | 111 | 883 | 20 | 1511 Central Ave. | Detroit | MI | 48220 |
| 302 | Rake | 222 | 212 | 18 | 6803 Alder St. | Dallas | TX | 97338 |

**FIGURE 3-5    Inventory data not normalized**

Examine the row for product 167, and observe the multiple values in the whse_id, bin, qty, whse_address, city, state, and zip columns. In this example, product number 167 is stored in two different warehouses. Having more than one value at the intersection of a row and column is referred to as having a repeating group. A table that contains a repeating group is called an **unnormalized table**.

The repeating groups can be eliminated by "filling in" the values in the vacant "cells" of the table as shown in Figure 3-6. Each column now contains only a single value, thus satisfying the first rule for first normal form.

The second rule for 1NF is to select a **primary key** that uniquely identifies each row in the table. In Figure 3-6, there is no one column that can represent the primary key because no one column uniquely identifies each row. As a result, the INVENTORY table contains a composite primary key of product_id and whse_id that uniquely identifies each row in the table. In addition, each column now contains only one value. In the figure, the primary key columns are in bold and underlined to identify them as the primary key.

| product id | prod_desc | whse id | bin | qty | whse_address | city | state | zip |
|---|---|---|---|---|---|---|---|---|
| 167 | Shovel | 111 | 150 | 19 | 1511 Central Ave. | Detroit | MI | 48220 |
| 167 | Shovel | 222 | 244 | 26 | 6803 Alder St. | Dallas | TX | 97338 |
| 448 | Hammer | 111 | 883 | 20 | 1511 Central Ave. | Detroit | MI | 48220 |
| 302 | Rake | 222 | 212 | 18 | 6803 Alder St. | Dallas | TX | 97338 |

**FIGURE 3-6    INVENTORY table**

Now that the primary key has been identified, the columns can be adjusted so the primary key, a composite key in this example, can be listed as the first two columns. Figure 3-7 represents the table in first normal form with whse_id and product_id as the primary key.

| whse id | product id | prod_desc | bin | qty | whse_address | city | state | zip |
|---|---|---|---|---|---|---|---|---|
| 111 | 167 | Shovel | 150 | 19 | 1511 Central Ave. | Detroit | MI | 48220 |
| 111 | 448 | Hammer | 883 | 20 | 1511 Central Ave. | Detroit | MI | 48220 |
| 222 | 167 | Shovel | 244 | 26 | 6803 Alder St. | Dallas | FL | 97338 |
| 222 | 302 | Rake | 212 | 18 | 6803 Alder St. | Dallas | FL | 97338 |

INVENTORY (whse_id, product_id, prod_desc, qty, bin, whse_address, city, state, zip)

**FIGURE 3-7    INVENTORY table in first normal form (1NF)**

A table in 1NF may not always be the ideal form for representing data because it may represent information redundantly. The INVENTORY table in Figure 3-7 really has not changed that much. There is still data redundancy in the prod_desc, whse_address, city, state, and zip columns.

## Second Normal Form (2NF)

Second normal form applies only to tables that have a concatenated primary key. A database table is in **second normal form (2NF)** when

- It is in first normal form (1NF).
- There are no partial dependencies. That is, each non-key attribute depends on the entire primary key. A non-key attribute cannot be determined by part of the primary key.

Take another look at the INVENTORY table in Figure 3-7, which is in first normal form (1NF). There are still problems with this table with what are referred to as partial dependencies.

### Partial Dependency

**Partial dependency** means that a non-key column is dependent on part of but not the entire primary key. In this example, the prod_desc column is dependent on the product_id key but has no connection with the whse_id key. Likewise, the whse_address column is dependent on the whse_id key and has no connection with the product_id key. Thus, the prod_desc and whse_address non-key columns do not depend on the entire composite primary key of product_id and whse_id.

The primary key for the INVENTORY table in Figure 3-7 includes both the whse_id and product_id columns (neither alone is unique). Because the whse_address column depends solely on the whse_id key and the prod_desc column depends solely on the product_id key, the table in this figure violates the 2NF requirement.

To remove the partial dependencies in the INVENTORY table, the PRODUCT and WAREHOUSE tables shown in Figure 3-8 are created. In addition, the INVENTORY table is modified so the dependent columns are moved to the appropriate tables. Thus, this figure shows the INVENTORY table split into three tables that eliminate the prod_desc and whse_address redundancy.

| product id | prod_desc |
|------------|-----------|
| 167 | Shovel |
| 302 | Rake |
| 448 | Hammer |

PRODUCT

| whse id | whse_address | city | state | zip |
|---------|--------------|------|-------|-----|
| 111 | 1511 Central Ave. | Detroit | MI | 48220 |
| 222 | 6803 Alder St. | Dallas | TX | 97338 |

WAREHOUSE

| whse id | product id | bin | qty |
|---------|------------|-----|-----|
| 111 | 167 | 159 | 19 |
| 111 | 448 | 883 | 20 |
| 222 | 167 | 244 | 26 |
| 222 | 302 | 212 | 18 |

INVENTORY

PRODUCT (**product_id**, prod_desc)

WAREHOUSE (**whse_id**, whse_address, city, state, zip)

INVENTORY (***whse_id***, ***product_id***, bin, qty)

FIGURE 3-8    **PRODUCT, WAREHOUSE, and INVENTORY tables represented in 2NF**

## REFERENTIAL INTEGRITY

Let us look at the warehouse example again to understand referential integrity. In Figure 3-8, a separate WAREHOUSE table is defined so that a warehouse address can be stored non-redundantly. The whse_id is stored as a column in the WAREHOUSE and INVENTORY tables so the whse_id value can be used in an INVENTORY row to reference, or look up, the appropriate WAREHOUSE row via the WAREHOUSE table's whse_id primary key. Thus, the rows in the two tables are interrelated, based on matching values in the whse_id columns in the two tables.

The whse_id column in the WAREHOUSE table serves as a primary key and can never be null. The whse_id column in the INVENTORY table is referred to as a **foreign key**; it addresses "foreign" rows that are usually outside the same table. A foreign key value can be null. This means that its related row is unknown. A foreign key value also can match exactly a primary key value in a related row. But a foreign key value cannot have some column values present (that is, at least one column value is not null) and not match the primary key value of an existing row in the related table. This requirement says nothing more than that if the foreign key points to a related row, the row must be there. A consequence of this rule is that composite foreign key values cannot be *partially* null because, by the entity integrity rule, no primary key column value can ever be null.

## What Is Meant by Redundancy?

It is important to be clear about the meaning of redundancy. First, any set of tables in a database will have some values repeated more than once. For example, in the tables in Figure 3-8, the warehouse IDs that appear in the INVENTORY table all appear in the WAREHOUSE table as well. This is one of the central features of the relational model: Rows are related by values. So the instances of warehouse number 111 and warehouse number 222 do not represent the type of redundancy with which we are concerned.

The redundancy we want to avoid is repeated representation of the same fact. For example, look back at Figure 3-7 and note that the fact that warehouse 111 is located at 1511 Central Avenue is repeated in two rows. If we actually created a database table with this structure, we would have to ensure that any change to the warehouse address was made consistently to *all* rows that stored the address.

Now, let us consider another example. Suppose we have the order data in Figure 3-9 for the items that are included in customers' orders.

| order_id | product_id | qty | cost_price |
|----------|------------|-----|------------|
| 9877 | 73 | 2 | 25.00 |
| 9878 | 52 | 1 | 10.00 |
| 9878 | 73 | 5 | 25.00 |
| 9879 | 73 | 3 | 25.00 |

**FIGURE 3-9**   Order data

This table appears to redundantly represent the fact that the product number determines the price. In many business systems, this might be true. But what if the price were negotiated on each order? Then it would be possible for the table in Figure 3-10 to have (at some point in time) a different cost price for the same product.

| order_id | product_id | qty | cost_price |
|----------|------------|-----|------------|
| 9877 | 73 | 2 | 25.00 |
| 9878 | 52 | 1 | 10.00 |
| 9878 | 73 | 5 | 19.00 |
| 9879 | 73 | 3 | 22.00 |

**FIGURE 3-10**   ORDER table

For the business model that this table represents, no fact redundancy exists. This example brings us to a crucial point in understanding normal forms: If the goal is to *unambiguously* represent various facts in a (logical) database model that uses tables, the tables *must* be structured so that they have no redundant representation of facts. The obvious consequence is that there is no mechanical method of normalizing tables. It is important to understand the facts that are to be represented and then define the tables accordingly.

## THIRD NORMAL FORM (3NF)

A database table is in **third normal form (3NF)** when:

- It is in second normal form (2NF).
- The table does not contain any non-key dependencies. A non-key dependency, also referred to as a transitive dependency, occurs when a non-key attribute determines the value of another non-key attribute. To conform to 3NF, every attribute must depend only on the primary key.

Let us consider the WAREHOUSE table shown in Figure 3-11. This WAREHOUSE table is a result of the second normal form step, so it satisfies the first rule of third normal form (3NF).

| whse_id | whse_address | city | state | zip |
|---------|--------------|------|-------|-----|
| 111 | 1511 Central Ave. | Detroit | MI | 48220 |
| 222 | 6803 Alder St. | Dallas | TX | 97338 |

FIGURE 3-11    WAREHOUSE table in second normal form

The second rule of third normal form is that each non-key column depends only on the primary key and not another non-key column. Consider the city and state columns. Do city and state depend on the primary key whse_id? In this application, the whse_id column is just an assigned number to identify each warehouse within the company. On the other hand, the zip column is used by the post office to identify city and state by Zip code. Thus, it can be said that the city and state columns are dependent on the zip column.

To satisfy the second rule of third normal form, the WAREHOUSE table can be split into two tables as shown in Figure 3-12.

| whse_id | whse_address | zip |
|---------|--------------|------|
| 111 | 1511 Central Ave. | 48220 |
| 222 | 6803 Alder St. | 97338 |

WAREHOUSE

| zip | city | state |
|-------|---------|-------|
| 48220 | Detroit | MI |
| 97338 | Dallas | TX |

ZIP

WAREHOUSE (**whse_id**, whse_address, *zip*)

ZIPS (**zip**, city, state)

**FIGURE 3-12** **WAREHOUSE** and **ZIP** tables in third normal form

Let us consider another example of third normal form. Consider the ORDER table in Figure 3-13, in which each row represents a customer order.

| order_id | cust_id | product_id | quantity | unit_price | total_amt |
|----------|---------|------------|----------|------------|-----------|
| 601 | 123 | 132 | 11 | 25.86 | 284.46 |
| 602 | 789 | 546 | 54 | 35.77 | 1931.58 |
| 603 | 123 | 758 | 33 | 22.10 | 729.30 |
| 604 | 198 | 910 | 87 | 91.59 | 7968.33 |

**FIGURE 3-13** **ORDER** table

To satisfy third normal form, all columns must be dependent on the primary key. In this example, this seems to be true except for the total_amt column, whose value is determined by multiplying the quantity by the unit_price. Thus, the total_amt column is not dependent on the primary key. To satisfy the second rule of third normal form, the total_amt column is removed from the table, as shown in Figure 3-14. The ORDER table is now in third normal form.

| order_id | cust_id | product_id | quantity | unit_price |
|----------|---------|------------|----------|------------|
| 601 | 123 | 132 | 11 | 25.86 |
| 602 | 789 | 546 | 54 | 35.77 |
| 603 | 123 | 758 | 33 | 22.10 |
| 604 | 198 | 910 | 87 | 91.59 |

**FIGURE 3-14** **ORDER** table in third normal form (3NF)

In this example, the total_amt column was removed from the table because it can be calculated during an SQL query by multiplying the quantity by the unit_price.

Understanding database normalization techniques is important to achieving a good database design. If the database design does not conform to at least the third normal form, it may be difficult to achieve a successful database application.

## BOYCE-CODD NORMAL FORM (BCNF)

A table is in Boyce-Codd normal form (BCNF) if every determinant is a candidate key. A **determinant** is any column within the row that determines the value of another column. The BCNF was developed to handle situations in which a non-key column determines the value of part of the primary key. Let us consider an example.

Bluewater Hospital assigns assessment rooms by the day so visiting doctors can meet with patients. Mary in the assessment office schedules the doctor visits and assigns each doctor to a specific assessment room. The schedule is posted on a board in the assessment entrance so doctors know which room they have been assigned for the day and patients know where their visit is scheduled. Figure 3-15 shows an example of the schedule. Mary wants this data converted into a database and needs to have it normalized to BCNF.

APPOINTMENT table

| patient_id | appt_date | app_time | doctor_id | room_id |
|---|---|---|---|---|
| 38963 | 05-16-2011 | 10:45 AM | D142 | E104 |
| 54321 | 05-17-2011 | 9:30 AM | D987 | E101 |
| 83691 | 05-17-2011 | 9:30 AM | D142 | E102 |
| 66301 | 05-17-2011 | 10:45 AM | D987 | E101 |
| 54321 | 05-17-2011 | 12:15 PM | D639 | E104 |
| 54321 | 05-17-2011 | 3:20 PM | D987 | E101 |
| 14682 | 05-18-2011 | 9:30 AM | D987 | E105 |
| 73811 | 05-19-2011 | 10:45 AM | D987 | E103 |
| 54321 | 05-20-2011 | 9:30 AM | D987 | E101 |

FIGURE 3-15   Appointment schedule

Let us consider the functional dependencies for this data, which are shown in Figure 3-16.

```
patient_id, appt_date, appt_time → doctor_id, room_id
doctor_id, appt_date, appt_time → patient_id, room_id
room_id, appt_date, appt_time → patient_id, doctor_id
```

FIGURE 3-16   Functional dependencies

These three functional dependencies are all candidate keys for this table. For example, if we know the values of `patient_id`, `appt_date`, and `appt_time`, we then know the values of `doctor_id` and `room_id`. Thus, they meet the requirements of BCNF. Now, consider the following functional dependency:

`doctor_id, appt_date → room_id`

This functional dependency is not a candidate key for the table because the concatenated key (`doctor_id` and `appt_date`) does not uniquely identify each row of the table. As a consequence, the `APPOINTMENT` table may result in update anomalies. For example, if the room number assigned to doctor D987 on May 17, 2011, needs to change, three rows have to be updated in the table.

To meet the requirements of BCNF, the `APPOINTMENT` table needs to be changed. The violating functional dependency needs to be removed by creating two new tables called `APPOINTMENT` and `DOCTOR_ROOM` as shown in Figure 3-17.

| patient_id | appt_date | app_time | doctor_id |
|---|---|---|---|
| 38963 | 05-16-2011 | 10:45 AM | D142 |
| 54321 | 05-17-2011 | 9:30 AM | D987 |
| 83691 | 05-17-2011 | 9:30 AM | D142 |
| 66301 | 05-17-2011 | 10:45 AM | D987 |
| 54321 | 05-17-2011 | 12:15 PM | D639 |
| 54321 | 05-17-2011 | 3:20 PM | D987 |
| 14682 | 05-18-2011 | 9:30 AM | D987 |
| 73811 | 05-19-2011 | 10:45 AM | D987 |
| 54321 | 05-20-2011 | 9:30 AM | D987 |

APPOINTMENT

| doctor_id | appt_date | room_id |
|---|---|---|
| D142 | 05-16-2011 | E104 |
| D987 | 05-17-2011 | E101 |
| D142 | 05-17-2011 | E102 |
| D639 | 05-17-2011 | E104 |
| D987 | 05-18-2011 | E105 |
| D987 | 05-19-2011 | E103 |
| D987 | 05-20-2011 | E101 |

DOCTOR_ROOM

Tables in BCNF:

APPOINTMENT (**patient id**, **appt date**, **appt time**, doctor_id)
　　FK doctor_id, app_date → DOCTOR_ROOMS

DOCTOR_ROOM (**doctor id**, **appt date**, room_id)

FIGURE 3-17　Example of tables in BCNF

A table is in **Boyce-Codd normal form (BCNF)** when:

- It is in third normal form (3NF).
- Every determinant in the table is a candidate key.

## FOURTH NORMAL FORM (4NF)

A database table is in **fourth normal form (4NF)** when:

- It is in third normal form (3NF).
- It has no multivalued dependencies. A multivalued fact is one in which several values for a column might be determined by one value for another column, such as the children of an employee or the courses taken by an employee.

The table in Figure 3-18 represents two multivalued facts.

| employee_id | child | course |
|---|---|---|
| 576 | Bonnie | Math 101 |
| 576 | Janice | Psych 203 |
| 576 | Sam | ? |
| 601 | Abigail | Art 101 |

**FIGURE 3-18    EMPLOYEE table with multivalued facts**

Let us consider the problem in this table. When an employee has an unequal number of children and courses, what value should be used as a placeholder? You cannot use null because all three columns are necessary in the primary key, and primary key columns cannot have null. The solution is to use two tables as shown in Figure 3-19.

| employee_id | child |
|---|---|
| 576 | Bonnie |
| 576 | Janice |
| 576 | Sam |
| 601 | Abigail |

| employee_id | course |
|---|---|
| 576 | Math 101 |
| 576 | Psych 203 |
| 601 | Art 101 |

**FIGURE 3-19    EMPLOYEE table split into two tables**

## Practical Example

The table in Figure 3-20 contains unnormalized data about college students. Let us consider the steps required to put this data into third normal form (3NF).

| student_id | student_name | credits | advisor_id | advisor_name | course_id | course_desc | grade |
|---|---|---|---|---|---|---|---|
| 12345 | Jane Smith | 12 | 654 | Shirley Jones | CIS 101<br>CIS 102<br>CIS 110 | Logic<br>XHTML<br>Visual Basic | A<br>B<br>A |
| 98765 | Thomas Last | 9 | 745 | Terry Evans | BUS 101<br>ENG 101<br>ENG 102 | Business I<br>English I<br>English II | B<br>C<br>C |
| 56789 | Robert Sim | 12 | 654 | Shirley Jones | ACC 101<br>ACC 102<br>ENG 101<br>ENG 102 | Accounting I<br>Accounting II<br>English I<br>English II | B<br>A<br>A<br>A |

STUDENT

STUDENT (student_id, student_name, credits, advisor_id, advisor_name, course_id, course_desc, grade)

FIGURE 3-20   Unnormalized **STUDENT** data

## First Normal Form (1NF)

*Step 1.* Remove the repeating groups. Every cell must have only one value.

| student_id | student_name | credits | advisor_id | advisor_name | course_id | course_desc | grade |
|---|---|---|---|---|---|---|---|
| 12345 | Jane Smith | 12 | 654 | Shirley Jones | CIS 101 | Logic | A |
| 12345 | Jane Smith | 12 | 654 | Shirley Jones | CIS 102 | XHTML | B |
| 12345 | Jane Smith | 12 | 654 | Shirley Jones | CIS 110 | Visual Basic | A |
| 98765 | Thomas Last | 9 | 745 | Terry Evans | BUS 101 | Business I | B |
| 98765 | Thomas Last | 9 | 745 | Terry Evans | ENG 101 | English I | C |
| 98765 | Thomas Last | 9 | 745 | Terry Evans | ENG 102 | English II | C |
| 56789 | Robert Sim | 12 | 654 | Shirley Jones | ACC 101 | Accounting I | B |
| 56789 | Robert Sim | 12 | 654 | Shirley Jones | ACC 102 | Accounting II | A |
| 56789 | Robert Sim | 12 | 654 | Shirley Jones | ENG 101 | English I | A |
| 56789 | Robert Sim | 12 | 654 | Shirley Jones | ENG 102 | English II | A |

STUDENT

*Step 2.* Identify the primary key. The primary key uniquely identifies every row. In this example, it requires two attributes to uniquely identify each row. Thus, `student_id` and `course_id` are concatenated to form the primary key.

| student_id | student_name | credits | advisor_id | advisor_name | course_id | course_desc | grade |
|---|---|---|---|---|---|---|---|
| 12345 | Jane Smith | 12 | 654 | Shirley Jones | CIS 101 | Logic | A |
| 12345 | Jane Smith | 12 | 654 | Shirley Jones | CIS 102 | XHTML | B |
| 12345 | Jane Smith | 12 | 654 | Shirley Jones | CIS 110 | Visual Basic | A |
| 98765 | Thomas Last | 9 | 745 | Terry Evans | BUS 101 | Business I | B |
| 98765 | Thomas Last | 9 | 745 | Terry Evans | ENG 101 | English I | C |
| 98765 | Thomas Last | 9 | 745 | Terry Evans | ENG 102 | English II | C |
| 56789 | Robert Sim | 12 | 654 | Shirley Jones | ACC 101 | Accounting I | B |
| 56789 | Robert Sim | 12 | 654 | Shirley Jones | ACC 102 | Accounting II | A |
| 56789 | Robert Sim | 12 | 654 | Shirley Jones | ENG 101 | English I | A |
| 56789 | Robert Sim | 12 | 654 | Shirley Jones | ENG 102 | English II | A |

STUDENT

STUDENT (**student id**, student_name, credits, advisor_id, advisor_name, **course id**, course_desc, grade)

The STUDENT table is now in 1NF because

- There are no repeating groups
- All of the primary key attributes have been identified
- All non-key attributes are dependent on the primary key

## SECOND NORMAL FORM (2NF)

*Step 1.* Eliminate partial dependencies. A partial dependency exists when a column is determined by only part of the primary key. This occurs in a table that contains a concatenated primary key. To resolve partial dependency, each component of the primary key identified in 1NF is used to create a new table. As a result, the original table is divided into the three tables shown in the dependency diagram below.

```
Partial Dependencies:

student_id → student_name, credits, advisor_id,
advisor_name
course_id → course_desc
```

*Step 2.* Move dependent attributes from the original table to the new tables.

| student_id | student_name | credits | advisor_id | advisor_name |
|------------|--------------|---------|------------|--------------|
| 12345 | Jane Smith | 12 | 654 | Shirley Jones |
| 98765 | Thomas Last | 9 | 745 | Terry Evans |
| 56789 | Robert Sim | 12 | 654 | Shirley Jones |

STUDENT

| course_id | course_desc |
|-----------|-------------|
| CIS 101 | Logic |
| CIS 102 | XHTML |
| CIS 110 | Visual Basic |
| BUS 101 | Business I |
| ENG 101 | English I |
| ENG 102 | English II |
| ACC 101 | Accounting I |
| ACC 102 | Accounting II |

COURSE

| student_id | course_id | grade |
|------------|-----------|-------|
| 12345 | CIS 101 | A |
| 12345 | CIS 102 | B |
| 12345 | CIS 110 | A |
| 98765 | BUS 101 | B |
| 98765 | ENG 101 | C |
| 98765 | ENG 102 | C |
| 56789 | ACC 101 | B |
| 56789 | ACC 102 | A |
| 56789 | ENG 101 | A |
| 56789 | ENG 102 | A |

STUDENT_COURSE

STUDENT (**student id**, student_name, credits, advisor_id, advisor_name)
COURSE (**course id**, course_desc)
STUDENT_COURSE (**student_id**, **course_id**, grade)
  FK student_id → STUDENT
  FK course_id → COURSE

The tables are now in 2NF because

- They are in 1NF
- There are no partial dependencies

## THIRD NORMAL FORM (3NF)

A table in 3NF is a table in which non-key columns determine the value of another non-key column. As mentioned, a determinant is any column within the row that determines the value of another column. In the STUDENT table, advisor_id is a determinant that determines the value of advisor_name. As a result, a new table is created with the determinant as the primary key. In addition, the determinant attribute advisor_id remains in the original table as a foreign key.

Non-Key Dependency:

advisor_id → advisor_name

| student_id | student_name | credits | advisor_id |
|------------|--------------|---------|------------|
| 12345 | Jane Smith | 12 | 654 |
| 98765 | Thomas Last | 9 | 745 |
| 56789 | Robert Sim | 12 | 654 |

STUDENT

| advisor_id | advisor_name |
|------------|--------------|
| 654 | Shirley Jones |
| 745 | Terry Evans |
| 654 | Shirley Jones |

ADVISOR

**Relational schema of tables in 3NF:**

STUDENT (**student_id,** student_name, credits, advisor_id)
   FK advisor_id → ADVISOR

ADVISOR (**advisor_id,** advisor_name)

COURSE (**course_id,** course_desc)

STUDENT_COURSE (**student_id, course_id,** grade)
   FK student_id → STUDENT
   FK course_id → COURSE

The tables are now in 3NF because

- They are in 2NF
- They do not contain non-key columns that determine the value of other non-key columns

## END-OF-CHAPTER

### CHAPTER SUMMARY

1. Normalization is a series of steps used to evaluate and modify table structures to reduce data redundancies.

2. There are two purposes for normalization:

   a. Eliminate redundant data; that is, eliminate the storing of the same data in more than one
   b. Ensure that data within a table are related

3. Eliminating redundant data is achieved by splitting tables with redundant data into two or more tables without the redundancy.

4. Normal forms:

   a. Tables that satisfy the requirements for normal forms (1NF through 4NF) represent certain facts unambiguously and non-redundantly.

   b. A database table is in first normal form (1NF) when:

      • All columns in the table contain a single value. That is, every intersection of a row and column in the table contains only one value.
      • A primary key has been defined that uniquely identifies each row in the table.

   c. A database table is in second normal form (2NF) when:

      • It is in first normal form (1NF).
      • Each non-key column depends on the entire primary key.

   d. A database table is in third normal form (3NF) when:

      • It is in second normal form (2NF).
      • Each non-key column depends only on the primary key. This rule is not satisfied when a non-key column determines the value of another non-key column.

   e. A table is in Boyce-Codd normal form (BCNF) if every determinant is a candidate key. A determinant is any column within the row that determines the value of another column. The BCNF was developed to handle situations in which a non-key column determines the value of part of the primary key.

f. A database table is in fourth normal form (4NF) when:

- It is in third normal form (3NF).
- There is no more than one multivalued fact in the table. A multivalued fact is one in which several values for a column might be determined by one value for another column, such as the children of an employee or the courses taken by an employee.

5. Referential integrity states that all foreign key values must either be null or match some existing row's primary key.

## KEY TERMS

| | |
|---|---|
| Boyce-Codd normal form (BCNF) | normalization |
| determinant | partial dependency |
| first normal form (1NF) | primary key |
| foreign key | relational schema |
| fourth normal form (4NF) | second normal form (2NF) |
| functional dependency | table form |
| multivalued fact | third normal form (3NF) |
| normal form | unnormalized table |

# CHAPTER 4

## PHYSICAL DATABASE DESIGN: CREATING TABLES

### CHAPTER OBJECTIVES

Upon completion of this chapter, you should be able to

- Explain what physical database design is
- Explain what a DBMS is
- Explain the hierarchy of database, tables, rows, and columns
- Explain the EBCDIC representation for storing data
- Explain what a schema is
- Create schemas and tables
- Explain and use different data types
- Explain the purpose of NULL values and how they are used in tables
- Insert (enter) data into tables
- Drop (delete) tables

## PHYSICAL DATABASE DESIGN

**Physical database design** provides the bridge between conceptual data modeling and implementation. This stage of an application development project determines how hardware and system software resources will be used to implement an efficient set of tables, views, and other application components that provide the capabilities specified in the data model. This chapter provides a series of steps that can be followed to produce a database design from a conceptual data model.

Conceptual data modeling analyzes an organization's information requirements to produce a data model that specifies entity types, attributes of entities, relationships among entities, and integrity rules. This conceptual data modeling terminology is mapped to the physical design as shown in Figure 4-1.

| Terminology mapping | | |
|---|:---:|---|
| **ER diagram** | ➜ | **Physical design** |
| Entity | ➜ | Table |
| Instance | ➜ | Row |
| Attribute | ➜ | Column |
| Primary unique identifier (UID) | ➜ | Primary key |
| Secondary unique identifier | ➜ | Unique key |
| Relationship | ➜ | Foreign key |
| Business rules or constraints | ➜ | Check constraints |

**FIGURE 4-1**   Technology mapping from conceptual design to physical design

As shown in the figure, changing from analysis (conceptual model) to design (physical implementation) means changing terminology:

- An entity becomes a table.
- An instance becomes a row.
- An attribute becomes a column.
- A primary unique identifier becomes a primary key.
- A secondary unique identifier becomes a unique key.
- A relationship is transformed into a foreign-key column and a foreign key constraint.
- Business rules become constraints.

As shown, a relationship is transformed into a foreign key, which also includes a foreign key column. Business rules are the rules that the database must follow to be consistent. Some of these business rules are translated into check constraints; other, more complex rules require additional programming in the database or application.

The data model provides a description of both individual end-user or department views and an integrated set of tables and integrity rules. Both levels of description are from the business perspective and do not state particular implementation techniques.

Specific database design decisions require a thorough understanding of the performance and complexity tradeoffs. Separating conceptual data modeling and physical database design into two distinct stages is the best approach. The conceptual aspects of the system can be focused on during the data modeling stage. Then, while working on the database design, one can focus on the numerous platform-specific details and design an efficient implementation without clouding the understanding of what the system needs to deliver.

Although physical database design tasks may proceed in parallel with conceptual data modeling tasks, conceptually the physical database design follows the conceptual data model; one must determine *what* one wants to do before one decides *how* to do it. Here is a guideline to help keep the two processes distinct: Once there is a data model, all database design decisions should be able to be made based on the functionality and performance of the DBMS and the estimated pattern of data access.

## TRANSFORMING CONCEPTUAL DESIGN TO PHYSICAL DESIGN

The conceptual model (ER diagram) is transformed into a physical model. The physical implementation is a relational database.

Each entity is represented in the data model as a table containing columns that represent the entity's attributes. The table name is the plural of the entity name. For example, the EMPLOYEE entity becomes the EMPLOYEES table in the physical design.

For a table, the following design information should be specified:

- Full table name (maximum of 128 characters)
- System table name (specify if the full table name is longer than 10 characters; maximum of 10 characters)
- The name of the entity in the related data model
- Descriptive text for the table
- Schema that will contain the table
- User profile that will own the table

For each column, the following design information should be specified:

- Name of column. Column names are identical to the attribute names except that special characters and spaces are replaced with underscores. For example, the attribute first name becomes a column called first_name. Column names often use more abbreviations than attribute names.
- Table name that contains the column.
- Descriptive text for the column (up to 2,000 characters for column comments).
- Reference to the name of a standard column data type.
- Default column heading(s) (up to three lines of 20 characters for column labels).
- Column data type, length, and decimal positions.
- Whether the null placeholder is allowed.
- Default value, if any.
- Default display and print formats (as for telephone numbers).

Most of the listed items are self-explanatory; however, a few require further discussion. Each object must be contained in a schema and must have one user profile as its owner. Companies use various approaches to organizing objects into schemas. For database objects, there are several considerations. Often, organizations group objects into multiple schemas.

Some companies also use schemas to group different types of objects. For example, they put executable programs, including stored procedures, in one schema and put database tables and views in another. In general, it is best to keep all database tables and views related to an application in one schema. If there are many different applications, keeping multiple, related applications in a single schema can avoid an excessive number of schemas.

For object ownership, a common practice at many companies is to have a single user profile that owns all database objects. Specific authority to access these objects is then granted to other user profiles, which are the user profiles that end users specify when they sign on to the system. For large companies, there may be several user profiles whose purpose is to own application objects; for example, the `PayrollOwn` user profile may own the payroll application objects, and the `SalesOwn` user profile may own the order-entry and marketing application objects.

The implementation of special values or placeholders for a column requires careful consideration during design. One question is whether to specify an explicit default value to be used when a new row is added and no value is supplied for the column. The default value might also be used as the basis for the initial value put in an input field on a data-entry display. SQL uses blank for character columns and zero for numeric columns. If some other value is appropriate, specify that value.

Two more difficult exceptional cases are not-applicable and unknown. The first arises when a column might not always have a sensible value, such as the Color column of a part that has no particular color. The second case is different in that a value for the column might make sense; it just is not known what the value is at some particular time. There are two choices for either or both of these situations: use the null placeholder, or use some designated value to represent the condition(s).

Null-capable columns are supported. For example, when several columns are added together, the result will be null if any column is null. Although null-capable columns have the advantage of being a system-supported way of identifying that a column contains no valid value, the use of nulls is not problem-free. One should never allow null with primary key columns and rarely, if ever, with candidate key and foreign key columns.

Instead of null, a value can be designated that represents not-applicable and/or unknown. For example, for a column that contains the date an employee received his or her undergraduate degree, `0000-01-01` might be used for not-applicable if the employee does not have a degree and `0001-01-02` might be used for unknown if he or she has a degree but the date when the degree was received is not known. A column's default value, if any, needs to be considered in conjunction with the way not-applicable and unknown are represented. In this case, the value for unknown, `0001-01-02`, might be specified as the default value.

When designing the implementation of views and processes that have computations involving numeric or date columns, be sure to consider the values used for default, not-applicable, and unknown. For example, to calculate the average age of employees, be sure to handle values that have the format of dates but are not really valid birth date values. If the column for an employee's birth date can be `0001-01-02` to represent unknown, any summary routine should exclude employee rows with this value. If null is allowed for a column, be sure to consider the SQL and high-level language (HLL) handling of null-capable columns.

## PRIMARY, CANDIDATE, AND FOREIGN KEYS

A primary key is one or more columns that uniquely identify rows. Candidate keys are other column(s) that are also unique for each row. A foreign key is one or more columns in a dependent table that reference the primary key in a parent table. Each of these types of keys requires some implementation technique to enforce the corresponding integrity constraints. The `CREATE TABLE` statement provides the `CONSTRAINT` clause to specify primary, unique, and foreign keys. For existing tables, the `ALTER TABLE` statement can be used to add a constraint.

The `CREATE TABLE` statement supports some, but not all, of the possible actions for foreign key rules. For example, `CREATE TABLE` supports a delete rule of "cascade" for the case when a row is deleted from a parent table. But `CREATE TABLE` supports only the "reject" rule when a row is inserted into the dependent table and the row's foreign key does not match an existing primary key in the parent table. For foreign key rules not available with the `CREATE TABLE` statement, one of these techniques can be used:

- Create a trigger program for the parent and/or dependent table.
- Create a table-access routine in a stored procedure, and use that exclusively to perform table updates.

Trigger programs are programs that are called when a table update is attempted. The trigger program is written in an HLL and is associated with the appropriate database table. When an update to the table is attempted, the trigger program is called and is passed "before" and "after" images of the updated row. The program can analyze the pending table update and reject or accept it, as well as perform other actions.

Stored procedures can be written, using either an HLL or the SQL stored procedure language, that perform database updates. Such stored procedures can check the validity of an update before performing it and return an error condition, such as no parent row with matching primary key for foreign key, to the program that calls the stored procedure. This technique is similar to the use of triggers but offers more flexibility because the called stored procedure can have any interface, or set of parameters, required to provide enough information to determine the validity of the table update. Trigger programs essentially get nothing more than the name of the table and the before and after row images. On the other hand, custom stored procedures are not called when a utility program is used to update the table, but trigger programs are.

## SPECIFY VIEW IMPLEMENTATION

Once the initial database design for the data model's tables is complete, it is time to specify how the database will provide for the necessary end users' views. Recall that end users may need to see only selected rows or columns from data that is stored in tables. Users also may need to see data from several tables combined in a view; for example, a CUSTOMERORDERS view may combine data from the CUSTOMERS, ORDERS, ORDERITEMS, and PARTS tables.

A view provides a way to select, transform, or combine data from one or more underlying tables. In general, views provide a good way to implement end users' views.

Earlier steps described how stored procedures can be used to implement integrity constraints. For this purpose, these stored procedures are called to perform table updates. Stored procedures can also be used to read one or more tables and derive the type of data required in an end-user view. This technique is particularly useful when the capabilities of a view are not adequate.

As part of a table-access stored procedure, or for use directly by an application, an embedded cursor provides another way to select, transform, and combine data. A few functional differences exist between cursors and views, the main one being that views are persistent objects, whereas a cursor exists only during the application that uses it. A cursor also lets a program specify the order in which rows are returned, whereas a view does not. In general, if a view provides the functionality needed to implement an end-user view, it is the simplest alternative. In some cases, however, a cursor may avoid the need for the database management system to maintain an access path and, thus, may be a desirable performance tradeoff.

A final alternative for implementing end users' views is the use of interactive data retrieval tools that can provide methods of access that satisfy the requirements of some end users' views.

After selecting the appropriate design to provide the information specified in an end-user view, the next step is to specify exactly how the view is implemented. This specification might take the form of the necessary definitions for a CREATE VIEW statement. Do not just stop at the general specification to "use a view." Provide the full description so there is no ambiguity when the person responsible for implementation does his or her job. Note that future steps may revise some table designs, so this step should be revisited when changes are made that affect the specification of a view or other implementation method for an end-user view.

## SPECIFY SECURITY IMPLEMENTATION

With the initial design for the implementation of tables and end-user views completed, the objects necessary to design the implementation of security are known. This database design step specifies how read and update access will be controlled for tables and views as well as for related objects such as programs that implement file-access routines.

The first step is to specify public and private, or individual user profile, authority for table and program objects. The GRANT statement or the GRTOBJAUT (Grant Object Authority) command can be used to grant authorities. In general, it is best to grant only the resource-level authorities that are intended to be used in an unrestricted manner. For example, grant update rights to a table only if the user profile should have the authority to update the table in any way, potentially changing any column in any row.

SQL also allows column-level security for UPDATE statements, providing a finer-grained level of security than table-level security. Views can implement access that is restricted to selected rows or a subset of columns. This technique is especially useful for restricted read-only access. Trigger programs can provide some additional options for implementing specific update constraints based on the user profile.

For more context-sensitive control of database access, stored procedures—in the form of either general-purpose table-access routines or more specialized, task-specific routines—can be used. These routines can employ program adopted authority to provide controlled access beyond what a user profile normally has. For example, users who do not have general update authority to a table can still perform certain types of changes if they are authorized to use a stored procedure that adopts update authority to the table while the stored procedure is in use.

A final technique to consider in the database design is the implementation of an audit trail for some or all of the database access. Journaling or trigger programs provide two system-supported ways to record who accesses various data and what changes they make.

## Specifying Additional Indexes for Performance

There is only one way to know for certain the performance consequences of a particular implementation technique: Measure the results. Any production-level approach to performance must include some means of measurement.

Let us consider indexes, which are one of the most common options for improving performance. An **index** usually provides an efficient way to access a specific row by key value or to process some or all of a table in a particular sequence. An index can be created by using the CREATE INDEX statement. The database design will already include at least one index for each primary key and potentially others for candidate and foreign keys. In most cases, the need to access individual rows using the value of one or more columns will correspond to a primary or other candidate key; thus, many additional indexes will not be needed for this purpose.

The two most common reasons to consider additional indexes are for retrieving groups of rows in a particular sequence and as an efficient way to select a subset of rows. For large tables, indexes can speed these two types of retrieval. Indexes, however, add overhead to update operations because the system must keep index entries up-to-date when it adds, deletes, or changes rows in a table with one or more indexes.

One good candidate for an index is a column that is used frequently in a view that defines a join. If sets of joined rows are retrieved based on the one table's primary key, an index over the related column(s) in the other table may significantly improve performance.

For selection purposes, an index provides the greatest performance improvement when the table contains a lot of rows and the selection criteria selects a small percentage. For small tables, or once the number of selected rows reaches about 20 percent of the file, an index offers little, if any, performance improvement.

One type of index to avoid, unless it has a high payoff for retrieval, is an index over a frequently updated column. This type of index requires frequent updating and adds to the overhead of table updates.

When designing multiple indexes over the same table, consider the ability for the database management system to share indexes (access paths). If possible, design multicolumn indexes so the major key columns are also the key columns for indexes with fewer key columns. For example, suppose an index needs to be defined to enforce uniqueness for a candidate key consisting of `employee_id` and `project_id` on a table that stores employee assignments to projects. To guarantee uniqueness, it does not matter whether the major key column in the index is `employee_id` or `project_id`. But if a view also exists that has a single-column key consisting of `project_id` (and no view is keyed on `employee_id`), it may be better to define the composite key with `project_id` as the major key column. With that done, the DBMS can share the same index for both purposes.

Permanent indexes are not the only way to design row selection and sequencing. If no appropriate index exists when a view or embedded cursor is used, the DBMS handles the request by creating a temporary index, sequentially scanning the table, or using a variety of other on-the-fly methods. If these methods provide satisfactory retrieval performance, the update overhead of a permanent index may not be worth incurring.

## HIERARCHY OF DATA

Computer languages provide the computer with the instructions to perform specific tasks. Normally, these instructions include accessing data. **Data** are unorganized raw facts. **Information**, on the other hand, is the result of data being processed into something meaningful. For example, suppose there is a database table stored on disk containing items of interest about each employee. These items of interest are considered unorganized raw facts that have been accumulated and stored about each employee. If a computer program retrieves specific data from the employee database table and produces a listing of employees and their current vacation status, this would be meaningful information.

### VARIABLES

An important aspect of a computer program is the ability to store and manipulate values in computer memory locations. The values stored in computer memory and in tables on disk are called **variables**. Variables are sometimes referred to as fields. Variable names are used to represent the actual computer memory locations. Every variable has a name, type, size, and value. As a program executes, data stored in a specific variable will often change. For example, a program that prints a report may contain the date and time in the report headings. Each time the program runs, the value in the variable containing the time is different. Another example is a program that lists employees of an organization. The memory location referenced by the employee number variable will contain a different value as each employee is processed.

## DATABASE, TABLES, ROWS, AND COLUMNS

In the relational database model, data are stored in tables. A **table**, sometimes referred to as a **file**, is organized into rows and columns in the same way a spreadsheet is represented. A **row**, sometimes referred to as a **record**, represents a group of related data; within each row are columns. A **column**, often referred to as a **field**, is a group of storage positions reserved for one specific item of data

Figure 4-2 illustrates a conceptual perspective of customer data in table form. In the customer table, each row contains related data about one customer, where each column contains specific data about that customer. A column is similar to a cell in a spreadsheet. Every row in a table has the same structure.

For example, customer number and customer name are two columns that represent data for a specific customer. In the customer table, the columns for each row are grouped together to form data relevant to a specific customer.

Note that the table rows in the figure are illustrated in table form for ease of reading. When stored in the computer, a row is stored as contiguous data without spaces, periods, or commas.

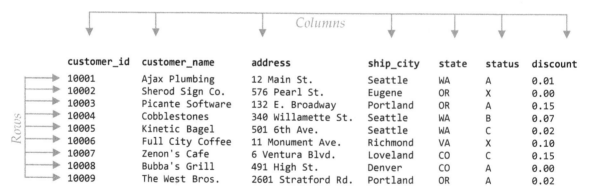

| | customer_id | customer_name | address | ship_city | state | status | discount |
|---|---|---|---|---|---|---|---|
| | 10001 | Ajax Plumbing | 12 Main St. | Seattle | WA | A | 0.01 |
| | 10002 | Sherod Sign Co. | 576 Pearl St. | Eugene | OR | X | 0.00 |
| | 10003 | Picante Software | 132 E. Broadway | Portland | OR | A | 0.15 |
| | 10004 | Cobblestones | 340 Willamette St. | Seattle | WA | B | 0.07 |
| | 10005 | Kinetic Bagel | 501 6th Ave. | Seattle | WA | C | 0.02 |
| | 10006 | Full City Coffee | 11 Monument Ave. | Richmond | VA | X | 0.10 |
| | 10007 | Zenon's Cafe | 6 Ventura Blvd. | Loveland | CO | C | 0.15 |
| | 10008 | Bubba's Grill | 491 High St. | Denver | CO | A | 0.00 |
| | 10009 | The West Bros. | 2601 Stratford Rd. | Portland | OR | A | 0.02 |

**FIGURE 4-2**   **Conceptual view of a customer table**

When stored on disk, each table contains object-header information. This header is often referred to as the table description, and it includes a description of the table's format, including the byte-by-byte layout of all the columns in the table.

The database management system uses the layout to know where specific columns are placed in a row that is to be added to the table or where specific columns should be retrieved from a row that has been read from the table. Once the layout of the table has been defined, the DBMS can reference all columns by their column names (e.g., customer_name); there is no need to deal with specific byte locations or other low-level storage details.

Figure 4-3 depicts a simple table layout for a customer table, along with a sample of data for one row. Not that the carat (^) symbol represents an implied decimal position.

| Column description | Type | Size | Start position | Storage (in bytes) | SQL name |
|---|---|---|---|---|---|
| Customer ID | Integer | 9,0 | 1 | 4 | customer_id |
| Customer Name | Character | 30 | 5 | 30 | name |
| Address | Character | 100 | 35 | 100 | address |
| Ship to City | Character | 30 | 135 | 30 | ship_city |
| Ship to State | Character | 2 | 165 | 2 | ship_state |
| Status | Character | 1 | 167 | 1 | status |
| Discount | Decimal | 3,2 | 168 | 2 | discount |

| 10001 | Ajax Plumbing | 12 Main St. | Seattle | WA | A | 0^01 |
|---|---|---|---|---|---|---|
| ↑ | ↑ | ↑ | ↑ | ↑ | ↑ | ↑ |
| 1 | 5 | 35 | 135 | 165 | 167 | 168 |

**FIGURE 4-3**    **Layout for customer table**

If a retail organization wanted to store data about its employees, it probably would want to include the following data elements: employee number, store number, employee name, department number, hourly rate, hours worked, sales, and so on. Each data element describes one specific aspect of the employee and is stored as a variable. Suppose an employee's number is 864955834; enough storage positions would be set aside to store this value in the employee number variable.

Examine the employee number variable in Figure 4-4, and observe that the value 864955834 is stored in a storage area allocated to employee number. Storage space is also allocated to store the employee's last name. In this example, the value "Hansen" is stored in the employee last name variable.

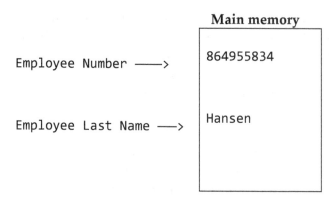

**FIGURE 4-4** Allocating storage positions for the employee number and last name variables

A row, sometimes referred to as a record, is a collection of related columns (fields) stored as a unit. In the example, the columns for each employee are grouped together to form one row in the employee pay table shown in Figure 4-5. Within each employee row is specific data relevant to one employee in the organization.

| Field —> | Employee ID | Store ID | First Name | Middle Initial | Last Name | Dept ID | Hourly Rate | Hours Worked | Sales |
|---|---|---|---|---|---|---|---|---|---|
| Sample data—> | 864955834 | 2257 | Laura | J | Hansen | 444 | 009^75 | 15^0 | 00024– |

**FIGURE 4-5** Group of related columns stored as one row in the employee pay table

Note that the figure illustrates the row in table form for ease of reading. When stored in the computer, a row exists as contiguous variables without spaces, periods, or commas. The carat symbol (^) shown in the values for Hourly Rate and Hours Worked represents an implied decimal point and is not stored in the actual variable. Also, the negative sign (–) shown in the Sales variable is used to represent a negative value. Later, this chapter discusses how negative values are stored in the computer.

A table, sometimes referred to as a file, is a collection of rows pertaining to a specific application. Figure 4-6 shows the first 15 rows from the employee pay table. Each row represents data for one employee of the organization. A payroll table, accounts receivable table, inventory table, and sales table are examples of commonly used tables in business applications.

| Employee ID | Store ID | First Name | Middle Initial | Last Name | Dept ID | Hourly Rate | Hours Worked | Sales |
|---|---|---|---|---|---|---|---|---|
| 827392161 | 7315 | Magdi | | Ali | 666 | 015^50 | 43^5 | 10400 |
| 228725876 | 5003 | Brenda | M | Fields | 666 | 009^85 | 40^0 | 04555 |
| 132135478 | 1133 | Janice | A | Porter | 333 | 008^55 | 10^0 | 00000 |
| 864955834 | 2257 | Laura | J | Hansen | 444 | 009^75 | 15^0 | 00024- |
| 103429376 | 4464 | Sang Yong | | Lee | 333 | 009^95 | 35^0 | 00563 |
| 314792638 | 1133 | Isabel | L | Houle | 666 | 023^60 | 45^0 | 21245 |
| 223649622 | 5003 | Tom | P | Simpson | 333 | 017^90 | 20^0 | 00099- |
| 123728964 | 1133 | Susan | P | Murphy | 111 | 023^21 | 45^0 | 10125 |
| 832476894 | 2257 | Stacey | V | Bond | 555 | 011^25 | 40^0 | 00740 |
| 235235658 | 4464 | Karl | C | Ryckman | 333 | 014^45 | 42^5 | 07866 |
| 336782368 | 2257 | Pabla | | Jorge | 333 | 021^45 | 17^5 | 00125- |
| 237289568 | 7315 | Theodore | P | Xavier | 666 | 025^00 | 35^0 | 01999 |
| 137298794 | 2257 | Jose | | Fernandes | 222 | 024^50 | 43^5 | 00899 |
| 443639268 | 5003 | Dave | M | Fergusan | 555 | 017^50 | 42^5 | 08797 |
| 246853789 | 1133 | Robert | M | Doyle | 444 | 012^45 | 13^5 | 00235- |

**FIGURE 4-6**    Group of related rows stored in the employee pay table

In most instances, a computer application system will include several related tables, collectively referred to as a database. Thus, a database is defined as the collection of related tables in a computer application system that can be joined.

## INTERNAL BINARY REPRESENTATION OF DATA

Internally, data are stored differently depending on the computer system used. The two computer codes used for internal binary representation are ASCII and EBCDIC. Microcomputers and non-IBM computer vendors use **ASCII**, which stands for *American Standard Code for Information Interchange.*

IBM enterprise computers use the EBCDIC coding system, which is the only coding system illustrated in this book. **EBCDIC** stands for *Extended Binary Coded Decimal Interchange Code* and is used to represent letters, digits, the blank character, and special characters. The chart in Figure 4-7 illustrates the EBCDIC codes for letters, numbers, and blank. It also displays the binary representation and hexadecimal (hex) codes used by the computer to represent EBCDIC codes. It is not necessary to memorize this chart, but it is important to be familiar with these methods for representing data.

There are times when it is necessary to display data as it is physically stored. However, it can be difficult to understand data in its binary form. Instead, each 8-bit EBCDIC byte is converted to a 2-character hexadecimal value as shown in Figure 4-8.

Each 4-bit portion of a byte is represented by one hexadecimal character. Hex characters can range from 0 (all 4 bits off = 0000) to F (all 4 bits on = 1111). Thus, this figure shows the full range of 4-bit binary combinations and their hexadecimal characters.

| | EBCDIC | | | | | | | | | | |
|---|---|---|---|---|---|---|---|---|---|---|---|
| | Binary | | | | Binary | | | | Binary | | |
| Char | Zone | Digit | Hex | Char | Zone | Digit | Hex | Char | Zone | Digit | Hex |
| blank | 0100 | 0000 | 40 | u | 1010 | 0100 | A4 | P | 1101 | 0111 | D7 |
| a | 1000 | 0001 | 81 | v | 1010 | 0101 | A5 | Q | 1101 | 1000 | D8 |
| b | 1000 | 0010 | 82 | w | 1010 | 0110 | A6 | R | 1101 | 1001 | D9 |
| c | 1000 | 0011 | 83 | x | 1010 | 0111 | A7 | S | 1110 | 0010 | E2 |
| d | 1000 | 0100 | 84 | y | 1010 | 1000 | A8 | T | 1110 | 0011 | E3 |
| e | 1000 | 0101 | 85 | z | 1010 | 1001 | A9 | U | 1110 | 0100 | E4 |
| f | 1000 | 0110 | 86 | A | 1100 | 0001 | C1 | V | 1110 | 0101 | E5 |
| g | 1000 | 0111 | 87 | B | 1100 | 0010 | C2 | W | 1110 | 0110 | E6 |
| h | 1000 | 1000 | 88 | C | 1100 | 0011 | C3 | X | 1110 | 0111 | E7 |
| i | 1000 | 1001 | 89 | D | 1100 | 0100 | C4 | Y | 1110 | 1000 | E8 |
| j | 1001 | 0001 | 91 | E | 1100 | 0101 | C5 | Z | 1110 | 1001 | E9 |
| k | 1001 | 0010 | 92 | F | 1100 | 0110 | C6 | 0 | 1111 | 0000 | F0 |
| l | 1001 | 0011 | 93 | G | 1100 | 0111 | C7 | 1 | 1111 | 0001 | F1 |
| m | 1001 | 0100 | 94 | H | 1100 | 1000 | C8 | 2 | 1111 | 0010 | F2 |
| n | 1001 | 0101 | 95 | I | 1100 | 1001 | C9 | 3 | 1111 | 0011 | F3 |
| o | 1001 | 0110 | 96 | J | 1101 | 0001 | D1 | 4 | 1111 | 0100 | F4 |
| p | 1001 | 0111 | 97 | K | 1101 | 0010 | D2 | 5 | 1111 | 0101 | F5 |
| q | 1001 | 1000 | 98 | L | 1101 | 0011 | D3 | 6 | 1111 | 0110 | F6 |
| r | 1001 | 1001 | 99 | M | 1101 | 0100 | D4 | 7 | 1111 | 0111 | F7 |
| s | 1010 | 0010 | A2 | N | 1101 | 0101 | D5 | 8 | 1111 | 1000 | F8 |
| t | 1010 | 0011 | A3 | O | 1101 | 0110 | D6 | 9 | 1111 | 1001 | F9 |

FIGURE 4-7     EBCDIC codes

| Binary | Hexadecimal |
|---|---|
| 0000 | 0 |
| 0001 | 1 |
| 0010 | 2 |
| 0011 | 3 |
| 0100 | 4 |
| 0101 | 5 |
| 0110 | 6 |
| 0111 | 7 |
| 1000 | 8 |
| 1001 | 9 |
| 1010 | A |
| 1011 | B |
| 1100 | C |
| 1101 | D |
| 1110 | E |
| 1111 | F |

FIGURE 4-8     4-bit binary combinations and corresponding hexadecimal characters

Figure 4-9 illustrates the binary and hexadecimal representations for the capital letter A.

| 8 | 4 | 2 | 1 | 8 | 4 | 2 | 1 | |
|---|---|---|---|---|---|---|---|---|
| | | | | | | | | |
| 1 | 1 | 0 | 0 | 0 | 0 | 0 | 1 | ← Binary value |
| C | | | | 1 | | | | ← Hex representation |
| Zone | | | | Digit | | | | |

**FIGURE 4-9**   **Binary representation of a single byte representing the letter A**

In EBCDIC, each storage position, or byte, consists of eight bits (binary digits). These eight bits are broken into two 4-bit segments. The high-order four bits are used to specify the *zone* portion, and the low-order four bits are used to specify the *digit* portion.

The four high-order zone bits are used to indicate whether the value stored in the byte is a letter, positive number, negative number, or special character. The four low-order digit bits are used to represent the numbers 0 through 9. Examine Figure 4-7 again, and observe that 1100 in the zone bits indicates that the value of the byte is one of the uppercase letters A through I. If 1100 appears in the four zone bits, the digit bits then will indicate which specific letter from A through I is being represented. The digit bits can represent 0 through 9 as 0000, 0001, 0010, 0011, . . . 1001.

A = 11000001

# DATA TYPES

Every variable must have a data type specified. A **data type** identifies what type of data can be stored in the variable and how large the value can be. Several different data types exist to store data. The method used to represent data depends on the type of processing to be performed on the data. The method used to define numeric data also affects a program's efficiency. Figure 4-10 identifies the most common data types.

## CHARACTER DATA TYPE

A **character data type** contains any combination of letters, digits, and special characters, such as $, %, @, or &. Simply, a character data type contains any printable characters. In the layout that was shown in Figure 4-3, the customer name, address, ship-to city, ship-to-state, and status are defined as character data types. In this format, a single position of storage, or byte, is used to store one character of data. A variable defined as a character data type cannot be used in arithmetic operations even though the field may contain only numeric digits.

| Data type | Description |
|---|---|
| CHAR(length) | The CHAR data type is a fixed-length character string that stores one character in each byte of the variable. The length (given as an integer) is specified in parentheses. If a character string that is 95 characters long is stored in a CHAR(150) column, it occupies 150 characters (95 characters for the actual data plus 55 blank spaces). The character data type can be used for variables that contain alphabetic or special characters and for columns containing numbers that are not used in calculations. If no length is specified, the default length of 1 is used. |
| VARCHAR(max-length) | The VARCHAR data type stores a variable-length character string. The maximum length of the string is specified in parentheses. Unlike the CHAR data type, the VARCHAR data type stores only the actual character string. For example, if a character string of 95 characters is stored in a VARCHAR(150) variable, it occupies only 95 characters.<br><br>In general, VARCHAR data types should be used for columns containing long descriptions or text that is seldom referenced. Fifty bytes is probably the smallest length that should be defined as a VARCHAR variable. DB2 does have to allocate some additional bytes for each row with variable-length variables to keep track of the varying length data, so these extra "tracking" bytes consume some of the space savings. Due to this overhead, the space savings is noticeable only on tables with a large number of rows. |
| DECIMAL(size,d) | The DECIMAL data type, sometimes referred to as packed decimal, is specified as two integers separated by a comma. The first integer (size) is the total number of digits, which can range from 1 to 31. The second integer (d) is the number of digits to the right of the decimal point, which can range from 0 to the size. For example, the data type DECIMAL(7,2) represents a variable that contains a number with five places to the left and two places to the right of the decimal (e.g., 12345.67). If the size is specified without the number of digits, the default for digits is 0. |
| SMALLINT | The SMALLINT (small integer) data type stores integers, which are whole numbers without a decimal, in a 2-byte binary field. The valid range is –32768 to 32767. |
| INTEGER | The INTEGER data type stores integers in a 4-byte binary field. The valid range is –2147483648 to 2147483647. |
| BIGINT | The BIGINT (big integer) data type stores integers in an 8-byte binary field. The valid range is –9,223,372,036,854,775,808 to 9,223,372,036,854,775,807. |
| DATE | The DATE data type stores a date. Dates are enclosed in single quotation marks (') and have the form *yyyy-mm-dd*; for example, '2011-10-15' is October 15, 2011. |
| Boolean | DB2 does not support a Boolean data type. However, a CHECK constraint can be used to simulate a Boolean data type. This technique is illustrated in the next chapter. |

**FIGURE 4-10    Common data types**

Each byte of a character data type is divided into two portions: the high-order, 4-bit zone portion and the low-order, 4-bit digit portion. The following example shows how a 1-byte character variable containing the value P is represented.

P = 1101 0111

| Zone | Digit | |
|------|-------|------------------|
| D | 7 | ← Hex value |
| 1101 | 0111 | ← Binary value |

*1 byte of character data containing the value P*

In Figure 4-11, the name Pam is stored in a variable defined as a 5-byte character data type. Note that the last two bytes contain spaces, which are represented as 40 in hexadecimal.

| | Byte 1 | | Byte 2 | | Byte 3 | | Byte 4 | | Byte 5 | |
|----------------|------|-------|------|-------|------|-------|------|-------|------|-------|
| | Zone | Digit | Zone | Digit | Zone | Digit | Zone | Digit | Zone | Digit |
| Hex value→ | D | 7 | 8 | 1 | 9 | 4 | 4 | 0 | 4 | 0 |
| Binary value→ | 1101 | 0111 | 1000 | 0001 | 1000 | 0100 | 0100 | 0000 | 0100 | 0000 |
| | P | | a | | m | | (space) | | (space) | |

**FIGURE 4-11**  **Five-byte character data type**

## NUMERIC DATA TYPES

A **numeric data type** contains the numeric digits 0 through 9 only. Two considerations apply when defining numeric data types:

1. If a variable is to be used in an arithmetic operation, it must be defined as a numeric data type.
2. Variables such as employee number, ZIP code, and part number will probably not be used in arithmetic operations but will contain numeric digits only. Thus, these variables could be defined as character fields or as numeric fields.

Two primary data types exist for defining numeric data: DECIMAL and INTEGER.

### DECIMAL FORMAT

Fields defined as the **DECIMAL data type** can be up to eight bytes (15 digits) in length. In the table layout in Figure 4-3, the discount column is defined as a DECIMAL data type.

DECIMAL data types provide a method that can be used where the zone portion is stripped from each byte (except for the low-order byte) so digits can be packed two per byte. In this way, the zone portion of each byte can be used to represent another digit. Thus, two digits are represented in a single byte. This technique is called *packing*.

### STORING DECIMAL DATA

When a numeric variable is defined as a DECIMAL data type:

- Two numeric digits are stored in each byte, except for the rightmost byte, which also contains the sign.
- The low-order four bits (digit portion) of the rightmost byte of a DECIMAL data type contain the sign (F = positive, D = negative).
- All other zones are stripped, and two digits are packed into each byte.

Consider the number 68254 in Example 1 of Figure 4-12. When a 5-digit number is stored in a variable defined as a DECIMAL data type, it occupies three bytes. This occurs because the zone portion of each byte (except the rightmost one) is removed, thereby permitting each byte to hold two digits. The low-order, or rightmost, byte contains only one digit because it also holds the sign of the field. In the DECIMAL data type, the hex "F" in the low-order four bits (digit portion) of the rightmost byte represents a positive sign. A negative number is represented with a hex "D" in the low-order four bits.

**Example 1** — DECIMAL data type containing the numeric value 68254

```
Zone  Digit │ Zone  Digit │ Zone  Digit │
  6     8   │   2     5   │   4     F   │ (hex)
0110   1000 │ 0010   0101 │ 0100   1111 │ (binary)
                                        └ positive sign
```
**DECIMAL representation of 68254 (three bytes)**

**Example 2** — DECIMAL data type containing the negative numeric value –65276

```
Zone  Digit │ Zone  Digit │ Zone  Digit │
  6     5   │   2     7   │   6     D   │ (hex)
0110   0101 │ 0010   0111 │ 0110   1101 │ (binary)
                                        └ negative sign
```
**DECIMAL representation of negative 65276 (three bytes)**

**Example 3** — DECIMAL data type containing the numeric value 835674

```
Zone  Digit │ Zone  Digit │ Zone  Digit │ Zone  Digit │
  0     8   │   3     5   │   6     7   │   4     F   │ (hex)
0000   1000 │ 0011   0101 │ 0110   0111 │ 0100   1111 │ (binary)
  └ zero fill                              └ positive sign
```
**DECIMAL representation of 835674 (four bytes)**

**FIGURE 4-12    DECIMAL data type**

Example 2 in the figure illustrates how a negative number is represented in the DECIMAL data type. Notice that the negative sign is represented with a hexadecimal value D (1101). In the DECIMAL data type, the negative sign (D) is placed in the digit portion of the rightmost byte.

Example 3 in the figure, the number 835674, occupies four bytes when stored in a DECIMAL data type. The computer must complete the packing operation by adding four zero bits to complete, or fill up, the high-order byte. This step occurs whenever the size of the variable is an even number of digits, as in 835674.

> **Tip**
> When defining a DECIMAL data type, define it as containing an odd number of digits. This practice eliminates the need for the operating system to zero-fill the high-order byte and lets the field contain a larger value without requiring additional storage.

### DETERMINING THE SIZE OF A DECIMAL DATA TYPE

When determining the storage size of a DECIMAL data type, compute as follows:

1. Divide the number of digits in the size of the variable by 2.
2. If there is a decimal remainder of .5, drop it (round down).
3. Add 1 to the result.

### Example 1
Calculate the storage size of a DECIMAL data type that will store a 5-digit variable containing 79645.

1. Divide 5 by 2; 2.5 is the quotient.
2. Round down to 2.
3. Add 1.

*Result:* Three bytes are needed for the DECIMAL data type.

### Example 2
Calculate the storage size of a DECIMAL data type that will store a 6-digit variable containing 937562.

1. Divide 6 by 2; 3 is the quotient.
2. Add 1.

*Result:* Four bytes are needed for the DECIMAL data type.

> **Note**
> Because 6 is an even number, the high-order four bits are zero-filled. Therefore, it is best to define this field as containing seven digits.

## INTEGER DATA TYPE

An **integer data type** is stored in binary, in which the bits are directly interpreted as a number. For example, the number 14 is **1110** when represented in binary.

The leftmost bit of an integer field is used to keep track of the sign. If the leftmost bit is a zero (**0**), the number is positive. If the leftmost bit is a one (**1**), the number is negative.

The size of a number that an integer data type can store is based on the number of bits it occupies. One byte of memory can store a number in the range **–128** to **127**. Two bytes can store the range **–32768** to **32767**. Four bytes can store **–2147483648** to **2147483647**. Eight bytes can store **–9223372036854775808** to **9223372036854775807**.

Integer data types are stored in the binary (base 2) number system, which has only two digits: 0 and 1. Each position in the number represents a power of 2. The rightmost digit represents 2 to the zero power, or 1. The preceding digit represents 2 to the first power, or 2. The digit preceding that one represents 2 to the second power, or 4, and so on. Therefore, the binary number 101 means (1 * 4) + (0 * 2) + (2 * 1), or 5. A 2-byte integer consists of 16 bits. The bits represent the following numbers:

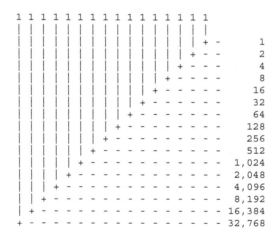

```
1 1 1 1 1 1 1 1 1 1 1 1 1 1 1 1
                        + -          1
                      + - -          2
                    + - - -          4
                  + - - - -          8
                + - - - - -         16
              + - - - - - -         32
            + - - - - - - -         64
          + - - - - - - - -        128
        + - - - - - - - - -        256
      + - - - - - - - - - -        512
    + - - - - - - - - - - -      1,024
  + - - - - - - - - - - - -      2,048
+ - - - - - - - - - - - - -      4,096
+ - - - - - - - - - - - - - -    8,192
+ - - - - - - - - - - - - - - - 16,384
+ - - - - - - - - - - - - - - - 32,768
```

If all the numbers are added, the sum is 65,535, the largest value a 2-byte integer can hold. Another way to calculate this value is to raise 2 to the 16th power and subtract 1. This is the value of a variable when all bits are set to 1.

Let us consider an example of a SMALLINT data type. In the employee pay table, the store number is defined as a SMALLINT, which means the store number variable occupies two bytes of storage and stores the value as a binary value. If the value 2257 were stored in the store number variable, if would be represented as follows:

| Byte 1 | | Byte 2 | |
|---|---|---|---|
| 0000 | 1000 | 1101 | 0001 |
| 0 | 2048 | 208 | 1 |

Integer variables differ in that the first digit is reserved for use as a sign bit. If the first bit is 0, the value is positive. If the first digit is 1, the value is negative. This form of storing numbers is known as *two's complement notation*. Because the first bit of a 4-byte integer is reserved for the sign, only 31 bits are available to store the number. Therefore, the greatest value of a 4-byte integer is 2 to the 31st power minus 1, or 2,147,483,647.

## SIMULATING A BOOLEAN DATA TYPE

A **Boolean data type** is a variable that can contain the values 1 or 0, representing true or false, respectively. DB2 does not support a Boolean data type. To create a database column (field) that simulates a Boolean data type, a check constraint is used with a SMALLINT column. This technique is illustrated in Chapter 5, Database Constraints.

## DATE FORMAT

A **date** data type is a variable that contains a valid date. Date variables have a predetermined size of 10 bytes and a predetermined format based on the internal format used in the application. Therefore, no data type or length is specified for date variables.

The default internal format for date fields is *ISO. **ISO** stands for **International Standards Organization**. When defined as an *ISO data type, the date variable is defined as a 10-byte variable using the format *yyyy-mm-dd*.

## TIMESTAMP FIELDS

A **timestamp data type** is a combination of the date and time variables. It contains a date and a time, as well as a fraction of a second. This makes a timestamp variable suitable for adding time durations that might cross over the date boundary or for keeping track of when something happened, such as the date and time when a row was updated.

## SAMPLE DATA FROM A TABLE

Examine the layout for the employee pay table in Figure 4-13. The figure's Description column contains a description for each column in the table. The Data type column identifies the data type of the column variable. The Size column contains the size of the data. For example, the employee number contains a number up to nine digits, the store number contains a 4-digit number (e.g., 2257), and sales contains a 9-digit number represented by seven places to the left of the decimal and two places to the right of the decimal (e.g., 1234567.89).

The Bytes column contains the internal storage of each column in bytes. For example, the employee number column is defined as an integer, which represents an internal storage of four bytes. The store number column is defined as a small integer and thus is stored internally as two bytes. The sales column, defined as a decimal, occupies five bytes of internal storage.

The Location column identifies the actual location of the data in the row. The employee number column, defined as an integer, occupies positions 1 through 4 in the row. The store number column, defined as a small integer, occupies positions 5 and 6 of each row. The sales column, which is a decimal, can store nine digits and occupies positions 65 through 69.

The SQL column name column contains the short name that is used to define each column in the row.

| Description | Data type | Size | Bytes | Location | SQL column name |
|---|---|---|---|---|---|
| Employee Number (PK) | INTEGER | | 4 | 1–4 | employee_id |
| Store Number | SMALLINT | | 2 | 5–6 | store_id |
| First Name | CHARACTER | 20 | 20 | 7–26 | first_name |
| Middle Initial | CHARACTER | 1 | 1 | 27–27 | m_initial |
| Last Name | CHARACTER | 20 | 20 | 28–47 | last_name |
| Hire Date | DATE | | 10 | 48–57 | hire_date |
| Department Number | SMALLINT | | 2 | 58–59 | department_id |
| Hourly Rate | DECIMAL | 5,2 | 3 | 60–62 | hourly_rate |
| Hours Worked | DECIMAL | 3,1 | 2 | 63–64 | hourh_worked |
| Sales | DECIMAL | 9,2 | 5 | 65–69 | sales |

FIGURE 4-13   Layout for employee pay table

Let us now consider Figure 4-14, which represents one row of data from the EMPLOYEES table, to illustrate how data are represented internally.

| Column description | Data type | Size | Bytes | Location | Sample data |
|---|---|---|---|---|---|
| Employee Number (PK) | INTEGER | | 4 | 1–4 | 244575315 |
| Store Number | SMALLINT | | 2 | 5–6 | 2257 |
| First Name | CHARACTER | 20 | 20 | 7–26 | Janice |
| Middle Initial | CHARACTER | 1 | 1 | 27–27 | H |
| Last Name | CHARACTER | 20 | 20 | 28–47 | Matheson |
| Hire Date | DATE | | 10 | 48–57 | 2009/01/15 |
| Department Number | SMALLINT | | 2 | 58–59 | 111 |
| Hourly Rate | DECIMAL | 5,2 | 3 | 60–62 | 015^70 |
| Hours Worked | DECIMAL | 3,1 | 2 | 63–64 | 22^5 |
| Sales | DECIMAL | 9,2 | 5 | 65–69 | 00056.75- |

**FIGURE 4-14**  Sample data for one row in the employee pay table EMPLOYEES

Figure 4-15 shows the row containing the actual data for this employee, Janice Matheson. Both the hexadecimal and character representations are used to represent internal EBCDIC codes. Character codes in the employee number, store number, and department number columns are represented with an asterisk (*) to indicate unknown characters because these variables are defined as INTEGER, SMALLINT, and SMALLINT, respectively.

| | | 1          2          3          4          5          6 |
|---|---|---|
| | | 12345678901234567890123456789012345678901234567890123456789 |
| Char: | | ******Janice        HMatheson        2009-01-15** |
| Hex: | Zone | 09E50DD89888844444444444444CD8A88A99444444444444FFFF6FF6FF060502500065 |
| | Digit | E3C3811159350000000000000084138526500000000000020090010150F17F2F0057D |

**FIGURE 4-15**  Hexadecimal and character representation of row data

Blanks are represented as hexadecimal 40. When a value is stored in a character field, the unused portion is padded with blanks, as shown in the first and last name fields.

The negative sign in the decimal sales field is represented with the value D in the low-order position of the byte (position 69).

Examine the first four bytes of data in the figure. These bytes represent the employee number of 244575315 defined as INTEGER. The hexadecimal representation for these four bytes is

0E|93|EC|53

When converted to binary, these hex numbers become

| 0 | 0000 |
|---|------|
| E | 1110 |
| 9 | 1001 |
| 3 | 0011 |
| E | 1110 |
| C | 1100 |
| 5 | 0101 |
| 3 | 0011 |

The chart in Figure 4-16 is used to determine the value of each binary digit. When the values are added, the result is **244575315**, the employee number for Janice Matheson.

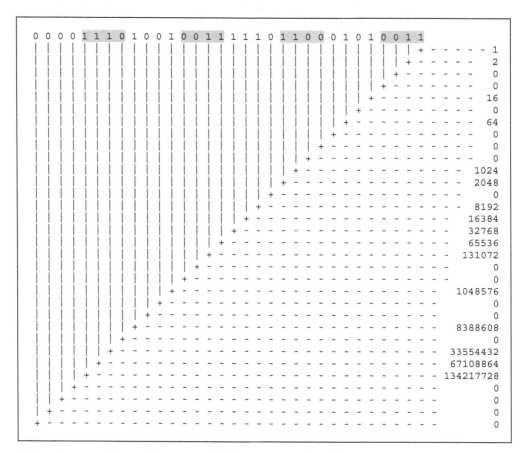

FIGURE 4-16    Converting an integer variable to a numeric value

## INTRODUCTION TO SQL

**SQL**, pronounced "S-Q-L," stands for **Structured Query Language** and is the standard language for relational database management systems. SQL commands are used to perform tasks such as creating and updating data in a table or retrieving data from a table. Although most DBMSs use SQL, they also have their own proprietary extensions that are usually used only on their system. In this book, we examine the DB2 version of SQL used on the IBM i system.

SQL contains commands that let users create schemas and tables, perform data manipulation (add, delete, and change) and data administration, and perform queries on tables that extract raw data into useful information for users.

There are two basic types of SQL statements. **Data Definition Language (DDL)** includes commands to create database objects such as tables, indexes, and views. **Data Manipulation Language (DML)** includes commands to insert, update, delete, and retrieve data within tables. In addition, SQL includes dynamic SQL and some miscellaneous commands.

With the use of SQL comes certain terminology. Throughout this book, the words keyword, clause, and statement are used:

- A **keyword** refers to an individual SQL element. For example, SELECT and FROM are keywords.
- A **clause** is part of an SQL statement. For example, SELECT product_id, product_description,... is a clause.
- A **statement** is a combination of two or more clauses. For example, SELECT product_id, product_description FROM products; is an SQL statement.

## RUNNING SQL COMMANDS

This textbook uses IBM Data Studio for the creation and running of SQL scripts. With IBM Data Studio, SQL scripts can be developed and run immediately or saved and accessed later.

### EDITOR PANE

The Data Studio window has several key areas. The Data Source Explorer pane provides for database connections. The upper-right portion of the window is the editor pane. The **editor pane** is used to create and edit the SQL commands that are to be run.

## SQL RESULTS PANE

The lower portion of the window is the **SQL Results pane**, which consists of the Results tab and the Status tab that display the output of the SQL commands that are run.

## CREATING A SCHEMA

A **schema** is an object that contains other objects, such as tables, views, indexes, stored procedures, and other object types. A schema must be created before the creation of tables and other SQL objects.

Schemas also consist of a journal, a journal receiver, and an SQL catalog. A schema can be used to group related objects and to find objects by name.

A schema is created by entering the CREATE SCHEMA command followed by the name of the schema. For example, to create a schema named MYSCHEMA, the CREATE SCHEMA command is entered:

```
CREATE SCHEMA myschema;
```

Some DBMS implementations of SQL require a semicolon (;) to signal the end of an SQL command. In DB2, the semicolon is optional, but it is recommended as a method to separate commands.

The preceding CREATE SCHEMA command creates a schema named MYSCHEMA. In addition, it generates a set of SQL views that reference the system catalog tables. A journal named QSqJrn and a journal receiver named QSqJrn0001 are also created. A **journal** is an object that records the activity of database changes (inserts, updates, and deletes). The journal records the activities on the specified objects in the form of journal entries. The journal writes the journal entries in another object called a journal receiver. By default, changes to tables in the schema are automatically journaled.

Once a schema is created, tables, views, and indexes, as well as other types of objects, can be created in the schema.

To create a schema:

1. *Click* in the SQL editor pane.
2. *Enter* the CREATE SCHEMA command shown in Figure 4-17, where myschema is the name of the schema that is be created.

```
CREATE SCHEMA myschema
```

**FIGURE 4-17    The CREATE SCHEMA command**

3.  *Click* the **Run All** icon, or select **Run/All** as shown here:

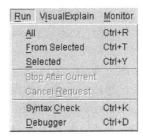

The messages pane displays the results of the SQL command.

After a schema has been created, tables, views, indexes, stored procedures, user-defined functions, and user-defined types can be created with the schema.

## CHANGING THE DEFAULT SCHEMA

To work with tables and other database objects that are stored in schemas, it is necessary to identify the schema in which the objects are stored. This task can be accomplished by using the SET SCHEMA command to change the default schema.

The SET SCHEMA command changes the default schema for all subsequent SQL commands. To change the default schema, enter the keywords SET SCHEMA followed by the name of the schema. For example, the following command changes the default schema to MYSCHEMA:

```
SET SCHEMA myschema;
```

Once the SET SCHEMA command is entered, the default schema is set for all subsequent SQL commands. Thus, there is no need to enter the SET SCHEMA command again unless it is necessary to work with objects in a different schema during the session. It is, however, necessary to enter the SET SCHEMA command at the start of each session to set the default schema.

Note that the system does not validate whether the schema exists at the time the SET SCHEMA command is executed. Thus, it is important to verify that the correct schema name was entered.

## Creating a Table

A *table* is a database object that is used to store data. Tables are stored in schemas and are uniquely identified by their names. Before data can be entered into a table and processed, the layout of the table must be described and created. This includes defining the characteristics of columns, including column names, column sizes, the type of data to be stored in each column, valid values the columns can contain, and so on. In addition, the format can define column headings and other textual information, range boundaries for numeric variables, validity-checking specifications, and other characteristics or attributes of the columns.

Consider the layout for the employee pay table in Figure 4-18. The letters PK identify the employee number as the primary key for this table.

| Column description | Data type | Size, digits | SQL name | NULL capable | Default |
|---|---|---|---|---|---|
| Employee ID (PK) | INTEGER | 4 | employee_id | No | |
| Store ID | SMALLINT | 2 | store_id | No | |
| First Name | CHAR | 15 | first_name | No | |
| Middle Initial | CHAR | 1 | m_initial | Yes | |
| Last Name | CHAR | 15 | last_name | No | |
| Hire Date | DATE | 10 | hire_date | No | Current date |
| Department ID | SMALLINT | 2 | department_id | No | |
| Hourly Rate | DECIMAL | 5,2 | hourly_rate | No | |
| Hours Worked | DECIMAL | 3,1 | hours_worked | No | |
| Sales | DECIMAL | 7,0 | sales | No | |

FIGURE 4-18    Layout for employee pay table

## CREATE TABLE Command

The **CREATE TABLE command** is used to create a table. To create a table, enter the keywords CREATE TABLE followed by the name of the table being created. Following the table name are the column names and their data types. Additional options for the CREATE TABLE command will be discussed later. Figure 4-19 shows the format for a CREATE TABLE command.

```
CREATE TABLE mySchema.employees
  ( employee_id    INTEGER         NOT NULL ,
    store_id       SMALLINT        NOT NULL ,
    first_name     CHARACTER (15)  NOT NULL ,
    m_initial      CHARACTER (1)   NOT NULL ,
    last_name      CHARACTER (15)  NOT NULL ,
    hire_date      DATE            NOT NULL ,
    department_id  SMALLINT        NOT NULL ,
    hourly_rate    DECIMAL (5, 2)  NOT NULL ,
    hours_worked   DECIMAL (3, 1)  NOT NULL ,
    sales          DECIMAL (7, 0)  NOT NULL ,
  PRIMARY KEY ( employee_id ) );
```

**FIGURE 4-19** **CREATE TABLE** command

Make sure there is an open parenthesis before the first column name and a closing parenthesis after the end of the last column definition. Each column definition should be separated with a comma. All SQL commands should end with a semicolon.

The rules for naming tables and columns are as follows:

- Names must start with a letter (A–Z).
- After position 1, names can contain letters, numbers, and underscores (_).
- Names cannot exceed 30 characters.
- Names cannot contain spaces.
- Do not use any SQL reserved keywords, such as "select," "create," or "insert," as names for tables or column names.

In addition, when a table is referenced, it can be referred to by its schema and table name. For example:

```
CREATE TABLE myschema.employees
```

To create a table:

1. *Click* in the SQL editor pane.
2. *Enter* the **CREATE TABLE** command as shown in Figure 4-20.

```
/* Create EmpPayTBL */

CREATE TABLE mySchema.empPayTBL
   ( EmployeeNo   INTEGER         NOT NULL ,
     StoreNo      SMALLINT        NOT NULL ,
     FirstName    CHARACTER (15)  NOT NULL ,
     MInitial     CHARACTER (1)   NOT NULL ,
     LastName     CHARACTER (15)  NOT NULL ,
     HireDate     DATE            NOT NULL ,
     DeptNo       SMALLINT        NOT NULL ,
     HourlyRate   DECIMAL (5, 2)  NOT NULL ,
     HrsWorked    DECIMAL (3, 1)  NOT NULL ,
     Sales        DECIMAL (7, 0)  NOT NULL ,
   PRIMARY KEY ( EmployeeNo ) );
```

**FIGURE 4-20** The **CREATE TABLE** command in the editor pane

---

**Note**

When more than one SQL command appears in the window, a specific command can be selected for running by placing the cursor in the command. When selected, the command is automatically run.

---

## VERIFY SYNTAX OF SQL SCRIPT

To verify the SQL script:

1. *Click* **Run/Syntax Check**.

## RUN SQL SCRIPT

To run the command:

1. *Click* the **Run All** icon [icon] or *select* **Run/All** from the menu bar. The results of the SQL command are displayed in the messages pane, as shown in Figure 4-21.

   SQL is a free-format language, and a statement can occupy multiple lines and include blanks between words. The example shows a coding style that puts each column definition on a separate line and aligns the similar parts of each definition. Although this columnar style is not required, it makes the statement much easier to read than an unaligned stream of text.

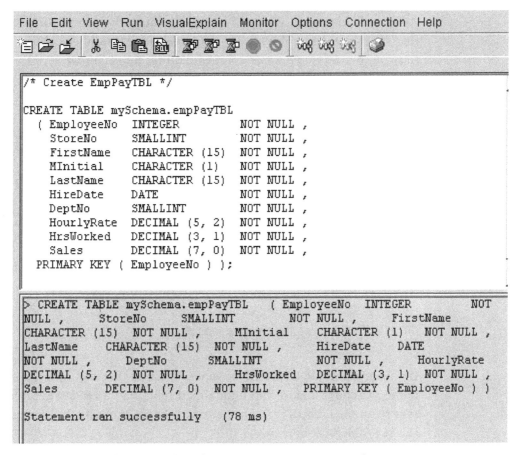

File   Edit   View   Run   VisualExplain   Monitor   Options   Connection   Help

```
/* Create EmpPayTBL */

CREATE TABLE mySchema.empPayTBL
  ( EmployeeNo   INTEGER          NOT NULL ,
    StoreNo      SMALLINT         NOT NULL ,
    FirstName    CHARACTER (15)   NOT NULL ,
    MInitial     CHARACTER (1)    NOT NULL ,
    LastName     CHARACTER (15)   NOT NULL ,
    HireDate     DATE             NOT NULL ,
    DeptNo       SMALLINT         NOT NULL ,
    HourlyRate   DECIMAL (5, 2)   NOT NULL ,
    HrsWorked    DECIMAL (3, 1)   NOT NULL ,
    Sales        DECIMAL (7, 0)   NOT NULL ,
  PRIMARY KEY ( EmployeeNo ) );
```

```
▷ CREATE TABLE mySchema.empPayTBL    ( EmployeeNo   INTEGER            NOT
NULL ,      StoreNo      SMALLINT           NOT NULL ,      FirstName
CHARACTER (15)   NOT NULL ,      MInitial      CHARACTER (1)    NOT NULL ,
LastName    CHARACTER (15)   NOT NULL ,      HireDate      DATE
NOT NULL ,      DeptNo       SMALLINT           NOT NULL ,      HourlyRate
DECIMAL (5, 2)   NOT NULL ,      HrsWorked    DECIMAL (3, 1)   NOT NULL ,
Sales         DECIMAL (7, 0)   NOT NULL ,    PRIMARY KEY ( EmployeeNo ) )

Statement ran successfully    (78 ms)
```

FIGURE 4-21    Results from running the **CREATE TABLE** command

SQL is not case-sensitive: "Create Table," "CREATE TABLE", and "CrEaTe TaBlE" will all work. Be aware, however, that string literals *are* case-sensitive, and 'x' is not generally treated the same as 'X'.

In addition, when tables are created, table and column names are stored in the system dictionary in upper case. Thus, if a list of the tables in the MYSCHEMA schema is displayed, the employee pay table will be listed as EMPLOYEES, in uppercase letters. However, the table can still be referred to as "EMPloyees" or "employees" in SQL commands.

## CONSTRAINTS

When tables are created, it is common for one or more columns to have constraints associated with them. A **constraint** is a rule associated with a column that the data entered into that column must follow. For example, a primary key constraint defines a unique identification of each row in a table. Another commonly used constraint is a unique constraint, which specifies that no two records can have the same value in a particular column. In the employee pay table, a primary key constraint specifies that no two rows will have the same employee number column value; this column thus serves as a unique identifier for each row.

## QUALIFIED NAMES

In the command

```
CREATE TABLE employees;
```

the table name EMPLOYEES is an unqualified name. When an unqualified table name is specified, SQL determines which schema to search for the table based on the default schema.

Database objects such as table names can also be specified as **qualified names**. For example, in the command

```
CREATE TABLE myschema.employees;
```

the table name EMPLOYEES is a qualified name that includes the schema name myschema before the unqualified table name EMPLOYEES. If qualified names are used, it is not necessary to set the default schema using the SET SCHEMA command.

## COMMENTS

There are two ways to include comments in a SQL script:

- To add a comment at the end of the line, two dashes (--) can be used to make the rest of the line a comment.
- To make longer comments, start the comment with /* and use */ to end it. Comments made in this manner can be any length.

## NULL VALUES

Occasionally, the actual data value for a column is unknown when a table row is inserted into a table or when an existing table row is modified. For example, consider an employee table that contains a column for the spouse's name. In this situation, a row could be inserted into the employee table even though the spouse column might never have an assigned value.

A special value called **NULL** is used to indicate that the value for the column is unknown. The NULL value is a data value; it is not blanks or zeros. In other words, if a column contains a NULL value, the actual value of the column is unknown.

The **NOT NULL** clause can be used in the CREATE TABLE command to indicate that a column cannot contain null values. If a column does not allow the null value, a value must be assigned to the column—either a default value or a user-supplied value. For example, in Figure 4-22, the employee_id, store_id, and first_name columns are defined with NOT NULL clauses. Thus, when a row is being inserted into the table, columns that are identified as NOT NULL must have an actual value or a default value.

```
CREATE TABLE mySchema.employees
  ( employee_id    INTEGER          NOT NULL ,
    store_id       SMALLINT         NOT NULL ,
    first_name     CHARACTER (15)   NOT NULL ,
    m_initial      CHARACTER (1)             ,
    last_name      CHARACTER (15)   NOT NULL ,
    hire_date      DATE             NOT NULL ,
    department_id  SMALLINT         NOT NULL ,
    hourly_rate    DECIMAL (5, 2)   NOT NULL ,
    hours_worked   DECIMAL (3, 1)   NOT NULL ,
    sales          DECIMAL (7, 0)   NOT NULL ,
  PRIMARY KAY ( employee_id ) );
```

**FIGURE 4-22**   Using **NULL** and **NOT NULL** values

It is important to understand that the store_id column can accept zeros and the first_name and last_name columns can accept spaces as values. This is because zeros and spaces are known quantities; they are not unknown, or NULL, values. Thus, the NOT NULL clause specifies that these columns cannot accept null values.

On the other hand, the m_initial column does not have a NOT NULL clause, and thus it defaults to being a null-capable column. This means that the m_initial column can be NULL, which indicates that the middle initial was unknown when the data was being entered.

## DEFAULT VALUES

A default value is assigned to a column when a row is added to a table and no value is specified for that column. Remember, NULL is a value. If a specific default value is not defined for a column, the system default value is used.

The **WITH DEFAULT clause** specifies a default column value, which is used for the column when an explicit value is not provided on an **INSERT** statement. The DBMS puts a default value in each column that is not in the **INSERT** statement's column list. In Figure 4-23, the customer_status column has a default of blank and the credit_limit column has a default of NULL.

The DEFAULT keyword can be specified with or without an explicit value. The following examples show both alternatives.

```
customer_status  CHAR (1)    NOT NULL
                             WITH DEFAULT ' ',
credit_limit     DEC (7,0 )  WITH DEFAULT NULL,
```

**FIGURE 4-23   WITH DEFAULT clause**

The table in Figure 4-24 shows the default values that the DBMS assigns to a column depending on the column type, whether a WITH DEFAULT is specified (with or without an explicit default value), and whether the NOT NULL clause is specified. Note that the DBMS does not assign any default for a column that specifies the NOT NULL clause but does not specify a WITH DEFAULT clause.

| Column data type | Default keyword specified? | Default value specified? | NOT NULL specified? | Column's default value |
|---|---|---|---|---|
| Numeric types | Yes | No | No | NULL |
| Fixed-length string (Char) types | Yes | No | Yes | Spaces |
| Variable-length string (VarChar) types | Yes | No | Yes | Zero-length string |
| Date or time | Yes | No | Yes | Current date or time |
| All types | No | No | No | NULL |
| All types | No | No | Yes | None |

**FIGURE 4-24   Default values for various column definitions**

## VARCHAR DATA TYPE

Character data can be defined using either the CHAR or the VARCHAR data type. The CHAR data type is a fixed-length data type for which the storage size is equal to the size defined for the column. The VARCHAR data type is a variable-length data type whose storage size is the actual length of the entered data, not the size of the column.

The VARCHAR data type does have an advantage on wildcard searches (LIKE '%RED%') because the DBMS stores the exact length of the VARCHAR string and stops searching after it reaches the end of the actual string. A wildcard search conducted on a CHAR data type must search through all the trailing blanks because the DBMS does not know the length of the actual string stored in the CHAR column. For example, if the wildcard search LIKE '%RED%' were conducted on a CHAR(200) column, the DBMS would search the entire 200 bytes.

## ALLOCATE CLAUSE

Quite often, when using a character data type, a large amount of storage needs to be allocated to accommodate the largest amount of data that could be stored. For example, a product description (product_ description) column might be defined as a 500-byte character data type. However, in many instances, the length of the product description could be much less. As a result, there would be many storage locations in the database table for product description that would contain spaces. To eliminate this unnecessary waste of storage, the ALLOCATE keyword can be specified. Although the ALLOCATE keyword can be used with several data types, it is used only with the VARCHAR data type in this book.

Data in a variable-length column is stored internally in two areas: a fixed-length or ALLOCATE area and an overflow area. If a default value is specified, the allocated length is at least as large as the value. The ALLOCATE clause specifies how many bytes should be reserved for data in the fixed portion of a row's data storage.

For example, the column definition

```
part_description VARCHAR( 500 ) ALLOCATE( 50 )
```

specifies that the part_description column can contain character strings up to 500 bytes long and that the first 50 bytes are stored in the fixed portion of the row. Values longer than 50 bytes have their first 50 bytes stored in the fixed portion of the row and additional data stored in the overflow area portion of the row.

The fixed-length ALLOCATE area for a VARCHAR column is the same length in every row for the particular column. A VARCHAR column always takes two bytes more than a CHAR data type for actual storage because it contains the actual length of data information (16-bit integer).

The ALLOCATE(N) keyword allocates N bytes in the fixed portion of the row and will store the column data in the overflow area only when the column value exceeds N. Setting N so that almost all of the column values are stored in the fixed portion of the row can improve performance by avoiding the extra I/O operation from the auxiliary overflow area.

The VARCHAR data type should be used when the data in a column are expected to vary considerably in length. On the other hand, use the CHAR data type in the following situations:

- If the significant data for a character column is always the same length or is very close to being the same length.
- When the length of the character column is 30 bytes or less. Any VARCHAR columns that are 30 bytes or less are converted into VARCHAR(n) ALLOCATE(n), where n is the defined length.

When a column is defined as variable-length data, the length of the ALLOCATE area should be considered. For example, if the primary goal is to save disk space, use ALLOCATE(0). ALLOCATE(0) is the default and causes the column value to be stored in the auxiliary overflow part of the row; this is the best value if the goal is to save space. If the primary goal is performance, the ALLOCATE area should be wide enough to incorporate at least 90 to 95 percent of the values for the column. It is possible to balance space savings and performance.

Consider the CREATE TABLE command in Figure 4-25, which contains an ALLOCATE clause. In this example of an electronic telephone directory, the following data is used:

- 8,600 names are identified by last, first, and middle name.
- The last_name, first_name, and m_initial columns are variable length.
- The shortest last name is 2 characters; the longest is 22 characters.

```
CREATE TABLE phonedir
  ( last_name   VARCHAR(40) ALLOCATE(10),
    first_name  VARCHAR(40) ALLOCATE(10),
    m_initial   VARCHAR(40) ALLOCATE(7) );
```

FIGURE 4-25    CREATE TABLE command with ALLOCATE clause

This example shows how space can be saved by using variable-length columns. Consider three scenarios of the ALLOCATE clause:

- The columns in the following table are defined as fixed-length columns of data type CHAR and use the most space.

```
CREATE TABLE phonedir
   ( last_name   CHAR(40),
     first_name  CHAR(40),
     m_initial   CHAR(40) );
```

- The table below, defined with carefully calculated allocated sizes, uses less disk space.

```
CREATE TABLE phonedir
   ( last_name   VARCHAR(40) ALLOCATE(10),
     first_name  VARCHAR(40) ALLOCATE(10),
     m_initial   VARCHAR(40) ALLOCATE(7) );
```

- A table defined with ALLOCATE(0) will have all the data stored in the overflow area and thus will use the least disk space.

```
CREATE TABLE PhoneDir
   ( last_name   VARCHAR(40) ALLOCATE(0),
     first_name  VARCHAR(40) ALLOCATE(0),
     m_initial   VARCHAR(40) ALLOCATE(0) );
```

In many applications, performance must be considered. If the default ALLOCATE(0) is used, it will double the disk access traffic. ALLOCATE(0) requires two reads: one to read the fixed-length portion of the row and one to read the overflow space. The variable-length implementation, with the carefully chosen ALLOCATEs, minimizes overflow and space and maximizes performance. The size of the table is 28 percent smaller than the fixed-length implementation. Because 1 percent of rows are in the overflow area, the access requiring two reads is minimized. The variable-length implementation performs about the same as the fixed-length implementation.

A VARCHAR column of 30 bytes or less is changed to

```
VARCHAR(30) ALLOCATE(30)
```

which results in the VARCHAR column always being stored in the fixed-length storage and the maximum length always allocated.

## ALTER TABLE COMMAND

The **ALTER TABLE command** adds, deletes, or modifies columns in an existing table. To add a column in a table, use the following syntax:

```
ALTER TABLE table_name
  ADD column_name datatype;
```

To delete a column in a table, use the following syntax:

```
ALTER TABLE table_name
  DROP COLUMN column_name;
```

To change the data type of a column in a table, use the following syntax:

```
ALTER TABLE table_name
  ALTER COLUMN column_name
    SET datatype;
```

## DROP (DELETE) TABLE COMMAND

If it becomes necessary to delete a table, the **DROP TABLE command** is used. To delete a table, the keywords DROP TABLE are entered followed by the name of the table that is to be dropped:

```
DROP TABLE employees;
```

In this example, the EMPLOYEES table is dropped. Dropping a table also deletes the data stored in the table.

## SAVING SQL SCRIPTS

Once an SQL script has been created and its syntax has been verified as correct, the script can be saved as a PC script file.

To save a script file:

1. *Click* **File/Save** from the File menu. IBM Navigator for i prompts for the name and location where the script is to be saved.

> **Tip**
> To check the syntax of the entire script before running Check Syntax, *select* **Smart Statement Selection** from the Options menu and *choose* **Select All** from the Edit menu.

> **Tip**
> The SQL scripts function can be used without starting IBM Navigator for i. Once a script file has been saved, double-clicking it runs the script without starting IBM Navigator for i.

## EDIT SQL SCRIPTS

To edit an SQL script:

1. *Open* **Run SQL Scripts**.
2. From the File menu, *select* **Open**.
3. In the File Open dialog box, *select* the SQL script to edit.
4. *Click* **OK**. The selected SQL script opens.
5. *Make* the desired changes in the SQL script.
6. To verify that the changes are correct, *select* **Check Syntax** from the Run menu.
7. *Select* **Save** from the File menu to save the file.

## ADDING DATA TO A TABLE

Several methods can be used to enter data into a table. The next section illustrates how the INSERT command is used to add or insert data into a table.

### THE INSERT COMMAND

The **INSERT INTO command** is used to insert or add a row of data into a table. The VALUES command specifies the actual data of the row that will be added to the table. These commands can be specified in two different ways.

#### SPECIFYING COLUMN NAMES WITH VALUES

In Figure 4-26, the keywords INSERT INTO are entered, followed by the table name, EMPLOYEES, followed by an open parenthesis, a list of column names separated by commas, and a closing parenthesis. Next, the VALUES command is specified, followed by the list of values enclosed in parentheses. The entered values are matched up with the specified column names. Strings must be enclosed in single quotation marks ('), and numbers should not be.

In this example, the column name `employee_id` matches up with the value `999999999`, and the column name `first_name` matches up with the value `'John'`.

### Specifying Values Without Column Names

To insert a row into a table without using column names, enter the keywords `INSERT INTO` followed by the name of the table into which a row of data is being added. The `VALUES` command follows the `INSERT INTO` command and specifies the values of the columns, as shown in Figure 4-27.

The keywords `INSERT INTO` are entered first, followed by the table name (`EMPLOYEES`). The names of the columns into which the data are being placed are not specified. Therefore, there must be data for each column specified with the `VALUES` command; otherwise, an error will be returned.

```
INSERT INTO myschema.employees
        ( employee_id,
          store_id,
          first_name,
          m_initial,
          last_name,
          hire_date,
          department_id,
          hourly_rate,
          hrs_worked,
          sales )
VALUES ( 999999999,
         2257,
         'John',
         ' ',
         'Alexander',
         '2007-04-15',
         333,
         14.50,
         37.5,
         342345);
```

FIGURE 4-26    Using the **INSERT INTO** and **VALUES** commands with column names

```
INSERT INTO myschema.employees
VALUES ( '123456789',
         '7315',
         'Amy',
         'Q',
         'Programmer',
         '2007-05-10',
         '666',
         '25.00',
         '40.5',
         '55555' );
```

FIGURE 4-27    Using the **INSERT INTO** and **VALUES** commands without column names

For example, in Figure 4-28, the hire date is missing and SQL returns the error message.

```
INSERT INTO myschema.employees
VALUES ( '123456789',
         '7315',
         'Amy',
         'Q',
         'Programmer',
         '2007-05-10',
         '666',
         '25.00',
         '40.5',
         '55555' );

SHOW ERROR MESSAGE
```

FIGURE 4-28    Error message for missing data

The **INSERT INTO** command is followed by the keyword **VALUES** accompanied by the list of values enclosed in parentheses. The entered values that are entered must match up with the columns that are defined in the table. Strings should be enclosed in single quotation marks; numbers should not be.

## The INSERT Command with NULLs

A slightly different form of the INSERT INTO command is used to enter a NULL value into a column. When a NULL value is entered into a column defined as null-capable, the column name is not specified on the INSERT INTO command. When no column name is specified for the null-capable column, a NULL value is automatically inserted into the column.

In the example shown in Figure 4-29, the m_initial column, which is null-capable, is not specified. By default, when the INSERT INTO command is executed, a row is inserted and the m_initial column contains a NULL value.

```
INSERT INTO myschema.employees
        ( employee_id,
          store_id,
          first_name,
          last_name,
          hire_date,
          department_id,
          hourly_rate,
          hours_worked,
          sales )
VALUES ( 999999999,
         2257,
         'John',
         'Alexander',
         '2007-04-15',
         333,
         14.50,
         37.5,
         342345);
```

FIGURE 4-29    INSERT INTO with NULL values

## The INSERT Command with Default Values

When a default value is specified for a column, the same format as inserting a NULL value is used. When a column name is not specified on the INSERT INTO command and it has been defined with a default value, the default value is automatically inserted into the column.

For example, let us assume that the store_id column has a default value of 1111 assigned to it. In the example in Figure 4-30, the store_id column is not specified. By default, when the INSERT INTO command is executed, a row is inserted and the store_id column contains the value 1111.

```
INSERT INTO myschema.employees
        ( employee_id,
          first_name,
          m_initial
          last_name,
          hire_date,
          department_id,
          hourly_rate,
          hours_worked,
          sales )
VALUES ( 999999999,
          'John',
          'P'
          'Alexander',
          '2011-09-15',
          333,
          14.50,
          37.5,
          342345);
```

FIGURE 4-30  **INSERT INTO default values**

## DISPLAYING DATA IN A TABLE

After the data have been entered into the table, the rows may be displayed to confirm the contents of the file. One simple way to display the data in a table is to use the SELECT command as follows:

```
SELECT * FROM employees;
```

The asterisk indicates that all columns are to be selected.

## DISPLAY TABLE DESCRIPTION INFORMATION

It is possible to view the table description information for a table. In the IBM Navigator for i window, expand the desired system.

1. *Expand* **Databases**.
2. *Expand* the database and schema to be worked with.
3. *Click* the **Tables** container.
4. *Right-click* the table, and *select* **Description**.

## Rename a Database Object

To rename a database object, expand the desired system in the IBM Navigator for i window.

1. *Expand* **Databases**.
2. *Expand* the database and schema to be worked with. Continue to expand until the object that is to be renamed is visible.
3. *Right-click* the object to be renamed.
4. *Select* **Rename**.
5. In the **Rename** dialog box, *enter* a new name for the object.
6. *Click* **OK**.

## End-of-Chapter

### Chapter Summary

1. Physical database design is the application development stage that produces a specification for the subsequent implementation.
2. Database design uses the conceptual data model that is produced in an earlier stage of the development project, along with estimates of data volume and access patterns and frequency, to plan an efficient database implementation that satisfies the requirements presented in the data model.
3. The major steps in database design are:

   Step 1. Create an SQL table for each entity.
   Step 2. Specify primary, candidate, and foreign keys.
   Step 3. Specify view implementation.
   Step 4. Specify security implementation.
   Step 5. Specify additional indexes for performance.

4. SQL:

   a. Stands for Structured Query Language
   b. Is a language used to define, retrieve, and manipulate databases

5. A database management system (DBMS):

   a. Is a set of software programs that controls the organization, storage, and retrieval of data in a database
   b. Uses a standard method of cataloging, retrieving, and running queries on data
   c. Manages incoming data, organizes it, and provides ways for the data to be modified or extracted by users or other programs

6. SQL has its own set of database terminology:

| SQL term | Description |
|---|---|
| Schema | A grouping consisting of a library, a journal, a journal receiver, an SQL catalog, and optionally a data dictionary. A schema groups related objects and lets the objects be found by name. |
| Table | A set of columns and rows. |
| Row | The horizontal part of a table containing a serial set of columns. |
| Column | The vertical part of a table of one data type. |
| View | A subset of columns and rows of one or more tables. |

7. Variables are values stored in computer memory and in tables on disk.

8. IBM enterprise computers use the EBCDIC coding system to represent letters, digits, and the character blank and special characters.

9. The most commonly used SQL data types are:

| Data type | Description |
|---|---|
| CHAR(length) | A fixed-length character string that stores one character in each byte of the variable. This type can be used for variables that contain alphabetic or special characters and for columns containing numbers that are not used in calculations. |
| VARCHAR(max-length) | A variable-length character string used for variables containing long descriptions or text that is seldom referenced. |
| DECIMAL(size,d) | The decimal data type, sometimes referred to as packed decimal; used to store numeric data in a packed format. |
| SMALLINT | The small integer data type; used to store integers, which are whole numbers without a decimal, in a 2-byte binary field. |
| INTEGER | The integer data type; stored as a 4-byte binary field. |
| BIGINT | The big integer data type; stores integers in an 8-byte binary field. |
| DATE | The data type used to store a date. Dates are enclosed in single quotation marks (') and have the form *yyyy-mm-dd*; for example, '2009-05-15' is May 15, 2009. |

10. The CREATE command is used to create schemas and tables.

11. A constraint is a rule associated with a column that the data entered into that column must follow.

12. NULL is a special value used to indicate that the value for a column is unknown.

13. The DROP TABLE command is used to delete a table.

14. The INSERT command is used to add a row of data to a table.

## KEY TERMS

| | |
|---|---|
| ALTER TABLE command | INSERT INTO command |
| ASCII | integer data type |
| Boolean data type | International Standards |
| character data type | Organization (ISO) |
| clause | journal |
| column | keyword |
| constraint | NOT NULL |
| CREATE TABLE command | NULL |
| data | numeric data type |
| Data Definition Language (DDL) | physical database design |
| Data Manipulation Language | qualified name |
| (DML) | record |
| data type | row |
| date data type | schema |
| DECIMAL data type | SQL Results pane |
| DROP TABLE command | statement |
| EBCDIC | Structured Query Language (SQL) |
| editor pane | table |
| field | timestamp data type |
| file | variable |
| index | WITH DEFAULT clause |
| information | |

# CHAPTER 5

## DATABASE CONSTRAINTS

## CHAPTER OBJECTIVES

Upon completion of this chapter, you should be able to

- Explain the purpose of constraints
- Use primary key constraints
- Use unique constraints
- Use foreign key constraints
- Use check constraints
- Create constraints using the CREATE TABLE and ALTER TABLE commands
- Use the ALTER TABLE command to add and drop constraints for an existing table

## INTRODUCTION TO CONSTRAINTS

**Constraints**, sometimes referred to as integrity constraints or integrity rules, are restrictions based on business rules and other business policies and procedures that ensure data in a database are acceptable and accurate.

A DBMS can provide features that can be used to specify integrity constraints. The features usually include range checks (e.g., "between 1 and 50") or allowable values (e.g., "equal to A or B or C"). More complex constraints may be specifiable as well; examples include relationships between columns within the same table (e.g., an employee's hire date must be greater than his or her birth date) or inter-row relationships (a customer number value in an order table must exist as a customer number value in exactly one customer table). The DBMS, which handles all updating of the database, checks these constraints when database rows are inserted, updated, or deleted. If a constraint is not met, the DBMS blocks the operation and signals an error.

Three integrity rule categories allow the specification of important constraints that a relational DBMS can enforce automatically whenever a database update occurs:

- Data integrity
- Entity integrity
- Referential integrity

These rules protect not only the specific values in columns but also the identity and interrelationships of rows.

## DATA INTEGRITY

**Data integrity** defines the possible values of a column. In a database system, data integrity is defined by

- Data type and length
- Null value acceptance
- Allowable values
- Default value

For example, if an **age** column in an **EMPLOYEES** table is defined as an integer, the value of every instance of that column must always be numeric and an integer. If this column is defined so that it must always be positive, a negative value is forbidden. The value of the column being mandatory indicates that the column can be NULL.

All these characteristics form the data integrity of this column. This type of data integrity warrants the following:

- The identity and purpose of the column are clear, and all the tables in which the column appears are properly identified.
- Column definitions are consistent throughout the database.
- The values of the column are consistent and valid.
- The types of modifications, comparisons, and operators that can be applied to the values in the column are clearly identified.

Each column in the model should be assigned attributes that include the following:

- *Data type*—Basic data types are integer, decimal, and character. Most databases support variants of these types plus special data types for date and time.
- *Length*—The length is the number of digits or characters in the value, such as a value of 5 digits or 40 characters.
- *Date format*—The date format specifies the format for date values, such as *dd/mm/yy, mm/dd/yyyy,* or *yy/mm/dd.*

- *Range*—The range specifies the lower and upper boundaries of the values that the column may legally have.
- *Constraints*—Constraints are special restrictions on allowable values. For example, the `retire_date` for an employee must always be greater than the `hire_date` for that employee.
- *Null support*—This attribute indicates whether the column can have null values.
- *Default value (if any)*—The default value is the value that a column will contain if no value is entered.

## ENTITY INTEGRITY

The second category of integrity essential to the relational database model is **entity integrity**. This is a fairly straightforward concept: Every row in a table represents an entity (i.e., an instance of an entity type) that must exist in the real world; therefore, every row must be uniquely identifiable. It follows that no completely duplicate rows (all column values identical) can exist in a table; otherwise, the unique existence of entities is not represented in the database.

From this property of uniqueness is derived the principle that there exists in every table some set of columns (possibly the entire table's columns) whose values are never duplicated entirely in any two rows in the table. If the set of columns includes no superfluous columns, or ones not needed to guarantee uniqueness, the set of columns can serve as the table's primary key. More than one possible set of columns may meet the criteria for a primary key; each of these is referred to as a **candidate key**, and one is picked arbitrarily as the primary key.

The **primary key** is a set of columns whose values are unique for all rows in a table. Because of this fact, the primary key forms the only means of addressing a specific row in the relational database model. A consequence of the requirement for unique primary key values is that none of the values in a row's primary key columns can be null; that is, none can be missing or unknown. None of the primary key columns can be null because otherwise this row's primary key value could not be guaranteed to be unequal to some other row's primary key value. In the relational model, null is essentially a placeholder that means the value of this column is unknown. There is no way to know that the null value is not also present in the same primary key column of some other row. Thus, if `employee_id` is the column serving as the primary key in the EMPLOYEES table and there exists a row with `employee_id = NULL`, there is no guarantee that another row might have a null value for `employee_id`. A similar argument holds for primary keys made up of more than one column, known as **composite primary keys**, which require all column values to guarantee uniqueness and hence cannot have null for any of the columns in the primary key.

## REFERENTIAL INTEGRITY

The third, and final, category of integrity fundamental to the relational database model is referential integrity. **Referential integrity** is a database concept that ensures that relationships between tables remain reliable. That is, when a table contains a foreign key associated with another table's primary key, the concept of referential integrity states that a row containing the foreign key may not be added to the table unless a matching value exists in the primary key column of the parent table. In addition, referential integrity includes the concepts of cascading updates and deletes, which ensure that changes made to the table with the foreign key, are reflected in the primary table.

## CONSTRAINT TYPES

In a DBMS, **database constraints** provide a way to guarantee that rows in a table have valid primary or unique key values, that rows in a dependent table have valid foreign key values that reference rows in a parent table, and that individual column values are valid. All constraints are enforced when rows are inserted or updated in the table. This chapter discusses five constraints, identified in Figure 5-1.

| Constraint | Description |
|---|---|
| PRIMARY KEY | Identifies which column is the unique identifier or primary key for each row in the table. The values in the primary key column must be unique for every row in the table. Since the primary key must be unique, it cannot be NULL. |
| FOREIGN KEY | Is what makes the relational database work. For every one-to-many (parent-child) relationship in the database, a foreign key constraint is added to the child (many) table. The foreign key in the child (many) table links to the parent (one) table. Thus, if a row is added to the child table, the value entered in the foreign key column must already exist as a primary key in the parent table. |
| UNIQUE | Identifies a column as containing unique values for the UNIQUE column in each row in the table. The UNIQUE constraint differs from a primary key in that it allows NULL values. |
| CHECK | Enforces a business rule on a column. Before a value can be entered into a CHECK column, the condition (business rule) specified in the CHECK constraint must be true. |
| NOT NULL | Ensures that a column identified as NOT NULL will not contain a NULL value. |

FIGURE 5-1   Constraint types

## PRIMARY KEY CONSTRAINTS

Each row in a table contains one or more columns that uniquely identify that row in the table. This single column or group of columns is referred to as the primary key and serves as the unique identifier for rows in the table. As shown in Figure 5-2, a **primary key constraint** can be added to a table with the CREATE TABLE or ALTER TABLE command.

```
CREATE TABLE customers
( customer_id   INTEGER                NOT NULL,
  customer_name CHARACTER( 30    )     NOT NULL,
  balance       DECIMAL  (  7, 2 )     NOT NULL DEFAULT 0,
  ship_city     CHARACTER( 30    )     NOT NULL,
  credit_limit  DECIMAL  (  7, 0 )     NOT NULL DEFAULT 100000,
  discount      DECIMAL  (  5, 3 )
  CONSTRAINT customers_customer_id_pk  PRIMARY KEY(customer_id) );
 ALTER TABLE customers
   ADD CONSTRAINT customers_customer_id_pk
       PRIMARY KEY(customer_id);
```

FIGURE 5-2   Example of a PRIMARY KEY constraint

When a constraint is defined, each constraint clause can optionally begin with the CONSTRAINT keyword followed by an optional constraint name. If a constraint name is not specified, the DBMS generates a name automatically. A constraint name must be unique within the schema that contains the table. For example, there cannot be two constraints with the name customers_customer_id_pk defined for two different tables in the same schema. Therefore, a standard naming convention should be used that helps prevent duplicate names.

In Figure 5-2, the primary key constraint is identified with the keyword CONSTRAINT. Following this keyword is the constraint name, customers_customer_id_pk. The constraint name is composed of three components separated by underscores:

| Component value | Description |
| --- | --- |
| customers | Table name |
| customer_id | Constraint name (usually the column name) |
| pk | Constraint type (primary key in this example) |

The first component, customers, is the name of the table or some standard short form that identifies the table for which the constraint applies. It is appended to the constraint name as a prefix.

The second component is the actual constraint name, which is customer_id in this example. The constraint name is usually the column name for which the constraint applies.

The third component is a suffix that identifies the constraint type. In this example, the constraint is a primary key constraint, so the suffix is _pk. The suffixes for the other constraints types are:

| Constraint | Suffix |
| --- | --- |
| PRIMARY KEY | _pk |
| FOREIGN KEY | _fk |
| UNIQUE | _uq |
| CHECK | _ck |
| NOT NULL | _nn |

Both examples in Figure 5-2 assign the primary key constraint to the CUSTOMERS table.

Every primary key constraint must include NOT NULL. For a table with a primary key constraint, the DBMS blocks any attempt to insert or update a row that would cause two rows in the same table to have identical value(s) for their primary key column(s). A table definition can have no more than one primary key constraint.

A constraint name is not required to drop a primary key constraint with the ALTER TABLE command. To drop a primary key constraint, simply specify the keywords Primary Key.

## UNIQUE CONSTRAINTS

A **unique constraint** is similar to a primary key constraint; however, a column listed as a unique constraint does not need to be defined with NOT NULL. It is recommended that a constraint name be specified for a unique constraint:

```
CONSTRAINT constraint-name UNIQUE ( column-name, ... )
```

Note that a unique constraint does not use the KEY keyword, as primary key and foreign key constraints do. In Figure 5-3, the employee_jobs_soc_sec_nbr_uq unique constraint specifies that the soc_sec_nbr column must be unique.

```
CREATE TABLE employee_jobs
   ( employee_id     INTEGER        NOT NULL,
     first_name      CHAR    (15)   NOT NULL,
     middle_initial  CHAR    (1)    NOT NULL,
     last_name       CHAR    (15)   NOT NULL,
     soc_sec_nbr     INTEGER        NOT NULL,
     birth_date      DATE           NOT NULL,
     hire_date       DATE           NOT NULL,
     work_department CHAR    (2)    NOT NULL,
     phone_ext       SMALLINT       NOT NULL,
     job_class       CHAR    (1)    NOT NULL,
     job_level       CHAR    (1)    NOT NULL,
     sex             CHAR    (1)    NOT NULL,
     salary          DECIMAL (9,2)  NOT NULL,
     bonus           DECIMAL (9,2)  NOT NULL,
     commission      DECIMAL (9,2)  NOT NULL,
CONSTRAINT employee_jobs_employee_id_pk
     PRIMARY KEY(employee_id) );

ALTER TABLE employee_jobs
     ADD CONSTRAINT employee_jobs_soc_sec_nbr_uq
        UNIQUE ( soc_sec_nbr );
```

FIGURE 5-3    Example of **CREATE TABLE** command with **UNIQUE** constraint

Figure 5-4 shows another example of a unique constraint; here, the Credit Authorization Number column (crd_authoridy_id) must be unique. The orders_crd_authoridy_id_uq unique constraint specifies that any non-null value for the crd_authoridy_id column must be unique. Allowing the crd_authoridy_id column to be null and specifying the orders_crd_authoridy_id_uq constraint together enforce a business rule that some orders (e.g., those paid by cash) may exist without a credit authorization number, but any order that does have a credit authorization number must have a unique value.

```
CREATE TABLE orders
  ( order_no          INTEGER     NOT NULL,
    order_date        DATE        NOT NULL,
    order_date        DATE        DEFAULT NULL,
    order_total       DEC( 7, 2 ) NOT NULL,
    crd_authoridy_id  INTEGER     DEFAULT NULL,
    customer_id       INTEGER     NOT NULL,
  CONSTRAINT orders_order_no_pk
    PRIMARY KEY( order_no) );

ALTER TABLE ORDERS
  ADD CONSTRAINT orders_crd_authoridy_id_uq
  UNIQUE ( crd_authoridy_id );
```

**FIGURE 5-4    Example of CREATE TABLE command with UNIQUE constraint**

A table can have multiple unique constraints; however, the same set of columns (regardless of order) can be listed on only one primary key or unique constraint. For example, it is not valid to have the following two constraints on the same table:

```
Primary Key( ColA, ColB ),
Unique     ( ColB, ColA )
```

With unique constraints, the DBMS also blocks any attempt to insert or update a row that would cause two rows in the same table to have identical, non-null value(s) for the column(s). If any of the constraint columns are null-capable, however, two rows can exist with unique constraint columns set to null. To have a unique constraint enforce the same rules as a primary key constraint (i.e., no identical values for the unique constraint columns), specify NOT NULL for the unique constraint columns' definitions.

## FOREIGN KEY CONSTRAINTS

A **foreign key** is one or more columns in the child (dependent) table that contain values that match the primary key of a parent table. When a logical model is translated to a physical database, the relationships between database tables are implemented as foreign key constraints, sometimes referred to as referential integrity. Referential integrity is a method of ensuring data integrity between tables related by primary and foreign keys. When a foreign key is specified for a column in a table, the values in that column must match one of the primary key values in another table.

A **foreign key constraint** specifies how records in different tables are related and how the DBMS should handle row insert, delete, and update operations that might violate the relationship. For example, order rows are generally related to the customers who place the orders. Although it might be valid for a customer row to exist without any corresponding order rows, it normally would be invalid for an order row not to have a reference to a valid customer. The foreign key constraint ties the primary key to the foreign key. The table with the primary key is called the **parent table**, and the table with the foreign key is called the **dependent** or **child table**. This relationship between rows in two tables is expressed by a foreign key in the dependent table.

## DEFINING FOREIGN KEY CONSTRAINTS

To define a foreign key constraint, a primary key is defined in the parent table and a foreign key in the dependent table. In Figure 5-5, the parent table in the relationship is the DEPARTMENTS table. The child table is the EMPLOYEE_JOBS table. Therefore, the primary key, department_code, resides in the DEPARTMENTS table, and a corresponding foreign key of the same data type and length, but not necessarily with same column name (work_department in this example), exists in the EMPLOYEE_JOBS table.

---

DEPARTMENTS table (parent)
- Primary key column: department_code

EMPLOYEE_JOBS table (dependent)
- Primary key column: employee_id
- Foreign key column: work_department

---

**FIGURE 5-5**    **Foreign key relationships**

For each row in the EMPLOYEE_JOBS table, the work_department column must contain the same value as the department_code column of some row in the DEPARTMENTS table because this value tells which department the employee works in. The purpose of specifying a foreign key constraint is to ensure that the EMPLOYEE_JOBS table never has a row with a non-null value in the work_department column that has no matching row in the DEPARTMENTS table.

Because a foreign key is a means of identifying a related row, in general the foreign key column(s) definition should be identical to the definition of the primary key column(s). A primary key constraint should be defined for the parent table before foreign key constraints are defined for any dependent tables.

A foreign key constraint is specified in the dependent table. The constraint specifies the foreign key column(s) in the same table as the constraint and specifies the column(s) of a primary key or unique constraint in the parent table. The corresponding primary and foreign key columns must have identical data type and length or precision.

Foreign key constraints are defined using the `FOREIGN KEY` clause, which consists of three components:

- A constraint name
- The columns making up the foreign key
- A references clause

The same constraint name cannot be specified more than once for the same table. If a constraint name is not explicitly defined, a unique name, derived from the name of the first column in the foreign key, is automatically created for the constraint. Consider the relationship between the `DEPARTMENTS` and `EMPLOYEE_JOBS` tables defined in Figure 5-6. The primary key of the `DEPARTMENTS` table is `department_code`, and the primary key of the `EMPLOYEE_JOBS` table is `employee_id`.

Let us examine the foreign key that relates the employee job table to the department table. The foreign key constraint, which is named `employee_jobs_work_department_fk`, in the employee jo table relates the `work_department` column to a specific `department_code` in the department table. This foreign key constraint ensures that no department code can exist in the `work_department` column of the employee job table before the department code exists as a primary key in the department table. The `work_department` column in each row of the employee job table must contain a value of a `department_code` column in the department table. This foreign key ensures that

- A value in the `work_department` column of the employee job table cannot subsequently be updated to a value that is not a valid `department_code` in the department table
- The primary key `department_code` of the department table cannot be deleted without the appropriate check for corresponding values in the employee job table foreign key column

```
CREATE TABLE departments
( department_code    CHAR     (2)    NOT NULL,
  department_name    CHAR     (30)   NOT NULL,
  Location           CHAR     (20)   NOT NULL,
  CONSTRAINT departments_department_code_pk
      PRIMARY KEY( department_code) );

CREATE TABLE employee_jobs
( employee_id      INTEGER          NOT NULL,
  first_name       CHAR     (15)    NOT NULL,
  middle_initial   CHAR     (1)     NOT NULL,
  last_name        CHAR     (15)    NOT NULL,
  soc_sec_nbr      INTEGER          NOT NULL,
  birth_date       DATE             NOT NULL,
  hire_date        DATE             NOT NULL,
  work_department  CHAR     (2)     NOT NULL,
  phone_ext        SMALLINT         NOT NULL,
  job_class        CHAR     (1)     NOT NULL,
  job_level        CHAR     (1)     NOT NULL,
  sex              CHAR     (1)     NOT NULL,
  salary           DECIMAL  (9,2)   NOT NULL,
  bonus            DECIMAL  (9,2)   NOT NULL,
  commission       DECIMAL  (9,2)   NOT NULL,
  CONSTRAINT employee_jobs_employee_id_pk
    PRIMARY KEY( employee_id) );

ALTER TABLE employee_jobs
  ADD CONSTRAINT employee_jobs_work_department_fk
    FOREIGN KEY ( work_department )
    REFERENCES departments( department_code );
```

FIGURE 5-6    Example of a **CREATE TABLE** command with a foreign key constraint

To ensure that this integrity remains intact, a series of rules for inserting, deleting, and updating applies:

- When inserting a row with a foreign key, the DBMS checks the values of the foreign key columns against the values of the primary key columns in the parent table. If no matching primary key columns are found, the insert is disallowed.
- A new primary key row can be inserted into the parent table as long as the primary key is unique for the table.
- When updating foreign key values, the DBMS performs the same checks as when inserting a row with a foreign key.
- If a primary key value is changed in the parent table, the DBMS does not allow existing foreign keys in the dependent table that refer back to the primary key that is changing. All foreign key

rows first must either be deleted or be set to NULL before the value of the primary key can be changed.

- Deleting a row in the dependent table with a foreign key is always permitted.

- When deleting a row with a primary key, the DBMS takes action as indicated in the command; it restricts deletion, cascades deletes to foreign key rows, or sets all referenced foreign keys to null.

## FOREIGN KEY ACTIONS

Foreign key constraints define the action that will be taken on foreign key rows when a primary key is deleted. Four options can be specified:

- RESTRICT: Disallows the deletion of the primary key row if any foreign keys relate to the row.

- CASCADE: Allows the deletion of the primary key row and also deletes the foreign key rows that relate to it.

- SET NULL: Allows the deletion of the primary key row and, instead of deleting all related foreign key rows, sets the foreign key columns to NULL.

- NO ACTION: Behaves similarly to RESTRICT. The only difference between RESTRICT and NO ACTION is when the foreign key constraint is enforced. The RESTRICT option enforces the delete rule immediately; NO ACTION enforces the delete rule at the end of the command.

The processing needs of the application dictate which delete option should be specified when the foreign key constraint is created. All these options are valid depending on the business rules that apply to the data.

## ADDITIONAL FOREIGN KEY CONSTRAINT CONSIDERATIONS

Consider the ORDERS table defined in Figure 5-7. This table contains rows with information about orders, including a customer_id column that contains the customer number of the customer who placed the order.

```
CREATE TABLE orders
  ( order_no          INTEGER      NOT NULL,
    order_date        DATE         NOT NULL,
    order_date        DATE         DEFAULT NULL,
    order_total       DEC( 9, 2 )  NOT NULL,
    crd_authoridy_id  INTEGER      DEFAULT NULL,
    customer_id       INTEGER      NOT NULL,
  CONSTRAINT orders_order_no_pk
    PRIMARY KEY( order_no) );

ALTER TABLE
  ADD CONSTRAINT orders_crd_authoridy_id_uq
    UNIQUE ( crd_authoridy_id );

ALTER TABLE
  ADD CONSTRAINT orders_customer_id_fk
    FOREIGN KEY ( customer_id )
    REFERENCES customers ( customer_id )
    ON DELETE CASCADE
    ON UPDATE RESTRICT;
```

FIGURE 5-7    Example of the **CREATE TABLE** command with a foreign key constraint

The **ORDERS** table's foreign key constraint, which is

```
CONSTRAINT orders_customer_id_fk
  FOREIGN KEY ( customer_id )
    REFERENCES customers ( customer_id )
    ON DELETE CASCADE
    ON UPDATE RESTRICT;
```

specifies that the customer_id column in the ORDERS table is a foreign key that references the customer_id primary key column in the CUSTOMERS table. With this constraint, the DBMS does not allow a new row to be inserted into the ORDERS table unless the row's customer_id column contains the value of some existing customer_id value in the CUSTOMERS table. This constraint also blocks any attempt to change the customer_id column of a row in the ORDERS table to a value that does not exist in any row in the CUSTOMERS table. In other words, a new or updated ORDERS row must have a parent CUSTOMERS row.

Although the ORDERS table's customer_id column in this example does not allow nulls, for a foreign key with one or more null-capable columns, the DBMS lets a row be inserted or updated in the dependent table if any foreign key column is set to null. The idea behind this aspect of a foreign key constraint is that if you let a foreign key field be null, you are implying it is valid for a dependent row to exist with an unknown parent or that a dependent row may not always require a parent. In most cases, however, the logical business model dictates that NOT NULL be specified for foreign key columns, thus requiring that every dependent row have a specific parent row.

The ON DELETE and ON UPDATE clauses determine the rules that the DBMS enforces when an attempt is made to delete or update a parent table row in a way that will leave dependent table rows that have invalid foreign key references. Both rules apply in cases in which one or more dependent table rows have a foreign key value that matches the parent key of the parent table row being deleted or updated. The ON DELETE and ON UPDATE rules are intended to prevent "orphan" rows or rows in the dependent table that have a non-null foreign key that does not reference an existing parent row.

In the example, the ON DELETE clause specifies what action should occur when an application tries to delete a row in the CUSTOMERS table and some row in the ORDERS table contains the customer_id value of the row being deleted. The CASCADE action used in this example causes the DBMS to propagate the delete operation to all ORDERS rows that have the same customer_id as the CUSTOMERS row that is being deleted. Thus, any ORDERS rows for the deleted CUSTOMERS row will also be deleted automatically.

The ON UPDATE clause in the example specifies what action should occur when an application tries to update the customer_id value in a row of the CUSTOMERS table and some row in the ORDERS table contains the customer_id value of the row being updated. The RESTRICT action used in this example causes the DBMS to block the update operation and return an error to the application.

If no ON DELETE or ON UPDATE clause is explicitly specified, the default action is the same as with the keywords NO ACTION. The NO ACTION alternative is similar to the RESTRICT action, but there is a subtle timing difference between RESTRICT and NO ACTION. With RESTRICT, the check for an unmatched foreign key occurs before an after-delete-event or after-update-event database trigger program is called, whereas with NO ACTION the check occurs after an after-delete-event or after-update-event trigger program is called.

Also, with set-at-a-time commands, the DBMS checks the RESTRICT rule immediately after each row update (or delete) but checks the NO ACTION rule only after command execution is completed and all rows have been updated or deleted. It is possible (although uncommon) to have an update command that changes a set of rows' parent key values (e.g., by adding 1 to each parent key value) such that as each row is changed, some foreign key value has no match, but when all the parent rows have been changed, all foreign key values are once again matched. In this situation, specifying ON UPDATE NO ACTION (or ON DELETE NO ACTION) is the appropriate choice.

The ON UPDATE clause allows only the two choices: RESTRICT or NO ACTION. The ON DELETE clause allows CASCADE, RESTRICT, NO ACTION, SET DEFAULT, and SET NULL.

When SET DEFAULT is specified for the DELETE action and a parent row is deleted, the DBMS sets all foreign key columns of dependent rows to their respective default values. If none of the foreign key columns has a default of NULL, the parent table must contain a row with a primary key value that is the same as the foreign key column default(s). After the delete operation is completed, the original parent will be deleted, and the dependent rows will subsequently reference the "default" parent row.

As an example of this technique, suppose inactive customers are allowed to be deleted but their old order information is to be kept (i.e., rows) for statistical purposes. The default value could be defined for the customer_id column in the ORDERS table as 0, and then one CUSTOMERS row with a customer_id (primary key) value of 0 and some dummy customer name, such as "Placeholder for Deleted Customers," could be created. If ON DELETE SET DEFAULT is specified for the previous example's foreign key constraint, when a CUSTOMERS row is deleted, its ORDERS rows would be updated to have 0 for their customer_id (foreign key) value.

If any foreign key column is null-capable, another ON DELETE alternative is SET NULL, which causes all null-capable foreign key columns to be set to null.

A dependent table in one foreign key constraint can be the parent table in another foreign key constraint. For example, the ORDERS table might be the parent table in a foreign key constraint that exists for the ORDER_ITEMS dependent table. This raises the possibility that a cascaded delete might delete dependent rows that are also parent rows for some other table.

For example, if ON DELETE CASCADE were specified for the previous example, deleting a CUSTOMERS row could delete some ORDERS rows that were parents of ORDER_ITEMS rows. If a foreign key constraint for the ORDER_ITEMS table specifies RESTRICT or NO ACTION and the DBMS blocks the deletion of the ORDERS rows, the DBMS also blocks the attempted deletion of the CUSTOMERS row. In general, with ON DELETE CASCADE, if the DBMS blocks any operation caused by the cascading delete, all operations are blocked. Similar rules apply when SET DEFAULT or SET NULL is specified and a resulting change in a foreign key value would violate some other constraint.

A foreign key constraint can specify the same table for the dependent and parent tables. Suppose an EMPLOYEES table with an employee_id primary key column and manager_id column holds the employee number for the person's manager. The following could be used to specify the foreign key constraint to express this relationship:

```
CREATE TABLE employees
  ( employee_id INTEGER NOT NULL,
    manager_id  INTEGER NOT NULL,
    other column definitions ... ,
  PRIMARY KEY ( employee_id ),
  CONSTRAINT employees_manager_id_fk
    FOREIGN KEY ( manager_id )
    REFERENCES employees ( employee_id )
      ON UPDATE RESTRICT
      ON DELETE RESTRICT ) );
```

To handle the case of an employee who had no real manager (e.g., the president of the company), a dummy employee row could be inserted with the name "No manager" and the employee_id and manager_id values set to 0 (or any other value not used by real employees). The manager_id for any employee with no manager could be set to 0 to satisfy the foreign key constraint.

Depending on how one wanted to implement the removal of an employee (who might be a manager), a DEFAULT 0 clause could be added to the manager_id column definition and ON DELETE SET DEFAULT specified. Another option would be to define manager_id as null-capable and consider a null manager_id to mean "no manager." In this case, ON DELETE SET NULL could be specified to handle the deletion of a manager's row. A final alternative would be to change all the rows for the manager's employees so they had a new, valid manager_id value before the old manager's row is deleted.

A table can have multiple foreign key constraints, including overlapping foreign keys. If a foreign key constraint specifies ON DELETE SET DEFAULT and the constraint's foreign key has a column that is in another constraint's foreign key, deleting a row from the parent table of the first constraint may change the value of a foreign key column in the second constraint. If this happens and the new foreign key value for the second constraint does not match a parent key in the parent table of the second constraint, the DBMS blocks the dependent row updates and the parent row delete.

A table can also be the parent table for multiple foreign key constraints. The DBMS enforces all constraints when a row in such a table is updated or deleted. The order the DBMS follows to check constraints is based on the action specified for each constraint. For an update operation, the DBMS checks RESTRICT constraints and then NO ACTION constraints. For a delete action, the order of checking is

1. RESTRICT
2. CASCADE
3. SET NULL
4. SET DEFAULT
5. NO ACTION

If any constraints are violated, the DBMS blocks the operation and ends the constraint checking.

When a foreign key constraint has both ON UPDATE RESTRICT and ON DELETE RESTRICT specified, the DBMS could check the constraint before doing any actual table update or delete operations. With any other rules, the DBMS must perform some operations, and then, if the constraint check fails, the DBMS must back out the partial changes to the table(s). As a result, you must journal both the dependent and parent tables in any foreign key constraint other than one with RESTRICT specified for both the update and delete rules. Both tables must be journaled to the same journal. The simplest way to ensure that a parent table and its dependent tables are journaled to the same journal is to create them all in the same schema. Note that commitment control need not be explicitly started. When necessary, the DBMS implicitly uses a commitment control cycle to ensure that table changes occur on an all-or-nothing basis.

## AVOID FOREIGN KEY CONSTRAINTS FOR READ-ONLY TABLES

Do not use foreign key constraints if tables are read-only. Tables containing static data that is loaded and then never or only rarely modified are not good candidates for foreign key constraints. The data should be analyzed and validated before loading so that it is referentially intact. Because of the stability of the data, there is no need for ongoing foreign key constraints to be applied to the data. For data that is rarely updated, using application programs to enforce foreign key constraints is usually preferable to employing DBMS foreign key constraints.

Sometimes, to validate the data when loading, it may be desirable to use the DBMS reference key constraints.

## CHECK CONSTRAINTS

**Check constraints** are used to enforce business rules by placing restrictions on the data that can be entered into a column. Any attempt to modify the column data (e.g. during INSERT or UPDATE processing) will cause the check constraint to be evaluated. If the modification conforms to the check condition, the modification is permitted to continue; if not, the command will fail with a constraint violation.

Check constraints consist of the keyword CONSTRAINT followed by the constraint name, followed by the keyword CHECK, followed by the check condition:

```
CONSTRAINT constraint-name
  CHECK check-condition;
```

## CHECK CONSTRAINT GUIDELINES

Several considerations and restrictions apply when defining check constraints:

- The same constraint name cannot be specified more than once for the same table.
- If a constraint name is not explicitly coded, a unique name, derived from the name of the first column in the check condition, is automatically created for the constraint.
- The constraint can refer only to columns in the table in which it is created.
- The first operand specified in the check condition *must be* the name of a column contained in the table. The second operand must be either another column name or a constant.
- If the second operand is a constant, it must be compatible with the data type of the first operand. If the second operand is a column, it must be the same data type as the first column specified.
- The check condition defines the actual constraint logic. The check condition can be defined using >, <, =, <>, <=, >= as well as BETWEEN, IN, LIKE, and NULL. Furthermore, AND and OR can be used to string conditions together.
- The NOT logical operator cannot be used.

## DEFINING CHECK CONSTRAINTS

Let us consider the check constraints for the EMPLOYEE_JOBS table in Figure 5-8. Following this example, each check constraint is explained.

```
CREATE TABLE departments
( department_code CHAR      (2)   NOT NULL,
  department_name CHAR      (30)  NOT NULL,
  Location        CHAR      (20)  NOT NULL,
  CONSTRAINT departments_department_code_pk
    PRIMARY KEY( department_code ) );


CREATE TABLE employee_jobs
( employee_id     INTEGER         NOT NULL,
  first_name      CHAR      (15)  NOT NULL,
  middle_initial  CHAR      (1)   NOT NULL,
  last_name       CHAR      (15)  NOT NULL,
  soc_sec_nbr     INTEGER         NOT NULL,
  birth_date      DATE            NOT NULL,
  hire_date       DATE            NOT NULL,
  work_department CHAR      (2)   NOT NULL,
  phone_ext       SMALLINT        NOT NULL,
  job_class       CHAR      (1)   NOT NULL,
  job_level       CHAR      (1)   NOT NULL,
  sex             CHAR      (1)   NOT NULL,
  salary          DECIMAL   (9,2) NOT NULL,
  bonus           DECIMAL   (9,2) NOT NULL,
  commission      DECIMAL   (9,2) NOT NULL,
CONSTRAINT employee_jobs_employee_id_pk
  PRIMARY KEY( employee_id ) );

ALTER TABLE employee_jobs
  ADD CONSTRAINT employee_jobs_soc_sec_nbr_uq
    UNIQUE ( soc_sec_nbr );

ALTER TABLE employee_jobs
  ADD CONSTRAINT employee_jobs_work_department_fk
    FOREIGN KEY (work_department)
    REFERENCES departments( department_code );

ALTER TABLE employee_jobs
  ADD CONSTRAINT employee_jobs_soc_sec_nbr_ck
  CHECK ( soc_sec_nbr > 0 AND soc_sec_nbr < 999999999 );

ALTER TABLE employee_jobs
  ADD CONSTRAINT employee_jobs_Birth_hire_date_ck
    CHECK ( hire_date > birth_date );

ALTER TABLE employee_jobs
  ADD CONSTRAINT employee_jobs_job_class_ck
    CHECK ( job_class IN ( 'T', 'J', 'C', 'M' ));

ALTER TABLE employee_jobs
  ADD CONSTRAINT employee_jobs_job_level_ck
```

```
        CHECK ( job_level > 0 AND job_level < 10 );

ALTER TABLE employee_jobs
  ADD CONSTRAINT employee_jobs_sex_ck
  CHECK ( sex IN ( 'F', 'M' ));

ALTER TABLE employee_jobs
  ADD CONSTRAINT employee_jobs_salary_ck
    CHECK ( salary < 92000.00 );

ALTER TABLE employee_jobs
  ADD CONSTRAINT  employee_jobs_comm_salary_ck
    CHECK ( salary > commission );

ALTER TABLE employee_jobs
  ADD CONSTRAINT employee_jobs_comm_bonus_ck
    CHECK ( commission > 0 OR bonus > 0 );
```

**FIGURE 5-8**    **Example of creating a table with check constraints**

A check constraint can compare a column to a constant. For example, the `employee_jobs_soc_sec_nbr_ck` check constraint compares the `soc_sec_nbr` column with two numeric constants to ensure that the Social Security number is a positive number between 1 and 999999999:

```
ALTER TABLE employee_jobs
  ADD CONSTRAINT employee_jobs_soc_sec_nbr_ck
    CHECK ( soc_sec_nbr > 0 AND soc_sec_nbr < 999999999 );
```

A check constraint can compare two columns in the same table. For example, the `employee_jobs_Birth_hire_date_ck` check constraint compares two columns to ensure that the employee's hire date (`hire_date`) is more recent than the birth date (`birth_date`). In other words, we want to make sure that the employee was hired after he or she was born:

```
ALTER TABLE employee_jobs
  ADD CONSTRAINT employee_jobs_Birth_hire_date_ck
    CHECK ( hire_date > birth_date );
```

The Job Class (`job_class`) column identifies the position of the employee within the company. Valid job classifications are T=Training, J=Junior, C=Clerk, and M=Manager. The `employee_jobs_job_class_ck` check constraint compares the `job_class` column with four alphanumeric constants to ensure that the Job Class column contains a valid job class:

```
ALTER TABLE employee_jobs
  ADD CONSTRAINT employee_jobs_job_class_ck
    CHECK ( job_class IN ('T', 'J', 'C', 'M'));
ALTER TABLE employee_jobs
  ADD CONSTRAINT employee_jobs_job_class_ck
    CHECK ( job_class = 'T'
         OR job_class = 'J'
         OR job_class = 'C'
         OR job_class = 'M' );
```

The Job Level (`job_level`) column contains a number from 1 to 9 that identifies the pay level within the Job Class. The `employee_jobs_job_level_ck` check constraint ensures that the Job Level (`job_level`) column contains a valid number from 1 through 9:

```
ALTER TABLE employee_jobs
  ADD CONSTRAINT employee_jobs_job_level_ck
    CHECK ( job_level > 0 AND job_level < 10 );
```

The `employees_jobs_sex_ck` check constraint ensures that the sex column contains F (female) or M (male):

```
ALTER TABLE employee_jobs
  ADD CONSTRAINT employee_jobs_sex_ck
    CHECK ( sex in ( 'F', 'M' );
```

At present, no one at the company has a salary greater than $92,000.00. The `employee_jobs_salary_ck` check constraint ensures that no employee has a salary greater than this limit:

```
ALTER TABLE employee_jobs
  ADD CONSTRAINT employee_jobs_salary_ck
    CHECK ( salary < 92000.00 );
```

Commission earned is based on a percentage of an employee's current salary. The `employee_jobs_comm_salary_ck` check constraint ensures that the value in the employee's salary column is greater than the value in the commission column:

```
ALTER TABLE employee_jobs
  ADD CONSTRAINT employee_jobs_comm_salary_ck
    CHECK ( salary > commission );
```

Every employee receives either a commission or a bonus. The `employee_jobs_comm_bonus_ck` check constraint compares two columns against the numeric constant 0 (zero) to ensure that each employee has a commission or a bonus:

```
ALTER TABLE employee_jobs
  ADD CONSTRAINT employee_jobs_comm_bonus_ck
    CHECK ( commission > 0 OR bonus > 0 );
```

The DBMS checks to make sure a new or changed row does not violate any of the table's check constraints before allowing an insert or update operation. If a check constraint condition evaluates to true, the DBMS considers the constraint satisfied; if the condition evaluates to false, the DBMS considers the constraint violated.

Conditions such as those used in check constraints can evaluate to true, false, or unknown. One way that a condition can evaluate to unknown is when the column is null. In the next example, the `ship_date` column can contain a `NULL` value, indicating that the `ship_date` is unknown, or it can contain a date indicating the shipping date. If the `ship_date` column contains a date, that date needs to be validated to ensure that it is greater than the `order_date` column, which contains the date of the sale.

```
ALTER TABLE orders
  ADD CONSTRAINT orders_ship_date_ck
    CHECK( ship_date IS NULL OR ship_date >= order_date );
```

When a check constraint condition evaluates to unknown, the DBMS considers the constraint satisfied. To prevent a null value in a column and avoid the possibility of an unknown condition, simply add `NOT NULL` to the column definition. If a column is to be tested for null, use the `IS NULL` or `IS NOT NULL` test, as in the `orders_ship_date_ck` check constraint.

Check constraints can combine more than one column into a single check constraint, as in this example:

```
ALTER TABLE shipTBL
  ADD CONSTRAINT shiptbl_status_name_ck
    CHECK ( ( status = 'A' OR status = 'I' )
  AND  ( name  <> ' ' ) );
```

However, when the DBMS detects a constraint violation, it provides only the constraint name in the error message, not the specific condition that was violated. If this constraint were violated, one could not easily determine whether the `status` or the `name` column was invalid. It is easier to handle constraint violations if each logical constraint has its own name and separate definition.

Expressions can also be used in check constraints. In the following example, the `commission` column contains the amount of commission that the person has earned. This commission value cannot be more than five percent of the person's salary. The `employee_jobs_comm_salary_ck` check constraint ensures that the value in the commission column is less than five percent of the salary column.

```
ALTER TABLE employee_jobs
  ADD CONSTRAINT employee_jobs_comm_salary_ck
    CHECK ( commission < salary * .05 ),
```

The primary benefit of check constraints is the ability to enforce business rules directly in each database. Once defined, a business rule is physically implemented and cannot be bypassed. Check constraints also provide the following benefits:

- Check constraints provide better data integrity because a check constraint is always executed whenever the data is modified. Without a check constraint, critical business rules could be bypassed during ad hoc data modification.
- Check constraints promote consistency. Because check constraints are implemented once, in the table command, each constraint is always enforced.

## Representing Boolean Data Types

As mentioned in a prior chapter, DB2 does not support a Boolean data type. However, Boolean data types can be represented using a `CHECK` constraint. Consider a `CUSTOMERS` table that contains a column called `Status` that identifies whether the customer is currently active or inactive in their account. There are only two values that this column can contain, '1' and '0'. The value `1` indicates that the customer is currently active, while the value 0 indicates that the customer is currently inactive. The CHECK constraint would be written as follows:

```
status  INTEGER NOT NULL DEFAULT 0,

ALTER TABLE customers
  ADD CONSTRAINT customers_status_ck
    CHECK (ACTIVE IN (0, 1);
```

In this example, the check constraint requires the value of the status column to contain a 0 or 1. This is similar to other databases that support Boolean data types. Of course, DEFAULT will give the column a default value of 0 if one is not explicitly given.

A Boolean data type can also be emulated with a character data type that contains the values 'A' or 'I', such as:

```
status  CHARACTER(1)  NOT NULL DEFAULT 'I',

ALTER TABLE customers
  ADD CONSTRAINT customers_status_ck
    CHECK (ACTIVE IN ('A', 'I');
```

When a value that is not allowed by the check constraint is inserted or updated into the status column, the following error is returned:

```
SQL0545 INSERT or UPDATE not allowed by CHECK constraint.
```

If a table has multiple columns with the same CHECK requirements, all three columns can be implemented within one constraint, as shown here:

```
CREATE TABLE test_boolean
( boolean1 INTEGER NOT NULL DEFAULT 0,
  boolean2 INTEGER NOT NULL DEFAULT 0,
  boolean3 INTEGER NOT NULL DEFAULT 0,
 CONSTRAINT check_flags_ck CHECK(boolean1 IN (1,0)
                            AND boolean2 IN (1,0)
                            AND boolean3 IN (1,0)));
```

## BEWARE OF SEMANTICS WITH CHECK CONSTRAINTS

The DBMS performs no semantic checking on constraints and defaults. It allows the definition of CHECK constraints that contradict one another. Care must be taken to avoid creating this type of problem.

In the following example, the `employee_jobs_dependents_ck` constraint checks that the `dependents` column contains a value that is both greater than 10 and less than 9, so nothing could ever be inserted. However, the DBMS will allow this constraint to be defined.

```
ALTER TABLE employee_jobs
  ADD CONSTRAINT employee_jobs_dependents_ck
    CHECK (dependents > 10 AND dependents < 9),
```

In the next example, the default value (`'N'`) for the Job Class (`job_class`) column is not one of the permitted values according to the CHECK constraint `employee_jobs_job_class_ck`. Therefore, no defaults would ever be inserted.

```
job_class    CHAR (1) DEFAULT 'N' NOT NULL,
.
.
ALTER TABLE employee_jobs
  ADD CONSTRAINT employee_jobs_job_class_ck
    CHECK (  job_class = 'T'
          OR job_class = 'J'
          OR job_class = 'C'
          OR job_class = 'M');
```

## DEFINING CHECK CONSTRAINTS AT THE TABLE LEVEL

Most constraints can be specified as part of a column definition or as a separate clause. In Figure 5-9, the primary key and the `employee_jobs_soc_sec_nbr_uq` check constraint are defined as part of the column definitions.

```
CREATE TABLE employee_jobs
( employee_id    INTEGER       NOT NULL Primary Key,
  first_name     CHAR    (15)  NOT NULL,
  middle_initial CHAR    ( 1)  NOT NULL,
  last_name      CHAR    (15)  NOT NULL,
  soc_sec_nbr    INTEGER       NOT NULL,
    CONSTRAINT employee_jobs_soc_sec_nbr_uq
      UNIQUE ( soc_sec_nbr ),
  birth_date     DATE          NOT NULL,
.
.
```

FIGURE 5-9   Constraints defined as part of the column definition

Although single constraints (primary keys, unique keys, foreign keys, and check constraints) can be specified at the column level, avoid doing so. In terms of functionality, no difference exists between an integrity constraint defined at the table level and the same constraint defined at the column level. All constraints can be coded at the table level; only single-column constraints can be coded at the column level. When all constraints are coded at the table level, maintenance is easier and clarity is improved.

## ADDING AND REMOVING CHECK CONSTRAINTS FROM AN EXISTING TABLE

After a table is created, the ALTER TABLE command can be used to add or remove a primary key, unique, foreign key, or check constraint, as the following examples illustrate.

To drop a table's primary key constraint, just specify the PRIMARY KEY keywords:

```
ALTER TABLE employee_jobs
  DROP PRIMARY KEY;
```

To drop a unique, foreign key, or check constraint, you must specify the constraint name:

```
ALTER TABLE employee_jobs
  DROP CONSTRAINT employee_jobs_Empsoc_sec_nbr_uq;
```

To add a new constraint, use the following ADD CONSTRAINT syntax with the ALTER TABLE command:

```
ALTER TABLE employee_jobs
  ADD CONSTRAINT employee_jobs_Empsoc_sec_nbr_ck
    CHECK (soc_sec_nbr > 0 AND soc_sec_nbr < 999999999);
```

When a new table is created with constraints, data does not yet exist in the table and thus all the constraints are enabled immediately. When the ALTER TABLE command is used to add a constraint, the command succeeds only if all existing rows satisfy the constraint.

## END-OF-CHAPTER

### CHAPTER SUMMARY

1. Database constraints consist of

   a. Primary key constraint
   b. Unique constraint
   c. Foreign key constraint (referential integrity)
   d. Check constraint

2. A primary key constraint

   a. Serves as the unique identifier for rows in a table
   b. Is used as the target identifier to a foreign key in another database table

3. A unique constraint

   a. Is similar to a primary key constraint
   b. Does not have to be defined with NOT NULL

4. A foreign key constraint

   a. Is a method of ensuring data integrity between tables related by primary and foreign keys

5. Check constraints

   a. Are used to enforce business rules by placing restrictions on the data that can be entered into a column

### KEY TERMS

| | |
|---|---|
| candidate key | entity integrity |
| check constraint | foreign key |
| child table | foreign key constraint |
| composite primary key | parent table |
| constraint | primary key |
| data integrity | primary key constraint |
| database constraint | referential integrity |
| dependent table | unique constraint |

# CHAPTER 6

## SINGLE-TABLE QUERIES

### CHAPTER OBJECTIVES

Upon completion of this chapter, you should be able to

- Use SQL commands to retrieve data from a database table
- Use literals in the select list
- Use computed columns in the select list
- Use the AS clause
- Use simple and compound conditions in WHERE clauses
- Use the DISTINCT keyword
- Use the CONCAT, BETWEEN, LIKE, and IN operators
- Sort the results of a SELECT statement using the ORDER BY clause
- Use SQL functions
- Group the results of a SELECT statement using a GROUP BY clause
- Select groups of data in a SELECT statement using the HAVING clause

### BASIC FORMAT OF THE SELECT STATEMENT

The SQL **SELECT statement** is used to query a database and return a **result set** containing rows from one or more tables or views. Figure 6-1 shows the basic format and syntax of the SELECT statement, which consists of several required and optional clauses. The SELECT and FROM keywords must be specified; the other keywords are optional.

```
SELECT column_names
  FROM table or view_name
  WHERE search_condition
  GROUP BY column_names
  HAVING search_condition
  ORDER BY column_name;
```

FIGURE 6-1    Basic format of the SELECT statement

The parts of a SELECT statement serve the following purposes:

| Portion of select statement | Description |
|---|---|
| SELECT column-names | Specifies the columns in the SELECT statement's result set |
| FROM table-list | Specifies tables and/or views from which the result set data is returned |
| WHERE search-condition | Specifies a logical condition that must be true for a row to be included in the result set |
| GROUP BY grouping-column-list | Specifies the column(s) whose values are used to group the rows |
| HAVING search-condition | Specifies a logical condition that must be true for a group to be included in the result set |
| ORDER BY order-by-column-list | Specifies a list of columns with ascending or descending (with the DESC keyword) sequence |

Figure 6-2 shows the simplest form of the SELECT statement, along with the result set retrieved. The asterisk following the SELECT keyword tells the database management system to select all the columns within each selected row from the table. The FROM clause specifies that the DEPARTMENTS table is being queried. The table name in the FROM clause can be qualified with a schema name, such as MYSCHEMA.DEPARTMENTS. In this example, no other clauses are specified in the SELECT statement; therefore, all columns within all rows are retrieved.

| Example 1 | Return all row and column values from the DEPARTMENTS table. |
|---|---|
| SQL | `SELECT *`<br>`  FROM departments;` |
| Results | |

```
DEPARTMENT_CODE DEPARTMENT_NAME            MANAGER_ID
--------------- ------------------------- ----------
AD              Administration                  NULL
AC              Accounting                      NULL
MK              Marketing                       NULL
TR              Training                         110
IT              Information Technology          NULL
CA              Cameras                         NULL
MA              Major Appliances                 111
SA              Small Appliances                 115
OP              Office Products                 NULL
VG              Video Games                      113
HT              Home Theatre                     112
```

FIGURE 6-2    **SELECT statement that returns all rows and columns from a table**

## SELECT ONE COLUMN FROM A TABLE

When specific columns are required, the required column names are specified following the SELECT statement. In Figure 6-3, the SELECT statement retrieves only the customer_name column for all rows in the CUSTOMERS table.

| Example 2 | Return the `customer_name` column for all rows in the CUSTOMERS table. |
|---|---|
| **SQL** | `SELECT customer_name`<br>    `FROM customers;` |

**Results**

```
CUSTOMER_NAME
------------------------------
Smith Mfg.
Bolt Co.
Ajax Steel Inc.
Bluewater Inc.
Bell Bldg.
London Inc.
Alpine Inc.
Steelhead Tackle Co.
Nautilus Mfg.
Bluewater Mfg.
Seaworthy
John Steeling Products
Wood Bros.
```

**FIGURE 6-3**    Return the `customer_name` column for all rows in the CUSTOMERS table

SQL statements can be written on one line or several lines. For example, the SELECT statement in Figure 6-3 can be written on one line as follows:

```
SELECT customer_name FROM customers;
```

## SELECT MULTIPLE COLUMNS FROM A TABLE

When multiple columns are required, the column names are specified one after another separated by a column. In Figure 6-4, the `customer_id`, `customer_name`, and `discount` columns are retrieved for all rows in the CUSTOMERS table. The column values are retrieved in the order specified in the SELECT statement.

| Example 3 | Return the `customer_id`, `customer_name`, and `discount` column values for all rows in the CUSTOMERS table. |
|---|---|
| SQL | `SELECT customer_id, customer_name, discount`<br>`  FROM customers;` |

**Results**

```
CUSTOMER_ID CUSTOMER_NAME                    DISCOUNT
----------- ------------------------------- --------
     133568 Smith Mfg.                          0.050
     246900 Bolt Co.                            0.020
     275978 Ajax Steel Inc.                      NULL
     499320 Bluewater Inc.                      0.015
     499921 Bell Bldg.                          0.010
     518980 London Inc.                         0.050
     663456 Alpine Inc.                         0.010
     681065 Steelhead Tackle Co.                0.000
     687309 Nautilus Mfg.                       0.050
     781010 Bluewater Mfg.                       NULL
     888402 Seaworthy                           0.010
     890003 John Steeling Products              0.010
     905011 Wood Bros.                          0.010
```

FIGURE 6-4    Select multiple columns from a table

## NULL VALUES

A null value indicates the absence of a column value in a row. A null value is an unknown value; it is not the same as zero or all blanks.

When a row is inserted into a table and there is no data for a column defined as NULL capable, the value NULL is inserted into the column. For example, in the CUSTOMERS table, the `discount` column is NULL capable. Thus, in Figure 6-5, the value NULL appears in the `discount` column for each customer for whom the discount value is unknown.

| Example 4 | Return the customer_name and `discount` columns for all rows in the CUSTOMERS table. |
|---|---|
| SQL | ```
SELECT customer_name, discount
  FROM  customers;
``` |

**Results**

```
CUSTOMER_NAME                        DISCOUNT
------------------------------       --------
Smith Mfg.                            0.050
Bolt Co.                              0.020
Ajax Steel Inc.                        NULL
Bluewater Inc.                        0.015
Bell Bldg.                            0.010
London Inc.                           0.050
Alpine Inc.                           0.010
Steelhead Tackle Co.                  0.000
Nautilus Mfg.                         0.050
Bluewater Mfg.                         NULL
Seaworthy                             0.010
John Steeling Products                0.010
Wood Bros.                            0.010
```

**FIGURE 6-5**    Retrieve a column that contains NULL values

## DISTINCT KEYWORD

When the SELECT statement does not include the primary key column(s), the result set may contain duplicate rows. For example, the SELECT statement in Figure 6-6 returns the ship_city column for all rows. Since there can be several companies from each city, those cities that have multiple companies are listed more than one.
```

| Example 5 | Return the `ship_city` column for all rows in the CUSTOMERS table. |
|---|---|
| **SQL** | ```SELECT  ship_city<br>  FROM  customers;``` |

| **Results** | |
|---|---|

```
SHIP_CITY
-----------------------------
Chicago
Toronto
Albany
Portland
Detroit
Boston
Boston
Albany
San Diego
Boston
Albany
Houston
Dallas
```

**FIGURE 6-6**   **Retrieving a column that contains duplicate values**

Examine Figure 6-6 and observe that `Boston` and `Albany` are listed twice. To eliminate duplicate rows from the result set, the `SELECT` keyword is followed with the **DISTINCT keyword**, as shown in Figure 6-7. This statement returns a list of the cities (with no duplicates) in which at least one customer exists. Examine Figures 6-6 and 6-7 and note that in Figure 6-7 `Albany` and `Boston` each appear only once.

| Example 6 | Return the DISTINCT values for the ship_city column for all rows in the CUSTOMERS table. |
|---|---|
| SQL | `SELECT DISTINCT ship_city`<br>`   FROM customers;` |
| **Results** | |

```
SHIP_CITY
-------------------------------
Chicago
Toronto
Albany
Portland
Detroit
Boston
San Diego
Houston
Dallas
```

**FIGURE 6-7**   The DISTINCT operator

## COLUMN ALIASES

An alias name can be used to better describe the contents of a column in the result set. The alias name is returned in the result set as the column heading. In the example in Figure 6-8, the first_name, middle_initial, and last_name columns are returned from the EMPLOYEES table and displayed using alias names. Each alias name follows the column in which the alias name is associated with.

The AS clause is optional and if specified is placed between the column name and the column alias. Examine the first_name column and notice that the AS clause is used to identify the alias name. The AS clause can be helpful when identifying alias names in SQL queries.

Alias names can be specified within quotes. If quotes are used, the alias name is returned exactly as specified. If quotes are not used, no spaces can be used in the alias name and it is returned in uppercase letters.

| Example 7 | Return `first_name`, `middle_initial`, and `last_name` for all rows in the **EMPLOYEES** table. Use alias names for all three columns. |
|---|---|
| SQL | ``` SELECT first_name    AS "First Name",        middle_initial    Initial,        last_name        "Last Name"   FROM employees; ``` |

**Results**

```
First Name            INITIAL Last Name
-------------------- ------- ------------------------------
Lauren                M       Alexander
Lisa                  L       James
Dave                          Bernard
Steve                 L       Carr
Marg                  A       Horner
Scott                         Long
Jim                           Best
Sue                   A       McDonald
Trish                 S       Albert
Terry                 J       Maxwell
Dave                          Nisbet
Anne                  M       Richie
Jake                  L       Lee
Janice                B       Harper
Linda                 M       Johnson
William               J       Johnson
Sharron                       Evans
Robert                        Henry
Barb                  L       Gibbens
Greg                  J       Zimmerman
Dave                  R       Bernard
Trish                 S       Albert
Rick                  D       Peters
```

FIGURE 6-8    The **AS** (alias) clause

When an alias is defined within quotation marks, such as "`Discount Amount`", it appears in the result set heading exactly as it appears in the AS clause.

## CONCAT OPERATOR

The CONCAT (or | |) operator can be used to concatenate, or join together, two character strings. If an EMPLOYEES table has three columns (first_name, middle_initial, and last_name) to contain different parts of a person's name, the SELECT statement in Figure 6-9 shows how the values in the three columns can be concatenated into a single string.

| Example 8 | Return fullname as a concatenated alias consisting of the values for the first_name, middle_initial, and last_name columns for all rows in the EMPLOYEES table. |
|---|---|
| SQL | SELECT first_name     CONCAT<br>              middle_initial CONCAT<br>              last_name<br>                AS "Full Name"<br>        FROM employees; |
| **Results** | |

```
Full Name
---------------------------------------------------
Lauren          MAlexander
Lisa            LJames
Dave             Bernard
Steve           LCarr
Marg            AHorner
Scott            Long
Jim              Best
Sue             AMcDonald
Trish           SAlbert
Terry           JMaxwell
Dave             Nisbet
Anne            MRichie
Jake            LLee
Janice          BHarper
Linda           MJohnson
William         JJohnson
Sharron          Evans
Robert           Henry
Barb            LGibbens
Greg            JZimmerman
Dave            RBernard
Trish           SAlbert
Rick            DPeters
```

FIGURE 6-9    The CONCAT operator

Note that this example produces a result set with a single column that is the concatenated result of the three table columns.

The spaces between the `first_name` and `middle_initial` columns represent the padding in the `first_name` column. The length of the `first_name` column is `CHAR(20)`, and any value less than 20 characters is padded to the right of the value with spaces. Since the `middle_initial` column is only one character in length, there is no space between the `middle_initial` and the `last_name` columns. We will see later how spaces can be trimmed during a concatenation operation.

## USING LITERALS

The column-names list that follows the `SELECT` keyword can also include literals. For example, in Figure 6-10 the `SELECT` statement uses a literal in the select list, which is returned in the result set.

| Example 9 | Use a literal in the SELECT statement to return the customer_id and ship_city location. |
|---|---|
| SQL | ```
SELECT  'Customer '      CONCAT
        customer_id       CONCAT
        ' is located in ' CONCAT
        ship_city
           AS "Customer Cities"
   FROM  customers;
``` |
| Results | |

```
Customer Cities
----------------------------------------------------------
Customer 133568 is located in Chicago
Customer 246900 is located in Toronto
Customer 275978 is located in Albany
Customer 499320 is located in Portland
Customer 499921 is located in Detroit
Customer 518980 is located in Boston
Customer 663456 is located in Boston
Customer 681065 is located in Albany
Customer 687309 is located in San Diego
Customer 781010 is located in Boston
Customer 888402 is located in Albany
Customer 890003 is located in Houston
Customer 905011 is located in Dallas
```

FIGURE 6-10  Using a literal in the SELECT statement
```

## COMPUTED COLUMNS

A **computed column** is a column in the result set that does not exist in the table. Instead, a computed column is calculated using data from existing columns in the table. The computations on a computed column can include the arithmetic operators listed in Figure 6-11.

| Arithmetic operator | Description |
|:---:|---|
| + | Addition |
| – | Subtraction |
| * | Multiplication |
| / | Division |

FIGURE 6-11   **Arithmetic operators**

Computed columns can be used in SQL queries to provide a calculated value based on existing data from the table. In Figure 6-12, a computed column is used to calculate a discount based on 5 percent of the order_total column. In this example, the value in the order_total column is multiplied by 5 percent (.05).

| Example 10A | Return **order_id, customer_id, order_total,** and **discount (order_total * .05)** for all rows in the ORDERS table. |
|---|---|
| **SQL** | `SELECT order_id, customer_id, order_total,`<br>`    (order_total * .05) AS discount`<br>`FROM orders;` |
| **Results** | |

```
ORDER_ID CUSTOMER_ID ORDER_TOTAL DISCOUNT
-------- ----------- ----------- --------
  234112      499320       35.00   1.7500
  234113      888402      278.75  13.9375
  234114      499320       78.90   3.9450
  234115      890003     1000.00  50.0000
  234116      246900      678.00  33.9000
  234117      133568      550.00  27.5000
  234118      905011       89.50   4.4750
  234119      499320      201.00  10.0500
  234120      246900      399.70  19.9850
```

FIGURE 6-12   **Using a computed value in the SELECT statement**

Figure 6-13 provides another example of a computed value in a SELECT statement. Here, `balance` is subtracted from credit_limit to produce the available credit. As a result, the alias "Available Credit" is assigned to the computed value.

| Example 10B | Return customer_id, customer_name, and available_credit (credit_limit – balance) for all rows in the CUSTOMERS table. |
|---|---|
| **SQL** | SELECT   customer_id, customer_name,<br>          (credit_limit - balance) AS "Available Credit"<br>     FROM   customers; |
| **Results** | |

```
CUSTOMER_ID CUSTOMER_NAME                     Available Credit
----------- ------------------------------   ----------------
     133568 Smith Mfg.                              148002.00
     246900 Bolt Co.                                224896.45
     275978 Ajax Steel Inc.                         174867.00
     499320 Bluewater Inc.                          145124.00
     499921 Bell Bldg.                              142624.00
     518980 London Inc.                              99900.00
     663456 Alpine Inc.                              99900.00
     681065 Steelhead Tackle Co.                     99843.95
     687309 Nautilus Mfg.                            65324.00
     781010 Bluewater Mfg.                          164013.00
     888402 Seaworthy                                99002.00
     890003 John Steeling Products                   99899.88
     905011 Wood Bros.                               90145.99
```

FIGURE 6-13   **Returning a computed value as an alias**

## WHERE CLAUSE

In the previous examples, all rows are retrieved from the table. Sometimes, a request is made to retrieve only one row or a set of rows that meet a certain **search condition**. The WHERE clause used with a SELECT statement allows for simple and compound search conditions.

### SIMPLE SEARCH CONDITIONS

Suppose only those rows where the `ship_city` column contains the value `Boston` are to be retrieved. This objective can be accomplished using a WHERE clause that contains the simple condition shown in Figure

6-14. This WHERE clause contains a simple condition that states that all rows are to be retrieved when the ship_city column is equal to Boston.

Note that character strings enclosed in apostrophes ('), such as 'Boston', are case-sensitive; that is, uppercase characters must be entered in upper case, and lowercase characters must be entered in lower case.

| Example 11 | Return customer_id and customer_name for all rows in the CUSTOMERS table where ship_city is equal to Boston. |
|---|---|
| SQL | SELECT  customer_id, customer_name<br>  FROM  customers<br>  WHERE  ship_city = 'Boston'; |
| **Results** | |

```
CUSTOMER_ID CUSTOMER_NAME
----------- ------------------------------
     518980 London Inc.
     663456 Alpine Inc.
     781010 Bluewater Mfg.
```

FIGURE 6-14   Using the WHERE clause in a SELECT statement

The example in this figure might return any of the following results:

- No rows—If there are no customers in Boston
- One row—If there is exactly one customer in Boston
- Multiple rows—If there are two or more customers in Boston

Thus, a search condition can return zero, one, or more rows. The important point is that SQL has the ability to express conditions, such as ship_city = 'Boston', that define a multi-row result set and then to retrieve or update that set in a single statement.

The WHERE clause specifies which columns or rows will be returned, based on the criteria described after the WHERE keyword. A simple condition compares two values, using one of the comparison operators in listed Figure 6-15.

| Comparison operator | Description |
|---|---|
| = | Equal |
| > | Greater than |
| < | Less than |
| >= | Greater than or equal |
| <= | Less than or equal |
| <> | Not equal |

**FIGURE 6-15 Comparison operators**

## Using WHERE with a Primary Key

To return a specific row from a table, a WHERE clause is specified with a primary key value. In Figure 6-16, the WHERE clause is used to retrieve the customer name for customer 499320. Only one row is retrieved from the table because the customer_id column is the primary key that uniquely identifies each row in the table. This SELECT statement never returns more than a single row. It might return no rows, or an empty set, if no customer exists with the specified customer_id value.

| Example 12 | Return the customer_name for customer 499320 from the CUSTOMERS table. |
|---|---|
| SQL | ```
SELECT  customer_name
  FROM  customers
 WHERE customer_id = 499320;
``` |

| Results |
|---|
| ```
CUSTOMER_NAME
------------------------------
Bluewater Inc.
``` |

**FIGURE 6-16 Using a WHERE clause with a primary key value**

## Null Condition in WHERE Clause

An SQL condition is a logical condition that is true, false, or unknown for a given row. A condition is unknown if it involves a comparison and one or both of the values being compared is null. For example, the value of the condition ship_date = '2011-09-01' is unknown if ship_date is null.

A SELECT statement's result set contains only those rows for which the WHERE clause search condition is true. If the search condition is false or unknown, the row is not returned. So, in the query shown in Figure 6-17, if a row has a null ship_date and customer_id is 499320, the row is evaluated to unknown and the row is not selected. Thus, this search condition returns only one row from the ORDERS table. The other two rows for customer 499320 are evaluated to unknown, and the rows are not selected.

| Example 13 | Return customer_id, order_id, and order_total for all rows in the ORDERS table where ship_date > '2011-01-01' AND customer_id = 499320. |
|---|---|
| SQL | SELECT customer_id, order_id, order_total<br>　FROM orders<br>　WHERE ship_date  > '2011-01-01'<br>　　AND customer_id = 499320; |
| **Results** | |

```
CUSTOMER_ID ORDER_ID ORDER_TOTAL
----------- -------- -----------
     499320   234112       35.00
```

FIGURE 6-17   Query request on a column that is NULL-capable

A comparison between two values is unknown if either or both of the values is null. The **null condition** provides a way to test for null or not null, using syntax such as that shown in Figures 6-18 and 6-19.

## USING A COMPUTED VALUE WITH A WHERE CLAUSE

A computed value can be used in a WHERE clause. For example, in the WHERE clause in Figure 6-20, balance is subtracted from credit_limit to give an intermediate value for available credit. The available credit is then compared against the value 10000 so that only those customers with an available credit greater than $10,000 are returned in the result set.

| Example 14 | Return `customer_id`, `customer_name`, and `discount` for all rows in the **CUSTOMERS** table where `discount` is null. |
|---|---|
| **SQL** | ```SELECT  customer_id, customer_name, discount  FROM  customers  WHERE discount IS NULL;``` |
| **Results** | |

```
CUSTOMER_ID CUSTOMER_NAME                    DISCOUNT
----------- ------------------------------- --------
     275978 Ajax Steel Inc.                     NULL
     781010 Bluewater Mfg.                      NULL
```

FIGURE 6-18   Testing for a **NULL** condition

| Example 15A | Return `customer_id`, `customer_name`, and `discount` for all rows in the **CUSTOMERS** table where `discount` is not null. |
|---|---|
| **SQL** | ```SELECT customer_id, customer_name, discount  FROM customers  WHERE discount IS NOT NULL;``` |
| **Results** | |

```
CUSTOMER_ID CUSTOMER_NAME                    DISCOUNT
----------- ------------------------------- --------
     133568 Smith Mfg.                         0.050
     246900 Bolt Co.                           0.020
     499320 Bluewater Inc.                     0.015
     499921 Bell Bldg.                         0.010
     518980 London Inc.                        0.050
     663456 Alpine Inc.                        0.010
     681065 Steelhead Tackle Co.               0.000
     687309 Nautilus Mfg.                      0.050
     888402 Seaworthy                          0.010
     890003 John Steeling Products             0.010
     905011 Wood Bros.                         0.010
```

FIGURE 6-19   Testing for a **NOT NULL** condition

| | |
|---|---|
| Example 15B | Return `customer_id`, `customer_name`, and `available_credit (credit_limit – balance)` for all rows in the CUSTOMERS table where available credit is greater than 10000. |
| SQL | ```
SELECT customer_id AS "Customer",
       customer_name AS "Customer Name",
       credit_limit - balance AS "Available Credit"
   FROM customers
   WHERE (credit_limit - balance) > 100000;
``` |

**Results**

```
Customer Customer Name                      Available Credit
-------- ------------------------------     ----------------
  133568 Smith Mfg.                               148002.00
  246900 Bolt Co.                                 224896.45
  275978 Ajax Steel Inc.                          174867.00
  499320 Bluewater Inc.                           145124.00
  499921 Bell Bldg.                               142624.00
  781010 Bluewater Mfg.                           164013.00
```

FIGURE 6-20   Using a computed column with a WHERE clause

## USING COMPOUND CONDITIONS

The WHERE clause also may contain a **compound condition** that specifies two or more conditions with AND or OR connectors. The example in Figure 6-21 shows a compound search condition that contains two conditions connected by AND.

In this example, the `customer_name`, `ship_city`, and `discount` columns are retrieved for every row that meets these two conditions:

- `ship_city` is equal to Albany
  AND
- `discount` is greater than zero

## NEGATING A CONDITION

To negate a condition, the NOT logical operator can be specified at the beginning of any condition or before conditions connected by AND or OR. To use NOT to negate a compound condition, place parentheses around the condition. The condition in Figure 6-22 is true if `ship_city` is not equal to Albany.
```

| Example 16 | Return customer_name, ship_city, and discount for all rows in the CUSTOMERS table where ship_city = Albany AND discount > 0. |
|---|---|
| SQL | ```
SELECT  customer_name, ship_city, discount
  FROM  customers
 WHERE  ship_city = 'Albany'
   AND  discount > 0;
``` |

**Results**

```
CUSTOMER_NAME                    SHIP_CITY                 DISCOUNT
---------------------------      ------------------------- --------
Seaworthy                        Albany                       0.010
```

FIGURE 6-21   Compound search condition

| Example 17 | Using a NOT condition, return customer_name, ship_city, and discount for all rows in the CUSTOMERS table where the ship_city is not equal to Albany. |
|---|---|
| SQL | ```
SELECT  customer_name, ship_city, discount
  FROM  customers
 WHERE  NOT ( ship_city = 'Albany');
``` |

**Results**

```
CUSTOMER_NAME                    SHIP_CITY                 DISCOUNT
---------------------------      ------------------------- --------
Smith Mfg.                       Chicago                      0.050
Bolt Co.                         Toronto                      0.020
Bluewater Inc.                   Portland                     0.015
Bell Bldg.                       Detroit                      0.010
London Inc.                      Boston                       0.050
Alpine Inc.                      Boston                       0.010
Nautilus Mfg.                    San Diego                    0.050
Bluewater Mfg.                   Boston                        NULL
John Steeling Products           Houston                      0.010
Wood Bros.                       Dallas                       0.010
```

FIGURE 6-22   Using NOT to negate a search condition

## SPECIFYING ORDER OF EVALUATION

Parentheses can be used to specify the order of evaluation for a compound condition that contains both ANDs and ORs. In Figure 6-23, the compound condition

```
customer_id = 246900 AND order_total > 200.00
```

is evaluated first. The result of this compound condition connected by AND is then OR'd with the value of the simple condition

```
order_date > '2011-05-05'
```

| Example 18 | Return **customer_id, order_id, order_total,** and **order_date** for all rows in the ORDERS table where (**customer_id = 246900 AND order_total > 200.00**) OR **order_date > 2011-05-05.** |
|---|---|
| **SQL** | SELECT   customer_id, order_id, order_total, order_date<br>    FROM   orders<br>    WHERE ( customer_id = 246900 AND order_total > 200.00 )<br>        OR order_date > '2011-05-05'; |
| **Results** | |

```
CUSTOMER_ID ORDER_ID ORDER_TOTAL ORDER_DATE
----------- -------- ----------- ----------
     246900   234116      678.00 05/04/11
     246900   234120      399.70 05/06/11
```

FIGURE 6-23   Specifying order of evaluation

## BETWEEN OPERATOR

The **BETWEEN operator** is used to test whether a value specified before the BETWEEN keyword is between the two values specified after the BETWEEN keyword. For example, the search statement in Figure 6-24 retrieves only those rows where `discount` is greater than or equal to 0.01 and less than or equal to 0.02.

| Example 19 | Retrieve **customer_id, customer_name,** and **discount** for all rows in the CUSTOMERS table where **discount** is between 0.01 and 0.02. |
|---|---|
| SQL | SELECT  customer_id, customer_name, discount<br>    FROM  customers<br>    WHERE discount BETWEEN 0.01 AND 0.02; |
| **Results** | |

```
CUSTOMER_ID CUSTOMER_NAME                   DISCOUNT
----------- ------------------------------ --------
     246900 Bolt Co.                          0.020
     499320 Bluewater Inc.                    0.015
     499921 Bell Bldg.                        0.010
     663456 Alpine Inc.                       0.010
     888402 Seaworthy                         0.010
     890003 John Steeling Products            0.010
     905011 Wood Bros.                        0.010
```

FIGURE 6-24   Using the BETWEEN operator

The NOT keyword can also be specified before the BETWEEN keyword to negate the test. The search condition in Figure 6-25 retrieves only rows where discount is less than 0.01 and greater than 0.02.

| Example 20 | Retrieve **customer_id, customer_name,** and **discount** for all rows in the CUSTOMERS table where **discount** is NOT BETWEEN 0.01 and 0.02. |
|---|---|
| SQL | SELECT  customer_id, customer_name, discount<br>    FROM  customers<br>    WHERE discount NOT BETWEEN 0.01 AND 0.02; |
| **Results** | |

```
CUSTOMER_ID CUSTOMER_NAME                   DISCOUNT
----------- ------------------------------ --------
     133568 Smith Mfg.                        0.050
     518980 London Inc.                       0.050
     681065 Steelhead Tackle Co.              0.000
     687309 Nautilus Mfg.                     0.050
```

FIGURE 6-25   Using the NOT BETWEEN operator

## LIKE OPERATOR

Most search conditions involve performing an exact match between the value specified in the WHERE clause and the value in the table column. However, there are some searches in which an exact match may not be possible. In these situations, the LIKE operator can be used. The **LIKE operator** permits the use of wildcards in the WHERE clause to perform string pattern matching. Two patterns can be used:

- The percent sign (%) specifies a match to a string of any length (including zero length)
- Underscore (_) specifies a match on a single character

The SELECT statement in Figure 6-26 includes a search condition that returns customers containing the string Steel anywhere in the name column.

| Example 21 | Retrieve customer_id and customer_name for all rows in the CUSTOMERS table where customer_name is LIKE 'Steel' |
|---|---|
| SQL | SELECT customer_id, customer_name<br>  FROM customers<br>  WHERE customer_name LIKE '%Steel%'; |

| Results | |
|---|---|

```
CUSTOMER_ID CUSTOMER_NAME
----------- ------------------------------
     275978 Ajax Steel Inc.
     681065 Steelhead Tackle Co.
     890003 John Steeling Products
```

FIGURE 6-26   Using the LIKE % operator in a WHERE clause

The expression before the LIKE keyword must identify a string (e.g., a character column or a string function, such as SUBSTR). Following the LIKE keyword, a string literal provides the pattern to be matched. In the pattern, the percent character represents a substring of zero or more occurrences of any character.

The second wildcard symbol, the underscore, represents a substring of exactly one occurrence of any character. In Figure 6-27, the condition tests for first names that begin with the letter R. Since the first_name column is 20 characters long, the percent wildcard symbol is used to ignore the remaining characters in the first_name column.

| Example 22A | Retrieve `employee_id` and `first_name` for all rows in the EMPLOYEES table where `first_name` is LIKE `'R%'` |
|---|---|
| SQL | ```SELECT   employee_id, first_name   FROM   employees  WHERE   first_name LIKE 'R%';``` |
| **Results** | |

```
EMPLOYEE_ID FIRST_NAME
----------- --------------------
        116 Robert
        139 Rick
```

FIGURE 6-27   **Example of underscore wildcard symbol with LIKE operator**

The result set contains two employees that have a first name beginning with the letter R.

Let us consider another example. Suppose you have a need to list all employees for whom the first letter of the first name is unknown and the remaining letters are `ick`. In Figure 6-28, the condition ignores the first character of `first_name`, examines for the characters `ick` in positions 2 through 4, and ignores the remaining characters.

| Example 22B | Retrieve `employee_id` and `first_name` for all rows in the EMPLOYEES table where `first_name` is LIKE `'R%'` |
|---|---|
| SQL | ```SELECT   employee_id, first_name   FROM   employees  WHERE   first_name LIKE '_ick%';``` |
| **Results** | |

```
EMPLOYEE_ID FIRST_NAME
----------- --------------------
        139 Rick
```

FIGURE 6-28   **Example of underscore wildcard symbol with LIKE operator**

This pattern matches `Dick`, `Rick`, `Mick`, and `Nick`, as well as `dick`, `rick`, `mick`, `nick`, `kick`, and `lick`. This pattern does not match names such as `DICK` and `RICK` because of the wrong case.

## IN OPERATOR

The **IN operator** can be used if the exact value for a column to be returned is known. The IN operator is used to test whether a value specified before the IN keyword is in the list of values specified after the IN keyword. For example, in Figure 6-29, the IN operator is used to determine if the value of ship_city is Detroit, Portland, or Boston.

| Example 23 | Use the **IN operator to retrieve customer_id, customer_name, and ship_city for all rows in the CUSTOMERS table where ship_city is Detroit, Portland, or Boston.** |
|---|---|
| SQL | SELECT   customer_id, customer_name, ship_city<br>    FROM   customers<br>   WHERE ship_city IN ( 'Detroit', 'Portland', 'Boston' ); |

| Results | | |
|---|---|---|

```
CUSTOMER_ID CUSTOMER_NAME                      SHIP_CITY
----------- ---------------------------------- --------------------------
     499320 Bluewater Inc.                     Portland
     499921 Bell Bldg.                         Detroit
     518980 London Inc.                        Boston
     663456 Alpine Inc.                        Boston
     781010 Bluewater Mfg.                     Boston
```

FIGURE 6-29   Using the **IN** operator with a **WHERE** clause

The SELECT statement using the OR operator in Figure 6-30 is equivalent to the SELECT statement using the IN operator in Figure 6-29. This statement selects the customer_id and customer_name columns from the CUSTOMERS table where ship_city is equal to Detroit, Portland, OR Boston.

| Example 24 | Use the OR operator to retrieve customer_id, customer_name, and ship_city for all rows in the CUSTOMERS table where ship_city is Detroit, Portland, or Boston. |
|---|---|
| SQL | `SELECT customer_id, customer_name, ship_city`<br>`  FROM customers`<br>` WHERE ship_city = 'Detroit'`<br>`    OR ship_city = 'Portland'`<br>`    OR ship_city = 'Boston';` |

**Results**

```
CUSTOMER_ID CUSTOMER_NAME                   SHIP_CITY
----------- ------------------------------- ---------------------
     499320 Bluewater Inc.                  Portland
     499921 Bell Bldg.                      Detroit
     518980 London Inc.                     Boston
     663456 Alpine Inc.                     Boston
     781010 Bluewater Mfg.                  Boston
```

FIGURE 6-30   Using the OR operator with a WHERE clause

## ORDER BY CLAUSE

The **ORDER BY clause** is used to return the results of a query in a sorted order based on the columns specified with the clause. For example, in Figure 6-31, the SELECT statement retrieves the ship_city, customer_name, and customer_id columns for all rows in the CUSTOMERS table. The ORDER BY clause sorts the result set in ascending order by customer_name within ship_city. That is, customer_name is the minor sort column and is sorted first. Once the result set is sorted by customer_name, the rows are then sorted by ship_city, which is the major sort column.

| Example 25 | Retrieve ship_city, customer_name, and customer_id for all rows in the CUSTOMERS table and sequence in customer_name within ship_city order. |
|---|---|
| SQL | SELECT      ship_city, customer_name, customer_id<br>  FROM      customers<br>  ORDER BY ship_city, customer_name; |

**Results**

```
SHIP_CITY                     CUSTOMER_NAME                CUSTOMER_ID
--------------------------    --------------------------   -----------
Albany                        Ajax Steel Inc.                   275978
Albany                        Seaworthy                         888402
Albany                        Steelhead Tackle Co.              681065
Boston                        Alpine Inc.                       663456
Boston                        Bluewater Mfg.                    781010
Boston                        London Inc.                       518980
Chicago                       Smith Mfg.                        133568
Dallas                        Wood Bros.                        905011
Detroit                       Bell Bldg.                        499921
Houston                       John Steeling Products            890003
Portland                      Bluewater Inc.                    499320
San Diego                     Nautilus Mfg.                     687309
Toronto                       Bolt Co.                          246900
```

FIGURE 6-31   Using the ORDER BY clause

The sort order can be ascending or descending. An ORDER BY clause specifies a list of columns with ascending or descending sequence. When descending order is required, the DESC keyword is specified after the column that is to be sorted in descending order. In Figure 6-32, the result set is sorted by customer_name within ship_city, with ship_city sorted in descending order.

| Example 26 | Retrieve `ship_city`, `customer_name`, and `customer_id` for all rows in the CUSTOMERS table and sequence in `customer_name` within `ship_city` (descending) order. |
|---|---|
| SQL | SELECT     ship_city, customer_name, customer_id<br>  FROM     customers<br>  ORDER BY ship_city DESC, customer_name; |

**Results**

```
SHIP_CITY                       CUSTOMER_NAME                  CUSTOMER_ID
----------------------------    ----------------------------   -----------
Toronto                         Bolt Co.                            246900
San Diego                       Nautilus Mfg.                       687309
Portland                        Bluewater Inc.                      499320
Houston                         John Steeling Products              890003
Detroit                         Bell Bldg.                          499921
Dallas                          Wood Bros.                          905011
Chicago                         Smith Mfg.                          133568
Boston                          Alpine Inc.                         663456
Boston                          Bluewater Mfg.                      781010
Boston                          London Inc.                         518980
Albany                          Ajax Steel Inc.                     275978
Albany                          Seaworthy                           888402
Albany                          Steelhead Tackle Co.                681065
```

FIGURE 6-32   Using the ORDER BY clause with a column in descending sequence

## USING A RELATIVE COLUMN NUMBER

When a computed column is returned in the result set, a relative column number can be used instead of a column name to specify that the unnamed column is to be used to sequence the rows. In Figure 6-33, shipped orders are sequenced by customer number and, within customer number, by the number of days (longest interval first) that it took to ship the order.

| Example 27 | Retrieve **customer_id, order_id, order_date, ship_date**, and a calculated column (**ship_date – order_date** in days) for all rows in the ORDERS table where **ship_date** is not null. Sort the result set by **customer_id** (major) and calculated field (minor) in descending sequence. |
|---|---|
| SQL | ```
SELECT     customer_id, order_id, order_date, ship_date,
           DAYS( ship_date ) - DAYS( order_date )
FROM       orders
WHERE      ship_date IS NOT NULL
ORDER BY customer_id, 5 DESC;
``` |

**Results**

```
CUSTOMER_ID ORDER_ID ORDER_DATE SHIP_DATE 00005
----------- -------- ---------- --------- -----
     133568   234117 05/05/11   05/08/11      3
     246900   234116 05/04/11   05/08/11      4
     246900   234120 05/06/11   05/08/11      2
     499320   234112 05/01/11   05/15/11     14
     888402   234113 05/01/11   05/04/11      3
     890003   234115 05/04/11   05/10/11      6
     905011   234118 05/05/11   05/10/11      5
```

FIGURE 6-33   Using the ORDER BY clause with a relative column number

In this example, the unnamed fifth column that results from the expression DAYS(ship_date) – DAYS(order_date) is used to sequence rows within the same customer_id value.

As a more readable alternative to a relative column number, the AS keyword can be used to assign an alias name to the derived column. Figure 6-34 shows the preceding example rewritten to use this technique.
```

| Example 28 | Retrieve **customer_id, order_id, order_date, ship_date,** and "**Days To Ship**" as a calculated column (**ship_date** – **order_date** in days) for all rows in the **orders** table where **ship_date** is not null. Sort the result set by **customer_id** (major) and "**Days To Ship**" (minor) in descending sequence. |
|---|---|
| **SQL** | <pre>SELECT    customer_id, order_id, order_date, ship_date,<br>          DAYS( ship_date ) - DAYS( order_date )<br>            AS "Days To Ship"<br>  FROM    orders<br>  WHERE   ship_date IS NOT NULL<br>  ORDER BY customer_id, "Days To Ship" DESC;</pre> |

**Results**

```
CUSTOMER_ID ORDER_ID ORDER_DATE SHIP_DATE Days To Ship
----------- -------- ---------- --------- ------------
     133568   234117 05/05/11   05/08/11             3
     246900   234116 05/04/11   05/08/11             4
     246900   234120 05/06/11   05/08/11             2
     499320   234112 05/01/11   05/15/11            14
     888402   234113 05/01/11   05/04/11             3
     890003   234115 05/04/11   05/10/11             6
     905011   234118 05/05/11   05/10/11             5
```

FIGURE 6-34    Using **ORDER BY** with an alias name assigned to a derived column

## FUNCTIONS

SQL has many built-in **functions**. Some functions, referred to as character and numeric functions, affect character and numeric values from one row at a time. Other functions, called aggregate functions, produce a value from a set of rows.

### CHARACTER FUNCTIONS

A character function takes one or more arguments that can be literals, column names, or expressions. If a column name is used in a function, the function is applied to the column's value in each row in the result set and produces a value for the same row.

## TRIM FUNCTION

The **TRIM function** removes leading and trailing blanks from a string expression. Figure 6-35 shows the TRIM function used to remove (trim) leading and trailing blanks from the first_name column.

| Example 29 | Return Full Name (concatenated alias of the first_name, middle_initial, and last_name columns) for all rows in the employees table. Trim all blanks. |
|---|---|
| SQL | ```
SELECT TRIM( first_name )
       CONCAT ' '
       CONCAT middle_initial
       CONCAT ' '
       CONCAT TRIM( last_name )
         AS "Full Name"
    FROM employees;
``` |
| **Results** | |

```
Full Name
------------------
Lauren M Alexander
Lisa L James
Dave    Bernard
Steve L Carr
Marg A Horner
   .
   .
   .
```

FIGURE 6-35   The TRIM operator

If the TRIM function were not used here, the trailing blanks in the first_name column would not be removed. As a result, there would be a gap of blanks between the first_name and middle_initial column values. Using the TRIM function and concatenating a blank literal, the concatenation operation produces a more readable string.
```

## UPPER FUNCTION

The **UPPER function** returns a string in which all the characters have been converted to uppercase characters. The UCASE function can be used as well as UPPER. In Figure 6-36, the UPPER function is used to convert the company name to uppercase letters.

| Example 30A | Retrieve customer_id and customer_name for all rows in the CUSTOMERS table. Convert the customer_name column to upper case. |
|---|---|
| SQL | SELECT  customer_id AS "Customer",<br>        UPPER(customer_name) AS "Customer Name"<br>  FROM  customers; |
| Results | |

```
Customer Customer Name
-------- --------------------------------
  133568 SMITH MFG.
  246900 BOLT CO.
  275978 AJAX STEEL INC.
  499320 BLUEWATER INC.
  499921 BELL BLDG.
  518980 LONDON INC.
  663456 ALPINE INC.
  681065 STEELHEAD TACKLE CO.
  687309 NAUTILUS MFG.
  781010 BLUEWATER MFG.
  888402 SEAWORTHY
  890003 JOHN STEELING PRODUCTS
  905011 WOOD BROS.
```

FIGURE 6-36   Using the UPPER function

## LOWER FUNCTION

The **LOWER function** returns a string in which all the characters have been converted to lowercase characters. The LCASE function can be used as well as LOWER. In Figure 6-37, the LOWER function is used to convert the company name to lowercase letters.

| Example 30B | Retrieve customer_id and customer_name for all rows in the CUSTOMERS table. Convert the customer_name column to lower case. |
|---|---|
| SQL | SELECT  customer_id AS "Customer",<br>           LOWER(customer_name) AS "Customer Name"<br>  FROM  customers; |

**Results**

```
Customer Customer Name
-------- ------------------------------
  133568 smith mfg.
  246900 bolt co.
  275978 ajax steel inc.
  499320 bluewater inc.
  499921 bell bldg.
  518980 london inc.
  663456 alpine inc.
  681065 steelhead tackle co.
  687309 nautilus mfg.
  781010 bluewater mfg.
  888402 seaworthy
  890003 john steeling products
  905011 wood bros.
```

FIGURE 6-37  Example of the LOWER function

## NUMERIC FUNCTIONS

SQL also includes several functions that can be used on numeric data.

### ROUND FUNCTION

The **ROUND function** is used to round a numeric value to the number of decimals specified in the function. In Figure 6-38, the order_total column is retrieved as several alias columns to illustrate the ROUND function.

| Example 31A | Retrieve **order_total**, alias "**0 Decimals**" (order_total rounded to 0 decimals), alias "**1 Decimal**" (order_total rounded to 1 decimal), alias "**2 Decimals**" (order_total rounded to 2 decimals), and alias "**-1 Decimals**" (order_total rounded on the units position) for all rows in the **ORDERS** table. |
|---|---|
| SQL | ```
SELECT order_total AS "Order Total",
       ROUND(order_total,0)  AS "0 Decimals",
       ROUND(order_total,1)  AS "1 Decimal",
       ROUND(order_total,1)  AS "2 Decimals",
       ROUND(order_total,-1) AS "-1 Decimals"
  FROM orders;
``` |

**Results**

| Order Total | 0 Decimals | 1 Decimal | 2 Decimals | -1 Decimals |
|---|---|---|---|---|
| 35.00 | 35.00 | 35.00 | 35.00 | 40.00 |
| 278.75 | 279.00 | 278.80 | 278.70 | 280.00 |
| 78.90 | 79.00 | 78.90 | 78.90 | 80.00 |
| 1000.00 | 1000.00 | 1000.00 | 1000.00 | 1000.00 |
| 678.00 | 678.00 | 678.00 | 678.00 | 680.00 |
| 550.00 | 550.00 | 550.00 | 550.00 | 550.00 |
| 89.50 | 90.00 | 89.50 | 89.50 | 90.00 |
| 201.00 | 201.00 | 201.00 | 201.00 | 200.00 |
| 399.70 | 400.00 | 399.70 | 399.70 | 400.00 |

FIGURE 6-38   Using the ROUND function

## DECIMAL FUNCTION

The **DECIMAL function** returns a decimal representation of a number. The result of the function is a decimal number with precision and scale, where precision and scale are the second and third arguments, respectively. If the first argument can be null, the result can be null; if the first argument is null, the result is the null value.

In Figure 6-39, the discount column from the CUSTOMERS table is multiplied by 5.0125 to determine a new discount value. The result of the calculation is first rounded to three decimals. The result of the rounding operating is then converted to a decimal number with three decimals.
```

| Example 31B | Retrieve customer_name as "Customer Name" and "New Discount" (discount multiplied by 5.0125) for all rows in the CUSTOMERS table. Round the results to three decimal places and convert the results to a decimal number with three decimal numbers. |
|---|---|
| SQL | ```SELECT customer_name AS "Customer Name",\n       DECIMAL (ROUND(discount * 5.0125, 3), 3,3)\n          AS "New Discount"\n   FROM customers;``` |

**Results**

```
Customer Name                        New Discount
------------------------------       ------------
Smith Mfg.                                  0.251
Bolt Co.                                    0.100
Ajax Steel Inc.                              NULL
Bluewater Inc.                              0.075
Bell Bldg.                                  0.050
London Inc.                                 0.251
Alpine Inc.                                 0.050
Steelhead Tackle Co.                        0.000
Nautilus Mfg.                               0.251
Bluewater Mfg.                               NULL
Seaworthy                                   0.050
John Steeling Products                      0.050
Wood Bros.                                  0.050
```

FIGURE 6-39   Example of the DECIMAL function

## AGGREGATE FUNCTIONS

**Aggregate functions** produce a value from a set of rows. Figure 6-40 lists the available SQL aggregate functions.

| Function | Returns |
|----------|---------|
| AVG | The average value of a given column |
| COUNT | The total number of values in a given column |
| COUNT(*) | The total number of rows in a table |
| MAX | The largest value in a given column |
| MIN | The smallest value in a given column |
| SUM | The sum of the numeric values in a given column |

Figure 6-40: SQL aggregate functions

## COUNT FUNCTION

The **COUNT function** returns the number of rows in a result set. In Figure 6-41, the SELECT statement uses the COUNT function to return the number of customers in the city of Boston.

| Example 32 | **Retrieve the number of distinct customers in the CUSTOMERS table.** |
|------------|----------------------------------------------------------------------|
| SQL | `SELECT COUNT(*) AS "Count"`<br>`   FROM customers`<br>`   WHERE ship_city = 'Boston';` |
| Results | |
| Count<br>- - - - -<br>3 | |

FIGURE 6-41   Using the COUNT function

The DISTINCT keyword can optionally be specified immediately after the opening parenthesis of an aggregate function to eliminate duplicate expression values, as well as nulls, from the set of values to which the function is applied. The main practical use of this feature is with the COUNT function to count the number of different values for some column, as in Figure 6-42, which produces a one-row, one-column result set that contains the number of cities in which at least one customer exists.

| Example 33 | Retrieve the number of cities in the CUSTOMERS table. |
|---|---|
| SQL | SELECT COUNT(DISTINCT ship_city) AS "Number of cities"<br>   FROM customers; |
| Results | |

```
Number of cities
----------------
               9
```

FIGURE 6-42  Using DISTINCT with the COUNT function to eliminate duplicate values

### SUM FUNCTION

The **SUM function** returns the total sum of a column. In Figure 6-43, the SUM function returns the accumulated value for all sales in the ORDERS table.

| Example 34 | Return the total sales for all orders in the ORDERS table. |
|---|---|
| SQL | SELECT  SUM(order_total) AS "Total Sales"<br>   FROM  orders; |
| Results | |

```
Total Sales
-----------
    3310.85
```

FIGURE 6-43  Using the SUM function

The COUNT and SUM functions can easily be used together. In Figure 6-44, the alias Total Sales contains a string that indicates the number of customer sales and total sales.

| Example 35 | Retrieve **Total Sales**, which is an alias for a string containing a count of the number of sales transactions and total sales in the ORDERS table. |
|---|---|
| SQL | ```
SELECT 'Total sales for '    CONCAT
       COUNT( * )            CONCAT
       ' customer sales is ' CONCAT
       SUM( order_total )
         AS "Total Sales"
  FROM orders;
``` |
| **Results** | |
| ``` Total Sales
------------------------------------------
Total sales for 9 customer sales is 3310.85 ``` | |

FIGURE 6-44  Using the COUNT and SUM functions together (example 1 of 3)

Be careful when using aggregate functions with columns that allow null. For example, suppose that the discount column allows nulls and that at least one row in the CUSTOMERS table has a null discount column. In this case, the statement in Figure 6-45 returns surprising results.

| Example 36 | Retrieve **Customer Count, Average Discount,** and **Total Discount** for all rows in the CUSTOMERS table. |
|---|---|
| SQL | ```
SELECT COUNT( * )      AS "Customer Count",
       DECIMAL (ROUND(AVG( discount ),5), 5,5)
                        AS "Average Discount",
       SUM( discount ) AS "Total Discount"
  FROM customers;
``` |
| **Results** | |

```
Customer Count Average Discount Total Discount
-------------- ---------------- --------------
            13          0.02136          0.235
```

FIGURE 6-45  Using the COUNT and SUM functions together (example 2 of 3)

The sum is not equal to the average times the count. The COUNT(*) function includes all rows, but the AVG and SUM functions ignore any rows with a null discount column.

There are two solutions to this problem. The first solution, shown in Figure 6-46, is to use an alternative form of the COUNT function that does eliminate rows with a null discount column.

| Example 37 | Retrieve Customer Count (discount column), Average Discount, and Total Discount for all rows in the CUSTOMERS table. |
|---|---|
| SQL | `SELECT COUNT( discount ) AS "Customer Count",`<br>`       DECIMAL (ROUND(AVG( discount ),5), 5,5)`<br>`                          AS "Average Discount",`<br>`       SUM( discount )  AS "Total Discount"`<br>`  FROM customers;` |
| Results | |

```
Customer Count Average Discount Total Discount
-------------- ---------------- --------------
            11          0.02136          0.235
```

FIGURE 6-46   Using the COUNT and SUM functions together (example 3 of 3)

Or, a more general solution can be used. In Figure 6-47, the WHERE clause uses the IS NOT NULL clause to eliminate rows with null columns before the functions are applied.

| Example 38 | Retrieve **Customer Count, Average Discount, and Total** for discount for all rows in the **CUSTOMERS** table where the discount column is not null. |
|---|---|
| SQL | ```
SELECT COUNT( * )      AS "Customer Count",
       DECIMAL (ROUND(AVG( discount ),5), 5,5)
                        AS "Average Discount",
       SUM( discount ) AS "Total Discount"
  FROM customers
  WHERE discount IS NOT NULL;
``` |

| Results |
|---|

```
Customer Count Average Discount Total Discount
-------------- ---------------- --------------
            11          0.02136          0.235
```

FIGURE 6-47   Using **IS NOT NULL** in a search condition

When a select list uses an aggregate function and no GROUP BY clause (discussed later) is specified, the aggregate function applies to the entire set of records selected by the WHERE clause, and the SELECT statement's result set is always a single row. When a GROUP BY clause is specified, the SELECT statement's result set contains one row for each group, or, if a HAVING clause (also discussed later) is also specified, the result set contains one row for each group that satisfies the HAVING clause's condition, with the aggregate function applied to each row of the group.

If the set of rows to which an aggregate function is applied is empty (that is, there are no rows), the result of any aggregate function except COUNT(*) is null. COUNT(*) returns zero for an empty set.

## CASE FUNCTION

The **CASE function** provides a multi-condition test. The query shown in Figure 6-48 uses CASE to produce a table that categorizes sales into small, medium, and large.
```

| Example 39 | Retrieve `customer_id`, `order_id`, `order_total`, and `category` (determined by a CASE function) for all rows in the CUSTOMERS table ordered by `category` and `order_total` (DESC). |
|---|---|
| SQL | ```SELECT customer_id, order_id, order_total,
       CASE
           WHEN order_total <= 100 THEN 'Small'
           WHEN order_total <= 500 THEN 'Medium'
           ELSE                          'Large'
       END AS category
    FROM orders
    ORDER BY category, order_total DESC;``` |

**Results**

```
CUSTOMER_ID ORDER_ID ORDER_TOTAL CATEGORY
----------- -------- ----------- --------
     890003   234115     1000.00 Large
     246900   234116      678.00 Large
     133568   234117      550.00 Large
     246900   234120      399.70 Medium
     888402   234113      278.75 Medium
     499320   234119      201.00 Medium
     905011   234118       89.50 Small
     499320   234114       78.90 Small
     499320   234112       35.00 Small
```

FIGURE 6-48    Using a CASE function

In this example, each WHEN condition specifies a search condition, followed by the keyword THEN, followed by a value. For each selected row, the first WHEN condition that is true produces the result. The optional ELSE clause specifies the result if no prior WHEN condition is true. If none of the WHEN conditions are true and there is no ELSE clause, the result is null.

A slightly different form of the WHEN clause can be used if the need exists to test for a set of discrete values. The SELECT statement in Figure 6-49, for example, produces a table of customer names and their states.

| Example 40 | Retrieve customer_name and state (determined by a CASE function) for all rows in the CUSTOMERS table ordered by state. |
|---|---|
| SQL | ```
SELECT customer_name,
       CASE ship_city
           WHEN 'Albany'    THEN 'New York'
           WHEN 'Boston'    THEN 'Massachusetts'
           WHEN 'Chicago'   THEN 'Illinois'
           WHEN 'Dallas'    THEN 'Texas'
           WHEN 'Detroit'   THEN 'Michigan'
           WHEN 'Houston'   THEN 'Texas'
           WHEN 'Portland'  THEN 'Oregon'
           WHEN 'San Diego' THEN 'California'
           WHEN 'Toronto'   THEN 'Ontario'
       END AS state
   FROM customers
   ORDER BY state;
``` |

**Results**

```
CUSTOMER_NAME                       STATE
--------------------------------    -------------
Nautilus Mfg.                       California
Smith Mfg.                          Illinois
London Inc.                         Massachusetts
Alpine Inc.                         Massachusetts
Bluewater Mfg.                      Massachusetts
Bell Bldg.                          Michigan
Ajax Steel Inc.                     New York
Steelhead Tackle Co.                New York
Seaworthy                           New York
Bolt Co.                            Ontario
Bluewater Inc.                      Oregon
John Steeling Products              Texas
Wood Bros.                          Texas
```

FIGURE 6-49   Using a CASE function

The CASE function can be used in other SELECT statement clauses as well. The example in Figure 6-50 produces a result set of customers from Toronto that have a discount greater than or equal to .02 and customers from all other cities that have a discount greater than or equal to .03.
```

| Example 41 | Retrieve **customer_id, customer_name, ship_city, and discount** for Toronto customers with a discount > .02 or other cities with a discount > .03. |
|---|---|
| SQL | ```SELECT customer_id, customer_name, ship_city,
   discount
   FROM  customers
   WHERE discount >= CASE ship_city
                       WHEN 'Toronto' THEN .02
                       ELSE            .03
                     END;``` |

**Results**

```
CUSTOMER_ID CUSTOMER_NAME          SHIP_CITY            DISCOUNT
----------- ---------------------- -------------------- --------
     133568 Smith Mfg.             Chicago                 0.050
     246900 Bolt Co.               Toronto                 0.020
     518980 London Inc.            Boston                  0.050
     687309 Nautilus Mfg.          San Diego               0.050
```

FIGURE 6-50   Using **CASE** in the **WHERE** clause

## DATE AND TIME ARITHMETIC

SQL includes expressions and functions for working with date and time values. Externally, date values are character strings containing numbers for the year, month, and day and (in some formats) date separators. When a literal date is entered, the value is coded as a string. The format of the string depends on the values specified for the DATFMT and DATSEP parameters. For example, if *ISO format is specified, the following string represents May 1, 2011:

```
'2011-05-01'
```

With *USA format, the proper representation is

```
'05/01/2011'
```

SQL offers some flexibility in the format of date literals, and it automatically recognizes a literal that is coded in one of the standard formats listed in Figure 6-51. These formats can be used regardless of the value specified for the DATFMT parameter.

| Format name | Abbreviation | Format | Example |
|---|---|---|---|
| International Standards Organization (*ISO) | ISO | *yyyy-mm-dd* | '2011-04-07' |
| IBM USA Standard (*USA) | USA | *mm/dd/yyyy* | '04/07/2011' |
| IBM European Standard (*EUR) | EUR | *dd.mm.yyyy* | '07.04.2011' |
| Japanese Industrial Standard Christian era (*JIS) | JIS | *yyyy-mm-dd* | '2011-04-07' |

**FIGURE 6-51  Standard date literal formats**

SQL also provides date addition and subtraction and date functions. In the example in Figure 6-52, the **DAYS function** is used to obtain the number of days since January 1, 0001. The difference between the DAYS value for ShipDate and the DAYS value for order_date is then used to determine how long after the sale the order was shipped.

| Example 42 | Retrieve customer_id, order_id, order_date, ship_date, and Days To Ship (difference between ship_date and order_date in days) for all rows in the ORDERS table where ship_date is not null. |
|---|---|
| SQL | ```SELECT customer_id,`<br>`       order_id,`<br>`       order_date,`<br>`       ship_date,`<br>`       DAYS( ship_date ) - DAYS( order_date )`<br>`          AS "Days To Ship"`<br>`   FROM  orders`<br>`   WHERE ship_date IS NOT NULL;``` |
| Results | |

```
CUSTOMER_ID ORDER_ID ORDER_DATE SHIP_DATE Days To Ship
----------- -------- ---------- --------- ------------
     499320   234112 05/01/11   05/15/11            14
     888402   234113 05/01/11   05/04/11             3
     890003   234115 05/04/11   05/10/11             6
     246900   234116 05/04/11   05/08/11             4
     133568   234117 05/05/11   05/08/11             3
     905011   234118 05/05/11   05/10/11             5
     246900   234120 05/06/11   05/08/11             2
```

**FIGURE 6-52  Retrieval using dates and durations**

Notice how for the first row, order_date is 05/01/11 and ship_date is 05/15/11, which results in a difference of 14 days between the DAYS function values for the two columns. If order_date were 05/01/10 (notice the year) and `ship_date` were `05/15/11`, the difference between the `DAYS` value for the two columns would be 380 days (366 + 14).

Note also how the search condition in this example excludes rows with a `NULL` `ship_date`. Because the `ORDERS` table permits the `ship_date` column to be null, the query must consider the case in which a row has a null `ship_date`. For arithmetic expressions, if one of the operands is null, the result of the expression is null. This rule makes sense, as can be seen in this example, in which the difference between two dates is obviously unknown if one or both of the dates is unknown, or null. The `IS NOT NULL` search condition lets the query eliminate the cases where the `ship_date` is not known, as when an order has not yet been shipped.

As an alternative, the following expression could be used to calculate the difference between two dates as an SQL **date duration** value:

```
ship_date - order_date
```

The result of this expression for sample column values would be

| order_date | ship_date | ship_date - order_date |
|------------|-----------|------------------------|
| 2011-05-01 | 2011-05-15 | 00000014 |
| 2010-05-01 | 2011-05-15 | 00010014 *(1 year, 0 months, 14 days)* |

SQL represents date duration as an 8-digit decimal number in the form *yyyymmdd*, not as a number of days; do not confuse date duration with days duration.

Duration can also be added to or subtracted from a date. When `order_date` is `2011-05-01`, the result of the expression

```
order_date + 14 Days
```

is `2011-05-15`. In this example, the term `14 Days` is a **labeled duration**. The following keywords can be used to specify what a duration value represents: `YEARS`, `MONTHS`, `DAYS`, `HOURS`, `MINUTES`, `SECONDS`, or `MICROSECONDS`. The following expression adds one year, two months, and 14 days to a date:

```
order_date + 1 Year + 2 Months + 14 Days
```

SQL supports time and timestamp columns, literals, and arithmetic in a way similar to what has been covered for date arithmetic. To code a time value with SQL's ISO format, a string representation, such as '13.30.10' for 10 seconds after 1:30 p.m., is used. To use a colon (:) as the time separator (e.g., '13:30:10'), use the JIS format. Time duration is a 6-digit DECIMAL number with an *hhmmss* format. Labeled time durations can also be used, as in the following expression, which adds labeled time duration values to a time column:

```
WrkBgnTime + 1 Hour + 30 Minutes
```

## GROUP BY AND HAVING CLAUSES

The **GROUP BY clause** works with aggregate functions to group the data in the result set by columns. The rows in the result set are grouped together based on the columns specified in the GROUP BY clause. In addition, the GROUP BY clause can be used to apply aggregate functions to (sub)groups of the rows in the result set. For instance, in Figure 6-53, the statement returns one row for each group of customers in a different city.

| Example 43 | Retrieve Ship City, Count, and Average Discount for all rows in the CUSTOMERS table and group by ship_city. |
|---|---|
| SQL | `SELECT    ship_city AS "Ship City",`<br>`          COUNT( * ) AS "Count",`<br>`          DECIMAL(ROUND(AVG(discount),3), 3,3)`<br>`              AS "Average Discount"`<br>`FROM      customers`<br>`GROUP BY ship_city;` |

**Results**

```
Ship City                        Count Average Discount
------------------------------   ----- ----------------
Toronto                              1            0.020
Chicago                              1            0.050
Houston                              1            0.010
Boston                               3            0.030
Detroit                              1            0.010
Albany                               3            0.005
Dallas                               1            0.010
Portland                             1            0.015
San Diego                            1            0.050
```

FIGURE 6-53   Using the GROUP BY clause

In this example, ship_city is the **grouping column** that partitions the rows in the CUSTOMERS table into groups, one for each different ship_city value. The aggregate functions COUNT and AVG are applied to each group in turn and produce one row in the result set for each group. In this example, rows with a null discount column are intentionally not excluded, letting the result set have a complete count of the number of customers in each city. The average discount is for the customers with a non-null discount column. For any null-capable grouping column, all nulls are considered in the same (null) group.

Grouping column names are listed in the select list as well as in the GROUP BY clause so that each row in the final result set has the identifying column value(s) for the group. Any other columns that appear in the select list must be used as arguments of an aggregate function.

The **HAVING clause** can be used to restrict rows in the result set after aggregate functions have been applied to grouped rows. The HAVING clause takes a form similar to that of the WHERE clause, which selects rows before they are grouped. For example, the SELECT statement in Figure 6-54 can be used to retrieve the information for cities with an average discount above 1 percent.

| Example 44 | Retrieve **Ship City, Count,** and **Average Discount** for all rows in the CUSTOMERS table with an average discount greater than one percent. Group by ship_city. |
|---|---|
| SQL | ```
SELECT    ship_city, COUNT (*) AS "Count",
          DECIMAL ( ROUND(AVG( discount ),3), 3,3)
              AS "Average Discount"
   FROM    customers
   WHERE   discount IS NOT NULL
   GROUP   BY ship_city
   HAVING AVG(discount) > 0.01;
``` |

**Results**

```
SHIP_CITY                        Count Average Discount
------------------------------   ----- ----------------
Toronto                            1              0.020
Chicago                            1              0.050
Boston                             2              0.030
Portland                           1              0.015
San Diego                          1              0.050
```

**FIGURE 6-54  Retrieval using the HAVING clause**
```

The search condition for a HAVING clause can include grouping columns, such as ship_city in this example, or aggregate functions, such as AVG(discount).

The grouping clause can also contain an expression, as Figure 6-55 shows. In this example, the result set returns the total sales for each day.

| Example 45 | Retrieve the total sales for each day for all rows in the ORDERS table. |
|---|---|
| SQL | SELECT DAY( order_date )  AS "Day",<br>        MONTH( order_date ) AS "Month",<br>        SUM( order_total ) AS "Total"<br>    FROM orders<br>    GROUP BY DAY( order_date ), MONTH( order_date ); |
| Results | |

```
DAY MONTH TOTAL
--- ----- -------
  1     5  313.75
  3     5   78.90
  4     5 1678.00
  5     5  840.50
  6     5  399.70
```

FIGURE 6-55  Using an expression in the GROUP BY clause

There is a conceptual ordering to a SELECT statement that helps clarify when the search conditions of the WHERE and HAVING clauses are tested as well as how the other clauses are executed. Each step produces a hypothetical result set from the intermediate result set of the previous step. The steps are as follows:

*Step 1.* All combinations of all rows from all tables and views listed in the FROM clause are included in an intermediate result set produced by this step. (If the FROM clause specifies only one table or view, the intermediate result set's columns and rows are the same as those in the specified table or view.)

*Step 2.* If a WHERE clause is specified, the search condition is applied to each row in the result set produced by Step 1. Only those rows for which the search condition is true are included in the intermediate result set produced by this step. (If no WHERE clause is specified, all rows from the result set produced in Step 1 are included.)

*Step 3.* If a GROUP BY clause is specified, the rows from the result set produced in the previous steps are collected into separate groups such that all the rows in a group have the same values for all grouping columns. (If no GROUP BY clause is specified, all the rows are considered as one group.)

*Step 4.* If a HAVING clause is specified, the search condition is applied to each group. Only those groups of rows for which the search condition is true are included in the intermediate result set produced by this step. (If no HAVING clause is specified, all groups, and rows, from the result set produced in the previous steps are included.)

If a HAVING clause is specified but no GROUP BY clause is specified, the intermediate result set produced by this step is either empty or contains all rows produced in the previous steps.

*Step 5.* If neither a GROUP BY nor a HAVING clause is specified, the intermediate result set produced by this step includes the rows in the result set produced in Steps 1 and 2. Each row contains the direct and derived columns specified in the select list.

If either a GROUP BY or a HAVING clause or both clauses are specified, the intermediate result set produced by this step includes one row for each group of rows produced in Steps 1 through 4. (If the previous result set was empty, the result set produced by this step is also empty.) Each row contains any grouping columns included in the select list as well as the result of applying any aggregate function(s) in the select list to the group.

*Step 6.* If the DISTINCT keyword is specified for the select list, duplicate rows are eliminated in the result set produced in the preceding steps; otherwise, all rows are included in the final result set.

Note that although this sequence of steps provides a way to understand the result of a SELECT statement, it is not necessarily how SQL actually carries out a SELECT or other statement. The query optimizer may use a more efficient method to produce the results.

Because either a WHERE clause or a HAVING clause can be used to select rows based on the value of a grouping column, either of the statements shown in Figures 6-56 and 6-57 can be used to return the average discount of customers in Portland or Boston.

| Example 46 | Retrieve the average discount of customers in Portland and Boston using a WHERE clause. |
|---|---|
| SQL | ```
SELECT     ship_city AS "Ship City",
           DECIMAL (ROUND( AVG( discount ),3), 3,3)
                AS "Average Discount"
   FROM     customers
   WHERE    ship_city IN ('Portland', 'Boston')
   GROUP BY ship_city;
``` |

**Results**

```
Ship City                       Average Discount
-----------------------------   ----------------
Boston                                     0.030
Portland                                   0.015
```

FIGURE 6-56   **SELECT** statement using **WHERE** clause

| Example 47 | Retrieve the average discount of customers in Portland and Boston using a HAVING clause. |
|---|---|
| SQL | ```
SELECT     ship_city AS "Ship City",
           DECIMAL (ROUND( AVG( discount ),3 ), 3,3)
                AS "Average Discount"
   FROM     customers
   GROUP BY ship_city
   HAVING   ship_city IN ( 'Portland', 'Boston' );
``` |

**Results**

```
Ship City                       Average Discount
-----------------------------   ----------------
Boston                                     0.030
Portland                                   0.015
```

FIGURE 6-57   **SELECT** statement using **HAVING** clause

Using a WHERE clause is a clearer way to code this retrieval, and in many cases it performs significantly faster than using the HAVING clause because the database management system can eliminate rows before the grouping step and the calculation of the AVG aggregate function values.

## CODING SUGGESTIONS

- Use an **AS** clause to give a meaningful column name to an expression or function in the select list.
- Consider null-capable columns when specifying expressions, functions, or search conditions.
- In general, when specifying a **GROUP BY** clause, include all grouping columns in the select list so that each row in the result set has the identifying information for the group.
- Performance-related suggestions:

  o When possible, use a **WHERE** clause rather than a **HAVING** clause to select rows.

  o Avoid conversion between different numeric data types in conditions. For example, if a column's data type is **INTEGER**, use a comparison such as **column_1 = 1** rather than **column_1 = 1.0**.

  o If possible, avoid patterns that begin with % or _ in the **LIKE** condition so that the optimizer can use an index to select rows.

## END-OF-CHAPTER

### CHAPTER SUMMARY

1. The SELECT statement retrieves rows from one or more tables and/or views. The basic structure of a SELECT statement is

```
SELECT column_names
  FROM table or view_name
  WHERE search_condition
  GROUP BY column_names
  HAVING search_condition
ORDER BY column_name;
```

2. The parts of a SELECT statement serve the following purposes:

| Portion of select statement | Description |
|---|---|
| SELECT column-names | Specifies the columns in the SELECT statement's result set |
| FROM table-list | Specifies tables and/or views from which the result set data is returned |
| WHERE search-condition | Specifies a logical condition that must be true for a row to be included in the result set |
| GROUP BY grouping-column-list | Specifies the column(s) whose values are used to group the rows |
| HAVING search-condition | Specifies a logical condition that must be true for a group to be included in the result set |
| ORDER BY order-by-column-list | Specifies a list of columns with ascending or descending (with the DESC keyword) sequence |

The column list of a SELECT statement can specify either an asterisk (*), indicating all columns, or an explicit list of column names, literals, expressions, and functions.

3. SQL supports arithmetic, string, and date/time expressions. Character and numeric functions operate on a single value for each argument, and a value is produced for each row. Aggregate functions operate on a set of values, one value from each selected row.

4. A search condition is a simple condition or compound conditions connected by the AND or OR logical operator. Simple or compound conditions can be negated with the NOT operator. A condition is true, false, or unknown. A condition may be unknown if one or more

operands are null. A row is selected only if the search condition is true for the row.

5. Case expressions provide multi-condition tests. The first condition that is true (if any) produces the case expression's result value. If no condition is true, the value associated with the optional ELSE clause produces the result value. If no condition is true and there is no ELSE clause, the result is null.

6. Operators:

- NULL condition—Tests whether an expression is null
- BETWEEN operator—Tests whether an expression is within a range of values
- IN operator—Tests whether an expression is in a set of values
- LIKE operator—Performs a string comparison using pattern matching

7. When a GROUP BY clause is specified, the final result set consists of one row for each group. All rows in a group have the same value(s) for the specified grouping column(s). The result set columns can include the grouping column(s) and any aggregate functions.

8. The search condition of a HAVING clause is applied either to each (sub)group of rows (if a GROUP BY clause is also specified) or to the entire set of rows in the intermediate result set (if a GROUP BY clause is not specified). The final result set includes only those rows for groups for which the HAVING clause's search condition is true.

## KEY TERMS

| | |
|---|---|
| aggregate function | IN operator |
| BETWEEN operator | labeled duration |
| CASE function | LIKE operator |
| compound condition | LOWER function |
| computed column | null condition |
| COUNT function | ORDER BY clause |
| date duration | result set |
| DAYS function | ROUND function |
| DECIMAL function | search condition |
| DISTINCT keyword | SELECT statement |
| function | SUM function |
| GROUP BY clause | TRIM function |
| grouping column | UPPER function |
| HAVING clause | |

# CHAPTER 7

## UPDATING TABLES

## CHAPTER OBJECTIVES

Upon completion of this chapter, you should be able to

- Demonstrate the use of the INSERT statement
- Demonstrate the use of the UPDATE statement
- Demonstrate the use of the DELETE statement

## MODIFYING TABLE DATA

SQL has three statements that change table data: INSERT, UPDATE, and DELETE. All three statements can modify either a single row or a set of rows in a table. None of the statements can modify more than one table in a single statement. All three statements permit the use of a WHERE clause to specify the set of rows to be inserted, updated, or deleted.

An updatable view can be specified in an INSERT, UPDATE, or DELETE statement rather than a table. To be updatable, a view must be created over a single table or updatable view.

## INSERT STATEMENT

The **INSERT statement** adds new rows to a table. This statement requires three values:

- The name of the table.
- The names of the columns in the table to be populated. These names are listed explicitly or implicitly.
- Corresponding values for the columns that are being populated.

## EXPLICIT COLUMN NAMES

Before the DBMS can insert data into a column, it needs to know which column the data in being inserted into, too. In Example 1, Figure 7-1, the INSERT statement is used to add a new row into the CUSTOMERS table. Following the name of the table, the INSERT statement explicitly lists each column name as it appears in the table. The values to be inserted into each column are listed in the VALUES clause in the same order as the explicit column names list. Character values are enclosed in quotation marks, while numeric values are not.

| Example 1: |
| --- |
| **Insert data for customer 912637 into the CUSTOMERS table using an explicit column list.** |
| ```INSERT INTO customers<br>        ( customer_id, customer_name, balance, ship_city,<br>          credit_limit, discount )<br><br>  VALUES ( 912637, 'Brideview Inc.', 0.00, 'Dallas', 50000, .050 );``` |
| **Results:** |
| Succeeded. |

FIGURE 7-1    Example of an INSERT statement with an explicit column list

A column list in parentheses follows the table name, and the VALUES clause specifies a list of values, also in parentheses, for the corresponding columns in the column list.

Once a customer has been inserted into the table, the SELECT statement can be used as shown in Figure 7-2 to verify that the new customer was inserted.

| Example 2: |
| --- |

**Verify that customer 912637 was inserted into the CUSTOMERS table**

```
SELECT *
  FROM customers
  WHERE customer_id = 912637;
```

**Results:**

```
CUSTOMER_ID CUSTOMER_NAME        BALANCE SHIP_CITY            CREDIT_LIMIT DISCOUNT
----------- -------------------- ------- -------------------- ------------ --------
     912637 Brideview Inc.          0.00 Dallas                     50000    0.050
```

FIGURE 7-2     Verify that customer 912637 was added to CUSTOMERS table

## IMPLICIT COLUMN NAMES

The column list can be omitted from the INSERT statement as shown in Example 3, Figure 7-3. In this example, the values are inserted into the table implicitly by omitting the column names. The values are inserted as an implicit list with all columns in the order in which they were defined by CREATE TABLE, CREATE VIEW, and ALTER TABLE statements.

When using the implicit method, the values for each column must match exactly the default order in which they appear in the table, and a value must be provided for each column. In Figure 7-3, the INSERT statement was written without explicitly naming the columns. For clarity, however, it is best to use the column names and explicitly identify the column names with the INSERT statement.

| Example 3: |
| --- |

**Insert data for customer 984574 into the CUSTOMERS table using an implicit column list.**

```
INSERT INTO customers
  VALUES ( 984574, 'Quality One Inc.', 0.00, 'San Francisco', 125000, .055 );
```

**Results:**

```
Succeeded.
```

FIGURE 7-3     Example of INSERT statement with an implicit column list

Again, a SELECT statement can be used to verity the insert of customer 984574 into the CUSTOMERS table as shown in Figure 7-4.

| Example 4: |
| --- |
| Verify that customer 984574 was inserted into the CUSTOMERS table. |
| ``` SELECT *   FROM customers   WHERE customer_id = 984574; ``` |
| Results: |

```
CUSTOMER_ID CUSTOMER_NAME         BALANCE SHIP_CITY            CREDIT_LIMIT DISCOUNT
----------- --------------------- ------- -------------------- ------------ --------
     984574 Quality One Inc          0.00 San Francisco              125000    0.055
```

FIGURE 7-4    **Verify that customer 912637 was added to CUSTOMERS table**

When inserting a character value into a column that contains a single quote, a double quote is used to represent the single quote. For example, if an employee's last name was O'Brien, it would be inserted as follows:

```
'O''Brien'
```

## EXPLICIT DEFAULT WITH UPDATE

A column in a table can be given a default value. This option prevents null values from entering the columns if a row is inserted without a specified value for the column.

Explicit defaults can be used in UPDATE statements. When a table is created, columns can be assigned default values. For example, a default value of 100,000 can be assigned to the credit_limit column on the CREATE TABLE command as follows:

```
credit_limit  DECIMAL  ( 7, 0 ) DEFAULT 100000,
```

When a new customer is inserted into the CUSTOMERS table, a credit limit value may not be initially established. Moreover, it may be determined that those customers who do not have an initial credit limit will be assigned a credit limit of 100,000 as a default.

Instead of inserting the 100,000 value for each customer, the DEFAULT keyword can be used as shown in Figure 7-5. If the DEFAULT keyword is specified for a column on the VALUES clause of an INSERT statement, the default value for that column is inserted into the column. For example, in Figure 7-5, the balance and credit_limit columns have the DEFAULT keyword specified. As a result, the initial value of balance is set to 0.00 and credit_limit is set to 100,000.

**Example 5:**

**Insert a new customer into the CUSTOMERS table and specify the DEFAULT value for the balance and credit_limit columns.**

```
INSERT INTO customers
   (customer_id, customer_name, balance, ship_city, credit_limit, discount)
  VALUES ( 901758, 'ATD Inc.', DEFAULT, 'Jacksonville', DEFAULT, .060 );
```

**Results:**

Succeeded.

FIGURE 7-5    Example of using DEFAULT keyword to set the default value of a column

If default values were defined for the balance and credit_limit columns when the CUSTOMERS table was created, the DBMS sets these columns to the default values. However, if no default value was defined when a column was created, the DBMS inserts a null value. Both of these default values can be changed at any time with the UPDATE statement, but initially the new customer has a balance of zero and a credit limit of 100,000.

If a default for the column does not exist and the column allows NULLs, NULL will be inserted. If any column of the table does not have a default or does not allow NULL, an error will be returned and the INSERT statement rejected.

A value must be inserted for any column that specifies NOT NULL and that lacks an explicit default, as when the DEFAULT clause was not specified on the CREATE TABLE statement. A column's default value, or null, is used for any table column not specified on the INSERT statement.

Figure 7-6 verifies that the balance and credit_limit columns of customer 901758 are the default values 0.00 and 100,000.

| Example 6: |
|---|
| **Verify that customer 901758 was inserted into the CUSTOMERS table** |

```
SELECT *
  FROM customers
  WHERE customer_id = 901758;
```

| Results: |
|---|

```
CUSTOMER_ID CUSTOMER_NAME          BALANCE SHIP_CITY             CREDIT_LIMIT DISCOUNT
----------- ---------------------- ------- --------------------- ------------ --------
     901758 ATD Inc.                  0.00 Jacksonville                100000    0.060
```

**FIGURE 7-6**    **Verify that customer 901758 was added to CUSTOMERS table**

## INSERTING ROWS WITH NULL VALUES

A column that is set to null must have been defined *without* the NOT NULL clause in the CREATE TABLE statement. For example, the discount column is defined in the CUSTOMERS table as follows:

```
discount      DECIMAL  ( 5, 3 )
```

The absence of NOT NULL indicates that this column is null-capable.

If a column can hold null values, it can be omitted from the INSERT statement. An implicit insert will automatically insert a null value in that column. To explicitly add null values to a column, the NULL keyword is used in the VALUES list for those columns that can hold null values.

Figure 7-7 illustrates three ways the NULL keyword can be used to set the discount column to null when inserting a new customer. Examine the examples in the figure and observe the following:

1. In Example 7.1, the discount column name is not specified in the column list on the SELECT statement. As a result, NULL is inserted into this column because discount is a null-capable column.
2. In Example 7.2, the discount column name is specified in the column list of the SELECT statement and the DEFAULT keyword is specified for the column value in the VALUES clause. As a result, the default value NULL is inserted as the column value.
3. In Example 7.3, the discount column name is specified on the VALUES clause and the value NULL is specified for the column value. As a result, NULL is inserted into the discount column.

The NULL values can be verified with the SELECT statement shown in Figure 7-8.

**Example 7:**

Insert three new customers into the CUSTOMERS table. Use three methods to insert a NULL value into the **discount** column.

```
/*  Example 7.1  */
INSERT INTO customers
  ( customer_id, customer_name, balance, ship_city, credit_limit )
  VALUES ( 954934, 'Crane Inc.', DEFAULT, 'Detroit', 75000 );

/*  Example 7.2  */
INSERT INTO customers
  ( customer_id, customer_name, balance, ship_city, credit_limit, discount )
  VALUES ( 969124, 'KTS Consulting', DEFAULT, 'Dallas', 125000, DEFAULT );

/*  Example 7.3  */
INSERT INTO customers
  ( customer_id, customer_name, balance, ship_city, credit_limit, discount )
  VALUES ( 972753, 'RJ Young Company', DEFAULT, 'Houston', 85000, NULL );
```

**Results:**

```
Succeeded.
Succeeded.
Succeeded.
```

**FIGURE 7-7**    Three methods to insert a NULL value into a NULL-capable column

**Example 8:**

Verify that the three inserts in Example 7 contain NULL values in the **discount** column.

```
SELECT *
  FROM customers
  WHERE customer_id IN ( 954934, 969124, 972753 );
```

**Results:**

```
CUSTOMER_ID CUSTOMER_NAME                   BALANCE SHIP_CITY             CREDIT_LIMIT DISCOUNT
----------- ----------------------- ------- -------------------- ------------ --------
     954934 Crane Inc.                         0.00 Detroit                     75000 NULL
     969124 KTS Consulting                     0.00 Dallas                     125000 NULL
     972753 RJ Young Company                   0.00 Houston                     85000 NULL
```

**FIGURE 7-8**    Verify NULL values from INSERT statement

## SPECIFYING A DEFAULT DATE

There are many instances where a default date may be required. For example, all orders placed on a particular day might be inserted using the current date. In another situation, when new employees are inserted, their hire date defaults to the current date. The statement in Figure 7-9 illustrates how the CURRENT_DATE keyword is used to insert the current date into the retire_date.

| Example 9: |
|---|
| Insert customer 139 into the EMPLOYEES_RETIRED table. Use CURRENT_DATE for the retire_date column. |
| <pre>INSERT INTO employees_retired<br>  ( employee_id, first_name, middle_initial, last_name, retire_date )<br>  VALUES ( 139, 'Rick', 'D', 'Peters', CURRENT_DATE );</pre> |
| Results: |
| Succeeded. |

FIGURE 7-9    Example of inserting CURRENT_DATE with the INSERT statement

The SELECT statement in Figure 7-10 verifies the contents of the retire_date column for employee 139 in the EMPLOYEES_RETIRED table.

## MULTIPLE-ROW INSERT STATEMENT

A multiple-row INSERT statement copies data from one table to another table. In Figure 7-11, the INSERT statement copies all rows from the table called EMPLOYEES_RETIRED to a table called EMPLOYEES_RETIRED_NEW. In addition, the statement includes an additional column, last_job_code, in the EMPLOYEES_RETIRED_NEW table.

Initially, all rows in the EMPLOYEES_RETIRED_NEW table contain blank in the last_job_code column because the result set for the SELECT includes the ' ' literal as the final element in its select list.

**Example 10:**

Verify that the `retire_date` column is the current date for employee 139 in the **EMPLOYEES_RETIRED** table.

```
SELECT *
  FROM employees_retired
  WHERE employee_id = 139;
```

**Results:**

```
EMPLOYEE_ID FIRST_NAME    MIDDLE_INITIAL LAST_NAME              RETIRE_DATE
----------- ------------- -------------- ---------------------- -----------
        139 Rick          D              Peters                 12/31/12
```

FIGURE 7-10    Verify the value of the `retire_date` column after insert

**Example 11:**

Insert the rows from the **EMPLOYEES_RETIRED** table into the **EMPLOYEES_RETIRED_NEW** table. Insert a blank for the `last_job_code` column.

```
INSERT INTO employees_retired_new ( employee_id, first_name, middle_initial,
                                    last_name, retire_date, last_job_code )
  SELECT employee_id, first_name, middle_initial, last_name, retire_date, ' '
    FROM employees_retired;
```

**Results:**

```
Succeeded.
```

FIGURE 7-11    Example of a multiple-row insert

Although the INSERT statement can add rows to only a single table, the inserted rows can be constructed from more than one table. In Figure 7-12, the INSERT statement makes a temporary copy of combined CUSTOMERS and ORDERS data.

After this INSERT statement is executed, changes to the data in the CUSTOMERS or ORDERS table are not reflected in the TEMPORARY_ORDERS table. A multiple-row INSERT, unlike a view, copies the data from the tables referenced in the FROM clause.

| |
|---|
| **Example 12:** |
| **Insert rows from the CUSTOMERS and ORDERS tables into the TEMPORARY_ORDERS table.** |
| `INSERT INTO temporary_orders ( order_id, order_total, customer_name )`<br>`  SELECT  order_id, order_total, customer_name`<br>`    FROM customers JOIN orders`<br>`      ON customers.customer_id = orders_customer_id;` |
| **Results:** |
| `Succeeded.` |

**FIGURE 7-12**  **Example of a multiple-row insert from a JOIN of two tables**

Figures 7-11 and 7-12 also show how the SELECT statement can be used within an INSERT statement to specify the rows to be inserted. The nested SELECT statement can use all the clauses and operators, including FROM, WHERE, GROUP BY, HAVING, ORDER BY, and UNION.

If the target is a view, only insert-capable columns can be assigned values. A view column is not insert-capable if it is a literal, an expression, or a scalar function. An insert operation also cannot insert values into more than one column derived from the same table column. When a view is used, any table column not present as an updatable column in the view must have a default value, as discussed earlier, and the new row gets this default value for the column.

## UPDATE STATEMENT

The **UPDATE statement** modifies existing rows in a table. It requires four values:

- The name of the table
- The name of the column(s) whose values will be modified
- A new value for each column(s) being modified
- A condition that identifies which rows in the table will be modified

A specific row can be updated by using its primary key value in the WHERE clause of an UPDATE statement and assigning new values to one or more columns in the **SET clause**. The UPDATE statement shown in Figure 7-13 changes the customer name and adds 2 percent to a customer's current discount.

| Example 13: |
|---|
| Update customer number 969124. Change `customer_name` to KTS Consulting Inc. and add 2 percent to the `discount` column. |
| ```
UPDATE customers
  SET customer_name = 'KTS Consulting Inc.',
      discount = discount + .02
  WHERE customer_id = 969124;
``` |
| **Results:** |
| `Succeeded.` |

FIGURE 7-13    Example of updating a row using its primary key value in the WHERE clause

A *set* of rows can be updated by using a search condition that specifies more than one row. An UPDATE statement that does not contain a WHERE clause will update all rows. An UPDATE statement that contains a WHERE clause for a search condition will search for the rows to be updated.

The UPDATE statement in Figure 7-14 gives all Portland customers a 10 percent discount. If the WHERE clause is not used, all rows in the specified table are updated.

| Example 14: |
|---|
| Update all Portland customers to have a `discount` of 10 percent. |
| ```
UPDATE customers
  SET discount = .10
  WHERE ship_city = 'Portland';
``` |
| **Results:** |
| `Succeeded.` |

FIGURE 7-14    Example of updating a set of rows using a search condition in the WHERE clause

A null-capable column can be set to null by using the NULL keyword as shown in Figure 7-15.

| Example 15: |
| --- |
| Update all Portland customers to have a **discount** of NULL. |
| ```
UPDATE customers
  SET  discount = NULL
  WHERE ship_city = 'Portland';
``` |
| **Results:** |
| Succeeded. |

FIGURE 7-15    Example of setting a null-capable column to null

To set a column to its default value, the DEFAULT keyword is used. In Figure 7-16, the credit_limit for all customers in Portland is set to the default value of 100,000.

| Example 16: |
| --- |
| Update all Portland customers to set the **discount** column to the default value of 100,000. |
| ```
UPDATE customers
  SET  credit_limit = DEFAULT
  WHERE ship_city = 'Portland';
``` |
| **Results:** |
| Succeeded. |

FIGURE 7-16    Example of setting a column to its default value

## UPDATING A COLUMN WITH A VALUE FROM A SUBQUERY

The new value for a column in an UPDATE statement can be the result of a single-row subquery. Remember, a single-row subquery returns one column and one row.

The UPDATE statement in Figure 7-17 sets every customer's credit limit to the current average order total amount of all orders plus 10 percent. The subquery can contain references to columns in the target table, such as CUSTOMERS, in which case all values used in the subquery are from the table *before* it is updated. If the subquery does not return any rows, the updated column is set to null. If the subquery returns more than one row, an exception is generated.

| Example 17: |
| --- |
| **Set every customer's credit limit to the current average order total amount of all orders plus 10 percent.** |
| ```UPDATE customers  SET credit_limit =      ( SELECT AVG( order_total ) * 1.10        FROM orders );``` |
| **Results:** |
| Succeeded. |

FIGURE 7-17    Example of using a subquery with an update statement

Figure 7-18 illustrates another example of an UPDATE statement that uses a single-row subquery. In this example, each row in the CUSTOMERS table has a credit_rating column, which is used as a "lookup" value in the CREDIT_DISCOUNT_LIMITS table. Based on each customer's credit rating, the respective credit limit and discount columns are set to values from the CREDIT_DISCOUNT_LIMITS table. When this UPDATE statement is used, the subquery must have the same number of columns in the result set as exist in the SET clause column list. If the subquery returns no row, the updated columns are set to null. If the subquery returns more than one row, an exception is generated.

**Example 18:**

**Update each customer's credit limit and discount based on the customer's credit rating found in the CREDIT_DISCOUNT_LIMITS table.**

```
UPDATE customers
  SET (     credit_limit,
            discount ) =
  ( SELECT  credit_limit,
            discount
      FROM  credit_discount_limits
      WHERE customers.credit_rating =
            credit_discount_limits.credit_rating );
```

**Results:**

Succeeded.

FIGURE 7-18   Example of using a single-row subselect on the right side of a SET clause

## SET CLAUSE VARIATIONS

Several variations of the SET clause can be used. In Figure 7-19, column names and values are grouped into two lists.

**Example 19:**

**Update customer 905011.**

```
UPDATE customers
  SET ( customer_id, customer_name, ship_city, discount )
  = ( 905011, 'Wood Products', 'Chicago', discount = discount + .02 )
  WHERE customer_id = 905011;
```

**Results:**

Succeeded.

FIGURE 7-19   Example of grouping column names and values in a SET clause

To update multiple tables, more than one UPDATE statement must be used. In Figure 7-20, to increase the hourly rate of both employees and contractors, two UPDATE statements are used.

```
UPDATE employees
  SET  hourly_rate = hourly_rate * 1.08

UPDATE contractors
  SET  hourly_rate = hourly_rate * 1.05
```

FIGURE 7-20: **Updating multiple tables with multiple UPDATE statements**

## INTEGRITY CONSTRAINT ERRORS

Integrity constraints ensure that the update data conforms to a set of rules that are normally established when the table was created. All constraints for a column are automatically checked whenever a DML statement is executed against a column. If any constraint rule would be broken as a result of the update, the table is not updated and an error is returned.

When an UPDATE is performed, constraints, including primary key, unique, foreign key, and check constraints, must be taken into consideration. Consider Figure 7-21, where the EMPLOYEES table has a foreign key constraint on department_code, which references the department_code of the DEPARTMENTS table. This ensures that every employee belongs to a valid department. In this example, the department_code CP does not exist in the DEPARTMENTS table. As a result, the update fails because of a foreign key constraint on the department_code column in the EMPLOYEES table.

| Example 20: |
| --- |
| **Update the department code for employee 135 to CP.** |
| `UPDATE employees`<br>`  SET department_code = 'CP'`<br>`  WHERE employee_id = 135;` |
| **Results:** |
| `Failed.` |

FIGURE 7-21    **Example of a foreign key constraint check**

In another example, suppose we want to change a customer ID in the CUSTOMERS table. To do this, we must be sure that the customer_id column value is changed in the CUSTOMERS table's row as well as in all rows in tables that use customer_id as a foreign key. If no foreign key constraints exist, multiple UPDATE statements can simply be used, as shown in Figure 7-22.

```
UPDATE customers
   SET    customer_id = 123789
   WHERE customer_id = 888402

UPDATE orders
   SET    customer_id = 123789
   WHERE customers_id = 888402
```

FIGURE 7-22: Updating a customer number column in multiple tables

However, if the ORDERS table has a foreign key constraint specified for the customer_id column, both of these statements will cause an error because either statement by itself would result in unmatched ORDERS rows.

## DELETE STATEMENT

The **DELETE statement** removes a row from a table. The statement requires two values:

- The name of the table
- The condition that identifies the rows to be deleted

In Figure 7-23, the DELETE statement deletes the customer row with a customer_id (primary key) value of 905011.

| Example 21: |
| --- |
| **Delete customer 905011 from the CUSTOMERS table.** |
| ```
DELETE
  FROM   customers
  WHERE customer_id = 905011;
``` |
| **Results:** |
| Succeeded. |

FIGURE 7-23    Example of the DELETE statement to delete a row from a table
```

A set of rows can be deleted from a single table using a search condition that specifies more than one row as shown in Figure 7-24.

| Example 22: |
| --- |
| **Delete all customer from the CUSTOMERS table where the ship city is equal to Portland.** |
| ```
DELETE
  FROM  customers
  WHERE ship_city = 'Portland';
``` |
| **Results:** |
| ```
Succeeded.
``` |

FIGURE 7-24    Example of the DELETE statement to delete a set of rows from a table

All rows in a table can be cleared, intentionally or accidentally, by entering the DELETE statement in Figure 7-25 with no WHERE clause. Note that after all rows are cleared from a table, the table still exists; it is just an empty table. To clear and delete a table, the DROP statement is used.

| Example 23: |
| --- |
| **Delete (clear) all rows in the CUSTOMERS table.** |
| ```
DELETE
  FROM customers;
``` |
| **Results:** |
| ```
Succeeded.
``` |

FIGURE 7-25    Example of clearing all rows in a table

Deleting rows from multiple tables requires multiple DELETE statements to be executed. A foreign key constraint can be used with a DELETE CASCADE rule to delete all dependent rows along with a parent row. Thus, given the CUSTOMERS and ORDERS table definitions and sample data, the DELETE statement shown in Figure 7-26 deletes one row from the CUSTOMERS table and three rows from the ORDERS table.

| Example 23: |
| --- |
| Delete (clear) all rows in the CUSTOMERS table. |
| <pre>DELETE<br>  FROM  customers<br>  WHERE customer_id = 499320;</pre> |
| Results: |
| Succeeded. |

FIGURE 7-26   Example of deleting rows from multiple tables that contain a foreign key constraint

## CODING SUGGESTIONS

- Be sure that a subquery used on the right-hand side of the SET clause in an UPDATE statement can never have more than one row.
- Use an explicit list of columns in the INSERT statement to make clear which column each new value corresponds to.
- Be careful to include a WHERE clause in an UPDATE or DELETE statement unless the intention is to update or delete all rows in the table.
- Whenever updating or inserting a row into a table, be certain to adhere to any check constraints defined on the table.
- Be sure to consider the effect of primary key, unique, and foreign key constraints when updating a primary key, unique, or foreign key column or when deleting a row in a table referenced by a foreign key.

## END-OF-CHAPTER

### CHAPTER SUMMARY

1. Three SQL statements are used to manipulate table rows:

   a. INSERT

   b. UPDATE

   c. DELETE

2. The INSERT statement

   a. Can insert a single row using the VALUES clause

   b. Can insert multiple rows using a nested form of the SELECT statement

3. The UPDATE statement

   a. Changes the contents of one or more columns by specifying new values in a SET clause.

   b. The right-hand side of a SET clause assignment can be any expression, including a scalar subselect, that is compatible with the data type of the column being updated.

   c. Variations of the SET clause use column lists and/or a list of expressions or a multicolumn subselect.

4. The DELETE statement

   a. Can remove a single row from a table

   b. Can remove multiple rows using a search condition that specifies more than one row

   c. Can clear all rows from a table when the statement is specified with no WHERE clause

5. A WHERE clause can be used in an UPDATE or a DELETE statement to specify which subset of rows is changed or deleted. In both cases, if the WHERE clause is omitted, all rows in the table are updated or deleted.

### KEY TERMS

| | |
|---|---|
| DELETE statement | SET clause |
| INSERT statement | UPDATE statement |

# CHAPTER 8

## MULTIPLE-TABLE QUERIES

## CHAPTER OBJECTIVES

Upon completion of this chapter, you should be able to

- Explain the different types of joins
- Use joins to retrieve data from two or more tables
- Join a table to itself
- Uses aliases
- Use the UNION operator
- Join multiple tables with the WHERE clause

## INTRODUCTION TO JOINS

There are times when the required data for an application is stored in more than one table. In these situations, each row in the result set may consist of some columns from one table and some columns from another table. This type of selection can be accomplished with a join. A **join** creates a result set containing rows from two or more database tables by using columns that are common to each table.

### JOIN TYPES

The JOIN keyword is used in an SQL statement to query data from two tables. When a join is performed, one column is specified from each table that is to be joined. These two columns contain data that is common in both tables. Multiple joins can be used in the same SQL statement to query data from as many tables as needed. Figure 8-1 lists the different types of joins.

| Join type | Description |
|-----------|-------------|
| INNER JOIN | Returns only the rows from each table for which matching values exist in the join column. Any rows that do not have a match between the tables do not appear in the result set. |
| OUTER JOIN | |
|     LEFT OUTER JOIN (or LEFT JOIN) | Returns all rows from the first table (specified to the left of the JOIN keyword), even if no matching rows exist in the second table. |
|     RIGHT OUTER JOIN (or RIGHT JOIN) | Returns all rows from the second table (right of the JOIN keyword), even if no matching rows exist in the first table. |
|     FULL OUTER JOIN (or FULL JOIN) | Returns all rows from both tables, even if the rows do not match rows from the other table. |
| EXCEPTION JOIN | |
|     LEFT EXCEPTION JOIN | Returns only the rows from the first table that do not have a match in the second table. |
|     RIGHT EXCEPTION JOIN | Returns only the rows from the second table that do not have a match in the first table. |
| CROSS JOIN | Returns each row from the first table paired with each row of the second table. A CROSS JOIN is also known as a Cartesian product. |
| SELF-JOIN | Joins a table to itself. |

**FIGURE 8-1**   **Types of joins**

## JOINS AND KEYS

In a relational database, tables are related to each other using keys. A primary key is a column with a unique value for each row. Each primary key value must be unique within the table. One purpose of the primary key is to connect, or join, tables together without repeating all the data in every table.

In the DEPARTMENTS table, the department_code column is the primary key, meaning that no two rows can have the same department number. Likewise, the employee_id column is the primary key in the EMPLOYEES table. The employee_id distinguishes two customers even if they have the same name.

If one were to examine the DEPARTMENTS and EMPLOYEES tables (which are available on the companion website for this book), one would observe that

- The department_code column is the primary key of the DEPARTMENTS table
- The employee_id column is the primary key of the EMPLOYEES table
- The department_code column in the EMPLOYEES table is a foreign key that is used to connect to the departments in the DEPARTMENTS table

- The Cameras and Office Products departments currently do not have a supervisor

- The Cameras and Office Products departments currently do not have any employees

- At least one employee has not been assigned to any department yet

## INNER JOIN

An **inner join** creates a result set by combining column values of two tables based upon a join condition. There are two methods to specify an inner join statement: INNER JOIN/ON clauses and the WHERE clause.

### USING INNER JOIN/ON CLAUSES

The syntax for an INNER JOIN/ON or JOIN/ON is shown in Figure 8-2. The JOIN operator is not required, and, if omitted, an INNER join is performed by default. The INNER JOIN/ON clauses are used to join two tables. The FROM clause includes the JOIN operator to identify the two tables to be joined. The two tables are separated by the keywords INNER JOIN. The ON clause identifies the join condition by specifying the column in each table that is used to join the tables specified in the FROM clause.

An inner join selects only those rows in which columns from both tables have identical values; the inner join selects rows from Table 1 and Table 2 that match on the common or joining column. The INNER keyword is optional.

```
SELECT column1, column2, column3
  FROM table1 INNER JOIN table2
    ON table1.column_name = table2.column_name;
```

**FIGURE 8-2**     Syntax for inner join using INNER JOIN clause

Consider the example in Figure 8-3, which uses a SELECT statement to return the employee_id and last_name columns from the EMPLOYEES table and the department_name column from the DEPARTMENTS table. In this example, the INNER JOIN joins the EMPLOYEES and DEPARTMENTS tables using the department_code column.

| Example 1<br><br>INNER JOIN | Provide a list of employees who have been assigned to a department. List the employee_id, last_name, and department_name for each employee. Use the INNER JOIN clause. |
|---|---|
| SQL | SELECT employee_id, last_name, department_name<br>  FROM employees INNER JOIN departments<br>    ON employees.department_code =<br>      departments.department_code<br>  ORDER BY employee_id; |

**Results**

```
EMPLOYEE_ID LAST_NAME                          DEPARTMENT_NAME
----------- ------------------------------    ------------------------
        110 Alexander                         Training
        111 James                             Major Appliances
        112 Bernard                           Home Theatre
        113 Carr                              Video Games
        114 Horner                            Major Appliances
        115 Best                              Small Appliances
        116 Henry                             Major Appliances
        117 Albert                            Video Games
        118 Harper                            Home Theatre
        120 Richie                            Major Appliances
        122 Lee                               Video Games
        123 Johnson                           Major Appliances
        124 Long                              Video Games
        125 Maxwell                           Home Theatre
        127 Evans                             Major Appliances
        132 Bernard                           Information Technology
        135 Zimmerman                         Information Technology
        136 Albert                            Information Technology
        139 Peters                            Information Technology
```

FIGURE 8-3    Inner join using INNER JOIN clause

The INNER JOIN returns only those column values for each matched pair of rows from the EMPLOYEES and DEPARTMENTS tables that have matching values in the department_code column. Any rows that do not have a match in the department_code columns between the two tables do not appear in the result set.

The query compares the department_code from each row of the EMPLOYEES table with each row of the DEPARTMENTS table to find all pairs of rows that satisfy the join. When the join is satisfied, column values for each matched pair of rows from the EMPLOYEES and DEPARTMENTS tables are combined into a result row.

This INNER JOIN joins the EMPLOYEES and DEPARTMENTS tables using the department_code column of both tables. Where the department_code of these tables matches, the join condition is satisfied and the query will combine the employee_id, last_name, and department_name columns from the two tables into a result row that is returned with the result set. Where the department_code does not match, no result row is generated.

This INNER JOIN combines each row of the left table, EMPLOYEES, with every row of the right table, DEPARTMENTS, keeping only the rows where the join condition is true. Thus, the result set is missing rows from both of the joined tables. The result set does not include:

- Employee rows that have not been assigned to a department. This includes any employee where the department_code column in the EMPLOYEES table is NULL.
- Department rows that have not been assigned employees. That is, if there is a row in the DEPARTMENTS table but no corresponding row in the EMPLOYEES table with the same department_code, the row in the DEPARTMENTS table will not be returned in the result set of the INNER JOIN.

Special care should be taken when joining tables on columns that can contain NULL values because NULL will never match any other value (or even NULL itself) unless the join condition explicitly uses IS NULL or IS NOT NULL.

In example 1 in Figure 8-3, notice that employees 119, 121, 126, 130, and 131 do not appear in the query results. The reason for this is that the department_code column for these employees contain NULL and thus does not match any row in the DEPARTMENTS table.

Likewise, notice that the Cameras and Office Products departments do not appear in the query results. This is because these two departments do not have any employees assigned to them and thus there are no matches with the EMPLOYEES table.

## USING THE WHERE CLAUSE FOR INNER JOIN

An inner join can also be performed using the WHERE clause. The syntax for this method is shown in Figure 8-4. With the WHERE method, the tables to be joined are listed on the FROM clause separated by commas. The tables are joined using the join condition specified on the WHERE clause.

```
SELECT column1, column2, column3
  FROM table1, table2
  WHERE table1.column_name = table2.column_name;
```

**FIGURE 8-4**    Syntax for inner join using WHERE clause

The inner join in Figure 8-5 uses the WHERE method to return the same result set as the INNER JOIN in Figure 8-3. Again, these inner joins return only those rows from the EMPLOYEES and DEPARTMENTS tables that have matching values in the department_code column.

When this method is used for an inner join and the WHERE clause is omitted in error, a CROSS JOIN is generated instead of an inner join. We will discuss later in this chapter, in the section on cross joins, what the consequences are when this happens. For this reason, it is suggested that the INNER JOIN clause be used for queries that require an inner join operation.

| Example 2 WHERE | Provide a list of employees who have been assigned to a department. List the employee_id, last_name, and department_name for each employee. Use the WHERE clause. |
|---|---|
| SQL | SELECT employee_id, last_name, department_name<br>  FROM employees, departments<br>  WHERE employees.department_code =<br>     departments.department_code<br>  ORDER BY employee_id; |

**Results**

```
EMPLOYEE_ID LAST_NAME                         DEPARTMENT_NAME
----------- -------------------------------   ------------------------
        110 Alexander                         Training
        111 James                             Major Appliances
        112 Bernard                           Home Theatre
        113 Carr                              Video Games
        114 Horner                            Major Appliances
        115 Best                              Small Appliances
        116 Henry                             Major Appliances
        117 Albert                            Video Games
        118 Harper                            Home Theatre
        120 Richie                            Major Appliances
        122 Lee                               Video Games
        123 Johnson                           Major Appliances
        124 Long                              Video Games
        125 Maxwell                           Home Theatre
        127 Evans                             Major Appliances
        132 Bernard                           Information Technology
        135 Zimmerman                         Information Technology
        136 Albert                            Information Technology
        139 Peters                            Information Technology
```

FIGURE 8-5    Inner join using WHERE clause

## ALIAS NAMES

There are two types of aliases: column name alias and table name alias.

### COLUMN NAME ALIAS

Figure 8-6 provides a review of column name alias. In this example, the alias `Dept ID` is assigned to the `department_code` column, and the alias `Name` is assigned to the `department_name` column. When an alias is defined within quotation marks, it is not converted to upper case. Instead, it is returned in the result set exactly as stated in the alias clause. Thus, the column heading for the `department_code` is `Dept ID`.

| Example 3 | **Return the `department_code` (alias `Dept ID`) and `department_name` (alias `Name`) columns for all rows in the `DEPARTMENTS` table.** |
|---|---|
| **SQL** | `SELECT department_code AS "Dept ID",`<br>`        department_name AS "Name"`<br>`   FROM departments;` |

**Results**

```
Dept ID Name
------- --------------------------
AD      Administration
AC      Accounting
MK      Marketing
TR      Training
IT      Information Technology
CA      Cameras
MA      Major Appliances
SA      Small Appliances
OP      Office Products
VG      Video Games
HT      Home Theatre
```

**FIGURE 8-6**   Using column aliases

### TABLE NAME ALIAS

The syntax for a table name alias is

```
SELECT column FROM table AS table_alias
```

In Figure 8-7, the table alias E is used as the alias for the EMPLOYEES table.

| Example 4 | Return the employee_id, last_name, and department_code columns for all rows in the EMPLOYEES (alias e) table. |
|---|---|
| **SQL** | SELECT e.employee_id, e.last_name, e.department_code<br>    FROM employees AS e; |
| **Results** | |

```
EMPLOYEE_ID LAST_NAME                               DEPARTMENT_CODE
----------- -------------------------------- ----------------
        110 Alexander                        TR
        111 James                            MA
        112 Bernard                          HT
        113 Carr                             VG
        114 Horner                           MA
        124 Long                             VG
        115 Best                             SA
        126 McDonald                         NULL
        117 Albert                           VG
        125 Maxwell                          HT
        119 Nisbet                           NULL
        120 Richie                           MA
        122 Lee                              VG
        118 Harper                           HT
        123 Johnson                          MA
        121 Johnson                          NULL
        127 Evans                            MA
        116 Henry                            MA
        131 Gibbens                          NULL
        135 Zimmerman                        IT
        132 Bernard                          IT
        136 Albert                           IT
        139 Peters                           IT
```

FIGURE 8-7    Using table aliases

The AS keyword is optional when specifying an alias name. For example, the following defines EMP as the alias name for the EMPLOYEES table:

```
FROM employees emp;
```

## ALIAS NAMES ARE SOMETIMES REQUIRED

Let us consider an example where it is necessary to use alias names. In Figure 8-8, the department_code column is added to the SELECT statement. When this query is run, the error message

```
[SQL0203] Name DEPARTMENT_CODE is ambiguous.
```

is returned because the DBMS cannot determine which table to use for the department_code column specified on the SELECT statement. Because department_code is not qualified with the table name, that column is considered ambiguous.

| Example 5 | Return the last_name, department_code, and department_name columns for all matching rows in the EMPLOYEES and DEPARTMENTS tables. |
|---|---|
| SQL | `SELECT last_name, department_code, department_name`<br>`   FROM employees e INNER JOIN departments d`<br>`      ON e.department_code = d.department_code`<br>`   ORDER BY employee_id;` |
| Results | |
| `[SQL0203] Name DEPARTMENT_CODE is ambiguous.` | |

FIGURE 8-8    A column with an ambiguous error

To solve this ambiguous error, the department_code column in the SELECT statement must be qualified with the table name. Figure 8-9 illustrates two methods that can be used to qualify the column name. In the first method, the department_code column is qualified with the table name DEPARTMENTS. In the second method, the department_code column is qualified with the letter D, which has been assigned to the DEPARTMENTS table as a table alias. As this example illustrates, when a column with the same name exists in more than one table, a qualified column name is used in the form *table.column*.

Figure 8-10 illustrates the syntax to correct the ambiguous query specified in Figure 8-8. The department_code column is the only common column between the two tables. As a result, it is the only column that needs to be qualified with the table name or alias. The decision whether to qualify all columns or just the common columns is a developers preference.

```
Method 1:

      SELECT departments.department_code,

Method 2:

      SELECT d.department_code,
        FROM departments AS d
```

FIGURE 8-9    Two methods to qualify a column name

| Example 6 | Return the last_name, and department_code, department_name columns for all matching rows in the EMPLOYEES (alias E) and DEPARTMENTS (alias D) tables. |
|---|---|
| SQL | `SELECT e.last_name, d.department_code, d.department_name`<br>`  FROM employees AS e INNER JOIN departments AS d`<br>`    ON e.department_code = d.department_code`<br>`  ORDER BY e.employee_id;` |

**Results**

```
LAST_NAME                        DEPARTMENT_CODE  DEPARTMENT_NAME
------------------------------   ---------------  ----------------------
Alexander                        TR               Training
James                            MA               Major Appliances
Bernard                          HT               Home Theatre
Carr                             VG               Video Games
Horner                           MA               Major Appliances
Best                             SA               Small Appliances
Henry                            MA               Major Appliances
Albert                           VG               Video Games
Harper                           HT               Home Theatre
Richie                           MA               Major Appliances
Lee                              VG               Video Games
Johnson                          MA               Major Appliances
Long                             VG               Video Games
Maxwell                          HT               Home Theatre
Evans                            MA               Major Appliances
Bernard                          IT               Information Technology
Zimmerman                        IT               Information Technology
Albert                           IT               Information Technology
Peters                           IT               Information Technology
```

FIGURE 8-10    Using column and table aliases to prevent ambiguous errors

## USING THE WHERE CLAUSE WITH AN INNER JOIN

The WHERE clause can be specified with an INNER JOIN to identify a selection criteria. For example, in Figure 8-11, the CUSTOMERS table is joined with the ORDERS table to return a list of customers WHERE the value in the order_total column is greater than 500.00.

| Example 7 INNER JOIN | Provide a list of all sales that are $500.00 or more. Return the customer_name, order_id, and order_total in the result set. |
|---|---|
| SQL | ```SELECT c.customer_name, s.order_id, s.order_total FROM customers AS c INNER JOIN orders AS s ON c.customer_id = s.customer_id WHERE s.order_total > 500.00 ORDER BY c.customer_id;``` |

| Results |
|---|

```
CUSTOMER_NAME                    ORDER_ID ORDER_TOTAL
------------------------------- -------- -----------
Smith Mfg.                        234117      550.00
Bolt Co.                          234116      678.00
John Steeling Products            234115     1000.00
```

FIGURE 8-11   Using WHERE clause with INNER JOIN clause

Example 8 in Figure 8-12 illustrates the traditional WHERE clause method to perform the same query as that in Example 7, Figure 8-11. Note that the INNER JOIN query in Example 7 provides a better method than Example 8, where the join and selection criteria are combined into one WHERE clause. The INNER JOIN method separates the join clause from the conditional WHERE clause.

| Example 8 WHERE | Provide a list of all sales that are $500.00 or more. Return the customer_name, order_id, and order_total in the result set. |
|---|---|
| SQL | ```SELECT c.customer_name, s.order_id, s.order_total FROM customers AS c, orders AS s WHERE c.customer_id = s.customer_id AND s.order_total > 500.00 ORDER BY c.customer_id;``` |

**Results**

```
CUSTOMER_NAME                      ORDER_ID ORDER_TOTAL
---------------------------------- -------- -----------
Smith Mfg.                           234117      550.00
Bolt Co.                             234116      678.00
John Steeling Products               234115     1000.00
```

FIGURE 8-12   Traditional WHERE inner join with conditional WHERE clause

## OUTER JOIN

Outer joins are divided into left outer joins, right outer joins, and full outer joins. An **outer join** is similar to an inner join in that it creates a result set by combining column values of two tables based upon a join condition. However, an outer join does not require each row in the joined tables to have a matching value in the join columns. Instead, an outer join has the capability of returning all rows from the left table, the right table, or both tables.

For example, if the join is a LEFT OUTER JOIN, all rows from the left table will be returned even if there is no match with the right table. Likewise, a RIGHT OUTER JOIN returns all rows from the right table, and a FULL OUTER JOIN returns all rows from both tables. The OUTER JOIN includes the rows produced by the inner join as well as the missing rows, depending on the type of outer join:

- A LEFT OUTER JOIN or LEFT JOIN includes the rows from the left table that were missing from the inner join.
- A RIGHT OUTER JOIN or RIGHT JOIN includes the rows from the right table that were missing from the inner join.
- A FULL OUTER JOIN or FULL JOIN includes the rows from both tables that were missing from the inner join.

The keyword OUTER is optional in all three outer joins. There is no WHERE version for outer joins that allows the join condition to be specified on a WHERE clause.

## LEFT OUTER JOIN

Figure 8-13 shows the syntax for a LEFT OUTER JOIN.

```
SELECT column1, column2, column3
  FROM table1
    LEFT OUTER JOIN
      table2
    ON table1.column_name = table2.column_name;
```

**FIGURE 8-13**    Syntax for left join

A **left outer join** or **left join** is used when the intention is to retrieve all rows from the left table regardless of whether a match exists. In the example in Figure 8-14, the LEFT OUTER JOIN returns all rows from the EMPLOYEES table, even if no matching rows exist in the DEPARTMENTS table. If there are rows in the EMPLOYEES table that do not have matches in the DEPARTMENTS table, those rows are also returned to the result set.

The result of a LEFT OUTER JOIN for the EMPLOYEES and DEPARTMENTS tables always contains all records of the EMPLOYEES table, even if the join condition does not find any matching record in the DEPARTMENTS table. This means that if the ON clause matches 0 (zero) rows in the DEPARTMENTS table, the join will still return a row in the result set, but with NULL in each column from the DEPARTMENTS table. As a result, a LEFT OUTER JOIN returns all the values from the left table, plus matched values from the right table or NULL in case of no matching join. If the right table returns one row and the left table returns more than one matching row for it, the values in the right table will be repeated for each distinct row on the left table.

The LEFT OUTER JOIN in this example allows us to find an employee's department but still list the employees who have not been assigned to a department. This is contrary to the inner join shown earlier, where employees who have not been assigned a department are excluded from the result set.

The total number of rows in the result set is equal to the number of rows in the left table, the EMPLOYEES table in this example.

| Example 9 LEFT OUTER JOIN | Provide a list of employees and their department names. Include all employees, even if they have not been assigned to a department. Return the last_name and department_name. |
|---|---|
| SQL | SELECT e.last_name, d.department_name<br>    FROM employees e LEFT OUTER JOIN departments d<br>      ON e.department_code = d.department_code<br>    ORDER BY e.employee_id; |

**Results**

```
LAST_NAME                       DEPARTMENT_NAME
------------------------------  -------------------------
Alexander                       Training
James                           Major Appliances
Bernard                         Home Theatre
Carr                            Video Games
Horner                          Major Appliances
Best                            Small Appliances
Henry                           Major Appliances
Albert                          Video Games
Harper                          Home Theatre
Nisbet                          NULL
Richie                          Major Appliances
Johnson                         NULL
Lee                             Video Games
Johnson                         Major Appliances
Long                            Video Games
Maxwell                         Home Theatre
McDonald                        NULL
Evans                           Major Appliances
Gibbens                         NULL
Bernard                         Information Technology
Zimmerman                       Information Technology
Albert                          Information Technology
Peters                          Information Technology
```

FIGURE 8-14    Example of left outer join

In a left outer join, one row exists in the result set for each pair of rows satisfying the ON condition, just as with inner joins. In addition, the result set contains one row for each row in the first table that does not satisfy the ON condition, having no matching row in the second table. All columns from the second table in these unmatched rows are null. Note that a result set column for a left outer join may be null even when the column in the underlying table is not null-capable.

## RIGHT OUTER JOIN

Figure 8-15 shows the syntax for a **right outer join** or **right join**. The OUTER keyword is optional and is seldom used.

```
SELECT column1, column2, column3
  FROM table1
    RIGHT JOIN
      table2
    ON table1.column_name = table2.column_name;
```

**FIGURE 8-15**    **Syntax for right join**

In the example shown in Figure 8-16, the RIGHT OUTER JOIN returns all the rows from the DEPARTMENTS table even if there are no matches in the EMPLOYEES table.

The result set includes one row containing last_name and department_name when the two tables match on department_code. The result set also contains one row for each of the other rows in the DEPARTMENTS table that do not have a match on department_code in the EMPLOYEES table. The total number of rows in the result set is equal to the number of rows in the DEPARTMENTS table.

| Example 10<br><br>RIGHT OUTER JOIN | Use a RIGHT OUTER JOIN to provide a list of departments and their employees. Include all departments even if they have not been assigned any employees. Return the last_name and department_name. |
|---|---|
| SQL | ```SELECT e.last_name, d.department_name<br>   FROM employees E<br>      RIGHT OUTER JOIN departments d<br>      ON e.department_code = d.department_code<br>   ORDER BY d.department_name, e.last_name;``` |

**Results**

```
LAST_NAME                             DEPARTMENT_NAME
------------------------------------  -------------------------
NULL                                  Accounting
NULL                                  Administration
NULL                                  Cameras
Bernard                               Home Theatre
Harper                                Home Theatre
Maxwell                               Home Theatre
Albert                                Information Technology
Bernard                               Information Technology
Peters                                Information Technology
Zimmerman                             Information Technology
Evans                                 Major Appliances
Henry                                 Major Appliances
Horner                                Major Appliances
James                                 Major Appliances
Johnson                               Major Appliances
Richie                                Major Appliances
NULL                                  Marketing
NULL                                  Office Products
Best                                  Small Appliances
Alexander                             Training
Albert                                Video Games
Carr                                  Video Games
Lee                                   Video Games
Long                                  Video Games
```

FIGURE 8-16   Example of a right outer join

## FULL OUTER JOIN

Figure 8-17 shows the syntax for a full outer join. The OUTER keyword is optional.

```
SELECT column1, column2, column3
  FROM table1
    FULL OUTER JOIN table2
    ON table1.column_name = table2.column_name;
```

**FIGURE 8-17**     **Syntax for full outer join**

A **full outer join** or **full join** returns all rows from both tables, even if the rows do not match rows from the other table. Conceptually, the result set of a full outer join is the combined result sets from the left and right outer joins. When the rows in both tables match, a single row containing columns from both tables is returned in the result set. Where rows in the tables do not match, the result set contains NULL values for every column of the table that lacks a matching row.

Figure 8-18 shows the results of a full outer join on the EMPLOYEES and DEPARTMENTS tables.

## EXCEPTION JOIN

Exception joins include only the missing rows from an inner join, depending on the type of exception join:

- A LEFT EXCEPTION JOIN includes only the rows from the left table that were missing from the inner join.
- A RIGHT EXCEPTION JOIN includes only the rows from the right table that were missing from the inner join.

### LEFT EXCEPTION JOIN

A **left exception join** or **exception join** returns only the rows from the first table that do *not* have a match in the second table. A left exception join is the complement of an inner join in that it includes *only* unmatched rows. Figure 8-19 shows the syntax for a LEFT EXCEPTION JOIN. The keyword LEFT is the default and is optional.

| Example 11 FULL OUTER JOIN | Provide a list of employees and departments. Include all employees, even if they have not been assigned to a department. Also include all departments, even if they do not have any employees assigned to them. |
|---|---|
| SQL | ```SELECT e.last_name, d.department_name FROM employees e FULL OUTER JOIN departments d ON e.department_code = d.department_code ORDER BY e.employee_id;``` |

**Results**

```
LAST_NAME                      DEPARTMENT_NAME
-----------------------------  ---------------------------
Alexander                      Training
James                          Major Appliances
Bernard                        Home Theatre
Carr                           Video Games
Horner                         Major Appliances
Best                           Small Appliances
Henry                          Major Appliances
Albert                         Video Games
Harper                         Home Theatre
Nisbet                         NULL
Richie                         Major Appliances
Johnson                        NULL
Lee                            Video Games
Johnson                        Major Appliances
Long                           Video Games
Maxwell                        Home Theatre
McDonald                       NULL
Evans                          Major Appliances
Gibbens                        NULL
Bernard                        Information Technology
Zimmerman                      Information Technology
Albert                         Information Technology
Peters                         Information Technology
NULL                           Administration
NULL                           Accounting
NULL                           Marketing
NULL                           Cameras
NULL                           Office Products
```

FIGURE 8-18    Example of full outer join

```
SELECT column 1, column 2, column 3
  FROM table1
    LEFT EXCEPTION JOIN Table2
    ON table1.column_name = table2.column_name;
```

**FIGURE 8-19**   Syntax for left exception join

In the example in Figure 8-20, the LEFT EXCEPTION JOIN returns only the rows from the EMPLOYEES table that do not have a match in the DEPARTMENTS table. In other words, only those employees who are not assigned to any department are returned.

| Example 12 LEFT EXCEPTION JOIN | Provide a list of employees who have not been assigned to a department. Return the employee_id, last_name, and department_name. |
|---|---|
| SQL | SELECT e.employee_id, e.last_name, d.department_name<br>  FROM employees e<br>    LEFT EXCEPTION JOIN departments d<br>    ON e.department_code = d.department_code<br>  ORDER BY e.employee_id; |
| Results | |

```
EMPLOYEE_ID LAST_NAME                               DEPARTMENT_NAME
----------- -------------------------------------- ---------------
        119 Nisbet                                  NULL
        121 Johnson                                 NULL
        126 McDonald                                NULL
        131 Gibbens                                 NULL
```

**FIGURE 8-20**   Example of left exception join

## RIGHT EXCEPTION JOIN

A **right exception join** returns only the rows from the second table that do *not* have a match in the first table. The right exception join works just like a left exception join but with the tables reversed. Figure 8-21 shows the syntax for a RIGHT EXCEPTION JOIN.

```
SELECT column 1, column 2, column 3
  FROM table1
    RIGHT EXCEPTION JOIN Table2
    ON table1.column_name = table2.column_name;
```

FIGURE 8-21    Syntax for right exception join

In the example in Figure 8-22, the RIGHT EXCEPTION JOIN returns only the rows from the DEPARTMENTS table that do not have a match in the EMPLOYEES table.

| Example 13<br><br>RIGHT EXCEPTION JOIN | Provide a list of departments that do not contain employees. Return the employee_id, last_name, and department_name. |
|---|---|
| SQL | SELECT e.employee_id, e.last_name, d.department_name<br>  FROM employees e<br>    RIGHT EXCEPTION JOIN departments d<br>    ON e.department_code = d.department_code<br>  ORDER BY d.department_code; |
| **Results** | |

```
EMPLOYEE_ID LAST_NAME DEPARTMENT_NAME
----------- --------- -------------------------
       NULL NULL      Accounting
       NULL NULL      Administration
       NULL NULL      Cameras
       NULL NULL      Marketing
       NULL NULL      Office Products
```

FIGURE 8-22    Example of a right exception join

## CROSS JOIN

A **cross join** does not apply any join conditions to filter rows from the joined tables. As a result, the cross join, also known as a **Cartesian product**, returns a result set in which each row from the first table is combined with each row from the second table. The number of rows in the result set is the product of the number of rows in each table. If the tables are large, this join can take a very long time to run.

In many cases, a cross join is the result of an incorrect inner join that was intended to use the traditional WHERE method. For example, consider the inner join in Figure 8-23. In this example, the result set consists of matching rows between the EMPLOYEES and DEPARTMENTS tables.

| Example 14<br><br>INNER JOIN WHERE | Provide a list of employees and their assigned department. |
|---|---|
| SQL | SELECT e.employee_id, e.last_name, d.department_name<br>  FROM employees AS e, departments AS d<br>  WHERE e.department_code = d.department_code; |
| Results | |

```
EMPLOYEE_ID LAST_NAME                       DEPARTMENT_NAME
----------- ------------------------------- -------------------------
        110 Alexander                       Training
        135 Zimmerman                       Information Technology
        132 Bernard                         Information Technology
        136 Albert                          Information Technology
        139 Peters                          Information Technology
        111 James                           Major Appliances
        114 Horner                          Major Appliances
        120 Richie                          Major Appliances
        123 Johnson                         Major Appliances
        127 Evans                           Major Appliances
        116 Henry                           Major Appliances
        115 Best                            Small Appliances
        113 Carr                            Video Games
        124 Long                            Video Games
        117 Albert                          Video Games
        122 Lee                             Video Games
        112 Bernard                         Home Theatre
        125 Maxwell                         Home Theatre
        118 Harper                          Home Theatre
```

FIGURE 8-23    INNER JOIN using WHERE clause

Consider what happens in Figure 8-24 if the WHERE clause is mistakenly omitted. This error results in a cross join rather than an inner join, and the result set is the product of the number of rows in each table. For example, if the employee table contained 6,000 rows and the department table contained 20 rows, the result set of this cross join would be 120,000 rows (6000 * 20).

| Example 15 | **Provide a list of employees and their assigned department.** |
|---|---|
| SQL | SELECT employee_id, last_name, department_name<br>    FROM employees, departments; |
| Results | |

```
EMPLOYEE_ID LAST_NAME                        DEPARTMENT_NAME
----------- -------------------------------- -------------------------
        110 Alexander                        Administration
        110 Alexander                        Accounting
        110 Alexander                        Marketing
        110 Alexander                        Training
        110 Alexander                        Information Technology
        110 Alexander                        Cameras
        110 Alexander                        Major Appliances
        110 Alexander                        Small Appliances
        110 Alexander                        Office Products
        110 Alexander                        Video Games
        110 Alexander                        Home Theatre
        111 James                            Administration
        111 James                            Accounting
        111 James                            Marketing
        111 James                            Training
        111 James                            Information Technology
        111 James                            Cameras
        111 James                            Major Appliances
        111 James                            Small Appliances
        111 James                            Office Products
        111 James                            Video Games
        111 James                            Home Theatre
        112 Bernard                          Administration
        112 Bernard                          Accounting
        . . .   . . .                            . . .
```

FIGURE 8-24   Unintentional **CROSS JOIN** or an inner join with a missing **WHERE** clause

When the intention is to create an inner join between two tables using the traditional WHERE method and the WHERE clause is omitted, the result is a cross join. The preceding example illustrates a cross join, whether it is intentional or unintentional. The more appropriate method to create a cross join is shown in Figure 8-25.

| Example 16<br><br>CROSS JOIN | Return a CROSS JOIN of the EMPLOYEES and DEPARTMENTS tables. List the employee_id, last_name, and department_name columns. |
| --- | --- |
| SQL | `SELECT employee_id, last_name, department_name`<br>`    FROM employees`<br>`        CROSS JOIN departments;` |
| Results | |

```
EMPLOYEE_ID LAST_NAME                       DEPARTMENT_NAME
----------- ------------------------------- -------------------------
        110 Alexander                       Administration
        110 Alexander                       Accounting
        110 Alexander                       Marketing
        110 Alexander                       Training
        110 Alexander                       Information Technology
        110 Alexander                       Cameras
        110 Alexander                       Major Appliances
        110 Alexander                       Small Appliances
        110 Alexander                       Office Products
        110 Alexander                       Video Games
        110 Alexander                       Home Theatre
        111 James                           Administration
        111 James                           Accounting
        111 James                           Marketing
        111 James                           Training
        111 James                           Information Technology
        111 James                           Cameras
        111 James                           Major Appliances
        111 James                           Small Appliances
        111 James                           Office Products
        111 James                           Video Games
        111 James                           Home Theatre
        112 Bernard                         Administration
        112 Bernard                         Accounting
     . . .   . . .                            . . .
```

FIGURE 8-25   Example of CROSS JOIN

## SELF-JOIN

A **self-join** is a join in which a table is joined to itself. That is, a table assumes several roles in the FROM clause. To identify which table role is meant when specifying a column name in any of the other clauses, an alias name for any table listed more than once in a FROM clause must be used.

Let us consider an example where a list of employees and their assigned managers is requested. Recall that the EMPLOYEES table contains a row for each employee, and each row contains the manager number (ManagerNo) column indicating the manager to whom the employee reports. In Figure 8-26, the SELECT statement references the EMPLOYEES table to produce a list of employees and their manager's name.

| Example 17 SELF-JOIN | Provide a list of employees and their managers. List the employee_id, last_name (Emp), and last_name (Mgr) columns. |
|---|---|
| SQL | SELECT emp.employee_id, emp.last_name AS emp_last_name, mgr.last_name AS mgr_last_name<br>  From employees emp<br>    INNER JOIN<br>    employees mgr<br>      On emp.manager_id = mgr.employee_id<br>  ORDER BY emp.employee_id; |
| Results | |

```
EMPLOYEE_ID EMP_LAST_NAME                        MGR_LAST_NAME
----------- ------------------------------      -----------------------
        114 Horner                              James
        116 Henry                               James
        117 Albert                              Carr
        118 Harper                              Bernard
        119 Nisbet                              Alexander
        120 Richie                              James
        121 Johnson                             Alexander
        122 Lee                                 Carr
        123 Johnson                             Horner
        124 Long                                Carr
        125 Maxwell                             Bernard
        126 McDonald                            Alexander
        127 Evans                               Horner
```

FIGURE 8-26    Example of a self-join

In this example, the EMPLOYEES table is used in two roles: once to provide the set of employees (alias name Emp) and once to provide a lookup table to find the name for each ManagerNo value (alias name Mgr). Using a qualified column name such as emp.last_name makes it clear from which role of the EMPLOYEES table the column value is returned.

## SET OPERATORS

### THE UNION OPERATOR

The **UNION operator** is used to select related information from two tables, much like the JOIN command. While a JOIN combines columns from two or more tables, UNION combines rows from two or more result sets. In addition, with the UNION operator, the SELECT statement of both tables must have the same number of columns, and the corresponding columns need to be of the same data type. Basically, the join condition is determined by the columns identified on the SELECT statements. With UNION, only distinct values are selected. The syntax for the UNION operator is shown in Figure 8-27.

```
SQL statement 1
UNION
SQL statement 2
```

FIGURE 8-27  Syntax of UNION operator

An asterisk (*) or column list can be specified, as well as any of the other allowable subquery clauses for each of the subqueries specified in a UNION operation.

A JOIN operation combines data from two or more tables by combining column values from related rows into a single row in the result set. Another way to combine data is with the UNION operator. In the example in Figure 8-28, the UNION operator combines rows from the EMPLOYEES and EMPLOYEES_RETIRED tables. The SELECT statement for both tables must identify the same columns.

| Example 18 UNION | Combine all rows and columns from the EMPLOYEES and EMPLOYEES_RETIRED tables. Eliminate dublicates. |
|---|---|
| SQL | ```
SELECT employee_id, first_name, last_name
   FROM employees
UNION
  SELECT employee_id, first_name, last_name
    FROM employees_retired
ORDER BY employee_id;
``` |

**Results**

```
EMPLOYEE_ID FIRST_NAME           LAST_NAME
----------- -------------------- -----------------------------
        107 Lauren               Alexander
        108 Lisa                 James
        109 Dave                 Bernard
        110 Lauren               Alexander
        111 Lisa                 James
        112 Dave                 Bernard
        113 Steve                Carr
        114 Marg                 Horner
        115 Jim                  Best
        116 Robert               Henry
        117 Trish                Albert
        118 Janice               Harper
        119 Dave                 Nisbet
        120 Anne                 Richie
        120 Anne                 Tucker
        121 William              Johnson
        122 Jake                 Lee
        123 Linda                Johnson
        124 Scott                Long
        125 Terry                Maxwell
        126 Sue                  McDonald
        127 Sharron              Evans
        131 Barb                 Gibbens
        132 Dave                 Bernard
        135 Greg                 Zimmerman
        136 Trish                Albert
        139 Rick                 Peters
```

FIGURE 8-28    Example of UNION operator
```

This UNION statement produces a result set consisting of the employee_id, first_name, and last_name columns of all rows from the EMPLOYEES and EMPLOYEES_RETIRED table. Duplicate rows in the result set, or those with identical values in the select list, are eliminated.

Consider employees who have officially retired but have returned to work on contract. These employees will be in the EMPLOYEES table as active employees and also in the EMPLOYEES_RETIRED table as retired employees.

An examination of the data in the EMPLOYEES and EMPLOYEES_RETIRED tables (which are available on the companion website) reveals that employees 120 and 121 are in both tables. However, only employee 120 appears in the result set of the UNION operation. Employee 120 is selected from both tables because the last_name columns are different. Quite possibly she retired as Richie, got married, and returned to work on contract as Tucker.

Employee 121 is not selected twice because the employee_id, first_name, and last_name column values from the EMPLOYEES and EMPLOYEES_RETIRED tables are an exact match. Duplicate rows are omitted with the UNION operator.

## THE UNION ALL OPERATOR

The UNION ALL operator is equal to the UNION operator, except that UNION ALL selects all rows. In the preceding example, if duplicate rows were to be included, the UNION ALL operation in Figure 8-29 would be used. With the UNION operator, duplicate rows are omitted from the result set. When the UNION ALL operation is run, the two retired employees are listed twice in the result set because duplicates are not omitted in the UNION ALL operation.

| Example 19 **UNION ALL** | Combine all rows and columns from the EMPLOYEES and EMPLOYEES_RETIRED tables into a result set. Include duplicate values. |
|---|---|
| SQL | ``` SELECT employee_id, first_name, last_name FROM employees UNION ALL SELECT employee_id, first_name, last_name FROM employees_retired ORDER BY employee_id; ``` |

**Results**

```
EMPLOYEEID FIRSTNAME            LASTNAME
---------- -------------------- ----------------------------
       107 Lauren               Alexander
       108 Lisa                 James
       109 Dave                 Bernard
       110 Lauren               Alexander
       111 Lisa                 James
       112 Dave                 Bernard
       113 Steve                Carr
       114 Marg                 Horner
       115 Jim                  Best
       116 Robert               Henry
       117 Trish                Albert
       118 Janice               Harper
       119 Dave                 Nisbet
       120 Anne                 Richie
       120 Anne                 Tucker
       121 William              Johnson
       121 William              Johnson
       122 Jake                 Lee
       123 Linda                Johnson
       124 Scott                Long
       125 Terry                Maxwell
       126 Sue                  McDonald
       127 Sharron              Evans
       ...                      ...
```

FIGURE 8-29    Example of UNION ALL operator

In this example, two employees are listed twice. Similar to Example 18 in Figure 8-28, employee 120 is listed twice because of the different last name. In Example 19, employee 121 is also listed twice. Because both tables contain duplicate data for the columns listed on the SELECT statements, this employee was not listed in Example 18 in Figure 8-28. With the UNION ALL, however, the duplicate data is ignored, and all rows are returned in the result set.

## USING A SELECT LIST WITH A UNION OPERATOR

A WHERE clause can be specified with the UNION operator to filter the selection. For example, in Figure 8-30 only employees who are assigned to department MA are selected. In addition, only retired employees who have retired after 2011-05-01 are selected. The result set consists of the distinct values in the selected rows between the two tables.

| Example 20 | Return the employee_id , first_name, and last_name columns from a UNION of the EMPLOYEES and EMPLOYEES_RETIRED tables. |
|---|---|
| SQL | ```
SELECT employee_id, first_name, last_name
    FROM employees
    WHERE department_code = 'MA'
UNION
    SELECT employee_id, first_name, last_name
    FROM employees_retired
    WHERE retire_date > '2011-05-01'
ORDER BY employee_id;
``` |

**Results**

```
EMPLOYEE_ID FIRST_NAME              LAST_NAME
----------- --------------------    ------------------------------
        111 Lisa                    James
        114 Marg                    Horner
        116 Robert                  Henry
        120 Anne                    Richie
        121 William                 Johnson
        123 Linda                   Johnson
        127 Sharron                 Evans
```

FIGURE 8-30    Example of a select list with a UNION operator
```

When a UNION operator is used to combine rows from two or more result sets, the statement is called a **fullselect**. To specify the union of two SELECT statements, the queries' result sets must be **union-compatible**, which means they must have the same number of columns, and each pair of corresponding columns, by position in the respective select lists, must have compatible column definitions.

The other attributes of the fullselect's result set columns are determined as follows:

- If the two corresponding columns in the result sets have identical unqualified names, the fullselect's result set column has the same name; otherwise, the fullselect column is unnamed.
- If neither of the corresponding columns in the result sets allows nulls, the fullselect's result set column does not allow nulls; otherwise, the fullselect column allows nulls.

When a column in a fullselect has no name, or even if it does have a name, a name can be assigned by specifying the keyword AS followed by the name in the first select list. In Figure 8-31, the column Discount * 100 is assigned the alias Discount Pct in the first select list. This example specifies Discount Pct as the name of the calculated column.

## JOINING SEVERAL TABLES

A final example, showing how to join several tables, is shown in Figure 8-32.

| Example 21 | Return the customer_name and Discount Pct (Discount * 100) columns from a UNION between the CUSTOMERS and ARCHIVED_CUSTOMERS tables. |
|---|---|
| SQL | ```
    SELECT customer_name,
           DECIMAL( ROUND(discount * 100, 2), 3,2)
              AS "Discount Pct"
      FROM customers
UNION
    SELECT customer_name,
           DECIMAL( ROUND(discount * 100, 2), 3,2)
      FROM archived_customers;
``` |

**Results**

```
CUSTOMER_NAME                          Discount Pct
------------------------------ ------------
Smith Mfg.                                     5.00
Bolt Co.                                       2.00
Ajax Steel Inc.                                NULL
Bluewater Inc.                                 1.50
Bell Bldg.                                     1.00
London Inc.                                    5.00
Alpine Inc.                                    1.00
Steelhead Tackle Co.                           0.00
Nautilus Mfg.                                  5.00
Bluewater Mfg.                                 NULL
Seaworthy                                      1.00
John Steeling Products                         1.00
Wood Bros.                                     1.00
Mainstreet Mfg.                                1.00
Riverview Co.                                  1.50
```

FIGURE 8-31    Assigning an alias name to a calculated column in an UNION operation
```

| Example 22 | Provide a list of customers and their orders. List the customer_name, order_date, order_id, and product_description. |
|---|---|
| SQL | ```
SELECT c.customer_name, o.order_date, o.order_id,
       p.product_description
  FROM customers AS c
       INNER JOIN
       orders AS o
         ON c.customer_id = o.customer_id
       INNER JOIN
       order_lines AS ol
         ON o.order_id = ol.order_id
       INNER JOIN
       products AS p
         ON ol.product_id = p.product_id
 ORDER BY customer_name, order_date;
``` |

**Results**

```
CUSTOMER_NAME                        ORDER_DATE ORDER_ID PRODUCT_DESCRIPTION
------------------------------------ ---------- -------- ---------------------------------
Best Digital Products                02/05/10     1004   Portable Canister Cleaner
Best Digital Products                02/05/10     1004   Dual Fuel Range
Best Digital Products                02/05/10     1004   Freestanding Gas Range
Best Digital Products                02/05/10     1004   High Efficiency Front Load Washer
Best Digital Products                02/05/10     1004   High Efficiency Top Load Washer
Best Digital Products                02/17/10     1003   Dual Fuel Range
Best Digital Products                02/17/10     1003   Top Freezer Refrigerator
Best Digital Products                02/17/10     1003   Wet/Dry Hand Vacuum
Best Digital Products                02/17/10     1003   Stackable Washer and Dryer Combo
Best Digital Products                02/17/10     1003   High Efficiency Front Load Washer
Big Box Digital                      02/05/10     1000   Built-In Dishwasher
Big Box Digital                      02/05/10     1000   High Efficiency Top Load Washer
Everything Electronics               05/20/10     1005   Brushed Stainless Steel Blender
Everything Electronics               05/20/10     1005   Portable Air Conditioner
Everything Electronics               05/20/10     1005   Portable Canister Cleaner
Everything Electronics               05/20/10     1005   Extra-large Deep Fryer
Everything Electronics               05/20/10     1005   Full Digital Iron
Technology R Us                      02/17/10     1001   BrewStation 6 Cup Coffeemaker
Technology R Us                      02/17/10     1001   Extra-large Deep Fryer
Technology R Us                      02/17/10     1001   Top Freezer Refrigerator
Technology R Us                      02/17/10     1001   Wet/Dry Hand Vacuum
Worldwide Digital Inc.               02/17/10     1002   Brushed Stainless Steel Blender
Worldwide Digital Inc.               02/17/10     1002   Portable Air Conditioner
Worldwide Digital Inc.               02/17/10     1002   Full Digital Iron
Worldwide Digital Inc.               02/17/10     1002   Freestanding Gas Range
Worldwide Digital Inc.               02/17/10     1002   High Efficiency Top Load Washer
```

**FIGURE 8-32    Example of joining several tables**
```

## END-OF-CHAPTER

### CHAPTER SUMMARY

1. An SQL join combines related information from two or more tables or views. The join's ON condition specifies a basic condition that defines how rows are matched.

2. SQL provides the following join types:

| Join type | Description |
|---|---|
| Inner join | Returns only the rows from each table for which matching values exist in the join column. Any rows that do not have a match between the tables do not appear in the result set. |
| Left outer join (left join) | Returns all rows from the first table (specified to the left of the JOIN keyword), even if no matching rows exist in the second table. |
| Right outer join (right join) | Returns all rows from the second table (right of the JOIN keyword), even if no matching rows exist in the first table. |
| Full outer join (full join) | Returns all rows from both tables, even if the rows do not match rows from the other table. |
| Left exception join | Returns only the rows from the first table that do not have a match in the second table. |
| Right exception join | Returns only the rows from the second table that do not have a match in the first table. |
| Cross join | Returns each row from the first table paired with each row of the second table. A CROSS JOIN is also known as a Cartesian product. |
| Self-join | Joins a table to itself. |

3. For an inner join, unmatched rows from the first table are not included in the result set. A left outer join produces at least one row for each row in the first table specified. For rows from that first table that have no matching row in the second table, result set columns from the second table are set null.

### KEY TERMS

| | |
|---|---|
| Cartesian product | left join |
| cross join | left outer join |
| exception join | outer join |
| full join | right exception join |
| full outer join | right join |
| fullselect | right outer join |
| inner join | self-join |
| join | UNION operator |
| left exception join | union-compatible |

# CHAPTER 9

## SUBQUERIES

## CHAPTER OBJECTIVES

Upon completion of this chapter, you should be able to

- Use a subquery within a query
- Use the EXISTS operator
- Use the ALL and ANY operators

## INTRODUCTION TO SUBQUERIES

There are many times when a query requires more than one step to obtain the required results. That is, two queries need to be run where the second query depends on the result of the first query.

To resolve the problem of having to run two queries to produce the required results, a subquery is used. A **subquery** is a query that is placed inside another query—that is, a SELECT statement that is embedded within another SELECT statement.

A request requiring a subquery is a two-part statement that contains an inner query and an outer query. The query that is placed inside another query is called the inner query and is run first. The inner query returns a result set of value(s), which the outer query uses in its search condition.

There are two types of subqueries:

- Single-row subquery, which returns a single row to the outer query
- Multiple-row subquery, which returns multiple rows to the outer query

## SINGLE-ROW OR SINGLE-VALUE SUBQUERY

A **single-row** or **single-value subquery** is a nested inner subquery that uses the single-row operators >, =, >=, <, <=, and <> and returns only one row from the inner query. It is used when the result set of the outer query is determined on a single value from the inner query.

For example, what if we want a list of employees from the EMPLOYEES table for whom the employee salary is greater than the average salary for all employees? This would require two queries:

1. Determine the average salary for all employees.
2. Determine which employees have an above-average salary.

The first query, shown in Example 1, Figure 9-1, determines the average salary for all employees. As a result of this query, the average salary is determined to be 35423.91 (rounded to two decimals).

---

**Example 1:**

**Determine the average salary for all employees. Round to two decimals.**

```
SELECT DECIMAL( ROUND(AVG( salary ), 2), 7,2) AS "Average Salary"
  FROM employees;
```

**Results:**

```
Average Salary
--------------
      35423.91
```

FIGURE 9-1    Determine the average salary for all employees

Now that the average salary for all employees is known, that average can be used in another query to obtain a list of employees with an above-average salary.

The second query, shown in Example 2, Figure 9-2, produces a list of employees that have an above-average salary.

Every time the second request is run, the first request must be run first because the employee salaries in the EMPLOYEES table may have changed, which changes the average salary. Whenever two or more steps are required to obtain the desired results, a subquery can be used.

The query in Example 1 used to determine the average salary is considered the inner query because it must be run first. The query in Example 2 is the outer query because it uses the result from the inner query in Example 1 to return a list of employees with above-average salaries.

**Example 2:**

Return all employees from the EMPLOYEES table who have a salary greater than 35423.91 (the average salary for all employees determined in Example 1).

```
SELECT employee_id, last_name, salary
  FROM employees
  WHERE salary > 35423.91;
```

**Results:**

```
EMPLOYEE_ID LAST_NAME                       SALARY
----------- ------------------------------ --------
        110 Alexander                       45000.00
        111 James                           65000.00
        112 Bernard                         60000.00
        113 Carr                            55000.00
        114 Horner                          45000.00
        126 McDonald                        36000.00
        119 Nisbet                          39000.00
        120 Richie                          40000.00
        122 Lee                             45000.00
        116 Henry                           37000.00
```

FIGURE 9-2     List employees with an above-average salary

A subquery begins with the SELECT keyword followed by a list of columns or expressions, a FROM clause, and optional WHERE, GROUP BY, and HAVING clauses. A subquery does not allow an ORDER BY clause, nor does it allow a UNION operator.

The complete subquery request is shown in Example 3, Figure 9-3. The inner query defines a result set with a single row and one column, which contains the average salary for all employees. The search condition in the outer SELECT statement compares the salary column from each row of the EMPLOYEES table with the average salary and includes in the result set only those EMPLOYEES rows with a salary greater than the average.

**Example 3:**

List all employees who have a **salary** greater than the average salary of all employees.

```
SELECT employee_id, last_name, salary
 FROM employees
 WHERE salary > ( SELECT AVG( salary )
                  FROM employees );
```

**Results:**

```
EMPLOYEE_ID LAST_NAME                           SALARY
----------- ----------------------------------- --------
        110 Alexander                           45000.00
        111 James                               65000.00
        112 Bernard                             60000.00
        113 Carr                                55000.00
        114 Horner                              45000.00
        126 McDonald                            36000.00
        119 Nisbet                              39000.00
        120 Richie                              40000.00
        122 Lee                                 45000.00
        116 Henry                               37000.00
```

FIGURE 9-3    Subquery to list all employees who have an above-average salary

The outer query for Example 3 is shown in Figure 9-4.

```
SELECT employee_id, last_name, salary
 FROM employees
 WHERE salary >
```

FIGURE 9-4    Outer query

The inner query for Example 3 is shown in Figure 9-5.

```
( SELECT AVG( salary )
    FROM employees );
```

FIGURE 9-5    Inner query

## MULTIPLE-ROW SUBQUERIES

A **multiple-row subquery** is a subquery that uses the multiple-row operators IN, ANY, and ALL and returns more than one row in the result set to the outer query.

### THE IN OPERATOR

When the **IN operator** is used in a multiple-row subquery, the inner query returns multiple rows in the result set. The outer query then uses this list to determine whether the current row being processed is found in the list generated by the inner query. Let us consider an example where we wish to create a list of employees who have a salary equal to the highest salary of any department. For this request, a list containing the highest salary for each department is generated by an inner query. Next, the outer query uses the list to determine whether each employee's salary is equal to any of the salaries in the list.

The inner query is shown in Example 4, Figure 9-6. This query returns a list containing the highest salary for each department. Because the department_code column can be null for an employee not assigned a department, the IS NOT NULL clause is specified to prevent the highest salary being returned for those employees with a null value in the department_code column.

---

Example 4:

List the highest salary for each **department_code** in the **EMPLOYEES** table.

```
SELECT MAX(salary) AS "Max Salary by Department"
  FROM employees
  WHERE department_code IS NOT NULL
  GROUP BY department_code;
```

Results:

```
Max Salary by Department
-----------------------
             60000.00
             24000.00
             55000.00
             31500.00
             45000.00
             65000.00
```

---

FIGURE 9-6    Inner query to return the highest salary for each department

Once the inner query is run and a list of the highest salary for each department is returned, the multiple-row subquery in Example 5, Figure 9-7, uses the list to determine which employees have a salary that is equal to any of the salaries in the list. Notice that although Johnson works in the major appliance (MA) department, the value in the salary column for this employee matches the highest salary in the SA department. Since this salary matches one of the salaries returned from the inner query, the values in the Johnson row are retuned in the result set for the outer query.

---

**Example 5:**

List those employees in the **EMPLOYEES** table who have a salary equal to the highest salaries from any department.

```
SELECT last_name, salary, department_code
  FROM employees
  WHERE salary IN ( SELECT MAX(salary)
                FROM employees
                WHERE department_code IS NOT NULL
                GROUP BY department_code)
  ORDER BY department_code;
```

**Results:**

```
LAST_NAME                        SALARY   DEPARTMENT_CODE
-------------------------------  -------- ---------------
Bernard                          60000.00 HT
Zimmerman                        31500.00 IT
Bernard                          24000.00 IT
James                            65000.00 MA
Horner                           45000.00 MA
Johnson                          24000.00 MA
Best                             24000.00 SA
Alexander                        45000.00 TR
Carr                             55000.00 VG
Lee                              45000.00 VG
```

FIGURE 9-7     Example of multiple-row subquery with the IN operator

## ALL AND ANY OPERATORS

The **ALL and ANY operators** can be used with subqueries to produce a single column of numbers. If the subquery is preceded by the ALL operator, the resulting condition is true if it satisfies all values produced by the subquery. If the subquery is preceded by the ANY operator, the resulting condition is true if it satisfies any value produced by the subquery.

### ALL OPERATOR

The example in Figure 9-8 selects CUSTOMERS rows that have a discount greater than all the Albany customers.

---

**Example 6:**

**List all customers that have a discount greather than ALL (highest discount) of the Albany customers.**

```
SELECT   customer_id, customer_name, ship_city, discount
  FROM   customers
  WHERE discount >ALL ( SELECT  discount
                          FROM  customers
                         WHERE ship_city = 'Albany'
                           AND discount IS NOT NULL );
```

**Results:**

| CUSTOMER_ID | CUSTOMER_NAME | SHIP_CITY | DISCOUNT |
|---|---|---|---|
| 133568 | Smith Mfg. | Chicago | 0.050 |
| 246900 | Bolt Co. | Toronto | 0.020 |
| 499320 | Bluewater Inc. | Portland | 0.015 |
| 518980 | London Inc. | Boston | 0.050 |
| 687309 | Nautilus Mfg. | San Diego | 0.050 |

---

FIGURE 9-8    Using the ALL operator with a subquery

The inner query for this example is shown in Example 7, Figure 9-9. The inner query returns a list of discounts (not null) for all customers located in Albany. This list is used in the search operation of the outer query in Example 6, Figure 9-8, to return a result set containing all customers that have a discount greater than ALL of the Albany customers. Being higher than ALL values on the inner query list is the same as being higher than the highest value in the list, which is .010 in this example.

---

**Example 7:**

**List all discounts for customers in Albany.**

```
SELECT  discount
  FROM  customers
  WHERE ship_city = 'Albany'
    AND discount IS NOT NULL;
```

**Results:**

```
DISCOUNT
--------
   0.000
   0.010
```

---

**FIGURE 9-9**    **Inner query to produce a list of discounts for Albany customers**

This example's ALL condition is true if the subquery result set is empty or if the current customer's discount is greater than all the values in the subquery result set. The comparison test is applied to each value in the subquery result set.

In general, when the ALL operator is used, the condition is

- True if the subquery result set is empty or the comparison test is true for all values in the result set
- False if the comparison test is false for at least one value in the result set
- Unknown if the comparison test does not evaluate to false for at least one value in the result set and the comparison test is unknown for at least one value in the result set

### ANY OPERATOR

A similar query using the ANY operator is shown in Example 8, Figure 9-10. In this example, the outer query returns those customers that have a discount higher than ANY of the Albany customers. This is the same as requesting all customers that have a discount higher than the lowest discount of the Albany customers.

A condition with the ANY operator is

- True if the comparison test is true for at least one value in the result set
- False if the subquery result set is empty or the comparison test is false for all values in the result set

**Example 8:**

List all customers that have a **discount** higher than **ANY** (lowest discount) of any Albany customer.

```
SELECT  customer_id, customer_name, ship_city, discount
  FROM  customers
 WHERE discount > ANY ( SELECT discount
                          FROM  customers
                         WHERE ship_city = 'Albany'
                           AND discount IS NOT NULL );
```

**Results:**

```
CUSTOMER_ID CUSTOMER_NAME             SHIP_CITY               DISCOUNT
----------- ------------------------  ----------------------  --------
     133568 Smith Mfg.                Chicago                    0.050
     246900 Bolt Co.                  Toronto                    0.020
     499320 Bluewater Inc.            Portland                   0.015
     499921 Bell Bldg.                Detroit                    0.010
     518980 London Inc.               Boston                     0.050
     663456 Alpine Inc.               Boston                     0.010
     687309 Nautilus Mfg.             San Diego                  0.050
     888402 Seaworthy                 Albany                     0.010
     890003 John Steeling Products    Houston                    0.010
     905011 Wood Bros.                Dallas                     0.010
```

FIGURE 9-10    Example of using the **ANY** operator with a subquery

- Unknown if the comparison test does not evaluate to true for at least one value in the result set and the comparison test is unknown for at least one value in the result set

When using the **ALL** and **ANY** operators, be careful not to confuse informal ways of expressing a condition in English with the specific meanings of the **ALL** and **ANY** operators. For example, a user might ask for a list of customers who have a higher discount than any of the Albany customers. If the **SELECT** statement in Figure 9-10 is used, the retrieved list will include all customers who have a discount higher than the lowest discount of any Albany customer. This list obviously might include some customers in Albany, specifically those who have a **discount** that is not the lowest among Albany customers. Using the **ALL** operator, as in the preceding example, retrieves customers who have a **discount** greater than the highest **discount** of any Albany customer, which, of course, excludes all Albany customers.

## CORRELATED SUBQUERIES

In the previous subqueries, SQL evaluated the subquery once, substituted the result of the subquery in the search condition, and then evaluated the outer query based on the value of the search condition. These types of subqueries are called uncorrelated subqueries.

A subquery can be used where SQL may need to reevaluate the subquery as it examines each new row (WHERE clause) or group of rows (HAVING clause) in the outer query. This type of subquery is called a correlated subquery.

A **correlated subquery** is a SELECT statement nested inside another SQL statement, which contains a reference to one or more columns in the outer query. Figure 9-11 provides a comparison between uncorrelated and correlated subqueries.

| Uncorrelated subquery | Correlated subquery |
|---|---|
| Not dependent on the outer query | Dependent on the outer query |
| Can be run independently of the outer query | Cannot be run independently of the outer query |
| Will return a result set if run independently | Will not return a result set if run independently |

**FIGURE 9-11    Comparison between uncorrelated and correlated subquery**

A correlated subquery will be executed several times while the outer query statement that contains it is processed. The correlated subquery will be run once for each candidate row selected by the outer query. The outer query columns, referenced in the correlated subquery, are replaced with values from the candidate row before each execution. The results of the execution of the correlated subquery will determine whether the row of the outer query is returned in the final result set.

The effect of correlated subqueries can also be obtained using OUTER JOINs.

### USING THE WHERE CLAUSE WITH A CORRELATED SUBQUERY

Example 9, Figure 9-12, provides an example of a typical correlated subquery. In this example, a list of employees (employee_id, last_name, department_code, and salary) having a higher salary than the average salary of each employee's department is produced.

The inner query is executed for every employee row in the EMPLOYEES table as the department can change for every row.

**Example 9:**

**List all employees in the EMPLOYEES table whose salary is greather than the average salary for their department.**

```
SELECT employee_id, last_name, department_code, salary
 FROM employees AS emp
 WHERE salary > ( SELECT AVG( salary )
                  FROM employees
                  WHERE department_code = emp.department_code);
```

**Results:**

```
EMPLOYEE_ID LAST_NAME                          DEPARTMENT_CODE SALARY
----------- -------------------------------- --------------- --------
        111 James                             MA               65000.00
        112 Bernard                           HT               60000.00
        113 Carr                              VG               55000.00
        114 Horner                            MA               45000.00
        122 Lee                               VG               45000.00
        135 Zimmerman                         IT               31500.00
        139 Peters                            IT               28750.00
```

FIGURE 9-12    Example of using the WHERE clause with a subquery

The subquery used in the search condition is known as a correlated subquery because the inner subquery (the subquery following WHERE) refers to emp.department_code, which is a reference to a column of a table specified in the outer query statement. Thus, the evaluation of the inner subquery is correlated to the current row of the outer query.

Subqueries can also be used in an UPDATE, DELETE, or INSERT statement search condition. The UPDATE statement in Figure 9-13 uses a subquery to select rows to be updated. The statement in this example increases to 10 percent the discount of customers who currently receive less than a 10 percent discount and who have placed orders with a grand-total amount greater than 1000.00.

Note that if a subquery in an UPDATE, DELETE, or INSERT statement's search condition refers to the same table that is being updated, the subquery is evaluated completely before any rows are updated.

**Example 10:**

**Update customers to a 10 percent dicount if their current discount is less than 10 percent and they have placed orders with a grand total greater than 1000.00.**

```
UPDATE customers
  SET discount = .10
  WHERE ( discount < .10 OR discount IS NULL )
    AND 1000.00 < ( SELECT SUM( order_total )
                    FROM orders
                    WHERE orders.customer_id =
                          customers.customer_id );
```

**Results:**

Succeeded

FIGURE 9-13    Subquery to select rows to be updated

## EXISTS OPERATOR

The EXISTS operator *requires* a subquery. The syntax for the EXISTS operator is shown in Figure 9-14.

```
SELECT columns
  FROM tables
  WHERE EXISTS ( subquery );
```

FIGURE 9-14    Syntax for EXISTS operator

The condition specified with the **EXISTS operator** is true if the subquery result set contains one or more rows; otherwise, the condition is false. If the EXISTS condition does not return at least one row, the outer query is not executed, and the entire SQL statement returns nothing. The value of an EXISTS condition is never unknown; that is, it is never null.

The subquery SELECT list can specify any number of columns, but the column values are ignored, so generally an asterisk (*) is specified after the SELECT keyword. The EXISTS operator can be used in any valid SQL statement, such as SELECT, INSERT, UPDATE, or DELETE. In Figure 9-15, the SELECT statement returns all customer names from the CUSTOMERS table where there is at least one row in the ORDERS table with the same customer_id.

| Example 11: |
| --- |

List all customer names in the **CUSTOMERS** table where there is at least one row in the **ORDERS** table with the same **customer_id**.

```
SELECT customer_name AS "Customers with sales"
  FROM customers c
  WHERE EXISTS ( SELECT *
                   FROM orders o
                   WHERE c.customer_id = o.customer_id );
```

**Results:**

```
Customers with sales
-----------------------------
Smith Mfg.
Bolt Co.
Bluewater Inc.
Seaworthy
John Steeling Products
Wood Bros.
```

**FIGURE 9-15** Example of using the EXISTS operator

## NOT EXISTS OPERATOR

The NOT keyword can be specified before the EXISTS operator; in that case, the value of the negated condition will be true only if the subquery result set is empty. In Figure 9-16, the SELECT statement returns all rows from the CUSTOMERS table where no rows exist in the ORDERS table for the given customer_id.

The subquery used in the search condition is known as a correlated subquery because the inner subquery (the subquery following NOT EXISTS) refers to c.customer_id, which is a reference to a column of a table specified in the outer SELECT statement. Thus, the evaluation of the inner subquery is correlated to the current row of the outer SELECT.

A close look at this example can help clarify both correlated subqueries and the usefulness of the EXISTS operator. The example's EXISTS operator answers the question "Do any sales exist for this customer?" If the answer is No, the search condition, NOT EXISTS ..., is true, and the customer is selected. This EXISTS operator tests whether the customer has any sales by using a subquery that defines a result set containing all the CUSTOMERS rows for the customer. If this set of rows is not empty, the EXISTS condition is true; the customer has one or more sales.

---

**Example 12:**

---

**List all customers in the CUSTOMERS table where no rows exists in the ORDERS table.**

```
SELECT  c.customer_id, c.customer_name
  FROM  customers AS c
  WHERE NOT EXISTS ( SELECT *
                       FROM orders o
                       WHERE c.customer_id = o.customer_id );
```

**Results:**

```
CUSTOMER_ID CUSTOMER_NAME
----------- ------------------------------
     275978 Ajax Steel Inc.
     499921 Bell Bldg.
     518980 London Inc.
     663456 Alpine Inc.
     681065 Steelhead Tackle Co.
     687309 Nautilus Mfg.
     781010 Bluewater Mfg.
```

**FIGURE 9-16**    **Example of correlated subquery using a NOT EXISTS operator**

The result set with the customer's sales is defined by the subquery in Figure 9-17.

```
( SELECT *
    FROM orders o
    WHERE c.customer_id = o.customer_id )
```

**FIGURE 9-17**    **Subquery for customer sales**

Because we are interested only in whether or not the result set contains any rows, this subquery uses an asterisk (*) to specify an implicit list of columns rather than listing explicit column names. The search condition used for this subquery is quite simple: A CUSTOMERS row is included in the subquery result set if its o.customer_id column contains the same c.customer_id as the current CUSTOMER row being tested in the outer SELECT statement.

## COMBINING SUBQUERIES AND JOINS

JOINs can occur in subqueries as well as in an outer query. Consider Figure 9-18, where the SQL statement retrieves the desired list of customers.

**Example 13:**

**Retrieve the name and city for each customer who has placed any order with a total amount greater than the average total amount of orders placed by customers in the same city.**

```
SELECT  curCust.customer_name,
        curCust.ship_city
  FROM  customers curCust
  WHERE EXISTS
      ( SELECT  *
          FROM orders bigSale
          WHERE bigSale.customer_id = curCust.customer_id
            AND bigSale.order_total >
              ( SELECT AVG( avgSale.order_total )
                  FROM customers avgCust
                    JOIN
                    orders avgSale
                    ON avgCust.customer_id = avgSale.customer_id
                  WHERE avgCust.ship_city = curCust.ship_city ) );
```

**Results:**

```
CUSTOMER_NAME                   SHIP_CITY
------------------------------  ------------------------------
Bolt Co.                        Toronto
Bluewater Inc.                  Portland
```

FIGURE 9-18   Example of combining a subquery and join

A detailed look at how this statement is structured illustrates many of SQL's advanced retrieval capabilities.

The first FROM clause specifies that the result set comes from the CUSTOMERS table and that the alias name curCust is used elsewhere in the statement to qualify columns that come from this particular role of the CUSTOMERS table.

The first WHERE clause uses the EXISTS operator to see whether the customer has any orders that meet the specified criteria. The set of orders to be tested is specified by the first subquery, beginning with the second SELECT keyword. Remember, when a subquery is used, you can think of the subquery being executed for every row defined by the FROM clause in the outer SELECT statement. Thus, in this example, consider that for every row in CUSTOMERS, the subquery is executed and then tested to see whether its result contains any rows.

The first subquery retrieves rows from the ORDERS table. Because the only test made on the result of this subquery is whether it contains any rows, the * is specified for the column list: SELECT *. The FROM clause specifies that the rows from this use of ORDERS are qualified by the alias name bigSale. The only rows retrieved in this subquery are those that are for the current customer and that have an order total amount greater than the average total amount of orders placed by customers in the same city as the current customer.

The WHERE clause specifies the conjunction of two conditions that must be true for an ORDERS row to be in the subquery's result. The first condition is that an ORDERS row must have the same customer number as the current CUSTOMERS row's customer number.

The second condition is a basic condition that uses another subquery. The order total for each sale is compared with the average order total of a set of sales. In this example, the greater than (>) test is used, and because both values in a basic condition must be scalar, the set the subquery returns in this example must include no more than one value—that is, one row with one column. By specifying only the AVG column function in the subquery's list of result columns, the subquery retrieves a single row with a single column that has the desired average value. This value is then compared with the column value bigSale.order_total.

The second subquery, specified in the third SELECT statement, defines the set of rows from which the average is calculated. The rows come from the inner join of the CUSTOMERS and ORDERS tables: avgCust.customer_id = avgSale.customer_id. But only those rows that have customers from the same city as the current customer are included in the average. To evaluate this condition, the city of each row in the innermost subquery, avgCust.ship_city, is compared with the city for the current customer in the main query, curCust.ship_city.

## USING A NESTED VIEW

A **nested view** is a subquery specified in the FROM clause of an outer SELECT statement. Figure 9-19 shows an example. This nested view produces a result set that contains the ship_city, min_discount, and max_discount for each city in the CUSTOMERS table. From this result set, the outer SELECT includes only those rows where the minimum discount is less than .02 and the maximum discount is greater than .03.

**Example 14:**

Provide a nested view that returns **ship_city, min_discount,** and **max_discount** for each city in the CUSTOMERS table. Use the result set from the view to list only those cities where the minimum discount is less than .02 and the maximum discount is greater than .03.

```
SELECT ship_city,
       min_discount,
       max_discount
  FROM ( SELECT      ship_city,
                     MIN( discount ) AS min_discount,
                     MAX( discount ) AS max_discount
         FROM        customers
         GROUP BY ship_city )
       AS shipCityMinMaxDisc
 WHERE min_discount < .02
   AND max_discount > .03;
```

**Results:**

```
SHIP_CITY                        MIN_DISCOUNT MAX_DISCOUNT
-------------------------------- ------------ ------------
Boston                                  0.010        0.050
```

FIGURE 9-19    Example of a query using a nested view

The nested view is shown in Figure 9-20.

```
SELECT ship_city,
       MIN( discount ) AS min_discount,
       MAX( discount ) AS max_discount
  FROM      customers
 GROUP BY ship_city
```

FIGURE 9-20    Nested view from Example 14

If run separately, this nested view returns the result set in Figure 9-21.

```
SHIP_CITY                              MIN_DISCOUNT MAX_DISCOUNT
------------------------------------   ------------ ------------
Toronto                                     0.100        0.100
Chicago                                     0.050        0.050
Houston                                     0.010        0.010
Boston                                      0.010        0.050
Detroit                                     0.010        0.010
Albany                                      0.000        0.010
Dallas                                      0.010        0.010
Portland                                    0.015        0.015
San Diego                                   0.050        0.050
```

**FIGURE 9-21   Result set of the nested view**

The result set from the nested view returns the minimum discount and maximum discount for each city. The outer SELECT statement uses this result set from the view to determine which cities have a minimum discount that is less that .02 and a maximum discount greater than .03.

A nested view is a temporary view where no actual view is created. A temporary table may be created internally, if necessary. To use a nested view, the subquery is enclosed in parentheses followed by the AS keyword and an alias name for the result set. As the example shows, names can be specified for columns in the result set, such as min_discount.

The same query results can be produced without a nested view by using a HAVING clause instead of a WHERE clause, as shown in Figure 9-22.

But there are some cases when a nested view is essential. In Figure 9-23, the query produces a result set with rows consisting of maximum discounts found in each city with at least one customer and the number of cities having those maximums.

Example 15:

Rewrite Example 14 using a **HAVING** clause.

```
SELECT ship_city,
       MIN( discount ) AS min_discount,
       MAX( discount)  AS max_discount
  FROM customers
  GROUP BY ship_city
  HAVING MIN( discount) < .02
    AND MAX( discount ) > .03;
```

Results:

```
SHIP_CITY                        MIN_DISCOUNT MAX_DISCOUNT
-------------------------------- ------------ ------------
Boston                                  0.010        0.050
```

FIGURE 9-22    Alternate form to nested view using a **HAVING** clause

Example 16:

List the maximum discount for each city and the number of cities having those maximums.

```
SELECT  max_discount,
        COUNT( * ) AS "City Count"
  FROM  ( SELECT  ship_city,
                  MAX( discount ) AS max_discount
            FROM  customers
            GROUP BY ship_city )
         AS max_discount_group
  GROUP BY max_discount;
```

Results:

```
MAX_DISCOUNT City Count
------------ ----------
       0.050          3
       0.100          1
       0.010          4
       0.015          1
```

FIGURE 9-23    Resulting query for a query that requires a nested view

The SELECT statement for the view is shown in Figure 9-24.

```
SELECT  ship_city,
        MAX( discount ) AS MaxDiscount
  FROM  customers
  GROUP BY ship_city
```

**FIGURE 9-24**   **Nested view from Example 16**

This view returns the result set in Figure 9-25.

```
SHIP_CITY                         MAX_DISCOUNT
------------------------------    ------------
Toronto                                  0.100
Chicago                                  0.050
Houston                                  0.010
Boston                                   0.050
Detroit                                  0.010
Albany                                   0.010
Dallas                                   0.010
Portland                                 0.015
San Diego                                0.050
```

**FIGURE 9-25**   **Result set from the nested view**

This query could not be specified as a single SELECT statement without a nested view because there are two levels of grouping: by city and by maximum discount. When the database design does not require a permanent view, nested views provide a good solution.

## NAMED QUERY BLOCKS USING THE WITH KEYWORD

If you have to create a very complex query with JOINs and aggregations that are used several times, parts of the statement can be written as a named query block and then used in SELECT statements. A **named query block** is a named query that begins with the WITH keyword and is written in one statement. The WITH clause retrieves the results of one or more named query blocks and stores those results for the user who runs the query. In complex queries, the WITH clause can make the query easier to read.

A named query block is specified using the WITH keyword as a subquery before the main SELECT keyword. The result set is then available in any clause, not just the FROM clause. In the example in Figure 9-26, the named query block specifies a result set with the alias name dept_emp_count. The result set has two columns: department_code and employee_count, which are defined by a subquery using a form very much like the syntax of the CREATE VIEW statement. This named query can be referenced by its alias name anywhere a table name is valid in the main SELECT statement; in this example, dept_emp_count is referenced in both the FROM and WHERE clauses.

**Example 17:**

List the department_code and employee_count for each department in the EMPLOYEES table where the employee count is greater than the average employee count for the department.

```
WITH dept_emp_count
            ( department_code,
              employee_count )
  AS ( SELECT  department_code,
              COUNT( * )
        FROM  employees
        GROUP BY department_code )

  SELECT  department_code,
          employee_count
    FROM  dept_emp_count
   WHERE  employee_count > ( SELECT AVG( employee_count )
                              FROM dept_emp_count );
```

**Results:**

```
DEPARTMENT_CODE EMPLOYEE_COUNT
--------------- --------------
NULL                         4
VG                           4
IT                           4
MA                           6
```

FIGURE 9-26    Example of named query block using the WITH keyword

The query named `dept_emp_count` is shown in Figure 9-27.

```
WITH dept_emp_count
          ( department_code,
            employee_count )
  AS ( SELECT  department_code,
               COUNT( * )
          FROM  employees
          GROUP BY department_code )
```

**FIGURE 9-27**   **Named query from Example 17**

The named query `dept_emp_count` returns the result set in Figure 9-28.

```
DEPARTMENT_CODE 00002
--------------- -----
NULL                4
HT                  3
SA                  1
VG                  4
IT                  4
TR                  1
MA                  6
```

**FIGURE 9-28**   **Result set from the nested view**

Keep in mind that when applications have many queries that reference the same result set, a view may simplify the SELECT statements. But when a view is infrequently used, named query blocks provide a helpful alternative. Note that named query blocks also provide the flexibility of host variables when coded in SQL statements embedded in a program.

## End-of-Chapter

### Chapter Summary

1. Subqueries are subselects that are part of a search condition. Subqueries can be used with the following operators:

   a. *EXISTS operator*. This operator tests whether a subquery result set contains any rows.

   b. *ALL and ANY operators*. These operators compare an expression against all values in the subquery result set.

   All operators using a subquery can be preceded with NOT to negate the operator.

2. Correlated subqueries:

   a. A subquery and a correlated subquery are SELECT queries coded inside another query, known as the outer query.

   b. The correlated subquery and the subquery help determine the outcome of the result set returned by the complete query.

   c. A subquery, when executed independently of the outer query, will return a result set and is therefore not dependent on the outer query.

   d. A correlated subquery cannot be executed independently of the outer query because it uses one or more references to columns in the outer query to determine the result set returned from the correlated subquery.

3. Nested views define temporary result sets that can be referenced in a SELECT. A nested view can be used instead of a permanent view when the view would not be used frequently.

4. Named query blocks can be used to define a query with the WITH clause. Named query blocks can be used in complex JOINs by other SELECT statements.

### Key Terms

| | |
|---|---|
| ALL operator | named query block |
| ANY operator | nested view |
| correlated subquery | single-row subquery |
| EXISTS operator | single-value subquery |
| IN operator | subquery |
| multiple-row subquery | |

# CHAPTER 10

## VIEWS AND INDEXES

## CHAPTER OBJECTIVES

Upon completion of this chapter, you should be able to

- Create views
- Create indexes

## WHAT IS A VIEW?

There are times when a user needs to access a table in some manner other than the way the table is defined. For example, a user may want to access employee rows using either a Social Security number *or* a name as the key field. Similarly, a user may wish to group employees and print or display them by department number or city. An accounts receivable clerk may want to access only those accounts that exceed a certain balance. In another situation, a user may want to select or omit specific rows from a table or even select or omit columns within the rows. A view can be used to accomplish all of these tasks.

A **view** is an object that stores a query SELECT statement that defines an access path to data stored in one or more database base tables. A **base table** is a permanent database table that contains the actual data. A view or stored query is a virtual table derived from base tables. Once a view is defined, it can be referenced just as any other table in a database. Since a view is the result of a stored query, it does not contain any data itself. Instead, a view provides an alternative way to access the data in the underlying base tables. The view lets a user decide which data are to be retrieved from the table or tables and the format in which the data are to appear. Views can be used to

- Sequence data in a table in a different order
- Restrict access to data in base tables by selecting or omitting specific rows from tables
- Restrict access to data in base tables by selecting or omitting specific columns within rows from tables

- Combine data from two or more tables into a single virtual table that can be queried using basic statements
- Separate a complex table into multiple virtual tables that are simpler to query

Views provide a number of advantages:

- A view can provide additional security. By creating a view and establishing the necessarily privileges, users are only able to retrieve and modify data that is exposed by that view. Users will not be able to see or access data in the underlying base tables that is not exposed by the view.
- Views can reduce query complexities. By creating and storing complex queries and exposing them in the form of a view, the data from the view can be extracted using much simpler queries.
- Since a database view is a stored query, not a copy of the actual data, views consume very little space.

## CREATING A VIEW

A view is created with the `CREATE VIEW` command using the syntax shown in Figure 10-1.

```
CREATE VIEW viewname AS
  SELECT statement;
```

**FIGURE 10-1** **CREATE VIEW** syntax

To create a view, the `CREATE VIEW` command is specified, followed by the name of the view. A view must not have the same name as any object in the same schema. The view name is followed by the keyword `AS`, and the actual subquery used to define the view follows the `AS` keyword.

A **subquery** always begins with the `SELECT` keyword followed with either a list of column names or * to use an implicit list of all columns. The column names of the result set defined by the subquery are specified after the `SELECT` keyword. The column names are optional. If an asterisk is specified in the subquery, all columns are selected for each row returned in the result set. The subquery result set determines which columns and rows from one or more underlying tables or views are encompassed by the view being defined.

To create a view called `CUSTOMERS_CREDIT_LIMIT` that contains only the `customer_id`, `customer_name`, and `credit_limit` columns from the `CUSTOMERS` table, the `CREATE VIEW` statement in Figure 10-2 is used.

| Example 1: |
| --- |
| Create a view called **CUSTOMERS_CREDIT_LIMIT** that contains the **customer_id**, **customer_name**, and **credit_limit** columns for all customers in the **CUSTOMERS** table. |
| ``` CREATE VIEW customers_credit_limit AS SELECT customer_id, customer_name, credit_limit FROM customers; ``` |
| **Results:** |
| `View created.` |

FIGURE 10-2    Example of the **CREATE VIEW** command

The `CREATE VIEW` command in this example uses a subquery that defines a result set with all the rows from the `CUSTOMERS` table but only a subset of the columns. A similarity exists between the subquery and the `SELECT` statement.  A subquery is a limited form of the `SELECT` command that can use the `SELECT` command's `FROM`, `WHERE`, `GROUP BY`, and `HAVING` clauses; however, the `ORDER BY` clause cannot be used in a subquery.

You cannot specify column data types, `NOT NULL`, or `DEFAULT` for view columns. The data type of a view column is determined by the data type of the result set column. SQL includes several functions (e.g., `DECIMAL`, `SUBSTR`) to convert from one column data type or length to another in a derived column.

The `SELECT` statement shown in Figure 10-3 is a query against the `CUSTOMERS_CREDIT_LIMIT` view. The `CUSTOMERS_CREDIT_LIMIT` view in turn provides an access path to the data in the `CUSTOMERS` table.

**Example 2:**

List all rows and columns in the **CUSTOMERS_CREDIT_LIMIT** view.

```
SELECT *
  FROM customers_credit_limit;
```

**Results:**

```
CUSTOMER_ID CUSTOMER_NAME                   CREDIT_LIMIT
----------- ------------------------------ ------------
     133568 Smith Mfg.                            150000
     246900 Bolt Co.                              225000
     275978 Ajax Steel Inc.                       175000
     499320 Bluewater Inc.                        165000
     499921 Bell Bldg.                            155000
     518980 London Inc.                           100000
     663456 Alpine Inc.                           100000
     681065 Steelhead Tackle Co.                  100000
     687309 Nautilus Mfg.                         100000
     781010 Bluewater Mfg.                        165000
     888402 Seaworthy                             100000
     890003 John Steeling Products                100000
     905011 Wood Bros.                            100000
```

FIGURE 10-3    List all rows and columns in the **CUSTOMERS_CREDIT_LIMIT** view

## RENAMING COLUMNS IN A VIEW

The column names in a view do not have to be the same names as defined in the base table. The **CUSTOMERS_DISCOUNT** view in Figure 10-4 illustrates how to code view column names explicitly. The column list (if any) immediately follows the view name and is enclosed in parentheses, with commas used to separate each column's entry. The view column names correspond positionally to the columns in the subquery result set. In addition, the column names defined in the view have been renamed from those in the base table.

If a query is executed against a view that has column names that were renamed, the new column names appear in the result set. For example, the **SELECT** statement in Example 4, Figure 10-5, returns the new column names specified when the **CUSTOMERS_DISCOUNT** view was created.

Notice in this example how a view does not specify a particular order to the rows. Ordering of rows in SQL is always specified when the rows are retrieved (i.e., on a **SELECT** command), never when a table or view is defined.

**Example 3:**

Create a view called **CUSTOMERS_DISCOUNT** containing the **cust_id (customer_id)**, name **(customer_name)**, **customer_discount (discount)** columns for all rows from the **CUSTOMERS** table.

```
CREATE VIEW customers_discount ( cust_id, name, customer_discount ) AS
  SELECT customer_id, customer_name, discount
    FROM customers;
```

**Results:**

```
View created.
```

FIGURE 10-4    Renaming column names when creating a view

**Example 4:**

List all rows and columns in the **CUSTOMERS_DISCOUNT** view.

```
SELECT *
  FROM customers_discount;
```

**Results:**

```
CUST_ID NAME                              CUSTOMER_DISCOUNT
------- --------------------------------  -----------------
 133568 Smith Mfg.                                    0.050
 246900 Bolt Co.                                      0.020
 275978 Ajax Steel Inc.                                NULL
 499320 Bluewater Inc.                                0.015
 499921 Bell Bldg.                                    0.010
 518980 London Inc.                                   0.050
 663456 Alpine Inc.                                   0.010
 681065 Steelhead Tackle Co.                          0.000
 687309 Nautilus Mfg.                                 0.050
 781010 Bluewater Mfg.                                 NULL
 888402 Seaworthy                                     0.010
 890003 John Steeling Products                        0.010
 905011 Wood Bros.                                    0.010
```

FIGURE 10-5    Display all rows and columns from the **CUSTOMERS_DISCOUNT** view

## RESTRICTING ROWS WITH A WHERE CLAUSE

When creating a view, rows can also be restricted by using the WHERE clause on the subquery. For example, to create a view called CUSTOMERS_HIGH_CREDIT that contains only customers with a credit limit of at least 150,000, the CREATE VIEW statement in Figure 10-6 is used.

| Example 5: |
| --- |
| Create a view named CUSTOMERS_HIGH_CREDIT that contains customer_id, customer_name, ship_city, credit_limit, and discount for all customers in the CUSTOMERS table with a credit limit >= 150000. |
| ```<br>CREATE VIEW customers_high_credit AS<br>  SELECT customer_id, customer_name, ship_city, credit_limit, discount<br>    FROM customers<br>    WHERE credit_limit >= 150000;<br>``` |
| Results: |
| View created. |

FIGURE 10-6    Example of restricting rows with the WHERE clause

The SELECT statement in Figure 10-7 is a query against the CUSTOMERS_HIGH_CREDIT view. The CUSTOMERS_HIGH_CREDIT view in turn provides an access path to the data in the CUSTOMERS table.

## USING A WHERE CLAUSE WITH A VIEW

Once a view is created, it can be used in the same way other SQL commands are used to access base tables directly. Consider the SELECT statement in Example 7, Figure 10-8, and notice something important about the way this SELECT statement works with the view. Only those rows that meet both conditions are returned in the result set:

1. CreditLimit >= 150000
2. ShipCity = 'Boston'

**Example 6:**

List all rows and columns in the **CUSTOMERS_HIGH_CREDIT** view.

```
SELECT *
  FROM customers_high_credit;
```

**Results:**

```
CUSTOMER_ID CUSTOMER_NAME           SHIP_CITY           CREDIT_LIMIT DISCOUNT
----------- ----------------------- ------------------- ------------ --------
     133568 Smith Mfg.              Chicago                   150000    0.050
     246900 Bolt Co.                Toronto                   225000    0.020
     275978 Ajax Steel Inc.         Albany                    175000     NULL
     499320 Bluewater Inc.          Portland                  165000    0.015
     499921 Bell Bldg.              Detroit                   155000    0.010
     781010 Bluewater Mfg.          Boston                    165000     NULL
```

FIGURE 10-7     List all rows and columns in the **CUSTOMERS_HIGH_CREDIT** view

**Example 7:**

List the **customer_name** and **credit_limit** from the **CUSTOMERS_HIGH_CREDIT** view where the **ship_city** is Boston.

```
SELECT customer_name, credit_limit
  FROM customers_high_credit
  WHERE ship_city = 'Boston';
```

**Results:**

```
CUSTOMER_NAME                   CREDIT_LIMIT
------------------------------- ------------
Bluewater Mfg.                        165000
```

FIGURE 10-8     Example of using a **WHERE** clause against a view

When the **SELECT** statement is processed, only those rows that satisfy the **CUSTOMERS_HIGH_CREDIT** view's selection criteria are accessed—that is, only those customers that have a **credit_limit** value >= **150000**. To those rows, the **SELECT** command's selection criteria are applied to determine which customers have a **ship_city** value of **Boston**.

## USING A VIEW TO UPDATE DATA

Views can also be used in update commands. In Example 8, Figure 10-9, the UPDATE command is used to add 1.5 percent to the discount column for those customers that are in Toronto, have a current discount <= 2%, and have a credit_limit >= 150000.

---

**Example 8:**

Add 1.5% to the discount column for all customers in the CUSTOMERS_HIGH_CREDIT view that are in Toronto and have a discount <= 2%.

```
UPDATE customers_high_credit
  SET discount = ( discount + .015 )
  WHERE ship_city = 'Toronto'
    AND discount <= .020;
```

**Results:**

```
Update successful.
```

FIGURE 10-9    Example of using a view with the UPDATE command

Example 9, Figure 10-10, lists the customer_id, customer_name, and discount columns for all rows in the CUSTOMERS_HIGH_CREDIT view. Notice that the discount for Bolt Co. has increased to 3.5 percent.

---

**Example 9:**

List the customer_id, customer_name, and discount columns for all rows in the CUSTOMERS_HIGH_CREDIT view.

```
SELECT customer_id, customer_name, discount
  FROM customers_high_credit;
```

**Results:**

```
CUSTOMER_ID CUSTOMER_NAME                   DISCOUNT
----------- ------------------------------ --------
     133568 Smith Mfg.                         0.050
     246900 Bolt Co.                           0.035
     275978 Ajax Steel Inc.                     NULL
     499320 Bluewater Inc.                     0.015
     499921 Bell Bldg.                         0.010
     781010 Bluewater Mfg.                      NULL
```

FIGURE 10-10   Verify changes to discount column

As in the previous example, notice how this update works with the view. Only those rows that meet all three conditions will have their discount increased by 1.5 percent:

1. `credit_limit >= 150000`
2. `ship_city = 'Toronto'`
3. `discount <= .020`

When the UPDATE command is processed, only those rows that satisfy the CUSTOMERS_HIGH_CREDIT view's selection criteria are accessed. To those rows, the UPDATE command's selection criteria are applied to determine which rows to update. Although constraints cannot be defined for views, all constraints defined on the table or tables upon which a view is defined are enforced whenever an attempt to insert, update, or delete rows in the view occurs. As the preceding example demonstrates, a view can be thought of as a table that contains just those rows that meet the specified criteria.

## USING GROUP BY WITH A VIEW

The GROUP BY clause can also be used with views. The GROUP BY clause returns group or summary totals. In Figure 10-11, the GROUP BY clause is used to create a view that contains the total number of employees in each department.

**Example 10:**

Create a view called DEPT_COUNT containing dept_id and nbr_employees, which is a total count of employees in each department (COUNT(*)).

```
CREATE VIEW dept_count (dept_id, nbr_employees) AS
  SELECT department_code, COUNT(*)
    FROM employees
    WHERE department_code IS NOT NULL
    GROUP BY department_code;
```

**Results:**

```
View created.
```

FIGURE 10-11  Example of using the GROUP BY clause when creating a view

With a view like this, it would not make sense to let rows be inserted or updated through the view. If that were possible, which row(s) would be changed in the EMPLOYEES table, for instance, if the nbr_employees value of the Major Appliances (MA) department row in the DEPT_COUNT view were updated?

There are a variety of cases in which a view is read-only:

- Those in which the main (i.e., first) FROM clause specifies multiple tables and/or views or specifies another read-only view
- Those in which the first SELECT (following the AS keyword) specifies the DISTINCT keyword or a column function, such as MAX(discount)
- Those in which a nested subquery command specifies the same table as the outer subquery
- Those in which the outer subquery command contains a GROUP BY or HAVING clause
- Those in which the first SELECT does not contain at least one column that is derived directly (i.e., without an expression) from a column of the underlying table

You cannot use a read-only view as the target of an SQL INSERT, UPDATE, or DELETE command.

Example 11 in Figure 10-12 list all rows and columns from the DEPT_COUNT view.

| Example 11: |
| --- |
| List all rows and columns in the DEPT_COUNT. |
| ```
SELECT *
  FROM dept_count;
``` |
| Results: |
| ```
DEPT_ID NBR_EMPLOYEES
------- -------------
HT                  3
IT                  4
MA                  6
SA                  1
TR                  1
VG                  4
``` |

FIGURE 10-12  List all rows and columns in the DEPT_COUNT view

## USING JOINS WITH A VIEW

A `JOIN` can be used in a `CREATE VIEW` statement to create a view consisting of data from two or more tables. For example, in Example 12, Figure 10-13, the `DEPARTMENTS` and `EMPLOYEES` tables are joined to create a view containing the `department_code` and `department_name` from the `DEPARTMENTS` table and the `employee_id`, `last_name`, and `hire_date` from the `EMPLOYEES` table.

---

**Example 12:**

Create a view called **DEPT_EMP_HIRE_DATE** consisting of **dept_code, dept_name, emp_id, last_name,** and **hire_date** from the **DEPARTMENTS** and **EMPLOYEES** tables matching on **department_code.**

```
CREATE VIEW dept_emp_hire_date (dept_code, dept_name, emp_id,
                                last_name, hire_date) AS
  SELECT d.department_code, d.department_name, e.employee_id,
         e.last_name, e.hire_date
    FROM departments AS d JOIN employees AS e
    ON d.department_code = e.department_code;
```

**Results:**

```
View created.
```

---

FIGURE 10-13  **Example of using a JOIN in a CREATE VIEW statement**

When multiple tables and/or views are specified in the `FROM` clause, an intermediate result set is produced that has all combinations of all rows from all the listed tables and views. Each row has all the columns from all the tables as well. From this complete set of combinations, only those rows that satisfy the condition specified after the `ON` keyword, as well as the conditions specified in the `WHERE` and/or `HAVING` clauses (if any), are included in the subquery result set. And only those columns listed after the `SELECT` keyword are in the result set. In this example, only rows that contain matching `department_code` column values are in the result set. As a consequence, the result set contains one row for each department with a matching employee, and each row has both department data and employee data. Because the `CREATE VIEW` statement specifies an explicit list of columns after the `SELECT` keyword, the result set contains only the five columns listed.

Notice how each subquery column name in this example is qualified with the table alias name from which the column is taken. For example, d.department_code specifies that this column in the result set is the department_code column from the DEPARTMENTS table. To qualify a column name, the table or view name is specified followed by a period (.) before the column name.

In this example, the column names in the view have been renamed from those defined in the tables. As a result, these column names do not need an alias to identify them.

Figure 10-14 list all rows and columns from the DEPT_EMP_HIRE_DATE view.

---

**Example 13:**

---

**List all rows and columns in the DEPT_EMP_HIRE_DATE view.**

---

```
SELECT *
  FROM dept_emp_hire_date
  ORDER BY dept_name, hire_date, last_name;
```

---

**Results:**

---

```
DEPT_CODE DEPT_NAME                    EMP_ID LAST_NAME                      HIRE_DATE
--------- ---------------------------- ------ ------------------------------ ---------
HT        Home Theatre                    112 Bernard                        06/09/11
HT        Home Theatre                    118 Harper                         06/09/11
HT        Home Theatre                    125 Maxwell                        06/09/11
IT        Information Technology          136 Albert                         06/09/11
IT        Information Technology          132 Bernard                        06/09/11
IT        Information Technology          139 Peters                         06/09/11
IT        Information Technology          135 Zimmerman                      06/09/11
MA        Major Appliances                127 Evans                          06/09/11
MA        Major Appliances                116 Henry                          06/09/11
MA        Major Appliances                114 Horner                         06/09/11
MA        Major Appliances                111 James                          06/09/11
MA        Major Appliances                123 Johnson                        06/09/11
MA        Major Appliances                120 Richie                         06/09/11
SA        Small Appliances                115 Best                           06/09/11
TR        Training                        110 Alexander                      06/09/11
VG        Video Games                     117 Albert                         06/09/11
VG        Video Games                     113 Carr                           06/09/11
VG        Video Games                     122 Lee                            06/09/11
VG        Video Games                     124 Long                           06/09/11
```

**FIGURE 10-14  List all rows and columns in the DEPT_EMP_HIRE_DATE view**

# WITH CHECK OPTION AND WITH LOCAL CHECK OPTION

Other options for a `CREATE VIEW` command are **`WITH CHECK OPTION`** and **`WITH LOCAL CHECK OPTION`**. These options restrict row insert and update operations through an updatable view that selects a subset of rows. For example, in Figure 10-15 the view definition will not allow an `INSERT` or `UPDATE` that would create a row with `credit_limit < 150000`.

| |
|---|
| **Example 14:** |
| Create a view named `CUSTOMERS_HIGH_CREDIT_1` that contains `customer_id`, `customer_name`, `ship_city`, and `credit_limit` for all customers in the `CUSTOMERS` table with a credit limit >= `150000`. |
| ```<br>CREATE VIEW customers_high_credit_1 AS<br>  SELECT *<br>    FROM customers<br>    WHERE credit_limit >= 150000<br>    WITH CHECK OPTION;<br>``` |
| **Results:** |
| ```<br>View created.<br>``` |

FIGURE 10-15  Example of a `CREATE VIEW` command specifying `CHECK OPTION`

This restriction prevents so-called **phantom updates** in which a row is inserted or updated through a view but cannot subsequently be retrieved through the view. When a view specifies either `WITH CHECK OPTION` or `WITH LOCAL CHECK OPTION` and another view is defined over the view with the check option, the check option restrictions also apply to the dependent view.

For example, to insert a row into the `TORONTO_HIGH_CREDIT` view defined in Figure 10-16, the row must have `credit_limit >= 150000`, regardless of whether the `TORONTO_HIGH_CREDIT` view definition specifies `WITH CHECK OPTION`, `WITH LOCAL CHECK OPTION`, or neither check option.

---

**Example 15:**

Create a view named **TORONTO_HIGH_CREDIT** over the
**CUSTOMERS_HIGH_CREDIT_1** view that contains **customer_id**,
**customer_name**, **ship_city**, and **credit_limit** for all customers in the
**CUSTOMERS** table with a credit limit **>= 150000**.

```
CREATE VIEW toronto_high_credit AS
  SELECT *
    FROM customers_high_credit_1
    WHERE ship_city = 'Toronto';
```

**Results:**

```
View created.
```

---

**FIGURE 10-16** Example of dependent view restricted by CHECK OPTION from another view

If a view defined over another view specifies WITH CHECK OPTION, inserts and updates must satisfy all the lower-level views' search conditions in addition to the search condition, if any, specified on the view being defined. If a view defined over another view specifies WITH LOCAL CHECK OPTION, only the search conditions of the lower-level views that specify a check option must be met.

Additional processing is done when rows are inserted or updated through a view that has a direct or an indirect check option. Care should be taken when using such views for table updates when performance is critical. Before support for check constraints, views that had a WITH CHECK OPTION provided one means to define data integrity rules. Check constraints are a much better approach, however, because they are enforced whether the table is updated directly or through any view.

An SQL command referencing the TORONTO_HIGH_CREDIT view can treat the view as if it were a table consisting of just the listed columns and all the rows in the CUSTOMERS table. The FROM clause can name a view as well as a table.

The WHERE clauses are combined for a view defined over another view. Given the previous definition of the CUSTOMERS_HIGH_CREDIT_1 view, this definition of the TORONTO_HIGH_CREDIT view includes only those rows from the CUSTOMERS table for which credit_limit >= 150000 and ship_city = 'Toronto'.

## MORE VIEW EXAMPLES

Let us look at some additional examples of views. The example in Figure 10-17 uses BETWEEN and IN. Notice how these operators can improve the readability of search conditions.

| Example 16: |
| --- |
| Create a view named **CUSTOMERS_HIGH_CREDIT_2** over the **CUSTOMERS** table that contains all columns for all customers in the **CUSTOMERS** table with a **discount** not null, **credit_limit** between **100000** and **175000**, and **ship_city** either Dallas, Albany, or Boston. |
| <pre>CREATE VIEW customers_high_credit_2 AS<br>  SELECT *<br>    FROM customers<br>    WHERE discount IS NOT NULL<br>      AND credit_limit BETWEEN 100000 AND 175000<br>      AND ship_city IN ( 'Dallas', 'Albany', 'Boston' );</pre> |
| Results: |
| `View created.` |

FIGURE 10-17  Example of view specifying **BETWEEN** and **IN** operators

You can reorder and rename columns, as Figure 10-18 shows.

| Example 17: |
| --- |
| Create a view named **CUSTOMERS_NEW** over the **CUSTOMERS** table that contains all columns and rows for all customers in the **CUSTOMERS** table. Rename and resequence the columns in the new view. |
| <pre>CREATE VIEW customers_new ( name, id, crd_limit, city, dis, bal ) AS<br>  SELECT customer_id, customer_name, balance, ship_city,<br>        credit_limit, discount<br>    FROM customers;</pre> |
| Results: |
| `View created.` |

FIGURE 10-18  Example of reordering and renaming view columns

The example in Figure 10-19 illustrates how you can derive columns in an SQL view using a date function and concatenation operations.

---

**Example 18:**

Create a view named **EMPLOYEES_HIRE_YEAR** over the **EMPLOYEES** table that contains the `employee_id`, `hire_year`, and `full_name` (concatenated first, middle, and last names) columns for all rows from the **EMPLOYEES** table.

```
CREATE VIEW employees_hire_year ( emp_id, hire_year, fullname ) AS
  SELECT employee_id,
         year(hire_date),
         TRIM( first_name) CONCAT ' ' CONCAT middle_initial
         CONCAT ' ' CONCAT TRIM( last_name )
    FROM employees;
```

**Results:**

```
View created.
```

---

FIGURE 10-19   Example of using derived values in a view

Consider the view in Figure 10-20, which consists of the employee table joined with itself.

---

**Example 19:**

Create a view called **EMPLOYEES_MANAGER** containing employee ID, employee last name, manager ID, and manager last name.

```
CREATE VIEW employees_manager
    ( emp_id, emp_last_name, manager_id, mgr_last_name ) AS
  SELECT emp.employee_id, emp.last_name, emp.manager_id, mgr.last_name
    FROM employees emp JOIN employees mgr
    ON emp.manager_id = mgr.employee_id;
```

**Results:**

```
View created.
```

---

FIGURE 10-20   Example of view of table joined to itself

The FROM clause in this subquery lists the EMPLOYEES table twice. To have unambiguous references to the appropriate role of the table (that is, either the first role, which is the whole set of employees, or the second role, which is the set from which matching manager rows are retrieved), each EMPLOYEES table reference in the FROM clause is followed by an alias name: emp and mgr, respectively. These unique alias names are used as column qualifiers instead of the table name. Alias names can be used in any subquery, not just ones that specify a join. For nested or other long, complex subqueries, short alias names can make the SQL code more readable.

## INDEXES

When users perform a query on a database, they generally are searching for one or more rows that satisfy a certain search criteria. If every row of the database table has to be examined to determine which rows satisfy the query, that would be too time-consuming, especially for tables that contain thousands and thousands of rows that do not pertain to the search condition.

To solve this problem, indexes are created over tables that allow the DBMS to accelerate the searching process. Indexes do not contain data. The actual data is stored in the table. The index is just a method of sequencing the data for fast retrieval.

An index in a database is similar to an index in a book. The index at the end of a book lets readers find a specific location within the book without searching page by page. For example, if the reader of a barbeque book wants to know how to barbeque ribs, the index can direct that person to the exact location in the book. Instead of reading the book from the beginning until finding the section on ribs, it is much quicker to go to the index, locate which pages contain information about barbequing ribs, and then go to those pages directly. There is no need to search through the sections on barbequing chicken, beef, and seafood. The reader can simply look up ribs in the book's index and go directly to the ribs section in the book. Indexes save time and are more efficient for locating data.

The same principle applies to retrieving data from a database table. Without an index, the DBMS reads through the entire table to locate the desired data. When an index is built over the table, the DBMS can first go through the index to find out where the required data is located and then go to those locations directly to retrieve the data. This capability significantly increases the speed of data retrieval.

Indexes provide an alternative way to access data in one or more tables. You can use an index to

- Select a subset of the rows in a table (e.g., only customers in Toronto)
- Combine the rows from multiple tables (e.g., combine sales rows from a table for the year 2009 with rows from a table for the year 2010)
- Select a subset of a table's columns (e.g., only customer name and status)
- Combine ("join") related rows in two or more tables (e.g., combine detailed customer data with each of the sales rows for the customer)
- Provide an index so rows can be efficiently retrieved in a particular order (e.g., by customer name)

## ACCESSING DATA USING AN INDEX

Figure 10-21 shows the order in which the rows are stored in the employee pay table. Without an index, HLL programs receive the rows in the same sequence in which they are actually physically stored in the table, thus first-in, first-out.

| Record Sequence | Employee Number | Store Number | First Name | Init | Last Name | Dept | Hourly Rate | Hours Worked | Sales |
|---|---|---|---|---|---|---|---|---|---|
| 1 | 827392161 | 7315 | Magdi | | Ali | 666 | 015^50 | 43^5 | 10400 |
| 2 | 228725876 | 5003 | Brenda | M | Fields | 666 | 009^85 | 40^0 | 04555 |
| 3 | 132135478 | 1133 | Janice | A | Porter | 333 | 008^55 | 10^0 | 00000 |
| 4 | 864955834 | 2257 | Laura | J | Hansen | 444 | 009^75 | 15^0 | 00024- |
| 5 | 103429376 | 4464 | Sang Yong | | Lee | 333 | 009^95 | 35^0 | 00563 |
| 6 | 314792638 | 1133 | Isabel | L | Houle | 666 | 023^60 | 45^0 | 21245 |
| 7 | 223649622 | 5003 | Tom | P | Simpson | 333 | 017^90 | 20^0 | 00099- |
| 8 | 123728964 | 1133 | Susan | P | Murphy | 111 | 023^21 | 45^0 | 10125 |
| 9 | 832476894 | 2257 | Stacey | V | Bond | 555 | 011^25 | 40^0 | 00740 |
| 10 | 235235658 | 4464 | Karl | C | Ryckman | 333 | 014^45 | 42^5 | 07866 |

FIGURE 10-21   Sequence of first 10 rows in the EMPPAYTBL table

An **index** provides an access path in which the order of rows is based on ascending or descending values in one or more **keys** that are specified when a table or index is created.

A table defined with a primary key or index uses an access path in which rows are stored in sequence according to a key. When creating an index, the software developer must designate one or more columns that *uniquely* identify each row in the table. These columns, referred to as **key fields**, may be located anywhere in the row, and they do not have to be contiguous within the row. In addition, a key field may be either alphanumeric or numeric.

Figure 10-22 illustrates how the employee pay table appears when defined with an index. The employee number is the key field because it can be used to uniquely identify each row. When a table is created with a primary key, an index is created with the table, and thus the system establishes two files on disk:

- The *table* containing the actual data. When a table containing an index is created, the data is established on disk and contains the physical data rows stored in the sequence in which they are added to the table. In other words, the rows are stored in exactly the same manner as arrival sequence tables.

- An *index* containing the key field and a pointer field. The system uses the key field specified by the software developer to establish the index. The system uses the index to maintain the correct sequence of the rows by sorting the index in order by the key field. The *pointer field* within the index contains the disk address of where each row is physically located in the data table.

Indexes allow tables to be accessed randomly without accessing other rows in the table. This is accomplished by the DBMS first searching for a match on the key field in the index. Then, the address stored in the pointer field is used to go directly to the physical disk address to obtain the desired row. Thus, to randomly access a row in a payroll table, the user enters the employee number of the desired row. The system searches the index for the desired employee number. When a match is found, the system uses the address stored in the pointer field to retrieve the physical row from disk. This capability is very useful for interactive processing when users need to enter key fields that are not ordinarily entered in sequence.

Once the address of the row is obtained from the pointer field in the index, the disk drive's access mechanism can move directly to the physical address on the disk where the row is located. It is *not* necessary to read sequentially past all the previous rows in the table looking for the desired one.

An index is similar to a book's index with unique subjects (keys) and their corresponding page numbers (addresses). There would be two ways to find a topic in the book. One method would be to read the book sequentially, from the beginning, until the topic is found, but this approach would be time-consuming and inefficient. The better method would be to look up the topic in the index, find the corresponding page number, and go directly to that page. This is precisely the system accesses rows from a table using an index.

Table containing data
↓

| Data file | | | |
|-----------|---------|------------|---|
| Employee No | Store No | First Name | |
| 827392161 | 7315 | Magdi | . . . |
| 228725876 | 5003 | Brenda | . . . |
| 132135478 | 1133 | Janice | . . . |
| 864955834 | 2257 | Laura | . . . |
| 103429376 | 4464 | Sang Yong | . . . |
| 314792638 | 1133 | Isabel | . . . |
| 223649622 | 5003 | Tom | . . . |
| 123728964 | 1133 | Susan | . . . |
| 832476894 | 2257 | Stacey | . . . |
| 235235658 | 4464 | Karl | . . . |

↑

**Primary key used to identify each row
in the employee pay table**

Index keyed on employee number
↓

| Index file | |
|------------|---------|
| Employee No | Pointer |
| 103429376 | 05 |
| 123728964 | 08 |
| 132135478 | 03 |
| 223649622 | 07 |
| 235235658 | 10 |
| 228725876 | 02 |
| 314792638 | 06 |
| 827392161 | 01 |
| 832476894 | 09 |
| 864955834 | 04 |

← **1st row retrieved from the table.
The value (05) indicates that
this row is physically located
as the 5th row in the data file.**

← **10th row retrieved from the table.**

↑

**Physical disk address of the associated row
in the data portion of the employee pay table**

**FIGURE 10-22  Structure of a keyed sequence table**

When an index is created as illustrated in Figure 10-22, each row in the index contains two fields:

- The key field
- A pointer to the associated row in the table

The first field in each row of the index contains the value of the key field of the associated row in the table. For a payroll table, the key field may be employee number or Social Security number; for an inventory table, the key field may be product number; for an accounts receivable table, the key field may be customer number.

The second field, the **pointer**, is a field containing the location (actual physical disk address) of the row in the table that is identified by the key field.

When a table is created, key fields (indexes) provide the sequence in which rows are retrieved from the table. When rows are added to a table that has an index, the index is updated with a row containing the key field and pointer that contains the address of that row in the table. The DBMS places the new index rows in their proper sorted positions in the index and maintains the proper order by key field regardless of the physical address of the rows in the table. This permits random access of rows in the table. So while the table itself is in arrival sequence, not in order by any set of column values, the index effectively provides such orderings.

As noted, the rows in the index are stored and maintained in sequence according to the key field. During processing, the retrieval of rows from the table is performed by the DBMS using the index in a procedure that is *completely transparent* to the program. The table and the index may be thought of as one entity.

Each row occupies a unique location in the table, and the rows are not necessarily in any order based on their content. A row's location is identified by its relative record number (RRN), which starts at 1 for the first row in the table and increases by 1 for each location. When a row is deleted, the DBMS sets on an internal "deleted row" flag in the row's location. When a new row is added, the DBMS puts it either in the first available location with a "deleted row" flag set or after the last row in the table. As more space is needed for additional rows, the DBMS dynamically expands the size of the table.

## CREATING AN INDEX

Although a particular order of rows is not specified on either the CREATE TABLE or the CREATE VIEW statement, indexes are used for efficient row selection and ordering. The DBMS automatically selects which index to be used when an SQL statement, such as SELECT, is executed or when an SQL cursor embedded in an HLL program is opened. When a primary, unique, or foreign key constraint is specified, an internal index is created or shared as part of the table. Additional indexes can be created using the SQL CREATE INDEX statement. The CREATE INDEX statement has the syntax shown in Figure 10-23.

```
CREATE INDEX index-name
  ON table-name
    ( column1, column2, column3 )
```

FIGURE 10-23  Example of the **CREATE INDEX** command

The **CREATE INDEX** keywords are specified first, followed by the index name. Following the index name is the keyword **ON** and the name of the table on which the index is being built. Next, the column names that are to be included in the index are listed in parentheses. An index name cannot be the same as any table, view, alias, other index, or non-SQL table name in the same schema.

An index can be created on a single column or on several columns in a database table. An index is a database structure that arranges the values of one or more columns in a database table in a specific order. The index contains pointers to the values stored in the specified columns of the table. These pointers are ordered depending on the sort order specified in the index.

The **CREATE INDEX** example shown in Figure 10-24 creates an index called **EMP_LASTNAME_FIRSTNAME**. This index is built over the last_name and first_name columns of the **EMPLOYEES** base table.

**Example 20:**

Create an **INDEX** called **EMP_LASTNAME_FIRSTNAME** indexed on last_name as the major key and first_name as the minor key.

```
CREATE INDEX emp_lastname_firstname
  ON EMPLOYEES (last_name, first_name);
```

**Results:**

```
Index created.
```

FIGURE 10-24  Example **CREATE INDEX** statement

When an SQL index is created, a table is created with a keyed access path. You cannot access an SQL index directly with any SQL statement. In SQL, indexes are solely for internal use, and their purpose is generally related to performance.

The DESC keyword can optionally be added after any column name to specify a descending order. An index definition can also specify UNIQUE or UNIQUE WHERE NOT NULL, as Figure 10-25 illustrates.

---

**Example 21:**

Create an UNIQUE INDEX called DEPARTMENT_MANAGERS indexed on manager_id as the major key and department_name as the minor key.

```
CREATE UNIQUE INDEX DEPARTMENT_MANAGERS
  ON DEPARTMENTS
    ( manager_id, department_name );
```

**Results:**

```
Index created.
```

---

FIGURE 10-25  **Enforcing unique key values in an index**

The **UNIQUE keyword** enforces unique key values, including null, in the same way as explained earlier for a table primary key constraint. If you specify UNIQUE WHERE NOT NULL, unique values are enforced, except for null, as explained for unique constraints. In general, a primary key or unique constraint should be used on the CREATE TABLE statement for a table, which causes an internal index to be created. This practice, rather than creating a separate index with UNIQUE or UNIQUE WHERE NOT NULL, is preferred. Independent indexes are primarily useful for two cases:

- Unique indexes in addition to the primary key of a base table
- Non-unique indexes (as a performance aid)

Note that only one primary key constraint can be specified for each table; if it is necessary to enforce a second fully unique key (that is, including nulls) for the table, a CREATE UNIQUE INDEX statement must be used. Because multiple unique constraints (which exclude nulls) can be specified on a table, there is little reason to use a CREATE UNIQUE WHERE NOT NULL INDEX statement in SQL.

Indexes affect database performance both positively and negatively. In brief, indexes can speed data retrieval, but they may slow updates due to the time spent updating the entries in the index (or indexes) over a table as rows are inserted, deleted, or updated in the table. The system is fairly efficient at maintaining indexes, so there is generally no need to worry when five or fewer indexes exist over an active table, or 10 to 20 over a less frequently modified table. And, for tables that are primarily read-only, with little update activity, there is not likely to be any significant overhead from having numerous indexes. However, for actively updated tables, it is best to avoid an excessive amount of index maintenance, or the application's database updates may be slowed.

## Dropping an Index

The **DROP INDEX statement** is used to drop or delete an index. The format of the statement is shown in Figure 10-26.

| Example 22: |
| --- |
| **Drop the DEPARTMENT_MANAGERS index.** |
| DROP INDEX department_managers; |
| **Results:** |
| Index dropped. |

FIGURE 10-26  Example of dropping an index

## End-of-Chapter

### Chapter Summary

1. A view is an SQL object defined over one or more tables or other views that provides an alternative way to access the data in the underlying tables. Views can be used to

   - Sequence data in a table in a different order
   - Select or omit specific rows from tables
   - Select or omit specific columns within rows from tables
   - Access data from two or more tables

2. A subquery command is a limited form of SELECT command that plays a central part in view definition.

3. A subquery command is a specification of a result set with the following structure:

```
SELECT    select-list
   FROM    table-list
 [ WHERE   search-condition     ]
 [ GROUP BY grouping-column-list ]
 [ HAVING  search-condition     ]
```

(The brackets, or [], indicate clauses that are optional.)

4. The full power of the SQL subquery is available to define views. SQL view rows do not have any ordering.

5. You can change table data through a view only if the view is updatable (i.e., not read-only).

6. The `WITH CHECK OPTION` and `WITH LOCAL CHECK OPTION` clauses prevent "phantom updates," in which a row is inserted or updated through a view but cannot subsequently be retrieved through the view.

7. When a `SELECT` command is executed on a view, the conditions specified on the view's `WHERE` clause and the conditions specified on the `SELECT` command are combined.

8. The `CREATE INDEX` statement creates an SQL index, which is an object with a keyed access path.

9. An SQL index is created over a single table and specifies one or more key columns.

10. The `DROP INDEX` statement deletes an index.

## KEY TERMS

| | |
|---|---|
| base table | pointer |
| DROP INDEX statement | subquery |
| index | UNIQUE keyword |
| key | view |
| key field | WITH CHECK OPTION clause |
| phantom update | WITH LOCAL CHECK OPTION clause |

# CHAPTER 11
## EMBEDDED SQL

## CHAPTER OBJECTIVES

Upon completion of this chapter, you should be able to

- Use embedded SQL statements
- Use host variables
- Explain the purpose of the precompiler directive EXEC SQL
- Implement SQL error handling
- Use the SQLSTATE variable
- Create applications that INSERT, UPDATE, and DELETE rows in a database table

## INTRODUCTION TO EMBEDDED SQL

This chapter illustrates how to use **embedded SQL statements** in ILE RPG (source member type RPGLE) programs. In earlier chapters, SQL statements were used to query database tables and return one or more rows in a result set. In addition, SQL statements were used to modify database tables. For example, in Figure 11-1, the SQL statement queries the database table and returns one row.

```
SELECT  first_name, last_name, employee_id, hourly_rate
  FROM  employees
  WHERE employee_id = 10101;
```

FIGURE 11-1    Example of an SQL statement to return one row from a database table

In Figure 11-2, the UPDATE statement sets the hourly rate of all employees who work in department 333 at store 1133 to an increase of 2.5 percent in their hourly rate.

```
UPDATE   employees
  SET    hourly_rate = hourly_rate * 1.025
  WHERE store_id = 1133 AND department_id = 333;
```

**FIGURE 11-2**   **Example of SQL statements to update several rows in a database table**

Running SQL statements is quite useful for ad hoc retrieval and updates. However, there are times when it is necessary to control the execution of SQL statements from within a program rather than using the statements interactively.

The SELECT, INSERT, UPDATE, and DELETE statements can be embedded in RPGLE programs. When you code an SQL statement directly in a program, as in the examples illustrated thus far, the statement is known as a **static statement**, so called because the structure of the statement does not change; only the values supplied by host variables used in the statement may change.

### EXEC SQL COMPILER DIRECTIVE

During the compilation process of a program containing embedded SQL, the SQL precompiler requires some way to differentiate embedded SQL statements from the RPGLE programming language statements. For example, SQL and RPGLE have a delete statement; without some way to differentiate the two delete statements, the precompiler would not know whether to translate the statement as an SQL statement or to pass it on as an RPGLE statement.

As shown in Figure 11-3, every embedded SQL statement in RPGLE begins with the **precompiler directive** EXEC SQL. A semicolon (;) is used to identify the end of the embedded SQL statement.

```
EXEC SQL
  UPDATE   customers
  SET    discount = .10
  WHERE ship_city = 'Chicago';
```

**FIGURE 11-3**   **Using the precompiler directive with embedded SQL**

## HOST VARIABLES

A **host variable** is a program variable used in an embedded SQL statement. Host variables specified within SQL statements must be preceded by a colon (:).

Let us consider the example in Figure 11-4, where host variables are used with an UPDATE statement. This example illustrates a sequence of two RPGLE statements and an embedded UPDATE statement using the host variables newDisc and searchCity. Note that the colon is not used with the variables when coding normal RPGLE statements.

```
newDisc    = .10;
searchCity = 'Chicago';

EXEC SQL
  UPDATE  customers
    SET   discount = :newDisc
    WHERE ship_city = :searchCity;
```

FIGURE 11-4    Embedded SQL statement using host variables

Before the UPDATE statement, the program sets the values of the newDisc and searchCity variables. If these two variables were set to .10 and Chicago, respectively, the effect of this UPDATE statement would be that every customer in Chicago would have a discount of .10 after the UPDATE operation was completed. With the use of host variables, an application can both simplify and control the update action. For example, the user could be presented with a simple interface into which he or she enters the discount amount and city. The program could even provide a dropdown list of cities from which the user selects. The program could also check the discount the user enters, making sure it is not negative and not over some maximum allowed discount.

In general, when a host variable is used as a receiving variable or is compared with another variable, it is preferable to declare the host variable with a data type and size that matches the associated column's data type and size exactly.

An SQL statement can include host variable references in the WHERE clause, providing the ability to determine the selection criteria for which rows are selected. For example, when the UPDATE statement in Figure 11-4 is executed, the WHERE clause compares the ship_city column in the CUSTOMERS table with the searchCity host variable. The value in the ship_city column must be equal to the host variable searchCity for the row to be returned.

## USING COMMENTS WITH EMBEDDED SQL

Between the EXEC SQL and semicolon delimiters, blank lines or comment lines can be used. SQL comments can be used by beginning a comment anywhere in a line with two dashes (--); the comment then includes the rest of the line. SQL comments that span multiple lines can be used by beginning them with /* and ending them with */. The example in Figure 11-5 shows blank lines, an RPGLE comment, and SQL single- and multiple-line comments.

```
* Change the discount for all customers in Chicago
  EXEC SQL
    UPDATE   customers
      SET    discount = .10          -- New discount
      WHERE ship_city = 'Chicago';   -- Selected city

/* This UPDATE statement updates the customer discount
   for all customers in Chicago to 10%.
*/
```

FIGURE 11-5   Example of comments

## SQL ERROR HANDLING

Every time SQL performs an input/output operation on a database table, the system issues a return code to the program indicating the resulting state of the SQL statement. Two SQL variables, SQLCODE and SQLSTATE, contain the return code and can be monitored and tested to determine the result of the operation. Both SQLCODE and SQLSTATE are derived from the SQL standard, but SQLCODE has been marked deprecated. Therefore, it is strongly encouraged that SQLSTATE be used.

SQLSTATE is a five-character variable that contains five digits (0-9) or letters (A-Z). The five-character variable contains two parts that represent codes of various error and warning conditions. The first two characters indicate the general class of the condition; the last three characters indicate a subclass of the general condition. A successful state is indicated by the return code '`00000`'. The meanings of the general class values are Successful (`00`), Warning (`01`), No Data (`02`), and Error (`03` through `ZZ`).

When performing any SQL statement on a database, `SQLSTATE` should be tested to confirm that the SQL statement completed successfully. When the `SQLSTATE` variable contains a value of '`00000`', this means that the SQL statement was successful. Any other value indicates that the SQL statement was not successful.

When an embedded SQL statement is executed, several program variables are set to provide feedback about any exceptional conditions that occurred during execution. These variables should be checked to handle both anticipated conditions, such as no row found, and unexpected errors, such as a hardware failure. The SQL precompiler generates the SQL-related program variables automatically for `RPGLE` programs.

## THE SQL COMMUNICATION AREA

The DBMS sets values in a set of variables known as the **SQL communication area** (**SQLCA**) to provide feedback to `RPGLE` programs after executing an embedded SQL statement. In `RPGLE` programs, this area is stored in the `SQLCA` data structure. In `RPGLE` programs that contain embedded SQL, this data structure and its subfield declarations are generated automatically. Figure 11-6 shows the layout of the `RPGLE` `SQLCA` data structure. Figure 11-7 describes the contents of the SQL communication area.

Variables provide information about both normal and exceptional conditions and provide better diagnosis and reporting of exceptional conditions. Variables such as `SQLERRD(3)`, which contains the number of rows `FETCH`ed, `INSERT`ed, `UPDATE`ed, or `DELETE`ed, can also be used to provide user feedback for normal operations.

For now, let us focus on the `SQLSTATE` variable, which is a five-character return code set after the execution of an embedded SQL statement. The possible conditions that can result from executing an embedded SQL statement can be categorized as follows:

| Condition | SQLSTATE value |
|---|---|
| No warning or exception | '`00000`' |
| No row found | '`02000`' |
| Warning | '`01xxx`' |
| Error | '`yyxxx`', where yy is not 00, 01, or 02 |

```
    ....1....+....2....+....3....+....4....+....5
D*      SQL Communication Area
D SQLCA
D  SQLAID                 1       8A
D  SQLABC                 9      12B 0
D  SQLCOD                13      16B 0
D  SQLERL                17      18B 0
D  SQLERM                19      88A
D  SQLERP                89      96A
D  SQLERRD               97     120B 0 DIM(6)
D  SQLERR                97     120A
D   SQLER1               97     100B 0
D   SQLER2              101     104B 0
D   SQLER3              105     108B 0
D   SQLER4              109     112B 0
D   SQLER5              113     116B 0
D   SQLER6              117     120B 0
D  SQLWRN               121     131A
D   SQLWN0              121     121A
D   SQLWN1              122     122A
D   SQLWN2              123     123A
D   SQLWN3              124     124A
D   SQLWN4              125     125A
D   SQLWN5              126     126A
D   SQLWN6              127     127A
D   SQLWN7              128     128A
D   SQLWN8              129     129A
D   SQLWN9              130     130A
D   SQLWNA              131     131A
D  SQLSTT               132     136A
```

FIGURE 11-6    SQLCA data structure

| Variable | Data type | Purpose |
|---|---|---|
| SQLCAID | Char( 8 ) | Structure-identifying literal: "SQLCA" |
| SQLCABC | Integer | Length of SQLCA |
| SQLCODE | Integer | Return code:<br>    <0 = Error<br>     0 = Successful execution (SQLWARN indicators may have been set)<br>    >0 = Successful execution with warning |
| SQLERRMI | SmallInt | Length of SQLERRMC |
| SQLERRMC | Char( 70 ) | Message replacement text |
| SQLERRP | Char( 8 ) | For statements other than CONNECT, identifies the product and module returning the information. The first three characters identify the product (QSQ for DB2).<br>For a CONNECT statement, contains *pppvvrrm*, where *ppp* identifies the product, *vv* the version number, *rr* the release, and *m* the modification (e.g., QSQ06010 for DB2). |
| SQLERRD | Array of Integer | SQLERRD(1) — Treated as Char( 4 ); contains the last four characters of CPF or other escape message, if any.<br>SQLERRD(2) — Treated as Char( 4 ); contains the last four characters of CPD or other diagnostic message, if any.<br>SQLERRD(3) — For FETCH, INSERT, UPDATE, or DELETE, the number of rows retrieved or updated.<br>For PREPARE, the estimated number of rows affected.<br>For CONNECT (with no argument specified), returns the status of the connection:<br>    1 = Committable updates can be performed for the current unit of work.<br>    2 = Committable updates cannot be performed.<br>SQLERRD(4) — For FETCH, the length of the row retrieved.<br>For PREPARE, a relative number indicating estimated resources required for execution.<br>For CALL, the message key of the error that caused the procedure to fail (the message can be retrieved with the QMhRtvPm API).<br>For a trigger error in an UPDATE, INSERT, or DELETE statement, the message key of the error sent by the trigger program (the message can be retrieved with the QMhRtvPm API).<br>For CONNECT, indicates whether the conversation is protected and whether committable updates can be performed:<br>    1 = Protected/committable<br>    2 = Unprotected/not committable<br>    3 = Protected/unknown<br>    4 = Unprotected/unknown<br>    5 = Local connection or application requester driver program, unknown if committable |

*Continued*

| | | |
|---|---|---|
| | | SQLERRD(5) — For multiple-row FETCH, contains 100 if last available row is fetched.<br>For DELETE, the number of rows affected by referential constraints.<br>For PREPARE, the number of parameter markers in the prepared statement.<br>For CONNECT or SET CONNECTION, contains –1 if connection is unconnected, 0 if connection is local, or 1 if connection is remote.<br>SQLERRD(6) — When SQLCODE is 0, contains SQL completion message identifier. |
| SQLWARN | Char( 11 ) | Set of 11 warning indicators; each is blank, W, or N. (The following 11 items describe these warning indicators.) |
| SQLWARN0 | Char( 1 ) | Blank if all other SQLWARNx warning indicators are blank; W if any warning indicator contains W or N. |
| SQLWARN1 | Char( 1 ) | W if a string column was truncated when assigned to host variable; N if C program host variable was large enough for string but not for null terminator and *NoCNulRqd was specified for program. |
| SQLWARN2 | Char( 1 ) | W if null values were eliminated from a function. |
| SQLWARN3 | Char( 1 ) | W if number of columns is larger than number of host variables. |
| SQLWARN4 | Char( 1 ) | W if prepared UPDATE or DELETE statement does not include a WHERE clause. |
| SQLWARN5 | Char( 1 ) | Reserved. |
| SQLWARN6 | Char( 1 ) | W if date arithmetic results in end-of-month adjustment. |
| SQLWARN7 | Char( 1 ) | Reserved. |
| SQLWARN8 | Char( 1 ) | W if result of character conversion contains the substitution character. |
| SQLWARN9 | Char( 1 ) | Reserved. |
| SQLWARNA | Char( 1 ) | Reserved. |
| SQLSTATE | Char( 5 ) | Return code; 00000 if no error or warning. |

FIGURE 11-7    SQL Communication Area (SQLCA) structure contents

## MONITORSQL PROCEDURE

The monitorSQL procedure in Figure 11-8 can be used as a template to cover all categories. This procedure can easily be changed and included in any program.

Several common conditions that can result from executing an embedded SQL statement are shown in the figure. One of these, "No row found" (SQLSTATE = '02000'), occurs when no rows satisfy the search condition of a SELECT, UPDATE, or DELETE statement or when a FETCH statement has already retrieved the last available row from an open cursor. Another case is a duplicate value for a primary or unique key on an INSERT or UPDATE operation, in which case SQLSTATE is set to '42910'. To handle a specific exception, a condition can be added to the monitorSQL procedure.

```
D SUCCESSFUL       C                    Const('00000')
D NO_ROW           C                    Const('02000')

  EXEC SQL
  UPDATE  customers
      SET   discount  = :NewDisc
      WHERE ship_city = :SlcCusCity;
  monitorSQL();



P monitorSQL       B
D SUCCESSFUL       C                    Const('00000')
D NO_ROW           C                    Const('02000')
D NOT_FOUND        C                    Const('02600')
D DUPLICATE_KEY    C                    Const('42910')

 /free
  select;
      when SQLSTATE = SUCCESSFUL;
          processRow();
      when SQLSTATE = NO_ROW;
          processNoROW();
      when SQLSTATE = NOT_FOUND;
          processNotFound();
      when SQLSTATE = DUPLICATE_KEY;
          processDupKey();
      when %Subst(SQLSTATE : 1 : 2 ) = '01';
          processWarning();
      other;
          processSQLError();
  endSL;
 /end-free
P monitorSQL       E
```

FIGURE 11-8    **RPGLE error-handling procedure for embedded SQL**

## SELECT INTO STATEMENT

The SELECT INTO statement retrieves a single row into host variables. As mentioned, host variables are program variables that are preceded by a colon (:) and used in embedded SQL statements. The SELECT statement is an embedded statement within the RPGLE program that specifies the query that retrieves data from the database table. The column list following the SELECT keyword determines which columns from the database table are returned to the result set. The SELECT statement shown in Figure 11-9 selects the first_name, last_name, hourly_rate, and commission_pct columns from the EMPLOYEES database table. The order in which the columns are specified will be the order in which they are returned. As many columns as necessary can be selected from the database table, or an asterisk (*) can be used to select all columns. The table name specified in the FROM clause identifies the database table that is queried to retrieve the desired result set.

The WHERE clause includes the selection criteria used by the SELECT statement to determine which row is returned from the database table. The employeeID host variable is used in the WHERE clause to retrieve the required employee row from the EMPLOYEES table. The value in employee_id must be equal to the value in employeeID for the row to be returned. Once the row is retrieved, the data values are placed into the host variables firstName, lastName, hourlyRate, and commPct.

```
D emp            E DS
D  employeeID    S              10I 0 inz
D  firstName     S              20    inz varying
D  lastNname     S              20    inz varying
D  hourlyRate    S               5P 2 inz
D  commPct       S               3P 3 inz

  employeeID = 10101;

  EXEC SQL
  SELECT   first_name,  last_name,  hourly_rate, commission_pct
    INTO :firstName,  :lastName,  :hourlyRate,  commPct
    FROM   employees
    WHERE employee_id = :employeeID;
```

FIGURE 11-9   A SELECT INTO statement in a program

In addition to the FROM, WHERE, GROUP BY, HAVING, and ORDER BY clauses, a SELECT INTO statement has an INTO clause that follows the list of columns in the result set. The INTO clause must list one host variable, and optionally a null indicator variable, for each column in the column select list. When the SELECT INTO statement is executed, the result set must have only one row. If exactly one row is retrieved, its column values are assigned to the corresponding host variables listed in the INTO clause. If no row is retrieved, an SQL exception code is returned that indicates that no row was returned and the values in the host variables are undefined. If the result set contains two or more rows, a different SQL exception code is returned.

In addition to retrieving a single row by supplying its primary key value, as in the preceding example, another standard use of the SELECT INTO statement is to retrieve the count, average, and so on of a set of rows using a column function. The statement in Figure 11-10 retrieves the average discount for all customers into the avgDisc host variable. This SELECT INTO statement retrieves one row with one column.

```
D avgDisc              S              5P 3

  EXEC SQL
    SELECT AVG( discount )
      INTO :avgDisc
      FROM customers;
```

FIGURE 11-10  Using SELECT INTO to retrieve an average

### EXTERNAL DATA STRUCTURE

An **external data structure** provides a method of defining host variables within the program without having to define each column separately. As a result, each column from the database table becomes a subfield within the data structure.

Let us consider the example in Figure 11-11. For this example, assume that the EMPLOYEES table was created with the column names emp_id, first_name, last_name, m_initial, store_id, dept_id, hour_rate, and comm_pct. The data structure called EMP is based on the definition of the external EMPLOYEES database table where all of the columns of the EMPLOYEES table are defined as subfields within the EMP data structure. The SELECT INTO statement retrieves the values from the EMPLOYEES table for the stated columns and places the values into the host variables first_name, last_name, hour_rate, and comm_pct that are subfields within the external data structure.

```
D emp             E DS                    extName(employees)

  emp.emp_id = 10101;

  EXEC SQL
  SELECT   first_name,  last_name,  hour_rate,  comm_pct
    INTO   :first_name, :last_name, :hour_rate, :comm_pct
    FROM   employees
    WHERE  emp_id = :emp.emp_id;
```

FIGURE 11-11  Example of external data structure

### QUALIFYING AN EXTERNAL DATA STRUCTURE

As you can see in Figure 11-11, the names on the column list on the SELECT statement are the same names as the host variables that are subfields in the external data structure. The reason for this is that the values are being retrieved from the columns in the EMPLOYEES table and placed into the data structure subfields that are based on the column names in the EMPLOYEES table. To solve this confusion, the external data structure is QUALIFIED as shown in Figure 11-12.

```
D emp             E DS                    extName(employees) qualified

  emp.emp_id = 10101;

  EXEC SQL
  SELECT   first_name,  last_name,  hour_rate,  comm_pct
    INTO   :emp.first_name, :emp.last_name,
           :emp.hour_rate,  :emp.comm_pct
    FROM   employees
    WHERE  emp_id = :emp.emp_id;
```

FIGURE 11-12  Example of a qualified external data structure

Normally, the fields within the data structure are referenced using their simple name—that is, first_name, hour_rate, and so on. A **qualified data structure** further defines the subfields by the name of the data structure. For example, first_name becomes emp.first_name, hour_rate becomes emp.hour_rate, and so on. As a result, the names on the column list of the SELECT statement are distinguished from the host variable names, making the code must easier to understand.

However, the EMPLOYEES table being used in this book contains SQL column names that are longer than acceptable by RPGLE. For example, the column names in the EMPLOYEES table for hourly rate and commission percent are hourly_rate and commission_pct. To use the longer column names, the ALIAS keyword is used.

## ALIAS KEYWORD

In many cases, database tables created from the CREATE TABLE command contain column names longer than allowed by RPGLE. The **ALIAS keyword** on the external data structure definition allows the use of these longer SQL column names in embedded SQL programs.

Consider the example in Figure 11-13. This example illustrates a SELECT INTO statement where the values of first_name, last_name, hourly_rate, and commission_pct are retrieved from the EMPLOYEES table and are placed into the host variables :emp.first_name, :emp.last_name, :emp.hourly_rate, and :emp.commission_pct. Some of the host variable names are longer than allowed by RPGLE. The ALIAS keyword on the external data structure permits the use of the longer SQL column names in the embedded SQL.

```
D emp            E DS                    extName(employees) qualified alias

  emp.employee_id = 10101;

  EXEC SQL
  SELECT   first_name,  last_name,  hourly_rate,  commission_pct
    INTO   :emp.first_name,  :emp.last_name,
           :emp.hourly_rate, :emp.commission_pct
    FROM   employees
    WHERE  employee_id = :emp.employee_id;
```

FIGURE 11-13  Example of the ALIAS keyword

## INSERT STATEMENT

The **INSERT statement** inserts or adds a new row to a database table. This statement requires three values:

- The name of the table.
- The names of the columns in the table to be populated. These names are listed explicitly or implicitly.
- Corresponding values for the columns that are being populated.

Figure 11-14 provides an example of an embedded INSERT statement that uses explicit column names because not all of the columns are being inserted. In Figure 11-15, the embedded INSERT statement uses implicit column names and inserts data for all columns.

Inserting a row into a view also inserts the row into the table on which the view is based, if no INSTEAD OF trigger is defined for the insert operation on this view. If such a trigger is defined, the trigger will be executed instead.

```
D emp            E DS                    extName(employees) qualified alias

   EXEC SQL
      INSERT INTO employees
         ( employee_id,
           hourly_rate,
           commission_pct )
        VALUES
          ( :emp.employee_id,
            :emp.hourly_rate,
            :emp.commission_pct );
```

FIGURE 11-14  Example of an embedded INSERT statement with explicit column names

```
D emp            E DS                    extName(employees) qualified alias

   EXEC SQL
      INSERT INTO employees VALUES
         ( :emp.employee_id,
           :emp.store_id,
           :emp_first_name,
           :emp_m_Initial,
           :emp_last_name,
           :emp_hire_date,
           :emp_department_id,
           :emp_hourly_rate,
           :emp_commission_pct );
```

FIGURE 11-15  Example of an embedded INSERT statement with implicit column names

## UPDATE STATEMENT

The **UPDATE statement** modifies existing rows in a database table. It requires four values:

- The name of the table
- The name of the column(s) whose values will be modified
- A new value for each column(s) being modified
- A condition that identifies which rows in the table will be modified

An UPDATE statement that contains a WHERE clause for a search condition will search for the rows to be updated. A specific row can be updated by using its primary key value in the WHERE clause of an UPDATE statement and assigning new values to one or more columns. The UPDATE statement in Figure 11-16 increases the hourly rate by 2 percent and adds 2.5 percent to the commission percent.

```
D emp            E DS                    extName(employees) qualified alias
D rateInc        S            3P 2 inz
D commInc        S            3P 3 inz

  emp.employeeID = 10101;
  rateInc = 1.02;
  commInc = .025;
  EXEC SQL
      UPDATE employees
          SET hourly_rate     = hourly_rate * rateInc,
              commission_pct = commission_pct + commInc
          WHERE employee_id   = emp.employeeId;
```

FIGURE 11-16   Example of updating a row using its primary key value in the WHERE clause

A *set* of rows can be updated by using a search condition that specifies a group of rows in the WHERE clause. For example, in Figure 11-17, all employees that work at store 5003 are given a 2 percent raise.

```
D emp             E DS                        extName(employees) qualified alias
D rateInc           S             3P 2 inz

   emp.store_id = 5003;
   rateInc = 1.02;

   EXEC SQL
       UPDATE employees
           SET hourly_rate = hourly_rate * rateInc,
           WHERE store_id  = emp.store_id;
```

**FIGURE 11-17** Example of updating a group of rows with the WHERE clause

An UPDATE statement that does not contain a WHERE clause will update all rows in the database table. For example, in Figure 11-18, all employees in the EMPLOYEES table have their hourly rate increased by 2 percent.

```
D emp             E DS                        extName(employees) qualified alias
D rateInc           S             3P 2 inz

   rateInc = 1.02;

   EXEC SQL
       UPDATE employees
           SET hourly_rate = hourly_rate * rateInc;
```

**FIGURE 11-18** Example of updating all rows in the database table

## DELETE STATEMENT

The **DELETE statement** removes a row from a table. The statement requires two values:

- The name of the table
- The condition that identifies the rows to be deleted

In Figure 11-19, the DELETE statement deletes a row from the EMPLOYEES table with an employee_id (primary key) value of 10199. If no row exists with the specified employee_id, a no-row-found exception code is returned.

```
D emp            E DS                 extName(employees) qualified alias

   emp.employeeID = 10199;

   EXEC SQL
      DELETE from employees
         WHERE employee_id  = emp.employee_id;
```

FIGURE 11-19  Example of the DELETE statement to delete one row from a table

A set of rows can be deleted from a single table using a search condition that specifies more than one row. For example, if the company closed store 5003 and wanted to delete all the employees for that store, the statement in Figure 11-20 could be used. If no rows exist with the specified store_id, a no-row-found exception code is returned.

```
D emp            E DS                 extName(employees) qualified alias

   emp.store_id = 5003;

   EXEC SQL
      DELETE from employees
         WHERE store_id = emp.store_id;
```

FIGURE 11-20  Example of the DELETE statement to delete a set of rows from a table

All rows in a table can be cleared, intentionally or accidentally, by entering the DELETE statement in Figure 11-21 with no WHERE clause. Note that after all rows are cleared from a table, the table still exists; it is just an empty table. To clear and delete a table, the DROP statement should be used.

```
EXEC SQL
   DELETE from employees;
```

FIGURE 11-21  Example of a DELETE statement to delete all rows in a database table

## NULL VALUES

RPGLE variables cannot be null. To handle null values, SQL uses **null indicators**, which are two-byte (five-digit) integer variables that contain zero (0) or negative one (-1). Zero indicates a non-null value, and negative one indicates a null value.

### NULL INDICATORS

For the example in Figure 11-22, `commission_pct` is defined in the EMPLOYEES table as a null-capable column. Since RPGLE cannot recognize null, a null indicator called `commPctNull` is placed after `commission_pct` in the INTO clause. Both the data variable `commission_pct` and the null indicator `commPctNull` are prefixed with colons, as they are both host variables in the embedded SELECT INTO statement. In addition, there is no comma separating these two host variables. There can be a space between the host variable and null indicator, or they can be joined with no space.

```
D emp             E DS                     extName(employees) qualified alias
D commPctNull     S              5I 0 inz
  .
  .
  .
  EXEC SQL
  SELECT  first_name, last_name, hourly_rate, commission_pct
    INTO  :emp.first_name, :emp.last_name, :emp.hourly_rate,
          :emp.commission_pct:commPctNull
    FROM  employees
    WHERE employee_id = :emp.employee_id;
```

**FIGURE 11-22** Example of a NULL indicator

If the `commission_pct` column in the row that is retrieved is NULL, the corresponding null indicator, `commPctNull` is set to NULL (−1). If a column is non-null (i.e., has a valid value), the corresponding null indicator variable is set to 0. On a SELECT INTO statement, a null indicator variable should always be specified for a null-capable column because if no indicator variable is specified and the column is null, an exception occurs and an exception code is returned.

## USING AN ARRAY FOR NULL INDICATORS

If a data structure is used instead of individual variables, a null indicator array can be used to determine whether a variable is NULL or not. If a SELECT INTO statement is used to retrieve the column list into a data structure, each column from the database table becomes a subfield in the data structure. In this situation, an array of null indicators can be used to handle the null-capable subfields in the data structure. The array must have the same number of elements as the total number of columns in the external database table, even if all the columns do not support nulls. Each individual array element can be tested to determine whether a column returned is null or not.

In Figure 11-23, the array nullInds is defined as nine elements because there are nine columns in the EMPLOYEES table. In this case, only commission_pct, which is the ninth column and thus the ninth subfield in the data structure subfield, is null-capable. Thus, by referring to nullInds(9), commission_pct is being testing to determine whether it is null.

```
D emp            E DS                  extName(employees) qualified alias

D nullInds       S            5I 0 dim(9)
D NULL           C                 'null'
D NULL_VALUE     C                 const(-1)
D commPctValue   S            16A  inz varying

  EXEC SQL
  SELECT  * INTO :emp:nullInds
    FROM  employees
    WHERE employee_id = :emp.employee_id;

  if nullInds(9) = NULL_VALUE;
    commPctValue = NULL;
  else;
    commPctValue = %editW(emp.commission_pct:'0 .   ');
  endIf;
```

FIGURE 11-23  SQL1207.rpgle

## CODING SUGGESTIONS

- Always check SQLSTATE after each executable SQL statement to check for exceptions. Use standard error-handling routines to handle exceptions.

- In general, declare host variables so that they have the same data type and size as any column with which they are used.

- Use an INCLUDE, /COPY, or COPY to include commonly used declarations, SQL source code, or RPGLE source code in programs. Remember that the INCLUDE statement and RPGLE /COPY compiler directive include a source member during precompilation.

- For a search condition that is used in multiple embedded SQL statements within the same or multiple programs, consider creating a view and referencing that view in embedded SQL statements rather than repeating the search condition in multiple statements.

- As an alternative to using an explicit select list (i.e., a list of columns) that is used by multiple SELECT INTO statements, consider creating a view with the subset of columns used in these SELECT INTO statements. The SELECT INTO statements can then use an implicit select list, one that specifies * to select all columns, while specifying the view in the FROM clause.

- For any SQL statement executed in more than one place in a program, place the statement in a procedure or service program and execute that routine rather than coding the statement multiple times in the program.

- For any SQL statement that is used in multiple programs, consider putting the statement in a source member by itself and using an INCLUDE statement to include it during the precompilation phase.

- Never use a SELECT INTO statement with a search condition that might be satisfied by more than one row. In general, use SELECT INTO only to retrieve individual rows by primary or unique key or to retrieve column functions (without a GROUP BY clause).

- In a SELECT INTO statement, always use an indicator variable for null-capable columns.

- List only the columns you need to retrieve on a SELECT INTO statement.

## END-OF-CHAPTER

### CHAPTER SUMMARY

1. Embedded SQL statements are SQL statements coded in programs.
2. Each embedded statement begins with the precompiler directive EXEC SQL and ends with a semicolon. The SQL precompiler translates embedded SQL statements into RPGLE source code, which the RPGLE compiler then compiles.
3. Host variables can be used in embedded SQL statements.
4. Host variables:

   a. A host variable can be used to supply a value in a search condition or expression in the select column list.

   b. A host variable can also receive data returned by a SELECT INTO statement or can provide a value to be assigned to a column on an UPDATE or INSERT statement.

   c. Wherever a host variable is used, it can be followed by a null indicator variable, which is used to handle columns that are null (on the SELECT INTO statement) or that should be set to null (on the UPDATE and INSERT statements).

5. Static statements:

   a. Static statements have a fixed structure and can use host variables to supply new column values and search condition values.

   b. The SELECT INTO statement is the static form of the SELECT statement and can retrieve a single row's values into host variables.

   c. Static SELECT, UPDATE, and DELETE statements specify a search condition on a table's primary or unique key to provide direct access by key for input and update operations.

   d. The static INSERT statement provides a way to add new rows to a table.

6. The SQL communication area (SQLCA) provides a set of variables that provide completion and diagnostic feedback to the program after an SQL statement is executed. The SQLSTATE variable is the most important element of the SQLCA and indicates the completion status of the most recent statement.

7. After execution of every SQL statement, the SQLSTATE variable, and in some cases other variables that are part of the SQLCA, is set.

8. A program should always check SQLSTATE after each SQL statement.

9. The INCLUDE statement lets a program include external source statements during the precompile phase.
10. A null indicator variable should be specified for every null-capable column.

## KEY TERMS

| | |
|---|---|
| ALIAS keyword | precompiler directive |
| DELETE statement | qualified data structure |
| embedded SQL statement | SQL communication area (SQLCA) |
| external data structure | SQLSTATE |
| host variable | static statement |
| INSERT statement | UPDATE statement |
| null indicator | |

# CHAPTER 12
## SQL CURSORS

## CHAPTER OBJECTIVES

Upon completion of this chapter, you should be able to

- Explain the basic elements of SQL cursors
- Explain the different clauses that can be specified when defining cursors
- Use static and dynamic cursors

## BASIC ELEMENTS OF SQL CURSORS

SQL is excellent for processing groups of rows from a database table. For example, an UPDATE statement can be used to update several rows of data within a table at the same time. However, there are times when it is necessary to loop through a group of rows and perform some type of processing on each individual row. For this type of row-at-a-time processing, a cursor is used.

### CURSOR

A **cursor** is a technique whereby a temporary result set—a set of data rows—is created from a database and processed one row at a time. A cursor can be considered as a pointer that points to one row in a group of rows. The cursor is used to access only one row at a time, but it can be moved to other rows throughout the result set as needed.

### RESULT SET

A result set is required to process a group of rows with a cursor. A **result set** is a set of rows and columns from one or more database tables that were retrieved based on the criteria in a SELECT statement.

Let us consider a SELECT statement that could be used to build a cursor in a program. In Example 1, Figure 12-1, the SELECT statement returns a result set containing first_name, last_name, hire_date, and hourly_rate for employees in the EMPLOYEES table who work at store_id = 2257 and department_id = 222. If this SELECT statement were included in a cursor declaration in a program, the cursor would contain the result set determined by the SELECT statement.

---

**Example 1:**

Return a result set containing the first_name, last_name, hire_date, and hourly_rate for all employees working at store number 2257 in department 222 from the EMPLOYEES table. Order the result set by hire_date DESC, last_name, and first_name.

```
SELECT     first_name, last_name, hire_date, hourly_rate
  FROM     employees
  WHERE    store_id = 2257 AND department_id = 222
  ORDER BY hire_date DESC, last_name, first_name;
```

**Results:**

```
FIRST_NAME              LAST_NAME               HIRE_DATE HOURLY_RATE
--------------------    --------------------    --------- -----------
Jim                     Wellington              05/23/99      17.50
Albert                  Poole                   02/22/99      22.00
Henryo                  Anderson                02/15/97      24.75
Kelly                   Charrette               07/22/96      21.25
Anne                    Castle                  06/24/94      23.50
```

---

FIGURE 12-1    Example of a result set from a SELECT statement

## DEFINING AND USING A CURSOR

There are four steps when using a cursor in a program. They are:

1. Declare the cursor.
2. Open the cursor.
3. Fetch rows from the cursor.
4. Close the cursor.

Let us examine each step that is required when using a cursor in a program.

## STEP 1: DECLARE CURSOR

The DECLARE CURSOR statement in Figure 12-2 is a declaration statement, not an executable statement that declares an SQL cursor. The DECLARE keyword is followed by the cursor name cursor1. Following the FOR keyword, a SELECT statement is specified. This SELECT statement can include all the SELECT clauses, including FROM, WHERE, GROUP BY, HAVING, and ORDER BY, as well as the UNION operator; several other optional clauses are covered later. Because a cursor is defined with a SELECT statement, it can specify row selection, derived columns, and aggregation, such as the SUM column function, union, and other data manipulations.

SQL statements used in a program must be identified or delimited so the SQL precompiler can process them. SQL statements begin with EXEC SQL and end with a semicolon ( ; ).

```
EXEC SQL
 DECLARE  cursor1 CURSOR FOR
   SELECT first_name, last_name, hire_date, hourly_rate
   FROM   employees;
```

FIGURE 12-2    Example of a simple DECLARE CURSOR statement with SELECT statement

### SELECT STATEMENT

The DECLARE CURSOR statement includes a nested SELECT statement to specify the table(s) and/or view(s) that are accessed when the cursor is opened. The SELECT statement specifies the query used to retrieve data from the database table and create a result set. The column list following the SELECT keyword determines which columns from the database table(s) are returned in the result set.

No processing takes place with the DECLARE CURSOR statement. It simply defines the cursor that contains the result set containing rows and columns similar to the database tables from which the data is retrieved. In Figure 12-2, the DECLARE CURSOR statement defines a cursor called cursor1 and selects the first_name, last_name, hire_date, and hourly_rate columns from the EMPLOYEES table specified in the FROM clause. The order of the column list will determine the order in which columns are returned in the result set. As many columns as needed can be selected from the database table, or an asterisk (*) can be used to select all columns.

### WHERE CLAUSE

The WHERE clause in Figure 12-3 includes the selection criteria used by the SELECT statement to determine which rows are returned from the database table. If the WHERE clause is not specified, all rows are returned in the result set.

```
EXEC SQL
  DECLARE     cursor1 CURSOR FOR
    SELECT    first_name, last_name, hire_date, hourly_rate
      FROM    employees
     WHERE    store_id = 2257 AND department_id = 222;
```

**FIGURE 12-3** **Example of a DECLARE CURSOR statement with WHERE clause**

In this example, there are two comparisons linked together by the AND connector. The AND connector means that both comparisons must be true before a row is selected and returned. The WHERE clause compares the store_id column to a value of 2257 and the department_id column to a value of 222. If both comparisons are true, the row is returned from the EMPLOYEES table into the result set.

Hardcoding values in the WHERE clause makes the application impractical. Every time a user would want to select a different store or department, the program would have to be changed and recompiled. To solve this problem, host variables are used.

## USING HOST VARIABLES IN THE WHERE CLAUSE

In Figure 12-4, the variables emp.store_id and emp.department_id are used in place of the values 2257 and 222, respectively. The emp.store_id and emp.department_id variables are called **host variables** because they are variables defined in the host application in which the SQL is being executed. Host variables specified within SQL statements must be preceded by a colon (:).

In Figure 12-4, the EMPLOYEES table is specified as an external data structure called EMP. The variables in this data structure are qualified, as indicated by the QUALIFIED keyword. As a result, the two host variables, store_id and department_id, are qualified with the data structure name EMP as emp.store_id and emp.department_id.

A cursor's SELECT statement can include host variable references in the WHERE clause, providing the ability to determine the selection criteria for rows when the cursor is opened rather than when the program is created. These host variables are evaluated only when the cursor is opened.

When the SELECT statement is executed, the WHERE clause compares the store_id and department_id columns from the EMPLOYEES database table against the emp.store_id and emp.department_id host variables containing the selections made by the user. The values in the store_id and department_id columns must be equal to the host variables `emp.store_id` and `emp.department_id` for the row to be returned.

```
D emp              E DS                    extName(employees) qualified alias

  EXEC SQL
  DECLARE     cursor1 CURSOR FOR
    SELECT    first_name, last_name, hire_date, hourly_rate
    FROM      employees
    WHERE     store_id = :emp.store_id AND
              department_id = :emp.department_id;
```

**FIGURE 12-4**    Example of host variables in the **WHERE** clause

The `emp.store_id` and `emp.department_id` are host variables used in the search condition of the cursor's `SELECT` statement. If `emp.store_id` contains the value `1111` when the cursor is opened, subsequent `FETCH` operations retrieve only customers with a `store_id` value of `1111`. Host variables used in a cursor declaration are evaluated only when the `OPEN` statement opens the cursor; changing the value of a host variable has no effect on the cursor until the cursor is closed and reopened. By closing and reopening a cursor, the same cursor can be used to retrieve different sets of rows, such as store number `1111` and then store number `8888`, in the same program execution.

## ORDER BY CLAUSE

The `ORDER BY` clause in Figure 12-5 is used to sort the result set. In this example, the result set is sorted in `hire_date` (major sort), `last_name` (intermediate sort), and `first_name` (minor sort) sequence. In addition, `hire_date` is sorted in descending (DESC) order.

```
EXEC SQL
DECLARE cursor1 CURSOR FOR
    SELECT  first_name, last_name, hire_date, hourly_rate
    FROM    employees
    WHERE store_id = :emp.store_id AND
           department_id = :emp.department_id
    ORDER BY hire_date DESC, last_name, first_name;
```

**FIGURE 12-5**    Example of a **DECLARE CURSOR** statement with an **ORDER BY** clause

## STEP 2: OPEN STATEMENT

Cursors must be opened before they can be accessed. Only when an SQL OPEN statement is executed is the cursor opened. The OPEN statement has the following simple syntax

```
OPEN cursor-name
```

where *cursor-name* is the name specified on a DECLARE CURSOR statement.

A cursor must currently be closed when the OPEN statement is executed. As noted earlier, the cursor's SELECT statement, including any host variables, is evaluated when the OPEN statement is executed. If the OPEN is successful, the cursor is positioned before the first row in the result set. If the result set is empty, the cursor is effectively positioned after the last row. In this case, the first FETCH operation will fail with a "no row" condition.

The OPEN statement in Figure 12-6 allocates memory for the cursor1 cursor and performs any other housekeeping tasks depending on how the cursor is being used. The OPEN statement executes the SELECT statement for the DECLARE CURSOR. If necessary, the OPEN statement builds an access path. Once the access path is established, the result set is created based on the selection criteria.

```
EXEC SQL
    OPEN cursor1;
```

**FIGURE 12-6**    Example of an OPEN cursor statement

When the OPEN statement is executed, the values in the host variables emp.store_id and emp.department_id are used in the search condition of the cursor's SELECT statement.

## STEP 3: FETCH STATEMENT

The FETCH statement provides two capabilities: setting the position of the cursor for subsequent input or update operations and reading one or more rows into host variables. There are several variations of the FETCH statement, providing forward and backward positioning and input operations. This chapter covers only single-row input.

In Figure 12-7, the FETCH NEXT statement retrieves the next row (one row) from the cursor1 cursor and populates the host variables emp.first_name, emp.last_name, emp.hire_date, and emp.hourly_rate.

```
D emp            E DS                    extName(employees) qualified alias

  EXEC SQL
    FETCH NEXT
        FROM cursor1
        INTO :emp.first_name,
             :emp.last_name,
             :emp.hire_date,
             :emp.hourly_rate;
```

FIGURE 12-7    Fetching the next row from the cursor

The SELECT statement identifies the rows that contain the column values the program wants. However, SQL does not retrieve any data until the FETCH statement is issued. When the program retrieves data, the values are placed into the host variables specified with the INTO clause.

## STEP 4: CLOSE STATEMENT

The statement to close a cursor is

```
CLOSE cursor-name
```

A cursor must be open when the CLOSE statement is executed. Once the selected rows have been processed, the cursor should be closed. Cursors are closed automatically under certain conditions, but it is recommended that the cursor be closed when processing is finished. In Figure 12-8, the cursor cursor1 is closed.

```
EXEC SQL
  CLOSE cursor1;
```

FIGURE 12-8    Example of CLOSE cursor statement

## USING CLAUSES WITH THE CURSOR DECLARATION

There are several clauses that can be specified when a cursor is declared. The most common clauses are discussed in this section.

### FOR READ ONLY CLAUSE

If the FOR READ ONLY clause is added to the cursor's SELECT statement as shown in Figure 12-9, the cursor is read-only.

It is good practice to declare read-only cursors explicitly with the FOR READ ONLY clause because doing so provides better documentation and can sometimes improve performance.

```
EXEC SQL
DECLARE     cursor1 CURSOR FOR
    SELECT  first_name, last_name, hire_date, hourly_rate
    FROM    employees
    WHERE   store_id = :emp.store_id AND
            department_id = :emp.department_id
    ORDER BY hire_date DESC, last_name, first_name
    FOR READ ONLY;
```

**FIGURE 12-9**   Example of the **FOR READ ONLY** clause

### FOR UPDATE OF CLAUSE

To enable the use of a cursor for update operations, a FOR UPDATE OF clause is added to the cursor's SELECT statement as shown in Figure 12-10. In this example, a cursor is declared that allows updates of a customer's city and discount.

```
EXEC SQL
  DECLARE CustomerCursor CURSOR
    FOR SELECT *
        FROM customers
        FOR UPDATE OF ship_city, discount;
```

**FIGURE 12-10**   Example of the **FOR UPDATE OF** clause

The FOR UPDATE OF keywords are followed by a list of one or more columns that will be referenced in the SET clause of a subsequent UPDATE statement. Each column specified in the FOR UPDATE OF clause must belong to the table or view named in the FROM clause of the SELECT statement, although the columns listed in the FOR UPDATE OF clause do not need to be specified in the SELECT statement. No column may be named more than once in the FOR UPDATE OF clause. Column names in the FOR UPDATE OF clause may not be qualified by the name of the table or view; they are implicitly qualified by the table reference in the FROM clause of the select specification.

If the FOR UPDATE OF clause is specified without any columns, all updatable columns in the cursor's table or view are updatable. A column listed in the FOR UPDATE OF clause does not have to be included in the select list. That is, a column can be updated even if it is not in the result set defined by the cursor's SELECT statement.

If the cursor is used for DELETE operations but not for UPDATE operations, the FOR UPDATE OF clause should not be specified. As long as the cursor meets the requirements for an updatable cursor and the program contains a DELETE statement that references the cursor, the cursor is opened as a delete-capable cursor. Specifying a FOR UPDATE OF clause may hurt performance and will cause a cursor-open error if the user does not have update privileges to the table.

For an updatable cursor without a FOR UPDATE OF clause, a subsequent UPDATE statement can reference any updatable column, which means any column not derived using an expression, constant, or function. Limiting the columns that can be updated through a cursor provides some protection against coding mistakes and can also improve performance.

If the cursor's SELECT statement includes an ORDER BY clause and the cursor will be used for updates, the cursor's SELECT statement must specify a FOR UPDATE OF clause that does not include any of the columns listed in the ORDER BY clause. The example in Figure 12-11 provides a valid ORDER BY clause.

```
EXEC SQL
  DECLARE CustomerCursor CURSOR
    FOR SELECT *
          FROM customers
          ORDER BY customer_id
          FOR UPDATE OF ship_city, discount;
```

FIGURE 12-11  Using the ORDER BY clause with the FOR UPDATE OF clause

If there is no FOR READ ONLY or FOR UPDATE OF clause specified and the cursor satisfies the restrictions on updatable cursors, the cursor is opened as an updatable cursor if the program contains an UPDATE or DELETE statement that references the cursor or if it contains an EXECUTE or EXECUTE IMMEDIATE statement. It is much better, however, to explicitly code the FOR READ ONLY or FOR UPDATE OF clause so as not to rely on the default open mode. This practice also avoids unintentionally changing the nature of a cursor when the SQL statements are revised in a program.

## INSENSITIVE CLAUSE

Specifying INSENSITIVE in the cursor declaration guarantees that once the cursor is open, its result set remains unchanged until the cursor is closed. The DBMS insulates the result set by creating a temporary table with a copy of the result set data.

After the cursor declared in Figure 12-12 is opened, any insert, delete, or update operations to the CUSTOMERS table will not be reflected in the cursor's result set. A cursor specified with INSENSITIVE must be read-only, and therefore the FOR UPDATE OF clause cannot be specified. For documentation purposes, it is a good practice to specify an explicit FOR READ ONLY clause when the INSENSITIVE keyword is used. Also, the CrtSqlxxx command that is used to create the program must specify ALWCPYDTA(*OPTIMIZE) or ALWCPYDTA(*YES) to permit the DBMS to copy the result set data.

```
EXEC SQL
  DECLARE CustomerCursor INSENSITIVE CURSOR
    FOR SELECT customer_id, customer_name, discount
      FROM customers
      ORDER BY customer_name
    FOR READ ONLY;
```

FIGURE 12-12  Example of INSENSITIVE clause

## WITH HOLD CLAUSE

When a commitment control environment is active, cursor declarations should specify a WITH HOLD clause so that the cursor remains open when a COMMIT or ROLLBACK statement that lacks a WITH HOLD clause is executed. The WITH HOLD clause follows the CURSOR keyword, as shown in Figure 12-13.

```
EXEC SQL
  DECLARE CustomerCursor CURSOR
    WITH HOLD
    FOR SELECT        *
            FROM        customers
            ORDER BY    customer_id
            FOR UPDATE OF ship_city, discount;
```

FIGURE 12-13  Example of WITH HOLD clause

## OPTIMIZE CLAUSE

The OPTIMIZE clause can be used to improve performance when a small number of rows at a time are being processed from a result set. For example, consider a Web application in which only 20 rows are presented to the browser. The statement in Figure 12-14, which produces a cursor consisting of Atlanta customers, is optimized to retrieve the first 20 rows as quickly as possible.

```
EXEC SQL
  DECLARE CustomerCursor CURSOR
    FOR SELECT  *
            FROM customers
            WHERE ship_city = 'Atlanta'
            FOR READ ONLY
            OPTIMIZE FOR 20 ROWS;
```

FIGURE 12-14  Example of OPTIMIZE clause

The OPTIMIZE clause can also specify the number of rows to optimize as a host variable, as Figure 12-15 shows. Here, the host variable NbrRows contains the value for the number of rows to optimize.

```
EXEC SQL
  DECLARE CustomerCursor CURSOR
    FOR SELECT *
            FROM customers
            WHERE ship_city = 'Atlanta'
            FOR READ ONLY
            OPTIMIZE FOR :NbrRows ROWS;
```

FIGURE 12-15  Example of OPTIMIZE clause using a host variable

## READING BY KEY VALUE

A common sequence of operations is to position to the first row in a result set using a common partial key value, such as the first order in the set of orders for a customer, and then read (fetch) sequentially by full key through the set. In SQL, this type of task normally is implemented by repeated cursor open/close operations, with each cursor open selecting the desired subset based on host variable values, such as customer number. For example, in Figure 12-16 the cursor accesses, in order number sequence, only those ORDERS table rows for a particular customer.

```
D cus            E DS                    extName(customers) qualified alias

   EXEC SQL
     DECLARE OrderCursor CURSOR
       FOR SELECT    *
              FROM     orders
              WHERE    customer_id = :cus.customer_id
              ORDER BY order_id
              FOR READ ONLY;
```

FIGURE 12-16  **Reading by key value**

Before the cursor is opened, the appropriate customer number must be assigned to the cus.customer_id host variable.

## SCROLLABLE CURSORS

In addition to the NEXT keyword of the FETCH statement, any of the alternatives listed in Figure 12-17 can be specified if the SCROLL or DYNAMIC SCROLL option is added to the cursor declaration.

The example in Figure 12-18 shows the required DECLARE CURSOR and FETCH statements to read backward and retrieve the row prior to the current row.

| Keyword | Positions cursor |
|---|---|
| NEXT | On the next row after the current row |
| PRIOR | On the row before the current row |
| FIRST | On the first row |
| LAST | On the last row |
| BEFORE | Before the first row |
| AFTER | After the last row |
| CURRENT | On the current row (no change in position) |
| Relative n | $n < -1$     On the $n$th row before current<br>$n = -1$     Same as PRIOR keyword<br>$n = 0$     Same as CURRENT keyword<br>$n = 1$     Same as NEXT keyword<br>$n > 1$     The $n$th row after current |

**FIGURE 12-17 FETCH statement positioning keywords**

```
D cus            E DS                    extName(customers) qualified alias

  EXEC SQL
    DECLARE CustomerCursor SCROLL CURSOR
      FOR SELECT customer_id, customer_name, ship_city
           FROM customers
           ORDER BY customer_id
           FOR READ ONLY;
     .
     .
     .
  EXEC SQL
    FETCH PRIOR
      FROM CustomerCursor
        INTO  :cus.customer_id, :cus.customer_name, :cus_ship_city;
```

**FIGURE 12-18 Example of the FETCH PRIOR statement**

The SCROLL and DYNAMIC SCROLL options define a **scrollable cursor**, which is a cursor that enables the use of several FETCH operations in addition to FETCH NEXT. The SCROLL option, specified without the DYNAMIC keyword, implicitly defines the cursor as a read-only cursor, and because the DBMS may make temporary copies of the result set, changes to a row in the table made by another program or another SQL statement in the same program may not be reflected immediately in the data retrieved by a FETCH. The DYNAMIC SCROLL option can be used with an updatable cursor, and, in most cases, a dynamic scrollable cursor does immediately reflect changes to a row made by another job or SQL statement.

## FETCH WITHOUT INTO CLAUSE

When FETCH is specified without an INTO clause, the operation positions the cursor but does not return any data. The INTO clause cannot be used with the BEFORE and AFTER positioning keywords and is optional with all other positioning keywords. The purpose of the BEFORE and AFTER options is to reset the cursor position to the beginning or end of the result set. The FETCH statement in Figure 12-19 positions, without retrieving any data, the cursor at the end of the cursor's result set such that a subsequent FETCH PRIOR statement would retrieve the last row in the cursor's result set.

```
EXEC SQL
  FETCH AFTER
    FROM CustomerCursor;
```

FIGURE 12-19   Example of FETCH statement without an INTO clause

## POSITIONED UPDATE AND DELETE STATEMENTS

A **positioned UPDATE** or a **positioned DELETE statement** can be used to update or delete the current row of an updatable cursor. A successful FETCH must be executed before a positioned UPDATE or DELETE statement. Instead of a WHERE clause that specifies a search condition, positioned UPDATE and DELETE statements use a WHERE clause with the syntax

```
WHERE CURRENT OF cursor-name
```

The example in Figure 12-20 shows a DECLARE CURSOR, FETCH, and subsequent positioned UPDATE statement.

Other than the WHERE clause, the syntax of positioned UPDATE and DELETE statements is the same as for searched UPDATE and DELETE statements. The cursor name is specified in the WHERE clause of a positioned UPDATE or DELETE statement, but the table or view name that is specified in the FROM clause of the cursor's SELECT statement is specified after the UPDATE or DELETE FROM keywords. Any columns that are assigned values in the SET clause must either be listed in a FOR UPDATE OF clause in the cursor's SELECT statement or be an updatable column included in the cursor's select list, if there is no FOR UPDATE OF clause specified.

```
D cus            E DS                    extName(customers) qualified alias

   EXEC SQL
      DECLARE customerCursor CURSOR
          FOR SELECT     customer_id,
                         customer_name,
                         discount
            FROM         customers
          ORDER BY       customer_id
          FOR UPDATE OF discount;
            .
            .
   EXEC SQL
      FETCH NEXT
          FROM   CustomerCursor
          INTO   :cus.customer_id,
                 :cus.customer_name,
                 :cus_discount;
         .
         .
   EXEC SQL
      UPDATE customers
          SET discount = :new_discount
          WHERE CURRENT OF customerCursor;
```

FIGURE 12-20  Example of positioned UPDATE statement

A positioned UPDATE does not change the cursor's position; the updated row remains the current row. However, if the cursor is declared with the DYNAMIC SCROLL option and has an ORDER BY clause, and an update by a different program or through a different cursor in the same program changes one of the current row's ORDER BY column values such that the relative position of the current row changes within the result set, a subsequent attempt to use FETCH CURRENT will fail.

A positioned DELETE changes the current position to before the row, if any, following the current row.

There is no cursor-related INSERT statement; the static INSERT provides the SQL mechanism to add new rows to a table regardless of whether a cursor is also opened for the table.

## WEB APPLICATION SQL1201

This section describes a sample application that uses a cursor to process multiple rows from a database table.

> **Note**
> This application does not illustrate the HTML or routines to communicate between the client and server because each environment is different. Visit the book's companion website to run this application and view the entire source code.

The human resource manager wants an application where she can select and display employees by store and department. In addition, she wants the list to be sorted into hire date, last name, and first name sequence.

When SQL1201.html is launched, the page in Figure 12-21 loads into the browser. It waits for the user to select either a store or a department from the dropdown lists. There are two dropdown lists: one for selecting the store and one for selecting a department within a store.

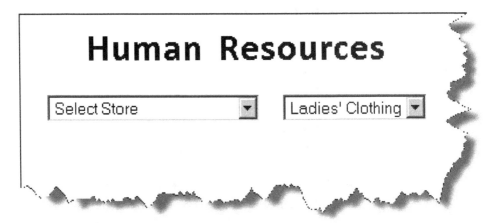

FIGURE 12-21  Initial output from SQL1201.html

Once the user selects *either* a store or a department, an AJAX request is made to the application server and program SQL1201.rpgle is executed. When a store is selected, an AJAX call is made using the selected store and the current department value. Likewise, if department is selected, an AJAX call is made using the selected department and the current value for store.

When the user selects a store or department, the program retrieves the required rows from the EMPLOYEES table and sends a JavaScript Object Notation (JSON) object to the browser, where the employee rows are displayed in the table grid. Figure 12-22 illustrates the results when store Chicago Michigan Ave (5003) and department Electronics (444) are selected. The rows are sorted by hire date, last name, and first name.

**Human Resources**

Chicago Michigan Ave ▾   Electronics        ▾

| Employee id | Store | Department | First name | Initial | Last name | Hire date | Hourly rate | Commission % |
|---|---|---|---|---|---|---|---|---|
| 10154 | 5003 | 444 | Alfred | L | Joseph | 06/23/2005 | 19.50 | 0.050 |
| 10158 | 5003 | 444 | Doug | W | Hardick | 06/19/2004 | 32.25 | 0.030 |
| 10112 | 5003 | 444 | James | | MacDonald | 06/01/1995 | 25.50 | 0.050 |

FIGURE 12-22   Output from SQL1201.html after AJAX call to program SQL1201.rpgle

The program uses the selected store and department and runs a query on the EMPLOYEES table. A cursor is created that includes all employee rows for those employees in the selected store and department. The program then processes the cursor to generate a JSON object that is returned to the browser.

Once the browser receives the response object containing JSON data, a jQuery loop is executed that generates an HTML table grid that is loaded into the browser.

Each row read from the JSON object is inserted into the HTML table grid. Although one of more rows appears in the HTML table, only *one* table row is defined in the HTML file. This single table row defines the first line of one or more identical lines to be displayed in the HTML table. As each row is read from the JSON object, a new row is inserted into the HTML table. Thus, the program uses the same table row repeatedly to build the HTML table that is rendered to the browser.

## PROGRAM SQL1201

Program SQL1201.rpgle in Figure 12-23 selects and processes multiple rows from the EMPLOYEES table depending on the store and department selected. The program's purpose is to build a cursor based on the store and department selected from the dropdown boxes. Once the cursor is built, it is used to build the JSON object that is returned to the browser.

When program `SQL1201.rpgle` executes, it performs the following steps:

1. Call procedure `getParms`, which retrieves the input data for store and department
2. Call procedure `declareCursor`:
   - `SELECT FROM` clause identifies the columns to be selected and the table being processed
   - `WHERE` clause uses host variables in the selection criteria
   - `ORDER BY` clause is used to sort the result set
   - `FOR READ ONLY` clause identifies this query as read-only
3. Call procedure `buildJson`:
   - Open cursor `cursor1`
   - Fetch the first row from the cursor
     - Monitor for no more rows condition (cursor empty)
   - Loop through the cursor processing one row at a time
     - *(Process row and build JSON object)*
     - Fetch next row and monitor for no-more-rows condition
   - *(Send the response object containing the JSON data to the browser)*
   - Close the cursor
4. Terminate the program:
   - Set `LR` to `*ON`
   - Return

Let us consider each step in more detail.

## DECLARECURSOR PROCEDURE

The `declareCursor` procedure in Figure 12-24 contains the `DECLARE CURSOR` statement that defines a cursor called `cursor1` that will hold the result set.

## SELECT STATEMENT

The `SELECT` statement is an SQL statement within the `DECLARE CURSOR` statement that specifies the query that retrieves data from the `EMPLOYEES` table and generates a result set.

```
H decedit('0.') datFmt(*USA)

D emp             E DS                    extName(employees) qualified alias
D totalRows         S           10U 0 inz
D rowStr            S           16384   inz varying
D comma             S               1   inz varying
D jsonData          S           16384   inz varying
D moreRows          S               N   Inz('1')
D YES               C                   Const('1')
D NO                C                   Const('0')

 /free

  getParms();
  declareCursor();
  buildJson();

  *INLR = *ON;
  return;
 /end-free

 //-----------------------------------------------------
P declareCursor    B
 /free
  EXEC SQL
    DECLARE      cursor1 CURSOR FOR
      SELECT     employee_id,
                 store_id,
                 first_name,
                 m_initial,
                 last_name,
                 hire_date,
                 department_id,
                 hourly_rate,
                 commission_pct
        FROM     employees
        WHERE    store_id = :emp.store_id AND
                 department_id = :emp.department_id
        ORDER BY hire_date DESC, last_name, first_name
        FOR READ ONLY;
 /end-free
P declareCursor    E

 //-----------------------------------------------------
P buildJson        B
 /free
  EXEC SQL OPEN cursor1;
  fetchNext();
  doW (moreRows = YES);
    .
    . (process row and build JSON object)
    .
    fetchNext();
  enddo;
```

*Continued*

```
    (Send JSON object to browser)

    EXEC SQL CLOSE cursor1;
  /end-free
P buildJson      E


  //-------------------------------------------------------
P fetchNext      B
 /free
   EXEC SQL
     FETCH NEXT
       FROM cursor1
       INTO :emp.employee_id,
            :emp.store_id,
            :emp.first_name,
            :emp.m_initial,
            :emp.last_name,
            :emp.hire_date,
            :emp.department_id,
            :emp.hourly_rate,
            :emp.commission_pct;
   monitorSQL();
 /end-free
P fetchNext      E


  //-------------------------------------------------------
P getParms       B
 /free
   (retrieve input parameters into emp.store_id and emp.department_id)
 /end-free
P getParms       E


  //-------------------------------------------------------
P monitorSQL     B
D SUCCESSFUL     C                   Const('00000')
D NO_ROW_FOUND   C                   Const('02000')

 /free
   select;
     when SQLSTATE = SUCCESSFUL;

     when SQLSTATE = NO_ROW_FOUND;
       moreRows = NO;
   endSL;
 /end-free
P monitorSQL     E
```

**FIGURE 12-23** `SQL1201.rpgle`

## WHERE Clause

The WHERE clause includes the selection criteria used by the SELECT statement to determine which rows are returned from the database table. When the SELECT statement is executed, the WHERE clause compares the store_id and department_id columns from the EMPLOYEES table with the

```
   P declareCursor    B
    /free
     EXEC SQL
       DECLARE      cursor1 CURSOR FOR
         SELECT     employee_id,
                    store_id,
                    first_name,
                    m_initial,
                    last_name,
                    hire_date,
                    department_id,
                    hourly_rate,
                    commission_pct
          FROM      employees
          WHERE     store_id = :emp.store_id AND
                    department_id = :emp.department_id
          ORDER BY hire_date DESC, last_name, first_name
          FOR READ ONLY;
    /end-free
   P declareCursor    E
```

FIGURE 12-24  **declareCursor** procedure

emp.store_id and emp.department_id host variables containing the selections made by the user. The store_id and department_id in the EMPLOYEES table must be equal to the emp.store_id and emp.department_id host variables for the row to be returned.

### ORDER BY CLAUSE

The ORDER BY clause sorts the result set in hire date (major sort) in descending (DESC) order, last name (intermediate sort), and first name (minor sort) sequence.

### OPEN THE CURSOR

Once the cursor is declared, it must be opened before being processed. The OPEN statement in Figure 12-25 executes the SELECT statement for the DECLARE CURSOR.

```
EXEC SQL OPEN cursor1;
```

FIGURE 12-25  **OPEN** statement

## FETCHNEXT PROCEDURE

The SELECT statement identifies rows that contain the column values the program wants. However, SQL does not retrieve any data until the FETCH statement is issued. In Figure 12-26, the FETCH NEXT statement retrieves a single row from the cursor1 cursor and populates the variables in the external data structure called EMP defined in the D-specifications.

```
D emp            E DS                    extName(employees) qualified alias

P fetchNext       B
 /free
   EXEC SQL
   FETCH NEXT
     FROM cursor1
     INTO :emp.employee_id,
          :emp.store_id,
          :emp.first_name,
          :emp.m_initial,
          :emp.last_name,
          :emp.hire_date,
          :emp.department_id,
          :emp.hourly_rate,
          :emp.commission_pct;
   monitorSQL();
 /end-free
P fetchNext       E
```

FIGURE 12-26  FetchNext procedure

## MONITORSQL PROCEDURE

When accessing a group of rows from a result set, an at-end condition needs to be tested to determine when all the rows have been processed. When the SQLSTATE variable contains a value of '02000', this means that either the end of the result set has been reached or there were no rows in the result set to begin with. In Figure 12-27, SQLSTATE is tested against the named constant NO_ROW_FOUND to determine when the end of the result set is reached. This condition occurs when the FETCH NEXT statement has retrieved the last row in the result set and the program issues a subsequent FETCH NEXT.

There may be occasions when no employees are assigned to a particular department at a store. When this happens, the store and department selection does not return any rows to the result set. For this reason, the SQLSTATE return code is monitored after each FETCH NEXT statement for an at-end condition. If SQLSTATE returns a value of '02000', an at-end condition was detected. If the at-end condition occurs on the first FETCH NEXT statement, this indicates that no rows were selected with the SELECT statement.

```
P monitorSQL        B
   D SUCCESSFUL       C                    Const('00000')
   D NO_ROW_FOUND     C                    Const('02000')

    /free
     select;
       when SQLSTATE = SUCCESSFUL;

       when SQLSTATE = NO_ROW_FOUND;
         moreRows = NO;
     endSL;
    /end-free
    P monitorSQL       E
```

FIGURE 12-27  monitorSQL procedure

## PROCESS MULTIPLE ROWS FROM THE CURSOR

Cursors are usually controlled with a DOW loop. The loop allows each row to be fetched one at a time. Figure 12-28 illustrates the processing required as the program processes multiple rows from the result set. The moreRows = YES condition controls whether the DOW loop is executed. The moreRows variable is a Boolean data type that is initialized to a value of 1 to indicate that a row is successfully retrieved from the cursor1 cursor. The fetchNext() procedure is used to retrieve the next row before the next cycle of the DOW loop. This process continues one row at a time until all rows in the result set have been processed. When all the rows have been processed, SQLSTATE returns a value of '02000', indicating that the end of the result set has been reached.

```
fetchNext();
      doW (moreRows = YES);
         .
         . (process rows and build JSON object)
         .
         fetchNext();
      enddo;
```

FIGURE 12-28  Example of processing rows from the cursor

## CLOSE CURSOR

Once the selected rows have been processed from the result set, the cursor should be closed. The cursor1 cursor is closed in the closeCursor procedure in Figure 12-29.

```
EXEC SQL CLOSE cursor1;
```

**FIGURE 12-29** **CLOSE CURSOR statement**

## DYNAMIC SQL STATEMENTS

Static statements have a hard-coded structure, and host variables provide the ability to execute the same statement using different values in a search condition or as values assigned to a column on an INSERT or UPDATE statement. A static statement cannot, however, change its structure from one execution to the next. For example, the same static UPDATE statement cannot use a particular search condition, such as ship_city = :cus.ship_city, in one execution and use a different search condition, such as discount > :cus.discount, in a subsequent execution. Of course, two static Update statements can be specified and program logic can be used to decide which one is to be executed on a particular iteration through the program. **Dynamic SQL statements** provide greater flexibility and allow the construction of entire SQL statements dynamically as a program is executing.

The simplest form of dynamic SQL uses RPGLE string operations to construct an SQL statement as a string in a host variable and then executes the string using the SQL EXECUTE IMMEDIATE statement as shown in Figure 12-30.

```
D sqlStmt          S             256A    inz varying

  sqlStmt = 'DELETE FROM customers +
              WHERE ship_city IS NULL';
  EXEC SQL
    EXECUTE IMMEDIATE :sqlStmt;
```

**FIGURE 12-30** **Example of EXECUTE IMMEDIATE**

The sqlStmt variable is assigned a string that is a complete SQL DELETE statement. The host variable is then specified on an EXECUTE IMMEDIATE statement that executes the string contained in the variable. If the string in the sqlStmt variable does not contain a syntactically valid

SQL statement, or if an exception occurs when the statement is executed, the SQLSTATE and other SQLCA variables are set.

The example in Figure 12-31 shows how dynamic SQL can be used to add flexibility to SQL. This example lets the user input any valid SQL condition as a string that is stored in the sqlCond host variable.

```
D sqlStmt          S              256A    inz varying
D sqlCond          S              256A    inz varying

 * Get a search condition (as a string) from user input
 * and place the string in the sqlCond variable.
       .
       .
       .
  sqlStmt = 'DELETE FROM customers WHERE ' + sqlCond;
  EXEC SQL
    EXECUTE IMMEDIATE :sqlStmt;
```

**FIGURE 12-31  Example of dynamic SQL statement**

In this example, only the first part of the statement (DELETE FROM customers WHERE) is coded as a literal in the program. The user input is then concatenated to the literal to complete the statement. Thus, the user could enter "ship_city IS NULL", "discount < .01", or any other valid search condition, and the Delete statement would delete the rows that satisfied the search condition.

## DYNAMIC CURSORS

SQL lets the capabilities of dynamic execution and a cursor be combined by dynamically preparing the SELECT statement that is used for a cursor declaration. The code in Figure 12-32 shows a simplified example of the statements used for this type of dynamic cursor.

The DECLARE CURSOR statement's FOR clause specifies the dynSqlStmt statement name rather than a nested SELECT statement as shown earlier in the chapter. The dynSqlStmt statement is prepared from a SELECT statement that is contained in the sqlStmt host variable. The statement must be successfully prepared before the OPEN statement opens the cursor. At the time the OPEN statement is executed, the DBMS uses the SELECT statement that has been prepared to determine which rows are in the cursor's result set. Question marks (?) can be used as parameter markers in the SELECT statement string and then a USING clause specified

```
D cus            E DS                      extName(customers) qualified alias
D sqlStmt          S            256A       inz varying
D sqlCond          S            256A       inz varying

 * Get a search condition (as a string) from user
 * input and place the string in the sqlCond variable.
         .
         .
   sqlStmt = 'SELECT * FROM customers WHERE ' +
              sqlCond;

   EXEC SQL
       PREPARE dynSqlStmt FROM :sqlStmt;

   EXEC SQL
       DECLARE cusCursor Cursor
          FOR    dynSqlStmt;

   EXEC SQL
     OPEN cusCursor;

   EXEC SQL
     FETCH NEXT
       FROM   cusCursor
       INTO :cus.customer_id,
            :cus.customer_name,
            :cus.ship_city,
            :cus.discount;
```

FIGURE 12-32  Example of a dynamic cursor

with corresponding host variables on the OPEN statement. The host variables' values are used in place of the parameter markers.

Dynamic execution of a statement can be broken down into two steps, preparation and execution, as in the example in Figure 12-33. Here, the RPGLE statements to create a string with an SQL statement are the same. But the string is first prepared for execution by the SQL PREPARE statement. The PREPARE statement has the syntax

```
PREPARE statement-name FROM :host-variable
```

where *host-variable* is a string variable containing an SQL statement and *statement-name* is any name desired. The statement name does not have to be the name of a host variable; in fact, to avoid confusion, it generally should not be the same name. The statement name serves to identify an internal SQL structure that has the translated form of the statement.

```
D cus              E DS                 extName(customers) qualified alias
D sqlStmt          S        256A        inz varying
D sqlCond          S        256A        inz varying
D SUCCESSFUL       C                    const('00000')

 * Get a search condition (as a string) from user input
 * and place the string in the sqlCond variable.
       .
       .
   sqlStmt = 'DELETE FROM customers WHERE ' +
              sqlCond;

   EXEC SQL
     PREPARE dynSqlStmt FROM :sqlStmt;

   if SQLSTATE = SUCCESSFUL;
       EXEC SQL
          EXECUTE dynSqlStmt;
       if ( SQLSTATE <> SUCCESSFUL);
          sqlError();
       endIf;
   else;
     sqlError();
   endIf;
```

**FIGURE 12-33** Dynamic execution using the **PREPARE** statement

Be sure to check for successful completion of a PREPARE statement, as the example above does, before a subsequent EXECUTE statement. After an SQL statement has been successfully prepared from a string, the statement can be executed by the EXECUTE statement. Note how EXECUTE specifies a statement name, whereas EXECUTE IMMEDIATE specifies a host string variable; do not confuse the two forms.

Using separate PREPARE and EXECUTE statements enables the relatively time-consuming process of translating an SQL statement from a string into an executable form to be done just once; then the statement can be executed more efficiently multiple times during the same program execution.

Figure 12-34 lists the statements that can be executed using either EXECUTE IMMEDIATE or PREPARE and EXECUTE.

| | |
|---|---|
| ALTER TABLE | DROP |
| CALL | FREE LOCATOR |
| COMMENT ON | GRANT |
| COMMIT | INSERT |
| CREATE ALIAS | LABEL ON |
| CREATE COLLECTION | LOCK TABLE |
| CREATE DISTINCT TYPE | RENAME |
| CREATE FUNCTION | REVOKE |
| CREATE INDEX | ROLLBACK |
| CREATE PROCEDURE | SET PATH |
| CREATE TABLE | SET TRANSACTION |
| CREATE VIEW | UPDATE |
| DELETE | |

**FIGURE 12-34  SQL statements that can be executed dynamically**

Notice that neither method can be used to execute a SELECT statement; however, a SELECT statement can be prepared and used in a cursor declaration, a technique discussed elsewhere in this book.

When a statement is prepared for subsequent execution, one or more question marks (?) can be used as **parameter markers** in the statement to designate a place in the statement where a host variable, or a host variable and an indicator variable, will supply a value when the prepared statement is executed. This approach makes it possible to prepare a statement and still change search condition values or values assigned to columns when the statement is executed, providing flexibility similar to that gained by using host variables in static statements. Figure 12-35 shows how a parameter marker can be placed in a statement string and how a host variable is subsequently specified to supply the value at the location of the parameter marker.

The USING clause of the EXECUTE statement specifies one host variable for each question mark in the statement string that was prepared. The host variables in the USING clause correspond positionally to the parameter markers in the string. When the EXECUTE statement is executed, the value of the first host variable is used in place of the first question mark, and so on. An indicator variable can follow the host variable in the USING clause, but only one question mark should be used in the statement string; in other words, do not include one question mark for the host variable and another question mark for the indicator variable. SQL ignores the USING clause if the prepared statement has no parameter markers.

```
D slcShpCity        S               30A    inz varying
D sqlStmt           S              256A    inz varying
D SUCCESSFUL        C                      Const('00000')
D NO_ROW_FOUND      C                      Const('02000')


  stmtStr = 'DELETE FROM customers +
            WHERE ship_city = ?';
  EXEC SQL
    PREPARE dynSqlStmt FROM :sqlStmt;

  if SQLSTATE = SUCCESSFUL;

 * Get the selected city from user input and place
 * the value in the SlcShpCity variable.
     .
     .
     .
    EXEC SQL
      EXECUTE dynSqlStmt
        USING :slcShpCity;
    select;
      When SQLSTATE = SUCCESSFUL;
 *        Skip
      When SQLSTATE = NO_ROW_FOUND;
        sqlNoRow();
      When %subSt(SQLSTATE : 1 : 2) = '01';
        sqlWarning();
      Other;
        sqlError();
    endSl;
  else;
    sqlError;
  endIf;
```

FIGURE 12-35  Dynamic execution using parameter markers

Let us consider a more complex example. The RPGLE code segment in Figure 12-36 lets a user enter a search condition to select a category of customers to be updated, such as the customers in Chicago. Then, for this category, the user can repeatedly enter a pair of old and new discount values. The resulting UPDATE statement is executed once for each pair of old and new discount values and sets the discount for customers who meet the search condition and who have the specified old discount value.

```
D oldDisc          S                 5P 3
D newDisc          S                 5P 3
D sqlStmt          S               256A    inz varying
D sqlCond          S               256A    inz varying
D SUCCESSFUL       C                       Const('00000')
D NO_ROW_FOUND     C                       Const('02000')

 * Get a search condition (as a string) from user input
 * and place the string in the sqlCond variable.
    .
    .
  sqlStmt = 'UPDATE customers +
                SET discount = ? +
                WHERE discount = ? And (';
  sqlStmt = %trimR( sQLStmt ) + sqlCond + ')';
  EXEC SQL
    PREPARE DynSqlStmt FROM :sqlStmt;
  if SQLSTATE = SUCCESSFUL;
    excSqlStmt();
  else;
    sqlError();
  endIf;

P excSqlStmt      B
 /free
 * Repeat the following until done or error....
 * Get old and new discount values from user.
    .
    .
  newDisc = InpNewDisc;
  oldDisc = InpOldDisc;
  EXEC SQL
    EXECUTE dynSqlStmt
      USING :newDisc,
            :oldDisc;
  select;
    when SQLSTATE = SUCCESSFUL;
 *                    Skip
    when SQLSTATE = NO_ROW_FOUND;
        sqlNoRow();
    when %subSt(SQLSTATE : 1 : 2) = '01';
        sqlWarning();
    other;
      sqlError();
  endSl;
 * ...End of repeated loop
 /end-free
P execSqlStmt      E
```

FIGURE 12-36  Code segment to search and update customer rows

## WEB APPLICATION SQL1202

This application focuses on dynamic SQL statements in an RPGLE application to process multiple rows from a database table. The application contains HTML5 that may not be supported by all browsers yet. It is only a matter of time before all browsers will support HTML5. If the browser you are using does not display the employee grid correctly, use Firefox as this browser supports the HTML5 in this application.

> **Note**
>
> This application does not include the HTML or routines to communicate between the client and server because each environment is different. Visit the companion website to run this application and view the entire source code.

This application is similar to SQL1201 in that the human resource manager wants an application where she can select and display employees. However, in this application she wants to create a filter where she can select the employees based on any combination of store, department, last name, employee ID, low hourly rate, and high hourly rate. In addition, she wants the list to be sorted based on the selection criteria.

Figure 12-37 shows the available options the user can use to build the filter string that will be sent to the program with the request. When the user enters her selection criteria and clicks on the **Submit** button, an AJAX request is made to the server and program SQL1202.rpgle is executed.

FIGURE 12-37 Initial output from SQL1202.html

Once the request is processed by program SQL1202.rpgle, the JSON object is returned to the browser and the table grid is created as shown in Figure 12-38.

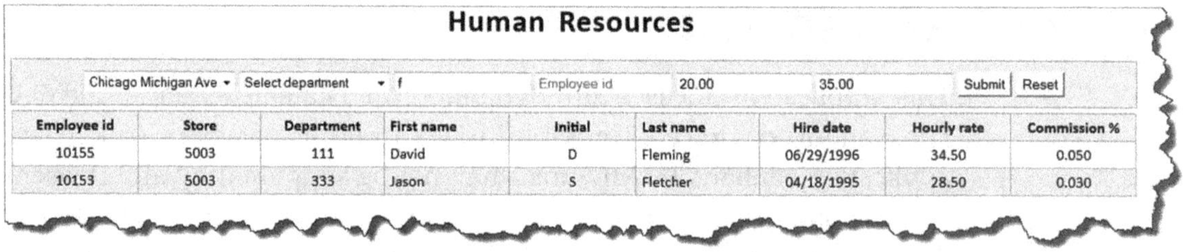


| Employee id | Store | Department | First name | Initial | Last name | Hire date | Hourly rate | Commission % |
|---|---|---|---|---|---|---|---|---|
| 10155 | 5003 | 111 | David | D | Fleming | 06/29/1996 | 34.50 | 0.050 |
| 10153 | 5003 | 333 | Jason | S | Fletcher | 04/18/1995 | 28.50 | 0.030 |

**FIGURE 12-38 Output from `SQL1202.html` after AJAX call to program `SQL1202.rpgle`**

As you can see in this example, the user selected the employees who

- Work at the `Chicago Michigan Ave` store.
- Have a last name starting with the letter `F`. (The last name field is not case-sensitive. Entering a lowercase `f` is the same as entering an uppercase `F`.)
- Have a hourly rate of `20.00` or higher.
- Have an hourly rate of `35.00` or less.

The `RPGLE` program for this application is shown in Figure 12-39.

```
H decEdit('0.') datFmt(*USA)

D emp             E DS                  extName(employees) qualified alias
D SQLStmt           S            256A       varying
D orderByClause     S            256A   inz varying
D WhereClause       S           1024A   varying
D rowCount          S             10U 0 Inz
D totalRows         S             10U 0 inz
D rowStr            S          32768    inz varying
D comma             S              1    inz varying
D jsonData          S          32768    inz varying
D sortNo            S              5U 0 inz
D moreRows          S               N   Inz('1')
D YES               C                   const('1')
D NO                C                   const('0')

 /free
  declareCursor();
  buildJson();

  *INLR = *ON;
  return;
 /end-free
```

```
//------------------------------------------------------------------------
P declareCursor     B
D sortDescData      DS
D                                50A    inz('store_id, department_id, +
D                                              last_name, first_name')
D                                50A    inz('department_id, last_name, +
D                                              first_name')
D                                50A    inz('last_name, first_name')
D                                50A    inz('employee_id')
D                                50A    inz('hourly_rate')
D  sortDesc                      50A    overlay(sortDescData)
D                                       dim(5)
 /free
  SQLStmt = 'SELECT * FROM employees';
  buildWhereClause();
  orderByClause = ' ORDER BY ' + sortDesc(sortNo);

  SQLStmt = SQLStmt + whereClause + orderByClause +
            ' FOR READ ONLY';

  EXEC SQL PREPARE C1Stmt FROM :SQLStmt;

  EXEC SQL DECLARE cursor1 INSENSITIVE CURSOR for C1Stmt;

 /end-free
P declareCursor     E

 //-----------------------------------------------------
P buildJson        B
 /free
  EXEC SQL OPEN cursor1;
  fetchNext();
  doW (moreRows = YES);
        .
        . (process row and build JSON object)
        .
        fetchNext();
      enddo;
        .
        . (send JSON object to browser)
        .

  EXEC SQL CLOSE cursor1;
 /end-free
P buildJson        E

 //-----------------------------------------------------
P fetchNext        B
 /free
  EXEC SQL
    FETCH NEXT
      FROM cursor1 INTO :emp;
```

*Continued*

```
    monitorSQL();
  /end-free
 P fetchNext        E


  //-------------------------------------------------------------------
 P buildWhereClause...
 P                 B
  /free
   whereClause = ' WHERE 1=1';

   clear sortNo;
   if reqStr( 'storeId' ) <> *BLANKS;
     whereClause = whereClause + ' AND store_id = ' +
                   reqStr( 'storeId' );
     sortNo = 1;
   endIf;

   if reqStr( 'deptId' ) <> *BLANKS;
     whereClause = whereClause +
                   ' AND department_id = ' + reqStr( 'deptId' );
     if sortNo = *ZERO;
       sortNo = 2;
     endIf;
   endIf;

   If reqStr( 'lastName' ) <> *BLANKS;
       whereClause = whereClause +
                   ' AND UPPER( last_name ) Like UPPER(''' +
                   (%trim( reqStr( 'lastName' ))) + '%' + ''')';
     sortNo = 3;
   EndIf;

   if reqStr( 'empId' ) <> *BLANKS;
       whereClause = whereClause +
           ' AND employee_id = ' + %char( reqNum( 'empId' ) );
     if sortNo = *ZERO;
       sortNo = 4;
     endIf;
   endIf;

   if reqStr( 'lowRate' ) <> *BLANKS;
       whereClause = whereClause +
           ' AND hourly_rate >= ' + %char( reqNum( 'lowRate' ) );
     if sortNo = *ZERO;
       sortNo = 5;
     endIf;
   endIf;
```

```
   if reqStr( 'highRate' ) <> *BLANKS;
      whereClause = whereClause +
          ' AND hourly_rate <= ' + %char( reqNum( 'highRate' ) );
    if sortNo = *ZERO;
      sortNo = 5;
    endIf;
  endIf;
  if sortNo = *ZERO;
    sortNo = 4;
  endIf;
 /end-free
P buildWhereClause...
P                     E


 //----------------------------------------------------
P monitorSQL      B
D SUCCESSFUL      C                       Const('00000')
D NO_ROW          C                       Const('02000')

 /free
  select;
    when SQLSTATE = SUCCESSFUL;

    when SQLSTATE = NO_ROW;
      moreRows = NO;
  endSL;
 /end-free
P monitorSQL      E
```

**FIGURE 12-39** `SQL1202.rpgle`

When program `SQL1202.rpgle` executes, it performs the following steps:

1. Call the `declareCursor` procedure:

   a. The `SQLStmt` variable is initialized with the `SELECT FROM` statement. This variable will be used to hold the entire dynamic SQL statement used to query the `EMPLOYEES` table.

   b. The `buildWhereClause` procedure is called. This is where the dynamic `WHERE` clause is built.

   c. The `ORDER BY` clause is created and placed in the `orderByClause` variable. The sort sequence is determined in the `WHERE` clause based on the filter selection.

   d. The `SQLStmt` variable is completed by concatenating the initial `SELECT FROM` statement plus the value in the `whereClause` variable plus the value in the `orderByClause` plus the string `FOR READ ONLY`.

   e. `C1Stmt` is prepared for execution from the `SQLStmt` host variable.

   f. The `cursor1` cursor is declared.

2. Call the `buildJson` procedure:
   a. Open the cursor.
   b. Fetch the first row from the cursor.
      o Monitor for no-more-rows condition (cursor empty).
   c. Loop through the result set (DOW):
      o Process the row and build the JSON object.
      o Fetch the next row and monitor for no-more-rows condition.
      o When the end of the cursor is reached and there are no more rows to process, terminate the loop.
   d. Send the response object containing the JSON data to the browser.
   e. Close the cursor.
3. End the program:
   a. Set LR to *ON.
   b. Return.

Let us consider the procedures that are different from those used in program `SQL1201.rpgle`.

### DECLARECURSOR PROCEDURE

The `declareCursor` procedure in Figure 12-40 contains the DECLARE CURSOR statement that defines a cursor called `cursor1` that will hold the result set.

### SELECT STATEMENT

The SELECT statement is an SQL statement within the DECLARE CURSOR statement that specifies the query that retrieves data from the EMPLOYEES table and generates a result set.

### BUILDWHERECLAUSE CLAUSE

The WHERE clause includes the selection criteria used by the SELECT statement to determine which rows are returned from the database table. In this example, it is unknown what the WHERE clause will be until the user enters the selection criteria. When this procedure is executed, each input parameter is examined for a value. If the parameter contains a value, it is concatenated to the WHERE clause. At the same time, a value is placed into the `sortNbr` variable that is used in the ORDER BY clause. The ORDER BY clause subsequently will determine the sort sequence of the grid when it is loaded in the browser.

```
P declareCursor    B
   D sortDescData       DS
   D                                   50A   inz('store_id, department_id, +
   D                                           last_name, first_name')
   D                                   50A   inz('department_id, last_name, +
   D                                           first_name')
   D                                   50A   inz('last_name, first_name')
   D                                   50A   inz('employee_id')
   D                                   50A   inz('hourly_rate')
   D   sortDesc                        50A   overlay(sortDescData)
   D                                         dim(5)
    /free
     SQLStmt = ('SELECT * FROM employees');
     buildWhereClause();
     orderByClause = ' ORDER BY ' + sortDesc(sortNo);

     SQLStmt = SQLStmt + whereClause + orderByClause +
                 ' FOR READ ONLY';

     EXEC SQL PREPARE C1Stmt FROM :SQLStmt;

     EXEC SQL DECLARE cursor1 INSENSITIVE CURSOR for C1Stmt;

    /end-free
P declareCursor    E
```

FIGURE 12-40  **declareCursor** procedure

## ORDER BY CLAUSE

The orderByClause variable in Figure 12-41 contains the ORDER BY clause that will be used in the SQL query against the EMPLOYEES table. The sort sequence is determined by the filter criteria of the WHERE clause.

```
orderByClause = ' ORDER BY ' + sortDesc(sortNo);
```

FIGURE 12-41  Building the ORDER BY clause

The actual value for the ORDER BY clause is contained in the array sortDesc and is accessed by the value of the sortNbr variable. The sortDesc array defined in Figure 12-42 contains the different sort sequence options and is controlled by the value of the sortNbr variable, which is set in the WHERE clause.

```
P declareCursor    B
    D sortDescData    DS
    D                              50A   inz('store_id, department_id, +
    D                                        last_name, first_name')
    D                              50A   inz('department_id, last_name, +
    D                                        first_name')
    D                              50A   inz('last_name, first_name')
    D                              50A   inz('employee_id')
    D                              50A   inz('hourly_rate')
    D    sortDesc                  50A   overlay(sortDescData)
    D                                    dim(5)
```

FIGURE 12-42  Array used for ORDER BY clause

## CODING SUGGESTIONS

- On cursor declarations:
  o For a read-only cursor, always specify the FOR READ ONLY clause.
  o For a cursor that will be referenced in an UPDATE statement, always specify the FOR UPDATE OF clause.
  o For a cursor that will be referenced in a DELETE statement but not in an UPDATE statement, do not specify either a FOR READ ONLY or a FOR UPDATE OF clause.
  o Specify the INSENSITIVE keyword if the contents of the cursor should remain unchanged after the cursor is opened. This step is not necessary for a cursor in which the SCROLL keyword has been specified (without the DYNAMIC keyword).
  o Explicitly close any open cursor when it is no longer needed. Be careful not to recursively execute SQL error handling when closing a cursor while still handling another SQL error.

- Performance-related suggestions:

  o List only the columns that need to be retrieved in a cursor declaration.

  o Add the OPTIMIZE FOR n ROWS clause to a cursor declaration when the number of rows to be fetched is known and when the number of rows is significantly fewer than the expected number of rows in the result set.

  o Do not use expressions in the SET clause of a positioned UPDATE. (The DBMS does an open for the first execution of a positioned UPDATE when the SET clause has an expression.) Calculate the new column value in a host variable, and use just the host variable in the SET clause assignment.

## END-OF-CHAPTER

### CHAPTER SUMMARY

1. An SQL cursor provides a result set through which a program can perform input, update, and delete operations.
2. A cursor uses a nested SELECT statement to define the result set. This SELECT statement can have a FROM, WHERE, GROUP BY, HAVING, and ORDER BY clause, as well as a UNION operator.
3. The WHERE and HAVING clauses can contain host variables that are evaluated when the cursor is opened. Thus, a cursor can be used to access different sets of rows depending on the value of host variables.
4. A cursor can also have a FOR READ ONLY clause to specify that the cursor is read-only or a FOR UPDATE OF clause to specify an updatable cursor.
5. The INSENSITIVE keyword can be used to define a read-only cursor whose result set will not be affected by database updates.
6. After a cursor is opened, the FETCH statement is used to retrieve one or more rows into host variables.
7. The FETCH NEXT statement reads rows sequentially in the order, if any, that is specified on the ORDER BY clause of the cursor's SELECT statement.
8. A positioned UPDATE or DELETE statement can be used to update the column values in an updatable cursor's current row or to delete the current row.

9.  A scrollable cursor:

    a.  Is a cursor defined with the SCROLL option (for read-only access) or with the DYNAMIC SCROLL option (which allows updates).

    b.  Allows other FETCH statement positioning options in addition to NEXT. With these positioning options, the cursor's current position can be moved forward or backward from the current position or set to the beginning or end of the result set.

10. Dynamic cursors let dynamically prepared SELECT statements be used with parameter markers. The name of this prepared SELECT statement is specified in the FOR clause of the DECLARE CURSOR statement.

## KEY TERMS

| | |
|---|---|
| cursor | positioned DELETE statement |
| dynamic SQL statement | positioned UPDATE statement |
| host variable | result set |
| parameter marker | scrollable cursor |

# CHAPTER 13

## THE CREATE SQL PROGRAM COMMAND

### CHAPTER OBJECTIVES

Upon completion of this chapter, you should be able to

- Explain the purpose of the CRTSQLRPGI command
- Explain the SQL translation process
- Demonstrate how to create an executable program object from a source member

### CREATING SQL PROGRAMS

After an RPG program containing SQL embedded statements is created, it must be compiled. The RPG source program type should be SQLRPGLE for RPG code with embedded SQL. The **CRTSQLRPGI (Create SQL ILE RPG Object) command** is used to compile the source program into a program, module, or service program object. The OBJTYPE (Object type) parameter, which can have the value *PGM (program object), *MODULE (module), or *SRVPGM (service program), determines which object is created.

The CRTSQLRPGI command can be entered from any display screen that allows CL commands, or it can be selected from the compile options within Rational Developer for Power (RDp). These commands can also be used in CL programs. The example in Figure 13-1 shows a typical command to create a program from RPG source containing embedded SQL.

```
CrtSqlRpgI Obj( AppExc/UpdCust )
           SrcFile( AppSrc/QRpgLeSrc )
           Option( *Sql )
           ObjType( *Pgm )
           IncFile( AppSrc/SqlIncSrc )
           Commit( *None )
```

FIGURE 13-1    **CRTSQLRPGI command to create a program from RPG source**

In this example, the object to be created is a program named UPDCUST in library APPEXC. The source for this program is in source file QRPGLESRC in library APPSRC. The command specifies the SQL naming option. The object type being produced from this command is a program (*PGM) object. The source file for INCLUDE statement members is SQLINCSRC in library APPSRC. No commitment control is in effect when this program is executed.

## CRTSQLRPGI COMMAND PARAMETERS

Figure 13-2 lists commonly used parameters and their default values for the CRTSQLRPGI command that creates RPG program objects. Online help provides a full description of all CRTSQLRPGI command parameters. This section discusses the more commonly used parameters.

| Parameter | Purpose | Default (Other values) |
|---|---|---|
| OBJ | Name of program, module, or service program to be created | — |
| SRCFILE | Source file that contains HLL and embedded SQL source | *LIBL/QCSRC, *LIBL/QCBLLESRC, or *LIBL/QRPGLESRC |
| SRCMBR | Source member that contains HLL and embedded SQL source | *OBJ |
| OBJTYPE | Type of object to create (program, module, or service program) | *PGM (*MODULE, *SRVPGM) |
| TEXT | Description of created object | *SRCMBRTXT |
| OPTION | Naming convention, object generation (and other options) | *SYS, *GEN (*SQL, *NOGEN) |
| INCFILE | Source file to use for embedded INCLUDE statements | *LIBL/*SRCFILE |
| COMMIT | Level of commitment control environment for program execution | *CHG (*NONE, *CS, *ALL, *RR, *UR, *RS, *NC) |
| RDB | Database name for distributed program | *LOCAL |
| DATFMT | Format used when accessing date result columns | *JOB (*USA, *ISO, *EUR, *JIS, *MDY, *DMY, *YMD, *JUL) |
| DATSEP | Separator used when accessing date result columns | *JOB (separator-character) |
| TIMFMT | Format used when accessing time result columns | *HMS (*USA, *ISO, *EUR, *JIS) |
| TIMSEP | Separator used when accessing time result columns | *JOB (*BLANK or separator-character) |
| ALWCPYDTA | Whether a copy of the data can be used in a SELECT statement | *OPTIMIZE (*YES, *NO) |

| CLOSQLCSR | Point when SQL cursors are implicitly closed, prepared statements are implicitly discarded, and LOCK TABLE locks are released | *ENDACTGRP (*ENDMOD) |
|---|---|---|
| ALWBLK | Allow blocking for read-only cursors | *ALLREAD (*READ, *NONE) |
| DFTRDBCOL | Default schema for unqualified names in static statements | *NONE (schema-name) |
| DYNDFTCOL | Whether to use DFTRDBCOL for dynamic statements | *NO (*YES) |
| SQLPATH | List of schemas to search for unqualified data type, stored procedure, or function names | *NAMING (*LIBL or list-of-schemas) |
| USRPRF | User profile for static statements | *NAMING (*USER, *OWNER) |
| DYNUSRPRF | User profile for dynamic statements | *USER (*OWNER) |
| TOSRCFILE | Source file to receive precompiled output | QTEMP/QSQLTEMP or QTEMP/QSQLTEMP1 |
| COMPILEOPT | Compiler options | character-value, *NONE |

**FIGURE 13-2**   **Commonly used command parameters for CRTSQLRPGI command**

The CRTSQLRPGI command's OBJ parameter specifies the name of the object being created. Normally, a qualified name is specified to ensure that the new object is placed in the correct library. The SRCFILE parameter identifies the source file in which the object's source code is stored. By default, all the CRTSQLRPGI commands use the same source member name as the object name specified in the OBJ parameter.

The OBJTYPE parameter indicates which type of object is to be produced. In addition to the default of *PGM, which means a program object is to be produced, a module (*MODULE) or service program (*SRVPGM) object can be created. The TEXT parameter lets up to 50 characters of descriptive text be specified for the object being created.

The OPTION (Precompiler options) parameter specifies the naming convention for SQL statements. Using the default value *SYS means that if tables are qualified with the schema name, a slash (/) is used to separate the schema and table names. If *SQL is specified, a period (.) is used to separate the two names. The naming convention also controls how unqualified database table objects will be located. The library list will be searched only when the *SYS option is used. This option is also important because some other parameters on the command have as their default value *NAMING, which means the behavior is determined by whether *SYS or *SQL naming is in effect. The sample command examined earlier (Figure 13-1) uses the OPTION parameter to specify that SQL naming (*SQL) is used. Another important CRTSQLRPGI option is *NOGEN, which tells the SQL precompiler to stop processing after the precompile step. This option is discussed further later in the chapter.

The INCFILE (Include file) parameter defines the source file that contains any source members that have been specified using the SQL INCLUDE statement. SQL INCLUDE works much like the /COPY or /INCLUDE directive in RPG but is required if SQL statements are to be copied into your program at compile time.

The COMMIT parameter specifies whether commitment control is in effect when the program is run, as well as which lock level, or isolation level, is used. Commitment control gives the programmer the capability to either "roll back," or reverse, a group of updates made to the files in an application or to "commit," or make those changes permanent. The default system value is set to *CHG, which means commitment control is assumed for programs that update database files using SQL. If commitment control is not to be used and/or the files updated with SQL are not being journaled, the programs may not work correctly unless *NONE is specified for this parameter.

The RDB (Remote database) parameter is used in distributed database applications to permit access to databases on other systems.

In general, when a program is created that accesses tables or views containing date or time columns, the CRTSQLRPGI command's DATFMT(*ISO) and TIMFMT(*ISO) parameters should be used. As an alternative, a SET OPTION statement can be coded in the program to set these two options. The DATSEP and TIMSEP parameters let date and time separator characters be specified. All SQL table and view columns with a Date or Time data type use the *ISO format. The performance overhead of converting between different formats can be avoided by using *ISO for the format of date and time values that are returned to the program, as by a FETCH statement, or that are passed by the program to the DBMS, as by an INSERT statement. The *ISO date and time format *must* be used when the program employs multiple-row FETCH or block INSERT; otherwise, hard-to-diagnose data errors may occur.

The ALWCPYDTA (Allow copy of data) parameter specifies when the query optimizer can make a copy of data to improve retrieval performance. Consider the query in Figure 13-3. If the CUSTOMER table is large, it may be faster for the DBMS to copy and sort the CUSTOMER table rather than using an index over the name column, if one exists.

```
Select     *
  From     Customer
  Order By Name;
```

**FIGURE 13-3**   Query on **CUSTOMER** table

Specifying the default, `ALWCPYDTA(*OPTIMIZE)`, for a `CRTSQLRPGI` command lets the query optimizer decide whether to create a copy of the data. When `ALWCPYDTA(*YES)` is specified, the query optimizer uses a copy of the data only if it must do so in order to run the query. Specifying `ALWCPYDTA(*NO)` prevents the query optimizer from making a copy of the data; if a query requires a copy to be made, an error occurs when the query is attempted.

The `CLOSQLCSR` (Close SQL cursor) parameter controls when SQL cursors are implicitly closed if they are not explicitly closed in the program. Specifying the default, `CLOSQLCSR(*ENDACTGRP)`, closes the cursor when the activation group is deleted; the `*ENDMOD` option does so when the module is exited.

The `ALWBLK` (Allow block) parameter controls record blocking. Specifying `ALWBLK(*NONE)` prevents blocking. The `*READ` option allows blocking for read-only cursors when `COMMIT(*NONE)` is also specified. The `*ALLREAD` option allows blocking for read-only cursors when `COMMIT(*NONE)` or `COMMIT(*CHG)` is also specified. In addition, this option causes SQL to open a cursor that is not explicitly updatable as a read-only cursor, even when the program contains `EXECUTE` or `EXECUTE IMMEDIATE` statements.

The `COMPILEOPT` (Compiler options) parameter specifies additional parameters to be used on the compiler command. The `COMPILEOPT` string is added to the compiler command built by the precompiler. No validation of the string occurs. The default option, `*NONE`, specifies that no additional parameters will be used on the compiler command. A character string can be specified that contains the additional options. These options are passed to the RPG compile process after a successful completion of the SQL precompile.

The `CRTSQLRPGI` command can be prompted for the command's parameter values. For example, Figure 13-4 shows the prompt screen displayed when Command Prompt is selected in RDp.

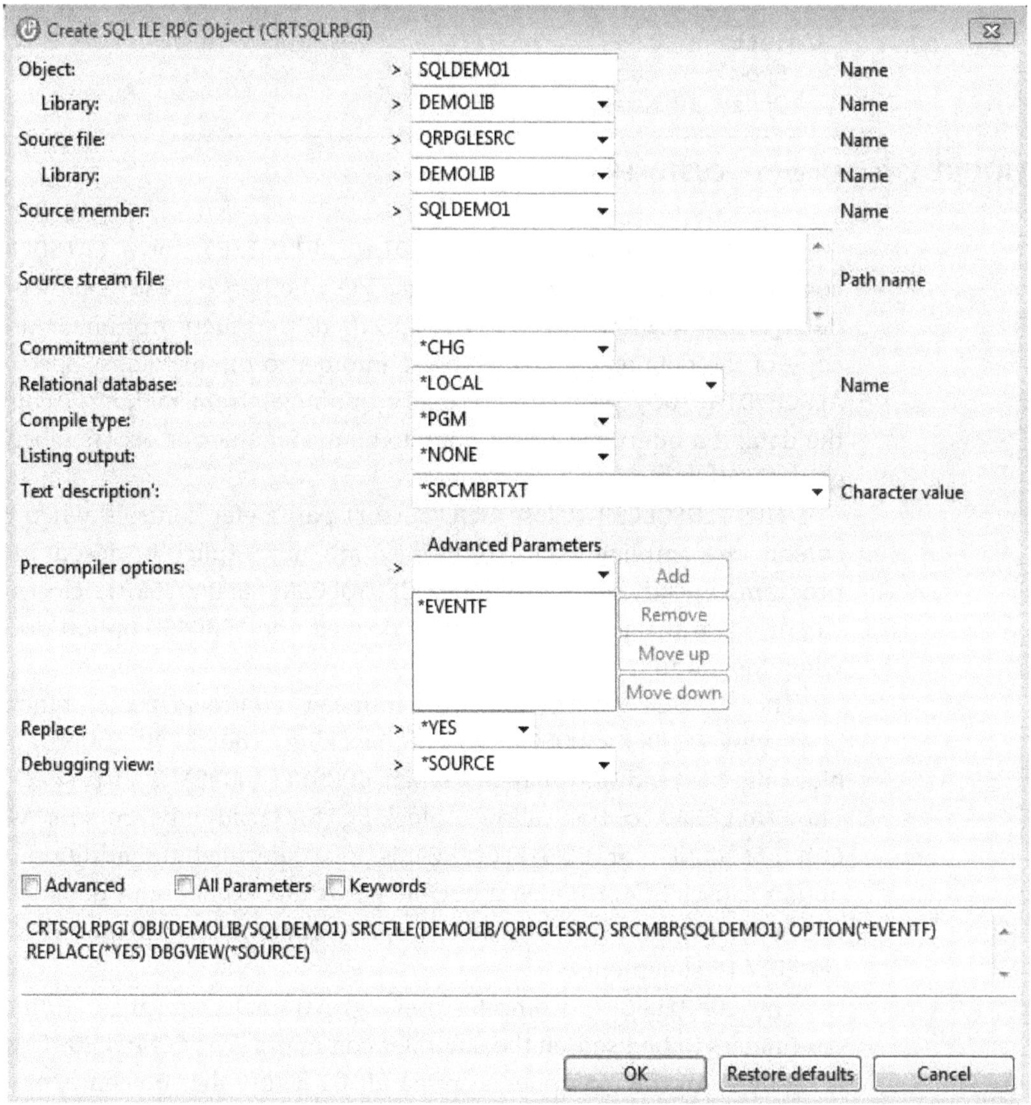

FIGURE 13-4    RDp prompt screen for `CRTSQLRPGI` command

## The SQL Translation Process

The process of creating a program object from a source member containing embedded SQL, known as the **SQL translation process**, consists of two major steps:

1. Precompilation, which precompiles RPG source containing SQL statements, producing a temporary source member

2. Compilation, in which the RPG compiler is called to create a module, program, or service program from the combined original RPG and translated SQL statements

## PRECOMPILATION STEP

The first step in the compile process, called **precompilation**, is the SQL pre-compile stage. The SQL compiler checks the syntax of the SQL statements, checks data definitions in the program, and verifies that all the SQL statements are correct, including that the necessary RPG variables have been defined. If everything at this stage is correct, the **SQL precompiler** comments the SQL statements and replaces them with API calls to database functions to accomplish the work. The resulting translated source is placed into a temporary source member with all the embedded SQL statements translated into HLL declarations and procedural statements. This temporary source member is then handed to the RPG complier to compile the rest of the code.

## COMPILATION STEP

In the second step, the normal HLL compilation process translates the temporary source member input into an executable program object. After the initial translation of embedded SQL statements, the precompiler invokes the appropriate HLL compiler (unless OPTION(*NOGEN) was specified), which reads the temporary source file member and produces a module object. If this step is successful, the compiler copies the processed SQL statements, which were built during the first step, from the temporary source file member's associated space to the associated space of the module object.

After a module is created, the precompiler invokes the operating system program binder (unless OPTION(*MODULE) was specified), which combines, or links, modules into a program object. The binder invokes a set of system routines that translate the processed SQL statements in the modules' associated spaces into the access plan, which is stored in the associated space of the program object. If OBJTYPE(*MODULE) is specified on the CRTSQLRPGI command, the precompiler does not invoke the program binder, and a CRTPGM (Create Program) command must subsequently be used to create a program from one or more module objects.

A distributed database program is one that accesses data on a remote system. A distributed database program requires an **SQL package** object on the remote system. The package contains the access plan to perform the program's SQL operations on the remote system's tables, views, and other objects. A package is created from a program object. The SQL precompiler invokes this step automatically when the RDB parameter of a CRTSQLRPGI command specifies a relational database name other than *LOCAL. As an alternative, the CRTSQLPKG (Create SQL Package) command can be used to create a package from a program object. Service program objects can also be created by specifying OBJTYPE(*SRVPGM) on the CRTSQLRPGI commands. A service program is somewhat like a dynamic link library (DLL) under Microsoft Windows®. Module objects created with the CRTSQLRPGI command can subsequently be bound into a service program using the CRTSRVPGM (Create Service Program) command.

## CODING SUGGESTIONS

- Specify the CRTSQLRPGI command's OPTION(*SQL) option to use the SQL naming convention. This practice renders the SQL portion of an embedded SQL program more portable.
- Specify the TEXT option to associate up to 50 characters of descriptive text with a program.
- Performance-related suggestions:
  - Use ALWBLK(*ALLREAD) to allow record blocking for read-only cursors.
  - Unless the application requires maximum data currency for read-only cursors, use the default of ALWCPYDTA(*OPTIMIZE).

- Specify *ISO for the DATFMT and TIMFMT parameters.
- To use compile options not available in the CRTSQLRPGI commands, specify OPTION(*NOGEN) and a permanent library and source file name in the TOSRCFILE parameter. When the precompiler finishes, its output source can be compiled using the HLL compiler with the desired compile options specified.

## END-OF-CHAPTER

### CHAPTER SUMMARY

1. The CRTSQLRPGI command is used to compile RPG programs that contain embedded SQL into program, module, or service program objects.
2. The SQL translation process, which is the process of producing an executable object, or module, from embedded source, consists of a precompile followed by a compile followed by a bind.
3. The precompiler creates HLL source into which non-SQL statements from the original source are copied unmodified and SQL statements are translated into calls to system routines. The SQL statements are also translated into structures saved in the output source member's associated space.
4. The source output of the precompiler is then compiled with the HLL compiler to produce a module object.
5. This module object is then bound into a program or service program. The SQL statement structures are carried forward in this process and in the final step, which produces the program or service program, are used to produce an access plan that is stored in the associated space of the program or service program object.

### KEY TERMS

| | |
|---|---|
| CRTSQLRPGI command | SQL precompiler |
| precompilation | SQL translation process |
| SQL package | |

# CHAPTER 14

## STORED PROCEDURES

## CHAPTER OBJECTIVES

Upon completion of this chapter, you should be able to

- Implement stored procedures
- Implement user-defined functions

## STORED PROCEDURES

SQL provides the ability to call an executable procedure, known as a stored procedure. A **stored procedure** is simply a program with or without embedded SQL statements. You can create the program for a stored procedure in two ways:

- By compiling RPGLE or other high-level language (HLL) source code
- By using **SQL Procedural Language (SPL)**

There is nothing special about an RPGLE program used as a stored procedure, and, as mentioned, the program itself does not even have to contain any SQL statements. If SPL is used to create a stored procedure, SQL actually translates the SPL code into ILE C source code with embedded SQL and then creates a normal RPGLE program object from the ILE C source.

A stored procedure can be called by an embedded SQL CALL statement, but this method is mainly useful for distributed processing, when the stored procedure exists on a different system. Otherwise, to call a program on the same system, an application can simply use the HLL's call operation. Also, an SPL procedure can call another program only if the program is also a stored procedure.

The following RPGLE example calls the MYPROCX procedure with three host variables, ARG1, ARG2, and ARG3, passed as arguments.

```
EXEC SQL
  Call MyProcX ( :Arg1,
                 :Arg2,
                 :Arg3 );
```

Rather than embedded SQL CALL statements, the most common scenario is for a client application, such as a Web or PC application, to use a Java Database Connectivity (JDBC) method or an Open Database Connectivity (ODBC) function to call a stored procedure. Because stored procedures can execute complex data access and business logic, they can benefit client applications in several ways: simplify coding the client application, increase performance, and improve security.

To use an RPGLE program as a stored procedure, a CREATE PROCEDURE statement must be executed before any call to the procedure. The **CREATE PROCEDURE statement** stores a permanent definition of a stored procedure's interface and the location of its associated program object in the SQL system catalog, and the DBMS uses this information to properly handle subsequent calls.

Here is an example for a procedure with three parameters:

```
CREATE PROCEDURE MyProcX
  ( In    Parm1    Int,
    InOut Parm2    Char( 10 ),
    Out   RtmMsgNo Char(  7 ) )
  Language RPGLE
  Specific MyProcXParam3
  Not Deterministic
  Reads SQL Data
  External Name MyPgmX
  Parameter Style General
```

The CREATE PROCEDURE statement specifies the procedure's parameter types and whether they are used for input, output, or both, from the perspective of the called procedure.

For the `MYPROCX` procedure defined in the example, the corresponding `RPGLE` program's parameter list would look like this:

```
....1....+....2....+....3....+....4....+....5....+....6
 * Parameters
 * - - - - - - - - - - - - - - - - - - - - - - - - - -
D Parm1           S               10I 0
D Parm2           S               10A
D RtnMsgNo        S                7A
 .
 .
 * Entry point
 * - - - - - - - - - - - - - - - - - - - - - - - - - -
C     *Entry      Plist
C                 Parm                        Parm1
C                 Parm                        Parm2
C                 Parm                        RtnMsgNo
```

The code in the `RPGLE` program should use `PARM1` only as an input value. The program can also use `PARM2` as an input value and can change the value of `PARM2` and `RTNMSGNO`. Otherwise, the program code can perform any valid `RPGLE` or embedded SQL operations.

A procedure can also return a read-only result set of rows by opening an SQL cursor in the program and leaving it open. The result set can be processed by JDBC methods or ODBC functions, topics beyond the scope of this book. If a procedure returns a result set, a `CREATE PROCEDURE` statement clause must specify how many result sets are returned, as in the following example:

```
Create Procedure MyProcY
  ( In  Parm1 Int )
  Result Set 1
  Language RPGLE
  Not Deterministic
  Modifies SQL Data
  External Name MyPgmY
  Parameter Style SQL
```

This example also illustrates use of the `PARAMETER STYLE SQL` clause, described in more detail later.

The corresponding `RPGLE` parameter list would look like this:

```
....1....+....2....+....3....+....4....+....5....+....6
 * Parameters
 * - - - - - - - - - - - - - - - - - - - - - - - - - -
D Parm1            S              10I 0

D Parm1NullInd     S               5I 0
D ParmSqlState     S               5A
D ParmProcName     S             517A    Varying
D ParmSpecName     S             128A    Varying
D ParmMsgText      S              70A    Varying
 .

 .
 * Entry point
 * - - - - - - - - - - - - - - - - - - - - - - - - - -
C     *Entry       Plist
C                  Parm                    Parm1
C                  Parm                    Parm1NullInd
C                  Parm                    ParmSqlState
C                  Parm                    ParmProcName
C                  Parm                    ParmSpecName
C                  Parm                    ParmMsgText
```

Both of these examples illustrate some of the other `CREATE PROCEDURE` clauses, covered briefly here.

### LANGUAGE language

Possible values for *Language* are

- `RPGLE`, `COBOLLE`, `C`, or another HLL name—For external HLL programs
- `SQL`—For SQL procedures that include a procedure body (that is, are written with SPL, as discussed below)

### SPECIFIC specific-name

This clause provides a unique name within the schema. If there is only one procedure with a particular procedure name, this clause can be omitted or the procedure name can be used as the specific name. Specify a different name here if several procedures have the same name but a different number of parameters.

### [NOT] DETERMINISTIC

- NOT DETERMINISTIC—For programs that may return different results for the same argument values. Use this setting if you are not sure (it is the default).
- DETERMINISTIC—For programs that always return the same results for the same argument values and have no side effects. (The client system may use a previously retrieved value and not actually call the program.)

### READS SQL DATA, MODIFIES SQL DATA, CONTAINS SQL, NO SQL

- READS SQL DATA—The program may use SQL statements to read data. It can contain any SQL statement other than DELETE, INSERT, UPDATE, COMMIT, ROLLBACK, SET TRANSACTION, ALTER TABLE, RENAME, COMMENT ON, LABEL ON, GRANT, REVOKE, CONNECT, DISCONNECT, RELEASE, SET CONNECTION, or any CREATE or DROP statement.
- MODIFIES SQL DATA—The program may use SQL statements to read and/or modify data. It can contain any SQL statement other than COMMIT, ROLLBACK, SET TRANSACTION, CONNECT, DISCONNECT, RELEASE, or SET CONNECTION.
- CONTAINS SQL—The program can contain SPL statements, such as DECLARE and SET, as well as COMMIT, ROLLBACK, SET TRANSACTION, CONNECT, DISCONNECT, RELEASE, and SET CONNECTION.
- NO SQL—The program should not contain any SQL statement.

The following two clauses can be specified only for an external HLL program (not a procedure written with SPL):

### EXTERNAL NAME HLL-program-name

Specify the external HLL program name. If no name is specified, the default is the procedure name. An unqualified or a qualified name can be specified.

### PARAMETER STYLE style

Possible values for *style* are

- GENERAL—Use this option for existing HLL programs (no extra parameters are passed). The following parameters are passed to the HLL program:
  - o One parameter for each parameter specified in the procedure's parameter list

- SQL—Use this option for newly implemented HLL programs that are (mainly) intended to be called from SQL, JDBC, or ODBC. The following parameters are passed to the HLL program:
  - One parameter for each parameter specified in the parameter list.
  - One indicator variable (INOUT SMALLINT) for each parameter in the list. Set by SQL runtime for IN and INOUT parameters to <0 for null, ≥0 for non-null; can be reset by the program for OUT and INOUT parameters.
  - INOUT CHAR(5)—SQLSTATE. Passed in as 00000; should be set by the program if
    - WARNING—Set to 01Hxx, where *xx* is any two digits or uppercase letters.
    - ERROR—Set to 38yxx, where *y* is an uppercase letter T–Z and *xx* is any two digits or uppercase letters.
  - IN CHAR(517)—The fully qualified procedure name, such as APPDTA.MYPROCX.
  - IN CHAR(128)—The specific name of the procedure, such as MYPROCXPARAMS.
  - InOut VarChar(70)—Initialized on input, can be set to message text by the program. If this parameter is set by the program, the SQLSTATE parameter (above) should be set to indicate a warning or error; otherwise, the message text is ignored.

To remove a procedure definition from the SQL catalog, a DROP PROCEDURE statement is executed:

```
Drop Procedure AppDta.MyProcX
```

If more than one procedure in the same schema has the same name, a list of parameter types can be specified along with the procedure name:

```
Drop Procedure
  AppDta.MyProcX( Int,
                  Char( 10 ),
                  Char(  7 ) )
```

As an alternative, the procedure's specific name can be used:

```
Drop Specific Procedure AppDta.MyProcXParam3
```

A procedure must be dropped before it can be re-created it using a CREATE PROCEDURE statement.

## SQL PROCEDURAL LANGUAGE

For portability to other relational database management systems, a procedure can be implemented with SPL. Figure 14-1 shows a simple stored procedure written with SPL. For simplicity, this example omits error handling and assumes the caller handles commitment control.

The first part of the CREATE PROCEDURE statement is similar to that for a stored procedure written with an HLL and specifies the parameter names, types, and usage. To use SPL for the implementation, SQL is specified as the language, and the procedure body is included within a pair of BEGIN/END delimiters. If the procedure body consists of only one SQL statement, the delimiters are not required.

The procedure body can contain comments, local variable declarations, assignment statements, SQL data manipulation statements, conditional tests, and a variety of other types of statements. SPL essentially provides a fairly complete programming language, although it does not include any user interface support. Keep in mind that an SQL CALL statement can be used within a stored procedure to call other stored procedures, including ones written in either SPL or an HLL. This capability lets a complex procedure be decomposed into a hierarchy of simpler procedures.

When a CREATE PROCEDURE statement that includes SPL for the procedure body is executed, the DBMS uses the multistep process depicted in Figure 14-2 to create a program (*PGM) object.

```
Create Procedure
  TransferPart ( In  XfrPartNo    Int,
                 In  XfrQtyRqs    Int,
                 In  FromWhsNo    Int,
                 In  ToWhsNo      Int,
                 Out XfrQtyActual Int )
  Language SQL

Begin
  -- Transfer up to XfrQtyRqs units of
  -- part XfrPartNo from FromWhsNo to
  -- ToWhsNo and return the actual units
  -- transferred in XfrQtyActual.

  Declare QtyToXfr Int;

  Set XfrQtyActual = 0;

  Select  Qty
    Into  QtyToXfr
    From  Inventory
    Where PartNo = XfrPartNo
      And WhsNo  = FromWhsNo;

  If QtyToXfr > XfrQtyRqs
    Then Set QtyToXfr = XfrQtyRqs;
  End If;

  Update  Inventory
    Set   Qty = Qty - QtyToXfr
    Where PartNo = XfrPartNo
      And WhsNo  = FromWhsNo;

  Update  Inventory
    Set   Qty = Qty + QtyToXfr
    Where PartNo = XfrPartNo
      And WhsNo  = ToWhsNo;

  Set XfrQtyActual = QtyToXfr;

End -- TransferPart
```

**FIGURE 14-1**  **TransferPart** stored procedure implemented in SPL

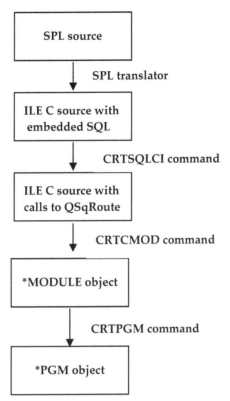

**FIGURE 14-2**    **Process to create a \*PGM object from SPL source**

The first step translates the SPL source into ILE C source code with embedded SQL statements. This source is then precompiled with the CRTSQLCI (Create SQL ILE C Object) command, which generates pure C code with the embedded SQL statements translated to function calls. Last, the CRTCMOD (Create C Module) and CRTPGM (Create Program) commands compile the C source into a program object with \*CALLER as its activation group.

This multistep process using C as an intermediate language has a couple of implications. First, to create a stored procedure with SPL, one must purchase and install IBM's ILE C product, as well as the IBM DB2 Query Manager and SQL Development Kit, to provide the necessary C compiler and precompiler. Second, the generated C program has hidden parameters used by DB2 to make the stored procedure call. These extra parameters mean one cannot call an SPL program with an HLL Call statement as one can with an HLL program used as a stored procedure.

The approach IBM took of creating a program object from SPL has an important security-related benefit. Program adopted authority can be used with an SPL stored procedure just as with HLL stored procedures. This capability enables the handling of a wide variety of security requirements that object and column-level security alone cannot completely handle.

A CREATE PROCEDURE statement with SPL also stores the procedure body's source in the SQL catalog. In any case, the whole CREATE PROCEDURE statement should generally be placed in a source member and the RUNSQLSTM (Run SQL Statements) command used to run the SQL statement from the source member. This approach lets the source be edited and the procedure re-created without the need to retrieve source from the catalog.

## SPL LANGUAGE FEATURES

The full SPL syntax and programming documentation is covered in the manuals. To give an idea of what is available, a brief review of some of the most important features of the language follows.

All SPL statements end with a semicolon (;). Comments can be coded following a double dash (--) and running to the end of the line:

```
-- This is a comment
```

### DECLARATIONS

As Figure 14-1 showed, SPL supports parameter and local variable declarations. These declarations can use any of the column data types available in the CREATE TABLE statement, such as CHAR, INT, or FLOAT. A default, or initial, value can also be declared:

```
Declare QtyToXfr Int Default 0;
```

Note that unlike all major HLLs, SPL does not support arrays.

### ASSIGNMENT

The SPL SET statement lets an expression value be assigned to a local variable or to an OUT or INOUT parameter. SPL also permits setting a local variable or parameter to NULL, as in the following statement:

```
Set XfrQtyActual = Null;
```

A local variable or parameter can also be tested for NULL:

```
If QtyToXfr Is Not Null Then ...
```

This feature makes it simpler to deal with null-capable columns because no separate null indicator variable need be provided, as is necessary when using embedded SQL SELECT, FETCH, UPDATE, and INSERT statements in an HLL program.

### SQL DATA DEFINITION AND MANIPULATION STATEMENTS

In SPL, SQL data definition and manipulation statements can be used in a similar way to embedded SQL statements in an HLL program. In SPL, however, the use of EXEC SQL is not required to delimit SQL statements, nor must variable or parameter names be prefixed with a colon (:), as is required with HLL host variables used in SQL statements.

### CONDITIONAL STATEMENTS

SPL has both IF and CASE conditional statements. An IF statement can have a series of tests, using ELSEIF clauses, as well as a final ELSE clause:

```
If XfrPartNo = 123 Then
  Set QtyToXfr = 1;
ElseIf XfrQtyRqs > 100 Then
  Set QtyToXfr = 100;
Else
  Set QtyToXfr = XfrQtyRqs;
End If;
```

The CASE statement can be used in two ways. The first form branches based on the value of a scalar expression:

```
Case PartNo
  When 123
    Set QTYTOXFR = 1;
  When 234
    Set QtyToXfr = 10;
  Else
    Set QtyToXfr = XfrQtyRqs;
End Case;
```

The second form of CASE is precisely equivalent to a multi-way IF/ELSEIF/ELSE:

```
Case
  When XfrPartNo = 123 Then
    Set QtyToXfr = 1;
  When XfrQtyRqs > 100 Then
    Set QtyToXfr = 100;
  Else
    Set QtyToXfr = XfrQtyRqs;
End If;
```

### LOOP CONTROL STRUCTURES

SPL has four loop structures:

- LOOP—Infinite loop (use the LEAVE statement to exit)
- WHILE—Test is at the beginning of the loop
- REPEAT—Test is at the end of the loop
- FOR—Iterate over a set of rows

The LOOP, WHILE, and REPEAT structures can be used the way comparable HLL loop structures are used to control program flow.

The example in Figure 14-3 shows a simple WHILE loop that conditionally allocates some of each warehouse's inventory. For simplicity, this example assumes warehouse numbers run from 1 to 10.

The REPEAT loop is similar to the WHILE loop, but the structure places the test at the end of the loop:

```
Repeat
  loop-body
Until condition
End Repeat;
```

The LOOP structure generally begins with a label and is exited by a LEAVE statement, as in this example:

```
AllocLoop: Loop
  ...
  If SQLSTATE <> SUCCESSFUL Then
    Leave AllocLoop;
  End If;
  ...
End Loop AllocLoop;
```

A LEAVE statement can also be used to exit from the middle of a WHILE or REPEAT loop, as long as a label is coded for the loop to be exited.

Just as in HLL programs, any of the loop structures just covered can be used to iterate over an open SQL cursor (declared with a DECLARE CURSOR statement earlier in the procedure), executing repeated FETCH statements. As a more convenient alternative, SPL also provides a special form of FOR loop to process a selected set of rows. Figure 14-4 shows a sample FOR loop that implements the same operation as the WHILE loop in Figure 14-3.

```
TotalAlloc = 0;
CurWhsNo   = 1;

While ( CurWhsNo    <= 10        ) And
      ( TotalAlloc <  RqsAlloc ) Do

  Select  Qty Into CurQty
    From  Inventory
    Where PartNo = CurPartNo
      And WhsNo  = CurWhsNo;

  If SQLSTATE = SUCCESSFUL Then
    Case
      When CurQty > 2 * (RqsAlloc - TotalAlloc) Then
        Set CurAlloc = RqsAlloc - TotalAlloc;
      When CurQty > (RqsAlloc - TotalAlloc) Then
        Set CurAlloc = (RqsAlloc - TotalAlloc) / 2;
      When CurQty > 0 Then
        Set CurAlloc = 1;
      Else
        Set CurAlloc = 0;
    End Case;
  End If;

  If CurAlloc > 0 Then
    Update  Inventory
      Set   Qty = Qty - CurAlloc
      Where PartNo = CurPartNo
        And WhsNo  = CurWhsNo;
    If SQLSTATE = SUCCESSFUL Then
      Set TotalAlloc = TotalAlloc + CurAlloc;
    End If;
  End If;

  Set CurWhsNo = CurWhsNo + 1;
End While;
```

**FIGURE 14-3   WHILE statement example**

```
TotalAlloc = 0;

For InvRow As InvCursor Cursor For
  Select  Qty
    From  Inventory
    Where PartNo = CurPartNo
Do
  Case
    When Qty > 2 * (RqsAlloc - TotalAlloc) Then
      Set CurAlloc = RqsAlloc - TotalAlloc;
    When Qty > (RqsAlloc - TotalAlloc) Then
      Set CurAlloc = (RqsAlloc - TotalAlloc) / 2;
    When Qty > 0 Then
      Set CurAlloc = 1;
    Else
      Set CurAlloc = 0;
  End Case;

  If CurAlloc > 0 Then
    Update  Inventory
      Set   Qty = Qty - CurAlloc
      Where Current Of InvCursor;
    If SQLSTATE + SUCCESSFUL Then
      Set TotalAlloc = TotalAlloc + CurAlloc;
    End If;
  End If;
End For;
```

**FIGURE 14-4**   **FOR statement example**

Notice how the first part of the FOR loop is a cursor specification. Within the loop body, any column defined in the cursor's SELECT list, such as Qty, can be referred to as a variable. The loop terminates when the last row in the cursor's result set has been processed. Note that the index variable, such as InvRow, in this form of the FOR loop is not used.

Note also that in a FOR loop, the same identifier, such as Qty, might be used for an implicit variable defined by the cursor's SELECT column list as well as for a column in a subsequent UPDATE statement. The SPL processor treats as a column name any unqualified identifier that names both a column and a variable. When this type of ambiguity arises, a label for a loop or compound statement (discussed next) can be used as a qualifier for a local variable within the scope of the loop or compound statement.

To branch out of a loop or to the next statement after the end of a compound statement, use the LEAVE statement.

## COMPOUND STATEMENTS

Any series of SPL statements can be combined within a BEGIN/END block, and the block can be treated as a single compound statement. Variables and condition handlers (discussed next) declared within a block are local to that block.

Optionally, the BEGIN keyword can be followed with the ATOMIC keyword to specify that if an error occurs during execution of any statement in the block, the effects of all prior statements in the block are rolled back. You must be at a commitment control boundary, for example by having just executed a COMMIT or ROLLBACK operation, when beginning execution of an atomic block. Because a stored procedure can be defined as a single block, atomic stored procedures can be created.

## CONDITIONS AND CONDITION HANDLERS

To provide a mechanism for handling exceptional conditions, SPL lets conditions and condition handlers be defined. A condition is just a name for a value of the SQLSTATE variable that is set for every SQL operation. The following statement declares CursorNotOpenState as a condition name for the corresponding SQLSTATE value:

```
Declare CursorNotOpenState
        Condition For '24501';
```

A condition handler specifies what to do when a condition occurs, as in the following example:

```
Declare Continue Handler For
  CursorNotOpenState
  Set RowCount = 0;
```

There are three main parts to a condition handler declaration. The first is a keyword: CONTINUE, EXIT, or UNDO. The keyword specifies which system-defined action to take when an exception occurs.

The second part is a list of one or more conditions. Each condition must be one of the following:

- A previously declared condition name
- The keyword SQLSTATE followed by an SQLSTATE string value
- One of the keywords SQLEXCEPTION, SQLWARNING, or NOT FOUND

The final part is a simple SQL statement that specifies user-defined actions to take. Figure 14-5 summarizes the effect of various condition handler options.

| System-defined actions | |
|---|---|
| CONTINUE | Perform user-defined actions and continue with the statement after the statement that raised the condition. |
| EXIT | Perform user-defined actions and continue at the end of the compound statement that contained the statement that raised the condition. |
| UNDO | First, roll back all changes made during execution of the compound statement that contained the statement that raised the condition. Then, perform user-defined actions and continue at the end of the compound statement that contained the statement that raised the condition. |

| Conditions | |
|---|---|
| Condition name | The handler is invoked when SQLSTATE is set to the value specified in the condition declaration. |
| SQLSTATE keyword followed by an SQLSTATE string value | The handler is invoked when SQLSTATE is set to the specified value. |
| SQLWARNING | The handler is invoked when SQLSTATE is set to 01xxx. |
| NOT FOUND | The handler is invoked when SQLSTATE is set to 02xxx. |
| SQLEXCEPTION | The handler is invoked when SQLSTATE is set to a value other than 00xxx, 01xxx, or 02xxx. |

**FIGURE 14-5   Condition handler options**

Note that this version of SPL does not support compound SQL statements in condition handlers; however, a one-pass loop can be coded as a workaround, as in the following example:

```
Declare Continue Handler For
   CursorNotOpenState
   CursorNotOpenStateLoop: Loop
     Set RowCount = 0;
     Set ErrMsg = 'Cursor not open';
     ...
     Leave CursorNotOpenStateLoop;
   End Loop CursorNotOpenStateLoop;
```

### SIGNALING USER-DEFINED WARNINGS AND EXCEPTIONS

To generate a user-defined condition to be handled by a program or procedure that calls a stored procedure, a stored procedure can execute a SIGNAL statement, such as the following:

```
Signal SqlState '99U002'
  Set Message_Text = 'Failed transfer of part.';
```

The statement can specify either the SQLSTATE keyword and value, as in this example, or a previously defined SQL condition name. The text can also be set for a message that will be placed in the SQLERRMC variable of the SQL Communication Area (SQLCA).

To avoid using system-defined SQLSTATE values to signal one's own application-defined errors, a digit from 7 through 9 or an uppercase character I through Z can be specified as the third character in the SQLSTATE values. Recall that the first two characters of SQLSTATE indicate the severity of the condition: 00 means no warning or error, 01 means a warning, 02 means no data, and other values mean error. When a SIGNAL is executed, if the same compound statement also includes a handler for that condition, control transfers to the handler. Otherwise, control transfers to the caller of the procedure. If a SIGNAL statement is executed within a handler, control also passes to the caller.

To handle a condition and then return to the procedure's caller with the same condition, a RESIGNAL statement can be executed within a handler:

```
Resignal
```

Optionally, user-defined message text can be provided by using a statement such as

```
Resignal
  Set Message_Text = 'Failed transfer of part.';
```

A RESIGNAL statement can also specify SQLSTATE or a condition, just as with the SIGNAL statement, but to specify your own SQL state, you should use a SIGNAL statement.

## Diagnostic Feedback

To obtain feedback in an SQL procedure, declare a variable for SQLSTATE:

```
Declare SqlState Char( 5 );
```

When either or both of these variables are declared, the SQL runtime sets them after every statement, except the following:

- An assignment that references the SQLSTATE variable, such as
  SET SQVESQLSTATE = SQLSTATE
- GET DIAGNOSTICS EXCEPTION 1 ...

In general, SQLSTATE should be saved immediately after any statement so it can be used in subsequent statements to diagnose the errors.

SPL includes the GET DIAGNOSTICS statement to retrieve information after a statement is executed. For DML statements, the following example shows how to retrieve the number of rows affected:

```
DECLARE RowCnt Integer;
  .
  .
  .
UPDATE   customers
  SET    discount = 0.0
  WHERE  status   = 'X';

Get Diagnostics RowCnt = Row_Count;
```

The ROW_COUNT built-in special register provides the same value as the SQLERRD(3) field of the SQL communication area.

When a statement is completed with a warning or exception, the message text, SQLERRMC, and message length, SQLERRML, can be retrieved using another form of the GET DIAGNOSTICS statement:

```
Declare MsgText    Char(70);
Declare MsgTextLen Integer;
  .
  .
  .
Get Diagnostics Exception 1
  MsgText    = Message_Text,
  MsgTextLen = Message_Length;
```

In general, if this statement is used, it should be the first statement in a condition handler. Otherwise, if other SPL statements precede it, you will not get the message for the appropriate statement.

# AN INTRODUCTION TO USER-DEFINED FUNCTIONS: SOURCED FUNCTIONS

SQL provides a variety of built-in scalar and column functions. These functions accept and return values defined by the built-in data types, such as Character and Integer. To handle values defined with distinct, or user-defined, types, SQL lets you create **user-defined functions (UDFs)** that are based on built-in functions. This type of function is known as a **sourced function**.

For example, consider the following DescriptionType distinct type definition and a partial PART table definition that uses that type:

```
Create Distinct Type DescriptionType
  As VarChar( 100 )

Create Table Part
  ( ...,
    Description DescriptionType Not Null,
    ... )
```

Although the description column is based on a VARCHAR(100) type, SQL does not permit the use of any built-in string functions, such as SUBSTR or CONCAT, on this column. However, a UDF can be created to handle the DescriptionType distinct type:

```
Create Function SubStr( DescriptionType, Int, Int )
  Returns VarChar( 100 )
    Specific DescriptSubStr
  Source SubStr( VarChar( 100 ), Int, Int )
```

This new function can then be used in a SELECT statement such as the following:

```
Select SubStr( Description, 1, 20 )
  From Part
```

For a sourced function, the SOURCE clause of the CREATE FUNCTION statement must specify the name of an SQL built-in function, such as SUBSTR, or another UDF, followed by a parenthesized list of the existing function's parameter types, which in this case is ( VARCHAR(100), INT, INT ). Together, the function name and the parameter types define exactly which function SQL should invoke when the new sourced function is called. Because an SQL function is uniquely identified within a schema by its name and the number and type of parameters, a UDF can have the same name as the function it is based on, as the one in this example does, as long as the parameter types are different. In fact, this is a common practice for sourced functions that merely make a built-in function available for a user-defined type (UDT).

In the example, CREATE FUNCTION SUBSTR is followed by a parenthesized list of data types—( DescriptionType, INT, INT )—for the sourced function's parameters. The sourced function must have the same number of parameters as the based-on function specified in the SOURCE clause, and each sourced function parameter type must be castable to the corresponding parameter type in the SOURCE clause.

The optional SPECIFIC clause provides a unique name to use when dropping this function, such as DescriptSubStr in this case. When an existing function name is used for a new sourced function, it is wise to provide a meaningful specific name.

Sourced UDFs are based on other existing functions. A sourced UDF always specifies the SOURCE clause in its CREATE FUNCTION statement. An external UDF is based on a user-written program and never uses the SOURCE clause in its CREATE FUNCTION statement. An SQL UDF uses SPL to implement the function and also does not use a SOURCE clause.

UDFs can be used almost everywhere built-in functions can be used. However, UDFs cannot be used in check constraints. Nor can external or SQL UDFs be used in an ORDER BY or a GROUP BY clause unless the SQL statement is read-only and is executed in an environment that allows temporary files for statement processing, such as when the CRTSQLxxx command's ALWCPYDTA parameter is *YES or *OPTIMIZE.

## USER-DEFINED FUNCTIONS

Like a stored procedure, a user-defined function can be implemented either with an HLL program (this is referred to as an **external function**) or by coding SPL (referred to as an **SQL function**). Many of the principles that apply to stored procedures also apply to scalar UDFs.

For example, the same SPL statements can be used for either a procedure or a function. Here is an example of creating a simple SPL function:

```
Create Function Right
  ( Str        VarChar ( 2000 ),
    SubStrLen Int )
  Returns  VarChar ( 2000 )
  Language SQL
  Returns  Null On Null Input
Begin
  -- Return a string that contains the rightmost
  -- SubStrLen characters of the Str string.

  Declare StrLen    Int;
  Declare RtnStrLen Int;
  Declare RtnStrBgn Int;
  Declare RtnStr    VarChar ( 2000 );

  Set StrLen    = Length( Str );
  Set RtnStrLen = Min( StrLen, SubStrLen );
  Set RtnStrBgn = ( StrLen - RtnStrLen ) + 1;
  Set RtnStr    = SubStr( Str, RtnStrBgn, RtnStrLen );

  Return RtnStr;

End -- Right
```

All parameters for a function are input parameters, so the IN, OUT, or INOUT keyword is not specified for function parameters as is done for procedure parameters. The RIGHT function has two parameters: the string and the length of the desired substring. A UDF always returns a single value, for which the data type, such as VARCHAR(2000) in this example, is specified on the RETURNS clause that follows the parameter list. The SPL RETURN expression statement exits the function and returns the function's value to its caller.

On the CREATE FUNCTION statement for an external or SQL function, the following clauses can be used, as explained previously for the CREATE PROCEDURE statement:

- LANGUAGE
- SPECIFIC
- [NOT] DETERMINISTIC
- READS SQL DATA, MODIFIES SQL DATA, CONTAINS SQL, or NO SQL
- EXTERNAL NAME
- PARAMETER STYLE

A RESULT SETS clause cannot be used because functions cannot return result sets. Also, instead of a program, a procedure in a service program can be specified on the EXTERNAL NAME clause, using the following form:

```
...
External Name 'APPDTA/APPFUNCS(RIGHT)'
```

Note a few particulars about this form of the EXTERNAL NAME clause. The name must be enclosed in apostrophes ('), and a library, service program, and procedure or function within the service program must be specified. In general, the library and program names, which are object names, should be all upper case. The procedure or function name should match the case of the name that is exported from the service program; typically, this means all upper case in RPGLE and COBOL and mixed case in C. In a quoted external name, the library and service program names must be separated by a slash (/), regardless of the naming option (discussed later). The procedure or function name is enclosed in parentheses following the service program name.

One clause that can optionally be specified for UDFs, but not for procedures, is RETURNS NULL ON NULL INPUT. When this clause is specified, the DBMS does not call the function if any of its arguments are null. Instead, null is returned. The default, or coding an explicit CALLED ON NULL INPUT clause, causes the function to be called even when one or more arguments are null.

For an external function, the correspondence between the function definition's parameter list and the HLL program or service program procedure or function is slightly different than for a stored procedure, as explained above. When PARAMETER STYLE SQL is specified, the stored procedure can be implemented with either an HLL program or an HLL procedure in a service program. In the program or procedure, declare one input parameter for each of the function's parameters, followed by an output parameter for the function's return value. Next, the HLL program or procedure should declare indicator parameters for the function's parameters followed by an additional indicator parameter for the function's return value. The HLL program or procedure should *not* change any of the input parameters or their respective indicator parameters and should always set the output parameter and its indicator parameter. Following the return value indicators are the additional parameters for SQLSTATE, function name, specific name, and message text as described above for stored procedures.

When PARAMETER STYLE GENERAL is specified, an HLL function coded as part of a service program must be used. The function's parameters and return value correspond one-to-one with the UDF's parameters and return value, and there are no indicator or other additional parameters.

Keep in mind that the same function name can be used for different functions as long as the functions have different numbers and/or types of parameters. When the same function name is used for more than one function, it is a good idea to include the SPECIFIC clause to give each function a unique specific name.

## END-OF-CHAPTER

### CHAPTER SUMMARY

1. Stored procedures are a named chunk of code with optional parameters that can be called with an SQL CALL statement, with JDBC methods, or with ODBC functions. A stored procedure can be implemented as an HLL program or using the SQL Procedural Language (SPL). An HLL program that implements a stored procedure can optionally include embedded SQL. A stored procedure can return one or more result sets to a JDBC or ODBC client. To define a stored procedure in a schema, the CREATE PROCEDURE statement is used.

2. The CREATE FUNCTION statement creates a user-defined function (UDF) that can be used in SQL statements. A sourced function is a UDF that is based on an existing built-in function or other UDF. Sourced functions are especially useful for extending SQL built-in functions to operate on values that are defined as a distinct type.

3. Nonsourced, user-defined functions are similar to stored procedures, except a UDF always returns a value. A UDF can be used most places a built-in scalar function can be used. A UDF can be implemented with an HLL program or with a procedure or function in a service program. SPL can also be used to implement a UDF. To define a UDF in a schema, the CREATE FUNCTION statement is used.

### KEY TERMS

| | |
|---|---|
| CREATE PROCEDURE statement | SQL Procedural Language (SPL) |
| external function | stored procedure |
| sourced function | user-defined function (UDF) |
| SQL function | |

# CHAPTER 15

## TRIGGERS

## CHAPTER OBJECTIVES

Upon completion of this chapter, you should be able to

- Explain what triggers are
- Explain how triggers can be used to transparently enforce application logic in the database

## INTRODUCTION TO DATABASE TRIGGERS

A **trigger** is a condition that causes a procedure to be executed when a specified change operation is performed on a table or view. The procedure evoked by the trigger includes a set of actions to be performed. The change operation can be an SQL INSERT, UPDATE, or DELETE statement or an insert, update, or delete high-level language statement in an application program.

When a user or an application issues a change or read operation on a database table that has an associated trigger, the operation calls the appropriate **trigger program**.

The advantage of trigger programs is that they ensure that the actions of a trigger program occur regardless of which application or system utility tries to change the table. Trigger programs can be used to block table inserts, updates, and deletes that do not meet specified conditions. Also, for row inserts and updates, a trigger program can change the row being inserted or updated. Thus, trigger programs provide an important tool to extend capabilities for enforcing database integrity and providing other database functions.

## ADDING A TRIGGER

To add a trigger to a database table:

1. Create a trigger program. The trigger program can be

   - High-level language (HLL)
   - Structured Query Language (SQL)
   - Control Language (CL) program

2. Add the trigger using one of the following methods:

   - IBM Navigator for i.
   - The ADDPFTRG (Add Physical File Trigger) CL command. The name of the trigger program must be specified in the command's trigger PGM (Program) parameter.
   - The CREATE TRIGGER SQL statement.

### ADDING A TRIGGER USING IBM NAVIGATOR FOR I

To add a trigger using IBM Navigator for i:

1. *Open* **IBM Navigator for i**.
2. *Expand* the **system name**.
3. *Expand* **Databases**.
4. *Expand* **Schemas**.
5. *Click* the **schema** that contains the table to which the trigger is being added.
6. *Click* **Tables**.
7. *Right-click* the **table** to which the trigger is being added.
8. *Click* **New**.
9. *Click* **Trigger**.
10. *Click* **External** (or **SQL**). The External option will add a system trigger. The SQL option will add an SQL trigger.
11. Follow the wizard to add the trigger.

### THE ADD TRIGGER COMMAND

To add a trigger using the ADDPFTRG command, a trigger program is first created and compiled like any other HLL program. The ADDPFTRG command then is used to associate the trigger program with a table.

Six trigger conditions are supported for a table:

- Before insert
- Before update
- Before delete
- After insert
- After update
- After delete

The ADDPFTRG command associates a trigger program with one or more of these conditions for a table. When a trigger condition is true (that is, right before or right after an insert, update, or delete event), the trigger program that was specified for the associated table and condition is automatically called.

The same trigger program can be used for multiple conditions or even for multiple tables. Because the second step is simpler, we cover that first.

Suppose a trigger program named CustChk is created to make additional integrity checks before permitting a row insert or update, and we want to associate the trigger program with the CUSTOMERS table. The ADDPFTRG commands shown in Figure 15-1 make the proper association.

```
AddPfTrg  File( AppDta/customers )
          TrgTime( *Before )
          TrgEvent( *Insert )
          Pgm( AppExc/CustChk )
          RplTrg( *Yes )

AddPfTrg  File( AppDta/customers )
          TrgTime( *Before )
          TrgEvent( *Update )
          Pgm( AppExc/CustChk )
          RplTrg( *Yes )
```

FIGURE 15-1   The ADDPFTRG (Add Physical File Trigger) command

For the TRGTIME (Trigger time) parameter, the option *BEFORE or *AFTER can be specified. A trigger program that is called before table changes occur can perform actions before the table constraints, such as foreign key constraints, are checked. Because a trigger program can itself perform table I/O, a before trigger program can take necessary actions to ensure that the constraints are satisfied. When TRGTIME(*AFTER) is specified, the trigger program is called after the table is updated.

The choices for the TRGEVENT (Trigger event) parameter are *INSERT, *UPDATE, and *DELETE. Any of the six combinations of TRGTIME and TRGEVENT values can be specified on an ADDPFTRG command. To associate the same program with multiple conditions, multiple ADDPFTRG commands are used, as in this example.

The RPLTRG (Replace trigger) parameter determines whether the trigger program replaces an existing trigger program for the same table and condition. If *NO is specified for this parameter, the ADDPFTRG command fails if the specified condition already has an associated trigger program.

Each of the six possible trigger conditions for a table can have only one trigger program.

An optional TRGUPDCND (Trigger update condition) parameter lets *CHANGE be specified so that a trigger program is called for an update event only if the update is changing the contents of the row. Or the default *ALWAYS can be specified to have a trigger program called for an update event whether or not the row is changed.

Another optional parameter is ALWREPCHG (Allow repeated change). Specifying ALWREPCHG(*YES) for a before-insert or before-update trigger lets the trigger program change the affected row by modifying the trigger buffer's after image before the insert or update. The ALWREPCHG parameter also determines whether an after-insert or after-update trigger program can directly update, via an SQL UPDATE statement, the row that the application program is inserting or updating. With ALWREPCHG(*NO), which is the default, the trigger program cannot perform I/O to the same row; with ALWREPCHG(*YES), it can.

A trigger program must exist when the ADDPFTRG command is executed, as well as when an attempt is made to call it for subsequent table operations. If the command omits the library or specifies *LIBL for the library on the PGM parameter, the library list is searched for the program at the time the ADDPFTRG command is executed. The name of the library in which the program is found is stored in the table object's description so that subsequent calls to the trigger program are explicitly qualified. If a trigger program is moved from one library to another, the ADDPFTRG command must be executed to replace the trigger program with the program in the new library. However, after a trigger program has been associated with a table, the program can be deleted and re-created without the need to re-execute the ADDPFTRG command.

## REMOVING TRIGGERS

Triggers can be removed by using

- The RMVPFTRG (Remove Physical File Trigger) command
- The SQL DROP TRIGGER statement
- IBM Navigator for i

## THE REMOVE TRIGGER COMMAND

The RMVPFTRG command is used to remove the association between a trigger program and the table with which the trigger is associated. After the association is removed, the system takes no action when a change or read operation occurs to the table. The trigger program, however, remains on the system.

The following example shows how to remove the before-insert trigger program for the CUSTOMERS table:

```
RmvPfTrg  File( AppDta/customers )
          TrgTime( *Before )
          TrgEvent( *Insert )
```

The RMVPFTRG command's TRGTIME and TRGEVENT parameters permit the same values as the parameters for the ADDPFTRG command as well as *ALL for all times and/or events. Trigger programs cannot be added or removed while a table is open.

Two trigger program restrictions are imposed on a table with a foreign key constraint:

- A table with an ON DELETE CASCADE foreign key rule cannot have a before- or after-delete trigger program.
- A table with an ON DELETE SET NULL or ON DELETE SET DEFAULT foreign key rule cannot have a before- or after-update trigger program.

These restrictions prevent a cascaded delete or indirect update to a dependent table from firing a trigger program for that table. These restrictions are necessary because delete rule actions are implemented at a lower operating-system level than triggers are, so a cascaded delete or indirect update cannot fire a trigger program under the current architecture.

## CODING A TRIGGER PROGRAM

The only requirement for a trigger program is that it has two parameters that conform to the interface for trigger programs. These two parameters provide the trigger buffer and the trigger buffer length.

When a trigger program is called, it fills the trigger buffer with the before and/or after image of the affected row, along with some control information. The length of this buffer is placed in the trigger buffer length parameter. The trigger program can use these parameters to inspect and, if the ALWREPCHG(*YES) parameter is specified for the trigger program, change the row's contents.

Figure 15-2 shows the layout of the trigger buffer.

| Field | Description | Codes | Type | Length | Starting position |
|-------|-------------|-------|------|--------|-------------------|
| TbFile | Table (file) name | — | Char | 10 | 1 |
| TbLib | Library (schema) name | — | Char | 10 | 11 |
| TbMbr | Member name | — | Char | 10 | 21 |
| TbTrgEvt | Trigger event | '1' = Insert<br>'2' = Delete<br>'3' = Update | Char | 1 | 31 |
| TbTrgTime | Trigger time | '1' = After<br>'2' = Before | Char | 1 | 32 |
| TbCmtLvl | Commit lock level | '0' = *None<br>'1' = *Chg<br>'2' = *CS<br>'3' = *All<br>(or Repeatable Read) | Char | 1 | 33 |
| — | Reserved | — | Char | 3 | 34 |
| TbCcsId | Coded Character Set Identifier (CCSID) | — | Binary | 4 | 37 |
| TbRrn | Relative record number | — | Binary | 4 | 41 |
| | Reserved | — | Char | 4 | 45 |
| TbBfrOfs | Before row image offset | — | Binary | 4 | 49 |
| TbBfrLen | Before row image length | — | Binary | 4 | 53 |
| TbBfrNulOf | Before null column map offset | — | Binary | 4 | 57 |
| TbBfrNulLn | Before null column map length | — | Binary | 4 | 61 |
| TbAftOfs | After row image offset | — | Binary | 4 | 65 |

| TbAftLen | After row image length | — | Binary | 4 | 69 |
|---|---|---|---|---|---|
| TbAftNulOf | After null column map offset | — | Binary | 4 | 73 |
| TbAftNulLn | After null column map length | — | Binary | 4 | 77 |
| — | Reserved | — | Char | 16 | 81 |
| TbBfrRcd | Before row image (update and delete events) | — | Char | Varies (physical file record length) | Varies (TbBfrOfs) |
| TbBfrNul | Before null column map (update and delete events) | '0' = Not null<br>'1' = Null | Char | Varies (equal to number of columns in the table) | Varies (TbBfrNulOf) |
| TbAftRcd | After row image (insert and update events) | — | Char | Varies (physical file record length) | Varies (TbAftOfs) |
| TbAftNul | After null column map (insert and update events) | '0' = Not null<br>'1' = Null | Char | Varies (equal to number of columns in the table) | Varies (TbAftNulOf) |

**FIGURE 15-2** **Trigger buffer layout**

The buffer starts with fixed-length fields that name and describe the table and the trigger condition (event and time). The buffer ends with four variable-length fields that contain the before and after images of the row and null column maps for the images. Each null column map is a series of one-character flags that indicate whether the corresponding column (in the before or after image) is null ('1') or not null ('0').

Because different tables can have different numbers of columns and column sizes and, thus, the before and after image fields in the trigger buffer can vary in length, the starting positions of the images and the null column maps can vary as well. The fixed part of the trigger buffer provides eight fields that contain the offsets and lengths of the four variable fields. An offset is the number of bytes from the start of the trigger buffer to the first byte of the field.

```
CREATE TABLE customers
  ( customer_id   Dec(   7, 0 ) Not Null,
    customer_name Char( 30     ) Not Null,
    credit_limit  Dec(   7, 0 ) Not Null,
  Primary Key ( customer_id ) )
```

**FIGURE 15.3    CUSTOMERS table**

For a simplified CUSTOMERS table such as the one shown in Figure 15-3, the starting positions and lengths are as follows:

| Field | Starting position | Length |
|---|---|---|
| Before image | 97 | 38 |
| Before null column map | 135 | 3 |
| After image | 138 | 38 |
| After null column map | 176 | 3 |

With this information, the definition of the trigger buffer parameter can be coded. Figure 15-4 shows a simple RPGLE trigger program called CustChk that prevents setting a customer's credit limit to a negative value.

In this example, the only trigger buffer fields defined are the before and after image fields and null column maps. The AfCrdLimit field is the only essential field; the others are coded to illustrate the trigger buffer layout. This trigger program should be associated with the before-insert and before-update conditions.

The sample CustChk trigger program tests the after image's credit limit column and, if it is less than zero, calls the CrdLmtMsg CL program shown in Figure 15-5.

The CrdLmtMsg program sends an escape message to the program that called trigger program CustChk. The DBMS handles this message and returns an error to the application program that attempted the I/O operation. In RPGLE, the %ERROR built-in function can be used to test for an error. Also, the RPGLE file status value, which can be retrieved using the %STATUS built-in function, is set to '1023' for before-event trigger programs and to '1024' for after-event trigger programs. In SQL, the SQLSTATE variable is set to '38501'. An application program should be designed to handle errors signaled by a trigger program just like other I/O errors.

```
   // CustChk --    Sample trigger program to check for non-negative
   //               values in the CrdLimit field in the customers table.

   // Requirements: This trigger program must be associated only with
   // before-insert and before-update conditions. If associated with
   // other conditions (e.g., a delete event), errors may occur.
   // Prototype for CrdLmtMsg program
 D CrdLmtMsg       PR                          ExtPgm( 'CRDLMTMSG' )
 D  AfCrdLimit                   15P 5 Const

   // Data structure for trigger buffer parameter, including:
   //   The trigger buffer header fields (bytes 1-96)
   //   Before image fields     (prefix Bf)
   //   Before null column map (prefix Bn)
   //   After  image fields     (prefix Af)
   //   After  null column map (prefix An)

 D TrgBuf          DS
 D  TrgBufHdr                    96A
 D  BfCustID                      7P 0
 D  BfName                       30A
 D  BfCrdLimit                    7P 0
 D  BnCustID                      1A
 D  BnName                        1A
 D  BnCrdLimit                    1A
 D  AfCustID                      7P 0
 D  AfName                       30A
 D  AfCrdLimit                    7P 0
 D  AnCustID                      1A
 D  AnName                        1A
 D  AnCrdLimit                    1A

   // Trigger buffer length parameter
 D TrgBufLen       S             10U 0

   // - - - - - - - - - - - - - - - - - - - - - - - - - - - - - - - -
 C     *Entry       PList
 C                  Parm                        TrgBuf
 C                  Parm                        TrgBufLen

 /Free
   // Check after image value; valid only for insert and update events.
   // Credit limit error

   If AfCrdLimit < 0;
     CrdLmtMsg(AfCrdLimit);
   EndIf;

   Return;

 /End-Free
```

FIGURE 15-4    RPGLE trigger program CustChk

```
/* CrdLmtMsg -- Send escape message to caller of CustChk trigger    */
/*              program                                              */

Pgm Parm( &CrdLmt )

Dcl &CrdLmt     *Dec  ( 15 5 )   /* Input parameter                 */
Dcl &CrdLmtChr  *Char  8         /* Credit limit in character format */
Dcl &MsgDta     *Char 256        /* Message data for escape message  */
Dcl &Blank      *Char  1         VALUE( ' ' )    /* Mnemonic         */

/* Convert credit limit to character, leave room for minus sign.    */
/* If error occurs, just use blank for the value in the message.    */

ChgVar     &CrdLmtChr  &CrdLmt
           MonMsg ( CPF9999 ) Exec( Do )
                   ChgVar &CrdLmtChr &Blank
           EndDo

ChgVar     &MsgDta ( 'Invalid credit limit value: ' *Cat &CrdLmtChr )


SndPgmMsg MsgId( CPF9898 )                                          +
          MsgF( QCpfMsg )                                           +
          ToPgmQ( *Prv ( CustChk ) )                               +
          MsgDta( &MsgDta )                                        +
          MsgType( *Escape )

          MonMsg MsgId( CPF0000 MCH0000 ) /* Ignore error           */

Return
EndPgm
```

FIGURE 15-5  **CrdLmtMsg CL program**

## SOFT-CODING THE TRIGGER BUFFER

The preceding example provides an introduction to how a trigger program works, but production applications can benefit from a somewhat more advanced set of programming techniques. The basic idea in the next example is that the trigger buffer is "soft-coded" so that changes to the table's row can be incorporated by simply recompiling the trigger program. This example also shows how RPGLE /COPY source members enable reuse of standard source code for parts of trigger programs.

The sample trigger program uses three /COPY source members. The DtaType member in Figure 15-6 declares a set of RPGLE variables of various data types. These are used as the basis for other declarations in the program. The TrgDcl member in Figure 15-7 declares an RPGLE data structure for the trigger buffer parameter along with several other variables used with this technique. The TrgEntry member in Figure 15-8 declares the trigger program's parameter list and includes some initial setup code.

The CustLog trigger program in Figure 15-9 uses three /COPY directives to incorporate the standard code into the program. CustLog is a simple program that checks to see whether the value of the customer credit limit has been changed and, if it has, calls another program (not shown) to write the change to a log file.

The CustLog trigger program declares two externally defined record structures (BfCustomer and AfCustomer). Notice that the PREFIX keyword is used on the declarations to provide a unique two-character prefix for every field name (Bf for the before image fields and Af for the after image fields). The trigger program picks up the layouts for the trigger buffer's before and after images from these declarations. For any table's trigger program, similar declarations that refer to the table with which the trigger program is associated must be coded.

```
....1....+....2....+....3....+....4....+....5....+....6....+
  // DtaType -- Standard data type definitions
  //
  // Note that the Based keyword is just a technique to
  // avoid any storage being allocated for the variables
  // because they are never referenced during execution.

D NulTypePtr      S                   *

D TypeBin2        S              5U 0 Based( NulTypePtr )
D TypeBin4        S             10U 0 Based( NulTypePtr )
D TypeChr         S              1A   Based( NulTypePtr )
D TypeIdx         S              7P 0 Based( NulTypePtr )
D TypeLgl         S              1A   Based( NulTypePtr )
D TypeSysNam      S             10A   Based( NulTypePtr )
D TypePtr         S               *   Based( NulTypePtr )
D TypeQlfNam      S             20A   Based( NulTypePtr )
D TypeTxt         S             50A   Based( NulTypePtr )
```

FIGURE 15-6    RPGLE /COPY source member DtaType

```
....1....+....2....+....3....+....4....+....5....+....6....+
// TrgDcl -- Trigger program standard declarations
//
// Requires copy modules: DtaType

D TbBufDs         DS
D  TbFile                               Like( TypeSysNam )
D  TbLib                                Like( TypeSysNam )
D  TbMbr                                Like( TypeSysNam )
D  TbTrgEvt                             Like( TypeChr )
D  TbTrgTime                            Like( TypeChr )
D  TbCmtLvl                             Like( TypeChr )
D  TbReserve1                  3A
D  TbCcsId                              Like( TypeBin4 )
D  TbRrn                                Like( TypeBin4 )
D  TbReserve2                  4A
D  TbBfrOfs                             Like( TypeBin4 )
D  TbBfrLen                             Like( TypeBin4 )
D  TbBfrNulOf                           Like( TypeBin4 )
D  TbBfrNulLn                           Like( TypeBin4 )
D  TbAftOfs                             Like( TypeBin4 )
D  TbAftLen                             Like( TypeBin4 )
D  TbAftNulOf                           Like( TypeBin4 )
D  TbAftNulLn                           Like( TypeBin4 )
   // -- End of TbBufDs --

D TbBufLen        S                     Like( TypeBin4 )

D TbBfrPtr        S                     Like( TypePtr )
D TbAftPtr        S                     Like( TypePtr )

D TbEvtIns        C                     Const( '1' )
D TbEvtDlt        C                     Const( '2' )
D TbEvtUpd        C                     Const( '3' )
D TbTimeBfr       C                     Const( '2' )
D TbTimeAft       C                     Const( '1' )
```

**FIGURE 15-7**    **RPGLE /COPY source member TrgDcl**

Both declarations use the BASED keyword, which specifies that a declaration is a template for storage that begins at the address contained in the pointer variable coded as the BASED keyword argument. As a result, the compiler will not allocate storage for the BfCustomer data structure but instead treats whatever storage starts at the address in TbBfrPtr as if it were the data structure. Obviously, this requires the program to place an appropriate address in the TbBfrPtr variable before referencing any of the data structure's subfields.

```
....1....+....2....+....3....+....4....+....5....+....6....+....7....
   // TrgEntry -- Trigger program standard entry and setup code

   // Requires copy module: TrgDcl
   //
   // Side effects:
   //   Sets TbBfrPtr   Pointer to before image in trigger buffer
   //   Sets TbAftPtr   Pointer to after  image in trigger buffer

   // - - - - - - - - - - - - - - - - - - - - - - - - - - - - - -
C     *Entry        PList
C                   Parm                    TbBufDs
C                   Parm                    TbBufLen

 /Free
  TbBfrPtr = %Addr( TbBufDs ) + TbBfrOfs;
  TbAftPtr = %Addr( TbBufDs ) + TbAftOfs;
 /End-Free
```

**FIGURE 15-8    RPGLE /COPY source member TrgEntry**

```
....1....+....2....+....3....+....4....+....5....+....6....+....
   // CustLog --    Sample trigger program to log changes to
   //               CrdLimit column in the customers table.

   // Prototype for LOGCRDCHG program
D LogCrdChg        PR                  ExtPgm( 'LOGCRDCHG' )
D  CustomerId                          Like( CustId )
D                                      Const
D  BeforeLimit                         Like( CrdLimit )
D                                      Const
D  AfterLimit                          Like( CrdLimit )
D                                      Const

   // Standard data types and trigger program declarations
   /Copy DtaType
   /Copy TrgDcl

   // Data structures to provide templates for before and after images
D BfCustomer    E DS                   ExtName( Customer )
D                                      Prefix ( Bf )
D                                      Based( TbBfrPtr )

D AfCustomer    E DS                   ExtName( Customer )
D                                      Prefix ( Af )
D                                      Based( TbAftPtr )
```

*Continued*

```
// Mnemonics and constants
D CrdLimit0        S                     Like( BfCrdLimit )
D                                        Inz( 0 )


// - - - - - - - - - - - - - - - - - - - - - - - - - - -
 // Entry point and setup code

 /Copy TrgEntry

 /Free
 // Dispatch on event (insert, update, or delete).

  Select;

    When TbTrgEvt = TbEvtIns;
 // Log first credit limit assigned to new customer.
 // Use after image (new record) for customer ID and
 // zero for "before" credit limit.
       Callp(E) LogCrdChg( AfCustId : CrdLimit0 : AfCrdLimit );

    When (TbTrgEvt = TbEvtUpd) And (AfCrdLimit <> BfCrdLimit);
 // Log changed credit limit for customer.
 // Use before image (old record) for customer ID.
       Callp(E) LogCrdChg( BfCustId : BfCrdLimit : AfCrdLimit );

    When TbTrgEvt = TbEvtDlt;
 // Log last credit limit assigned to customer being deleted.
 // Use before image (old record) for customer ID and
 // zero for "after" credit limit.
       Callp(E) LogCrdChg( BfCustId : BfCrdLimit : CrdLimit0 );

  EndSl;

  Return;
```

**FIGURE 15-9    RPGLE trigger program CustLog**

The same considerations apply to the AfCustomer data structure and the TbAftPtr variable. In a moment, we will look at how these two pointer variables are set.

Following the data structure declarations, two /COPY directives incorporate the DtaType and TrgDcl source members. The declarations in the TrgDcl member in Figure 15-7 include the TbBufDs data structure, which has subfields for the fixed portions of the trigger buffer. This declaration corresponds to the layout described in Figure 15-1. Two crucial subfields of the TbBufDs data structure are TbBfrOfs and TbAftOfs, which are used in the calculation of the address of the before and after images described shortly. The subfield declarations use RPGLE's LIKE keyword to specify each subfield's data type using one of the standard data types declared in the DtaType source member in Figure 15-6.

The rest of the declarations in TrgDcl include the trigger buffer length parameter (TbBufLen), the two pointers discussed earlier, and constants for the codes that are used for the trigger event and time fields in the trigger buffer.

Looking back at Figure 15-9, the next /COPY directive incorporates the code from the TrgEntry source member in Figure 15-8. This code declares the program's entry point with the two parameters, TbBufDs and TbBufLen, which are required. The copied code sets the two pointers. The TbBfrPtr pointer variable is set to the address of the first byte in the before image part of the trigger buffer parameter. This is done by adding the offset to the before image (TbBfrOfs) to the address of the buffer itself (using the %ADDR built-in function to obtain the trigger buffer address). A similar calculation is done to set the TbAftPtr pointer variable. After these two pointers are set, subsequent statements in the trigger program can refer to the subfields of the BfCustomer and AfCustomer data structures, and the references will be to the appropriate fields in the trigger buffer.

The statements in the CustLog program's UpdRcdEvt subroutine illustrate this technique. If the after-image credit limit is not the same as the before-image credit limit, the before-image customer ID and the before- and after-image credit limit values are passed to the LogCrdChg program (not shown) to log the change.

With the techniques illustrated in this sample trigger program, when columns are added, deleted, or changed in the table, one need only recompile the trigger program to synchronize its declarations with the new row definition. This approach substantially reduces maintenance effort and the possibility of errors when making these kinds of changes to a table.

## CONSIDERATIONS FOR USING TRIGGER PROGRAMS

Trigger programs should be created to perform their own I/O, executing within the same activation group and using the same commitment control environment as the application program. With this approach, the application program executes all commit and rollback operations, and any I/O that the trigger program performs is included in the transaction managed by the application program.

Keep in mind that any I/O performed by a trigger program may in turn cause another trigger program to be called. Trigger programs should be carefully designed so they do not result in infinite recursive calls of the same trigger program. Also, be sure to properly handle all errors that might occur when a trigger program performs its own I/O.

In addition, be aware of the performance implications of trigger programs. Each call to a trigger program adds some overhead, of course. If trigger programs are run in the caller's activation group and are not deactivated (for example, if the RPGLE LR indicator is left off upon return from a trigger program), the call overhead is not large compared with the time the system takes for a database I/O operation. The biggest impact comes because record blocking is not used when rows are inserted into a table with an insert-event trigger. This restriction is enforced so that the trigger program is called for each table insert, not just when the database tries to write a block of rows to the table. For batch jobs that sequentially insert large numbers of rows, unblocked access may be significantly slower than blocked access. One approach to consider is locking a table and removing its insert-event trigger program(s) before executing a long-running batch job. After the batch job is completed, the trigger program(s) can be added to the table again and the table unlocked. Of course, care must be taken to ensure that any program that runs while trigger programs are not in effect performs all the integrity checks or other operations that the trigger programs normally carry out. Because this technique complicates application design, consider using it only when performance is critical.

## INTERACTION OF TRIGGERS WITH CONSTRAINTS

Because a trigger program can change the contents of a row before the row is inserted or updated, it is important to understand how the DBMS times the constraint enforcement to prevent a trigger program from making a change that would circumvent a constraint. Also, any trigger program that takes actions based on a successfully completed database operation must be executed at the right time in the sequence of steps the DBMS takes for each I/O.

The timing of I/O operation steps depends on whether the table is being accessed under commitment control. It is strongly recommended that commitment control be used for all applications that update tables. Commitment control provides important all-or-none transaction integrity as well as automated recovery. Commitment control also provides stronger row-locking protocols than database access not under commitment control. The following discussion provides the essential timing information for accessing tables under commitment control.

## INTERACTION OF INSERT TRIGGERS WITH CONSTRAINTS

The following steps describe the sequence of events when performing an insert to a table with an insert trigger and constraints defined for the table:

1. Call the before-insert trigger program.
2. Insert the new row, and perform checks other than constraints, such as member full.
3. Call the after-insert trigger program.
4. Check all this table's foreign key constraints. In other words, for each foreign key constraint, make sure that there is a matching value for the new row's foreign key in the parent table or that one or more of the foreign key columns is null.
5. Check the primary key, unique, and check constraints.

If the before-insert trigger program sends an escape message, the process stops. Likewise, if an error occurs during step 2, the process stops. If the after-insert trigger program sends an escape message or any constraint is violated, the inserted row is rolled back and removed from the table using the active commitment control environment, and the process stops.

Notice several important implications of this sequence:

- The before-insert trigger program can change the new row's column values before any constraints are checked. This lets the trigger program fix invalid data and also ensures that any changes are still subject to constraint enforcement.
- Either a before-insert or an after-insert trigger program can insert a parent table row, if necessary, to satisfy a foreign key constraint.
- Neither a before-insert nor an after-insert trigger program can be certain the row will be permanently inserted. A constraint violation or an application rollback operation, even after a successful insert, may block or roll back the insert. For this reason, it is generally a good idea for trigger programs that perform I/O to run in the same commitment control environment as the application. That way, the application's subsequent commit or rollback operation covers any I/O done by the trigger program as well.

## INTERACTION OF UPDATE TRIGGERS WITH CONSTRAINTS

Here is the sequence of events when updating a single row in a table that has an update trigger and constraints defined for the table:

1. Call the before-update trigger program.
2. Check foreign key constraints for all dependent tables that specify ON UPDATE RESTRICT. That is, make sure a change to a column in this row leaves no "orphan" rows in a dependent table.
3. Update the row, and perform checks other than constraints, such as for invalid decimal data.
4. Call the after-update trigger program.
5. Check foreign key constraints for all dependent tables that specify ON UPDATE NO ACTION.
6. Check all this table's foreign key constraints.
7. Check the primary key, unique, and check constraints.

Looking at this sequence, one can observe one of the differences between the ON UPDATE RESTRICT and ON UPDATE NO ACTION rules for a foreign key constraint. There is a subtle, but important, implication of the different times these constraints are checked. At present, an ON UPDATE CASCADE foreign key option is not supported for updates, as it is for deletes. However, this functionality can be implemented with an after-update trigger, as long as the foreign key specifies ON UPDATE NO ACTION. For example, to change all the dependent rows' foreign key values when changing a parent row's primary key, the after-update trigger can perform updates to the dependent table. By the time step 5 checks the dependent table for unmatched rows, all the dependent rows will match the updated parent row.

Notice that this approach cannot be implemented using a before-update trigger program. Assume a before-update trigger program tries to change the dependent rows' foreign key values to the parent row's *new* primary key value. The parent row is not yet changed, and the dependent row updates are blocked because their new foreign key values do not match any parent row. As a consequence, because an after-update trigger program must be used to implement a cascading update, ON UPDATE NO ACTION must also be used to defer the foreign key constraint check until the after-update program is completed.

An SQL UPDATE statement can specify that multiple rows be updated in one statement execution. When an UPDATE statement is executed without commitment control active, all constraints are evaluated completely as each row is updated. When an UPDATE statement is executed under commitment control, however, all primary key and unique constraint checking is deferred until *all* rows have been updated. Foreign key constraints are also deferred, except those that specify a RESTRICT rule. Thus, for a multi-row UPDATE statement under commitment control, the process occurs in two stages. First, for each row to be updated, the following steps are performed:

1. Call the before-update trigger program.
2. Check foreign key constraints for all dependent tables that specify ON UPDATE RESTRICT.
3. Update the row, and perform checks other than constraints, such as for invalid decimal data.
4. Call the after-update trigger program.
5. Check check constraints.

Once this part of the process is completed, the following steps are performed for each updated row:

1. Check foreign key constraints for all dependent tables that specify ON UPDATE NO ACTION.
2. Check all this table's foreign key constraints.
3. Check the primary key and unique constraints.

Although it would be unusual, an application could perform an SQL statement to update a set of rows' primary key column, as in this example:

```
UPDATE customers
   SET  customer_id = customer_id + 1
```

This statement might succeed if the CUSTOMERS table were the parent in a foreign key constraint that specified ON UPDATE NO ACTION. However, it would almost certainly fail if the foreign key constraint specified ON UPDATE RESTRICT. To succeed with NO ACTION specified, all dependent rows require a matching parent row at the end of the UPDATE statement. In the case of RESTRICT, the requirement is that no individual CUSTOMERS row update can leave any unmatched dependent rows, something that would require a very precise ordering of the CUSTOMERS row updates to succeed.

## INTERACTION OF DELETE TRIGGERS WITH CONSTRAINTS

The following is the sequence of events when deleting a row from a table with a delete trigger and constraints defined for the table:

1. Call the before-delete trigger.
2. Check foreign key constraints for all dependent tables that specify ON DELETE RESTRICT constraints for this table. That is, make sure that deleting a row in this table leaves no "orphan" row in a dependent table.
3. Delete the row, and perform checks other than constraints.
4. Call the after-delete trigger.
5. Perform cascaded row deletions for all dependent tables that specify ON DELETE CASCADE constraints for this table.
6. Update rows for all dependent tables that specify ON DELETE SET NULL or ON DELETE SET DEFAULT constraints for this table.
7. Check the foreign key constraints for all dependent tables that specify ON DELETE NO ACTION constraints for this table.

It is apparent that the sequence of steps for a delete operation is an expanded version of the steps for an update. The main additions are steps to handle the additional options (CASCADE, SET NULL, and SET DEFAULT) for the ON DELETE foreign key rule. DELETE operations, of course, can never violate a primary key, unique, or check constraint, so these are not part of the process.

When an ON DELETE CASCADE constraint is processed (step 5), it is possible that a dependent table is the parent table in another table's ON DELETE RESTRICT foreign key constraint. Consider the example illustrated in Figure 15-10, in which table Table1 is the parent of table Table2 in an ON DELETE CASCADE constraint and table Table2 is the parent of table Table3 in an ON DELETE RESTRICT constraint.

From step 2, above, one can see that an application cannot directly perform a delete operation on Table2 if doing so would leave any orphan rows in Table3. The DBMS also prevents the completion of any delete operation to Table1 if a resulting cascaded delete operation to Table2 would leave orphan rows in Table3.

However, it is possible that Table1 may also be the parent of table Table3 in an ON DELETE CASCADE constraint. That is, Table3 would have two foreign key constraints: an ON DELETE CASCADE constraint with Table1 as the parent and an ON DELETE RESTRICT constraint with Table2 as the parent. In this case, all the cascaded deletions in Table2 and Table3 are completed before evaluating the Table3 table's ON DELETE RESTRICT constraint with Table2 as the parent. Similar logic governs ON DELETE SET DEFAULT and ON DELETE SET NULL constraints.

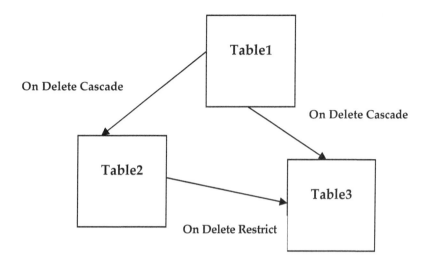

**FIGURE 15-10  Three tables with related delete rule actions**

In general, a delete operation is allowed as long as the final state of the database satisfies all foreign key constraints. There is one important exception: Any `ON DELETE RESTRICT` constraint for the main table (the one from which the application is directly deleting rows) is enforced immediately, one row at a time. Checking for an `ON DELETE RESTRICT` constraint is deferred until the end of the operation only when the constraint applies to cascaded deletions.

## CODING SUGGESTIONS

- In general, trigger programs should not deactivate themselves. In `RPGLE`, this means the trigger program should return without setting on `LR`.
- Consider specifying `SEQONLY(*YES n)` on an `OVRDBF` (Override with Database File) command to specify a blocking factor to use for large sequential table operations.
- Use the trigger buffer soft-coding technique to reduce future program maintenance when table columns are added, modified, or deleted.

## END-OF-CHAPTER

### CHAPTER SUMMARY

1. A trigger program is a program that is called when an application program tries to insert, update, or delete a database record. A trigger program is written and compiled just like any other HLL program, and the ADDPFTRG (Add Physical File Trigger) command is then used to associate the trigger program with a table. Six trigger conditions are supported for a table:

   - Before insert
   - Before update
   - Before delete

   - After insert
   - After update
   - After delete

2. The two steps for implementing a trigger program are coding it and then associating it with one or more tables using the ADDPFTRG command. A trigger can disallow the database action (insert, update, or delete). For insert and update, a trigger can modify the inserted or updated row.

3. A trigger program receives a trigger buffer and the length of the trigger buffer as its two parameters. The trigger buffer contains the before and after row image, null column maps for the before and after images, and other information about the trigger event.

4. There is a defined sequence for checking database constraints and calling trigger programs. Be sure to consider this sequence when using these two features.

### KEY TERMS

| trigger | trigger program |
|---------|-----------------|

# CHAPTER 16

## ADDITIONAL SQL TOPICS

## CHAPTER OBJECTIVES

Upon completion of this chapter, you should be able to

- Use the INCLUDE statement
- Discuss the importance of object and row locks and how they work
- Explain commitment control
- Discuss SQL naming options

## INCLUDE STATEMENT

The SQL **INCLUDE statement** inserts or includes source statements from an external source member into the source member containing the INCLUDE statement. Suppose a source member called SqlErrChk contains the error-checking code shown in Figure 16-1.

```
Select;
  When     SQLSTATE = '00000';
                                    ← (do nothing)

  When     SQLSTATE = '02000';
    ExSr   SqlNoRow;

  When     %SubSt( SQLSTATE : 1 : 2 ) = '01';
    ExSr   SqlWarning;

  Other;
    ExSr   SqlError;
EndSl;
```

FIGURE 16-1    Error-checking code

You can specify that the SQL precompiler include this code after an SQL statement by using an INCLUDE statement:

```
EXEC SQL
  UPDATE   customers
    SET    discount = :NewDisc
    WHERE ship_city = :SlcCusCity;

EXEC SQL
  INCLUDE SqlErrChk;
```

The source member name follows the INCLUDE keyword. The INCFILE parameter on the CRTSQLRPGI (Create SQL ILE RPG Object) or other command used to create the program specifies the schema and source file containing the member. For any single RPGLE source member, all SQL INCLUDE statements refer to members in the same include source file; there is no way to include members from two different source files when compiling an SQL program.

## OBJECT AND ROW LOCKS AND THE LOCK TABLE STATEMENT

Multiple users can access application objects simultaneously. To prevent one job's operations from interfering with another job's operations, the operating system provides object- and row-locking facilities. When one job holds an object or row lock, it restricts what other jobs can do with the locked object or row. The DBMS uses object and row locking to avoid conflicting database updates from multiple jobs. For many situations, default locking is adequate; however, in some cases explicit locks may need to be added to applications to prevent conflicts.

For example, imagine one user starts end-of-day batch transaction processing and another user, not knowing this, calls an interactive program to add a few last-minute transactions. Unless the program is designed to handle this situation, transactions entered by the interactive job may be lost as they are added behind those already processed by the batch job. The default object locking would let both jobs have update access to the table. However, the SQL LOCK TABLE statement or the ALCOBJ (Allocate Object) command can be used to let the batch job place a lock on the table so no other job can perform any updates until the lock is released. We will look at some examples of the LOCK TABLE statement after covering object-locking basics.

## OBJECT LOCKS

When an object is allocated during a job, the operating system places an **object lock** on the object. This lock serves two purposes:

- It guarantees to the job specific types of access to the object.
- It prevents other jobs from having specific types of access to the object.

The lock is released when a program executes a `DLCOBJ` (Deallocate Object) command, when the routing step ends, or when the object is deleted by the job holding the lock. Some additional cases will be covered later, in the discussion of the SQL `LOCK TABLE` statement. A routing step is one part of a job. Most jobs have a single routing step that starts when the job starts and ends when the job ends. For one-step jobs, it might be simpler to think of allocating an object to a job rather than to a routing step. Where this chapter uses the term "routing step," one can read "job" for most situations.

The type of lock placed on an object governs the way the object is shared among different jobs. This mechanism lets the system give different users a high degree of concurrent access to programs, data, and other objects. While sharing is allowed, the object is protected against simultaneous uses that would conflict; for example, a job cannot delete a table if another job is currently reading it.

Object allocation differs from object authorization, which is used to protect the security of shared objects. Object authorization allows a user profile specific types of access to an object; this authority generally remains in effect even when no job is active. (The exception is the authority that may be adopted while a program is executing.)

Object allocation, on the other hand, is used to protect the integrity of shared objects while they are in use. Object allocation grants a specific type of lock to the routing step that requests the allocation; objects are allocated only by active jobs. The allocation remains in effect only while the routing step is active. Here are some of the things an `ALCOBJ` command can be used for:

- To prevent a program from being deleted while someone is executing it
- To permit only one job at a time to execute a program
- To obtain database table locks that are not available with the SQL `LOCK TABLE` statement
- To guarantee access to a group of required objects before using any one of them

This discussion covers primarily those concepts related to locks for database tables and views.

## TYPES OF OBJECT LOCKS

When an object is allocated explicitly, the job is guaranteed a certain level of access to the object. Other jobs also are locked, to some degree, out of the object; the degree depends on the kind of lock obtained. There are five types of locks from which to choose:

- *Exclusive (*EXCL)*—Only the routing step holding the lock can use the object; routing steps in other jobs cannot access the object.
- *Exclusive-allow-read (*EXCLRD)*—The routing step that holds the lock can read or update the object, while routing steps in other jobs can only read it.
- *Shared-for-update (*SHRUPD)*—The routing step that holds the lock, as well as routing steps in other jobs, can read or update the object.
- *Shared-no-update (*SHRNUP)*—The routing step that holds the lock is guaranteed only read access to the object; routing steps in other jobs can only read the object.
- *Shared-for-read (*SHRRD)*—The routing step that holds the lock is guaranteed only read access to the object; routing steps in other jobs can read or update it.

The table in Figure 16-2 summarizes these locks.

| Your routing step needs this type of access | And you want to allow a routing step in another job the following access | | |
|---|---|---|---|
| | No access | Read-only | Update |
| None, but restrict other jobs | *EXCL | *SHRNUP | (No lock) |
| Read-only | *EXCL | *SHRNUP | *SHRRD |
| Update | *EXCL | *EXCLRD | *SHRUPD |

**FIGURE 16-2**  **Object lock types to use for required access control**

This table can help to quickly determine the type of lock to obtain in a given instance. Suppose you have decided to update a table, and while you are updating it you want other jobs or routing steps to be able to read the table but not update it. In the left column of the table in Figure 16-2, find "Update"; then move across the Update row to the "Read-only" column for routing steps in other jobs. The type of lock needed in this instance is *EXCLRD.

Although a lock gives the routing step that holds it a guarantee of access to an object and limits access by routing steps in other jobs, it does not limit subsequent access in the same routing step that holds the lock. For example, a program can execute an SQL LOCK TABLE statement to obtain an *EXCLRD lock on a table. A program in another job cannot open the locked table for updating. However, it is possible for the program holding the *EXCLRD lock to call a program that updates the same table. The point of object locking is to restrict *other* jobs, not the job holding the lock.

When a routing step attempts to obtain a lock, it gets the lock unless a routing step in another job already holds a conflicting lock on the same object. The operating system ensures proper sharing of an object by preventing conflicting locks. Figure 16-3 shows the types of locks that are allowed if a routing step in another job already holds a lock.

| *If a routing step already has this lock* | *A routing step in another job can obtain this lock* | | | | |
|---|---|---|---|---|---|
| | **\*EXCL** | **\*EXCLRD** | **\*SHRUPD** | **\*SHRNUP** | **\*SHRRD** |
| **\*EXCL** | No | No | No | No | No |
| **\*EXCLRD** | No | No | No | No | Yes |
| **\*SHRUPD** | No | No | Yes | No | Yes |
| **\*SHRNUP** | No | No | No | Yes | Yes |
| **\*SHRRD** | No | Yes | Yes | Yes | Yes |

**FIGURE 16-3**    **Allowable object lock combinations**

At different times in its processing, a routing step can obtain multiple locks of the same or a different type on an object. The system keeps a count of each type of lock placed on the object. Eventually, each lock must be released individually, even if the locks are of the same type. Thus, if at two different points in a routing step a *SHRRD lock is placed on an object, at some point both *SHRRD locks must be released on that object to return the system lock count to zero. Not until the count returns to zero is the *SHRRD lock totally removed from the object.

A routing step can use a single ALCOBJ command to obtain a lock on more than one object. Therefore, a group of objects required to complete an operation can be allocated at one time. Often, a program requires several tables, some for read-only access and others for updating. Allocating the tables before calling the program can simplify error handling. If explicit allocation is not used, either all tables must be opened before processing begins to ensure access to them all or a restart procedure must be used to continue at an interruption point (if one of the tables turns out to be unavailable).

The following statement shows an ALCOBJ command that allocates these objects: a daily transaction input table that no other job will be allowed to update, a CUSTOMERS table that will be read, a CUSTOMERS account table that will be updated, and a data area with the last transaction number processed that will be updated and can be read by other jobs:

```
AlcObj  Obj( ( daily_transactions *File    *ShrNUp )
            ( customer_name       *File    *ShrRd  )
            ( customer_account    *File    *ShrUpd )
            ( LstTrnNbr           *DtaAra *ExclRd ) )
        Wait( 10 )
```

If any one of these locks cannot be obtained, none of the objects will have locks placed on them by this ALCOBJ command. This all-or-none approach makes it easy to allocate the set of objects that is needed before starting to use any of them.

An ALCOBJ command succeeds if all the requested locks can be obtained. If any of the locks cannot be granted, an escape message (CPF1002) is sent to the program executing the ALCOBJ command. If the command is in a CL program, the message can be monitored for using the MONMSG (Monitor Message) command. If an RPGLE program's operation, such as an SQL cursor open or LOCK TABLE statement, cannot allocate an object, the program's exception procedures must handle the problem.

The WAIT(10) parameter in the example above specifies that the ALCOBJ command can wait up to 10 seconds for the locks. Such a wait may be necessary if a routing step in another job has one or more of the objects allocated with a lock that conflicts with the requested lock. If such a conflict exists and the conflicting locks are released within 10 seconds, this routing step obtains the locks it has requested unless a job with a higher dispatching priority also has requested locks on any of the objects.

A routing step also can release more than one lock with a single DLCOBJ command. When the objects in the preceding example are no longer needed, the following command deallocates them:

```
DlcObj  Obj( ( daily_transactions *File    *ShrNUp )
             ( customer_names      *File    *ShrRd  )
             ( customer_accounts   *File    *ShrUpd )
             ( LstTrnNbr           *DtaAra *ExclRd ) )
```

In general, for every ALCOBJ command in a job, there should be a corresponding DLCOBJ command with the same object list. However, if the job (or routing step) ends when the objects are no longer needed, no DLCOBJ command is necessary, and all objects are deallocated automatically.

Within a routing step, the type of lock held on an object may need to be changed. To do so, first obtain the new lock and then release the old lock. This technique prevents a routing step in another job from obtaining a conflicting lock before the new lock is obtained. For example, to use a table first for updating and then just to read, execute the following sequence of commands:

```
AlcObj  Obj( ( customers *File *ShrUpd ) )
   .
   . Call a program that updates the file.
   .
AlcObj  Obj( ( customers *File *ShrRd  ) )
DlcObj  Obj( ( customers *File *ShrUpd ) )
   .
   . Call a program that reads the file.
   .
DlcObj  Obj( ( customers *File *ShrRd ) )
```

Any time an SQL statement opens a table or view for access, the routing step obtains default locks determined by the type of open operation (input, output, input/output). When an open operation is executed on a table or view, a lock is placed on the table or view.

## THE LOCK TABLE STATEMENT

SQL uses object locks as the basis for table locking. In many cases, the default locks may be adequate; however, when two jobs access the same table, there is a possibility that one job's row updates might conflict with the other job's retrieval or update. For example, if one job (JobA) executes the SELECT INTO statement

```
SELECT  AVG( discount )
  INTO  :AvgDiscount
  FROM  customers
```

while another job (JobB) is executing the statement

```
UPDATE  customers
  SET   discount = .10
  WHERE ship-city = 'Portland'
```

to update the discount column, the first job may get an average based on the old discount value for some Portland customers and the new discount value for others. The DBMS does not automatically do anything to prevent these two jobs from interleaving the retrieval and update of individual rows.

The SQL **LOCK TABLE statement** provides an alternative to the ALCOBJ command to explicitly lock a table to prevent conflicting access. The LOCK TABLE statement can provide a shared lock to let other jobs read, but not modify, the table. For this example, the following statement could be executed to protect JobA's SELECT statement above from conflicting updates:

```
Lock Table customers In Share Mode
```

The SHARE keyword causes a *SHRNUP object lock to be placed on the table member for the table. A shared lock does *not* guarantee that the job holding the lock can update the table, which is not necessary in this case because JobA just needs to block JobB from doing updates while JobA reads the table.

Looking at the problem from JobB's perspective, JobB may want not only to prevent other jobs from updating the table but also to be assured of the ability to perform the updates. This requires a more restrictive exclusive-allow-read lock:

```
Lock Table customers In Exclusive Mode Allow Read
```

This type of lock prevents other jobs from performing conflicting updates and prevents them from getting an SQL shared lock as well. It places an *EXCLRD object lock on the table member for the table.

For the most restrictive lock, a LOCK TABLE statement can specify an exclusive lock to prevent any type of access to the table by another job. The following statement places a *EXCL object lock on the table member for the table and ensures that no other access to the CUSTOMERS table occurs while the job holds the lock:

```
Lock Table customers In Exclusive Mode
```

The basic rules for the LOCK TABLE statement's lock modes are:

- If a job holds a share table lock, other jobs can read, but not update, the table, and they can also obtain a share lock.
- If a job holds an exclusive-read table lock, other jobs can read the table but cannot use LOCK TABLE to obtain a share, exclusive-read, or exclusive lock.
- If a job holds an exclusive table lock, other jobs cannot access the table and cannot obtain any type of lock.

Refer to Figure 16-3 for the complete lock compatibility rules. If a lock cannot be placed because a different job already holds a conflicting lock, the LOCK TABLE fails and the SQLSTATE variable is set to 57033.

A lock placed by a LOCK TABLE statement can be removed with an SQL COMMIT or ROLLBACK statement that does not have the HOLD keyword specified, as discussed later. The DLCOBJ command can also be used to remove the lock. Table locks are also implicitly removed when the object is deleted, the routing step ends, the activation group ends, SQL closes its internal cursors for the table, or a remote connection is disconnected. In general, it is best to keep a table locked for the briefest time necessary because a table lock may block other jobs from executing their normal access to a table.

## ROW LOCKS

Locks placed on a table through the LOCK TABLE statement, with an ALCOBJ command, or implicitly by an SQL statement that accesses the table should not be confused with **row locks**. Table locks establish, for the entire table, allowable access methods by routing steps in different jobs. Row locks, on the other hand, restrict access to individual rows within a table. Without commitment control (discussed next), a row lock is generally obtained at the beginning of an I/O operation for the row and is held until the I/O statement for the next row begins, at which time the first row lock is released. If commitment control, which allows processing a series of database rows as a single transaction, is used, row locks are generally held from the I/O operation until the next commitment boundary, such as the next commit or rollback operation.

Without commitment control, an *update*-type row lock is held by an open data path (ODP), which is the control structure used to access database tables. An update row lock is similar to the *EXCLRD object lock in that it lets a locked row be read, but not updated or locked, through another ODP. If all ODPs for a table are in use under commitment control, the row lock is held by the commitment control environment. With commitment control, there are two types of row locks: read and update. The type of lock obtained and the allowable operations by other jobs depend on the **isolation level** for the commitment control environment in effect.

An important point to keep in mind is that, unlike object locks, row locks held by an ODP can conflict within the same routing step. This conflict can occur if the same row is accessed for updating through separate ODPs, as, for example, by having opened two views at the same time that are over the same table.

## TRANSACTION INTEGRITY AND
## THE COMMIT AND ROLLBACK STATEMENTS

An important consideration when updating a database is maintaining consistent data when multiple rows are modified. Suppose the following UPDATE statement is entered to increase the discount for all customers with a non-null discount:

```
UPDATE  customer
  SET   discount = discount + 0.001
  WHERE discount IS NOT NULL
```

To execute this statement, the DBMS retrieves, tests, and updates each row that satisfies the search condition. If the job in which this statement is being executed abruptly terminates, as in the case of a power failure, after some but not all CUSTOMERS rows have been processed, the CUSTOMERS table could be in an inconsistent state. Some rows might have the increase, but others would not. The UPDATE statement could not just be re-entered either, because that might add an additional discount to the customers who were already updated in the previous, possibly incomplete statement execution.

A facility called **commitment control** enables "all-or-none" execution of multi-row transactions to be specified. With this feature active, all row changes made by an update that fails before completion, and before being committed, will automatically be backed out by the DBMS, even if the system is shut down by a power failure. Under commitment control, after a failed update, all rows in the table are reset to exactly their values before the update was started. Thus, when a table is being updated under commitment control, the DBMS simply stores in a journal receiver object a before image, or copy, of each row just before the row is updated. If the whole update is not completed normally, the DBMS uses these before images to change each row back to its pre-update values. The same principle applies to multi-row DELETE and INSERT statements as well.

To use commitment control, a commitment environment is first defined by specifying *CHG (change), *CS (cursor stability), *ALL (all), or *RR (repeatable read) for the COMMIT parameter on the STRSQL (Start SQL), RUNSQLSTM (Run SQL Statement), or CRTSQLxxx command. The STRCMTCTL (Start Commitment Control) and ENDCMTCTL (End Commitment Control) commands provide another way to explicitly start and end commitment control. The STRCMTCTL command's LCKLVL (Lock level) parameter allows the isolation levels *CHG, *CS, and *ALL (but not *RR). When the interactive, batch, or embedded SQL statements are executed, they operate under commitment control at the specified isolation level (more about isolation levels in a moment).

Another way to specify that embedded SQL statements in a program are run under commitment control is to code a statement such as

```
SET OPTION COMMIT = *CS
```

as the first SQL statement in a program. The SET OPTION statement acts as a precompiler directive to set isolation level, date and time formats, sort sequence, and other options that are available as parameters on the CRTSQLxxx commands. The allowable SET OPTION COMMIT values are *CHG, *CS, *ALL, *RR, and *NONE.

The SQL SET TRANSACTION statement can also be used to establish (or end) a commitment environment and/or to change the isolation level at run time. The statement has the syntax

```
Set Transaction Isolation Level isolation-level
```

where *isolation-level* is one of the following values:

| *isolation-level* value | Equivalent COMMIT parameter value on a command |
|---|---|
| No Commit | *None |
| None | *None |
| NC | *None |
| Read Uncommitted, Read Write | *Chg |
| Chg | *Chg |
| UR | *Chg |
| Read Committed | *CS |
| CS | *CS |
| Repeatable Read | *All |
| All | *All |
| RS | *All |
| Serializable | *RR |
| RR | *RR |

Note that there are several synonymous keywords, such as REPEATABLE READ, ALL, and RS, for each isolation level. If a program executes a SET TRANSACTION ISOLATION LEVEL NONE, it effectively ends commitment control.

Some other considerations apply for the SET TRANSACTION ISOLATION LEVEL statement. For trigger programs:

- The SET TRANSACTION ISOLATION LEVEL statement can be used anywhere but should generally be executed at the beginning of the trigger program.
- The specified isolation level lasts only until the next COMMIT or ROLLBACK statement or until the trigger program returns.

For non-trigger programs:

- The SET TRANSACTION ISOLATION LEVEL statement can be executed only at the beginning of a transaction.
- The specified isolation level lasts only until the end of the transaction, such as until the next COMMIT or ROLLBACK statement.

To dynamically change the isolation level on an individual statement, a WITH isolation-level clause can be specified on SELECT, INSERT, UPDATE, and DELETE statements, as in this example:

```
UPDATE   customers
  SET    discount = discount + 0.001
  WHERE  discount IS NOT NULL
  WITH CS
```

For this clause, isolation-level is one of the values NC, UR, CS, RS, or RR, corresponding to the levels shown in the preceding table. The isolation level specified on an individual statement lasts just for the duration of the statement. This level is in effect regardless of any value specified on a command's COMMIT parameter, a SET OPTION COMMIT statement, or a SET TRANSACTION ISOLATION LEVEL statement.

An isolation clause can also be used on a DECLARE CURSOR statement. In that case, the isolation level applies just to the table(s) accessed via the cursor and lasts while the table(s) are open.

## DETERMINING WHICH COMMITMENT CONTROL ENVIRONMENT IS USED

A job can actually have multiple commitment control environments, including

- One *job-level* commitment control environment
- One *activation-group–level* commitment control environment for each activation group

When an SQL program that was created with a CRTSQLxxx command that specified a COMMIT parameter other than *NONE (or a corresponding SET OPTION statement) begins, the system follows this sequence to determine which commitment control environment to use for statements in the program:

1. Use the activation-group–level environment, if the activation group of the program calling the SQL program is using an activation-group–level environment.
2. Use the job-level environment, if the activation group of the program calling the SQL program is using the job-level environment.
3. Use the job-level environment, if one exists.
4. Start a new activation-group–level environment.

The program's COMMIT value is used to (re)set the isolation level. When the program returns, if there was a previous commitment environment, the isolation level is returned to the previous level.

## THE **COMMIT** AND **ROLLBACK** STATEMENTS

When a commitment environment is active, individual update statements or groups of update statements are followed with a COMMIT or ROLLBACK statement. Because the DBMS automatically backs out partially completed updates when the job ends, one must explicitly indicate when all related updates are ready to be committed, or made permanent. With the example shown earlier, the COMMIT statement would immediately follow the UPDATE statement, as in the following sequence:

```
UPDATE  customers
  SET   discount = discount + 0.001
  WHERE discount IS NOT NULL
COMMIT
```

If the UPDATE statement is completed successfully, the changes to the CUSTOMERS table are permanent as soon as the COMMIT statement is completed. Essentially, the DBMS just adds an entry to the journal that says that the updates for the rows whose before images were previously saved have now been completed and committed.

Commitment control can be used to group multiple update statements into a single **transaction**, also called a **logical unit of work**. All the database changes for all the UPDATE, INSERT, and DELETE statements in a transaction can then be guaranteed to execute all-or-none; in other words, either all the changes will be made, or none of them will be made.

Consider a classic banking transaction in which an amount is transferred from a savings account to a checking account. This transaction requires at least two UPDATE statements, and it is essential that both be completed or neither be completed. Using commitment control, the sequence of statements would be

```
UPDATE   saving
  SET    balance = balance - 100.00
  WHERE account_number = 123987
UPDATE   checking
  SET    balance = balance + 100.00
  WHERE account_number = 123987
COMMIT
```

If it is desirable to back out updates that have not yet been committed, a ROLLBACK statement can be executed:

```
Rollback
```

Both COMMIT and ROLLBACK statements are typically used in RPGLE programs rather than in interactive SQL interfaces. In particular, a ROLLBACK statement is usually coded to back out uncommitted updates when an error is detected. Here is a sketch of how the logic for the banking example would be coded when commitment control is used:

```
UPDATE   saving
  SET    balance = balance - 100.00
  WHERE account_number = 123987
If Error
   ROLLBACK
Else
  UPDATE   checking
    SET    balance = balance + 100.00
    WHERE account_number = 123987
  If Error
     ROLLBACK
  Else
     COMMIT
  EndIf
EndIf
```

The transaction is committed only if both parts of the funds transfer are completed successfully.

The HOLD keyword can optionally be specified after COMMIT or ROLLBACK, as in this example:

```
COMMIT HOLD
```

When HOLD is specified, all prepared statements are kept. (Without HOLD, they are discarded when a COMMIT or ROLLBACK statement is executed.) Also, the HOLD keyword avoids releasing a table lock (as discussed in a previous section). The HOLD keyword can also be added to avoid closing embedded SQL cursors. But, in most situations, a better solution to keep cursors open is to code the WITH HOLD option on the DECLARE CURSOR statement itself.

Notice that there is no "begin transaction" SQL statement. The DBMS always begins a transaction implicitly, either when a commitment control environment is started or when the previous transaction is ended with a COMMIT or ROLLBACK statement.

The main thing to consider with COMMIT and ROLLBACK statements that are embedded in RPGLE programs is where in the program logic to place these statements and what the impact of a commit or rollback will be on other resources, such as open cursors. In brief, try to code COMMIT and ROLLBACK at the point(s) in the application where all the SQL statements that are involved in a transaction have been completed, successfully or not. By checking for errors after each statement, the program can quit performing further update operations if an unrecoverable error occurs. At that point, program flow should return control to a higher-level statement, for example by returning from a subroutine or procedure call, where a ROLLBACK can be executed. The main mistake to avoid is coding lots of ROLLBACK statements at each point where an error might be detected. A program should contain few COMMIT and ROLLBACK statements, and these should be executed at the appropriate point where the overall transaction is started and ended.

## ISOLATION LEVELS

To use commitment control effectively, one must consider which isolation level to use and how row locking operates under commitment control. Otherwise, problems may occur with conflicting updates or conflicting row locks arising from concurrent access of the database by multiple jobs. The following discussion describes the general characteristics of each isolation level.

## NONE

Commitment control is not in effect with this level, and there is minimal protection against conflicting updates. In an application running without commitment control, each individual row update is effectively committed when it is completed, and there is no transaction rollback or recovery support. A job running without commitment control can retrieve rows that have been changed, but not yet committed, by another job. These are so-called "dirty reads" because they may read data that is subsequently rolled back by the other job. This is generally not a recommended isolation level except for read-only applications when an adequate object lock (as described above) is held on a table to protect against conflicting updates by another job.

## READ UNCOMMITTED, READ WRITE

This is the lowest isolation level that provides commitment control's all-or-none transaction support, including commit/rollback operations and transaction recovery. This level still allows dirty reads, so it should be used only when the application will not malfunction if it reads changes that are subsequently rolled back or when the application obtains an appropriate object lock to avoid conflicts.

## READ COMMITTED

This isolation level prevents an application from reading uncommitted data and is the minimum level to use unless object locking is also being used. Be careful, however, with applications that may re-retrieve rows (which were not updated) within the same transaction. With the READ COMMITTED isolation level, a job may obtain different results when it re-retrieves a row because it can see any *committed* changes (by another job) made to rows that are not updated in the transaction.

## REPEATABLE READ

An application running at this level is guaranteed to always see the same row contents for any row it retrieves more than once in the same transaction. It is possible, however, for a query result set, such as all the customers in Portland, to contain additional rows if the query is re-executed in the same transaction. With REPEATABLE READ, other jobs are allowed to insert new rows, known as "phantoms," into the range of a query made by another job running at the REPEATABLE READ isolation level.

## SERIALIZABLE

This isolation level guarantees that concurrent transactions will produce results exactly the same as if each transaction were run by itself—that is, as if all transactions were run serially, one after the other. Any query that is repeated within a transaction will always retrieve the same rows with the same contents. SQL ensures this outcome by placing an appropriate object lock on an accessed table as soon as any query references the table. The object lock is released when the transaction is committed or rolled back. A \*SHRNUP lock is placed on read-only tables, and an \*EXCLRD lock is placed on tables that are updated.

When considering which isolation level to use, do not jump immediately to SERIALIZABLE just because it offers the strongest guarantee that another job will not interfere with the application's transactions. The stronger isolation levels also increase the possibility of a different type of interference caused by conflicting row locks, a topic the next section examines. As a broad rule of thumb, most applications should use either the READ COMMITTED or the REPEATABLE READ isolation level, depending on whether or not they re-retrieve rows in the same transaction.

## ROW LOCKING WITH COMMITMENT CONTROL

To see more precisely how the various isolation levels work, it is worthwhile to take a closer look at the duration of row locks and the compatibility of different kinds of concurrent I/O operations under commitment control. As the previous section mentioned, with the SERIALIZABLE isolation level, an object lock may be placed on the entire table. All five isolation levels use row locks to provide different levels of isolation. Figure 16-4 shows when a row is locked and when the lock is released for each system-level I/O operation.

Keep in mind that an SQL set-at-a-time operation, such as a searched UPDATE, may cause a sequence of system-level I/O operations. In the case of an SQL UPDATE, for example, two system-level I/O operations, read-for-update and update, occur for each row that is updated.

As the last three rows of the table show, when commitment control is in effect, row locks on updated, added, and deleted rows are held until the next commitment boundary. In a non–commitment-control environment, the row lock is released as soon as a row is updated, added, or deleted. The first two rows of the table illustrate the different ways the four isolation levels handle locks for rows that are not updated.

Rows that are read for input are locked only when the READ COMMITTED, REPEATABLE READ, or SERIALIZABLE isolation level is used. The REPEATABLE READ and SERIALIZABLE isolation levels, but not READ COMMITTED, hold a row lock on all input-only rows until the next commitment boundary.

| System I/O operation | Isolation level | Time | | | | |
|---|---|---|---|---|---|---|
| | | This I/O ↓ | Release ↓ | Another read ↓ | Update or delete ↓ | Commit or Rollback ↓ |
| Read-for-input | None or Read Uncommitted, Read Write | ● | | | | |
| | | ●━━━━━━━━━━━━━━━━━━● | | | | |
| | Read Committed | Or, if no subsequent read operation; | | | | |
| | | ●━━━━━━━━━━━━━━━━━━━━━━━━━━━━━━━━━━━━━● | | | | |
| | Repeatable Read or Serializable | ●━━━━━━━━━━━━━━━━━━━━━━━━━━━━━━━━━━━━━● | | | | |
| Read-for update, then release | None or Read Uncommitted, Read Write | ●━━━━━━● | | | | |
| | | ●━━━━━━━━━━━━━━━━━━● | | | | |
| | Read Committed; | Or, if no subsequent read operation; | | | | |
| | | ●━━━━━━━━━━━━━━━━━━━━━━━━━━━━━━━━━━━━━● | | | | |
| | Repeatable Read or Serializable | ●━━━━━━━━━━━━━━━━━━━━━━━━━━━━━━━━━━━━━● | | | | |
| Read-for-update, then update or delete | None | ●━━━━━━━━━━━━━━━━━━━━━━━━━━━● | | | | |
| | Read Uncommitted, Read Write; Read Committed; Repeatable Read; or Serializable | ●━━━━━━━━━━━━━━━━━━━━━━━━━━━━━━━━━━━━━● | | | | |
| Add | None | ● | | | | |
| | Read Uncommitted, Read Write; Read Committed; Repeatable Read; or Serializable | ●━━━━━━━━━━━━━━━━━━━━━━━━━━━━━━━━━━━━━● | | | | |
| Delete | None | ● | | | | |
| | Read Uncommitted, Read Write; Read Committed; Repeatable Read; or Serializable | ●━━━━━━━━━━━━━━━━━━━━━━━━━━━━━━━━━━━━━● | | | | |

**FIGURE 16-4   Row lock duration**

Without commitment control or with the READ UNCOMMITTED, READ WRITE isolation level, rows fetched for update, but released without being updated, are unlocked when the release occurs. With the READ COMMITTED isolation level, however, the lock is retained until the next read to the table (or the next commitment boundary, if there is no subsequent read operation in the transaction). And with the REPEATABLE READ or the SERIALIZABLE isolation level, the lock is always retained until the next commitment boundary.

With no commitment control or with the READ UNCOMMITTED, READ WRITE or the READ COMMITTED isolation level, the lock on a row that has been read for update can be implicitly released by executing, before any update of the row, another read-for-update via the same ODP.

Figure 16-5 shows the allowable access of a row by a second job, Job B, when a job, Job A, has read the row either for input or for update and has not yet released the row lock (if any) by one of the actions listed in Figure 16-4.

| Job A | | Allowed type of access by Job B | | |
|---|---|---|---|---|
| Isolation level | Read row for | Non-commitment environment | Read Uncommitted, Read Write | Read Committed; Repeatable Read; or Serializable |
| None | Input | Update | Update | Update |
| | Update | Input | Input | None |
| Read Uncommitted, Read Write | Input | Update | Update | Update |
| | Update | Input | Input | None |
| Read Committed; Repeatable Read; or Serializable | Input | Input | Input | Input |
| | Update | Input | Input | None |

FIGURE 16-5  **Allowable row access**

As can be deduced from the lock duration rules of Figure 16-4, the rules for a second job's access are the same for a non–commitment-control environment and for the READ UNCOMMITTED, READ WRITE isolation level of commitment control. For simplicity, the figures and discussion refer to two different jobs, each with a job-scope commitment control environment. The same principles apply to any two commitment control environments, whether they have job scope or activation group scope.

Note, however, that the row lock for an updated, added, or deleted row is held until a commit or rollback with the READ UNCOMMITTED, READ WRITE isolation level. The READ COMMITTED and REPEATABLE READ isolation levels, on the other hand, require a read-type row lock to perform a read-for-input. Two jobs can hold read-type row locks on the same row, but there cannot be simultaneous read and update locks on a row.

Although it takes some planning to set up properly, commitment control offers substantial benefits in improved database integrity and recovery. Most production-level applications should be designed to run under commitment control.

## A GUIDE TO SQL NAMING

One of the challenges encountered in using SQL to create and access database objects is how to use the myriad naming features available with SQL. Among the most important decisions developers face are whether to explicitly qualify object names with the schema containing the object and whether to use **system naming** or **SQL naming**. The following sections provide explanations for the most important naming rules and lay out specific recommendations for all the major choices.

### SQL OBJECT NAMES

SQL includes a variety of object types, and most of them are implemented as object types. For example, an SQL table is a physical file. Figure 16-6 lists SQL objects and the corresponding system objects.

Every SQL object has a name. For all objects except a constraint, which is always part of a table definition, a name must be assigned when the object is created. A name can optionally be assigned to a constraint as well. Names for many types of SQL objects can be longer than the 10-character limit for system object names, and these types of SQL objects actually have two names: an *SQL name* and a *system name*. The SQL name is generally used in SQL statements; the system name is the name of the corresponding system object and is used with non-SQL interfaces, such as CL commands.

When executing one of the SQL Create statements to create an object with an SQL name of 10 characters or less, SQL creates the system name as the SQL name. When a longer SQL name is specified, SQL generates a system name using the first five characters of the SQL name and a five-digit sequence number. For example, for the SQL table name PART_SUPPLIERS, SQL would generate a table name such as PartS00001. Because some non-SQL interfaces, such as operating system save and restore commands, must be used in working with SQL objects, it helps to have more meaningful system names than those generated by SQL.

Figure 16-7 shows the maximum length of SQL object names and, where applicable, how to specify or rename the system name to a meaningful name. For example, to create a meaningful system name for a PART_SUPPLIERS table, an SQL RENAME statement such as this one could be used:

```
RENAME Table part_suppliers
    TO SYSTEM NAME PartSupplr
```

| SQL object | System object | System special value |
|---|---|---|
| Alias | Distributed Data Management (DDM) file | `*File` |
| Authorization ID | User profile | `*UsrPrf` |
| Schema | Library | `*Lib` |
| Constraint | Access path | Internal object owned by physical file for the table |
| Database | System | Entry in System i relational database directory |
| Server | System | Entry in System i relational database directory |
| Distinct type | SQL user-defined type | `*SqlUdt` |
| Function | Program or service program | `*Pgm` `*SrvPgm` |
| Index | Logical file | `*File` |
| Package | SQL package | `*SqlPkg` |
| Procedure | Program | `*Pgm` |
| Table | Physical file | `*File` |
| View | Logical file | `*File` |

FIGURE 16-6    SQL and system object types

| SQL object | Maximum length of name | How to set the system name |
|---|---|---|
| Alias | 128 | Not applicable (the whole point of an SQL alias is to provide another name for an object, so just specify the desired type of name). |
| Authorization ID | 10 | CRTUSRPRF command (there is no SQL statement to create a user profile). |
| Schema | 10 | Always the same as the SQL name. |
| Constraint | 128 | Not applicable (the system object is not visible, and the RMVPFCST command lets the SQL name be specified). |
| Database or Server | 18 | Not applicable (the name is an entry in the relational database directory). |
| Distinct type | 128 | Not possible (but SQL data types are used only in SQL statements). |
| Function or Procedure | 128 | Specify the system name on the CREATE FUNCTION or CREATE PROCEDURE statement's SPECIFIC clause. |
| Index | 128 | Use SQL's RENAME INDEX statement with a SYSTEM NAME clause. |
| Package | 10 | Always the same as the SQL name |
| Table or view | 128 | Use SQL's RENAME TABLE statement with a SYSTEM NAME clause. |

FIGURE 16-7    SQL and system names

The following recommendation makes it easier to work with SQL objects that have long names:

*Create meaningful system names for SQL names longer than 10 characters.*

To follow this standard, use the techniques listed in Figure 16-7. It is a good idea to create SQL objects by using the RUNSQLSTM command to run SQL scripts stored in a source member (or use a comparable approach with a software configuration management product). Both the CREATE and the RENAME SQL statements can be placed in the same source member, so the process is simple and foolproof.

## QUALIFIED NAMES AND UNIQUENESS

The following SQL objects can be referenced either by an **unqualified name**, such as CUSTOMERS, or by a **qualified name**, which includes the name of the schema containing the object, such as AppDta.customers or AppDta/customers:

- Alias
- Distinct type
- Function
- Index
- Procedure
- Table
- View

An alias, distinct type, index, table, or view is uniquely identified by its qualified name and its underlying system object type (*FILE or *SQLUDT). For any of these object types, two objects of the same underlying type can have identical names as long as they are in different schema. Put another way, you cannot have an alias, index, table, or view with the same name as another alias, index, table, or view in the same schema. Also, no two aliases, indexes, tables, or views in the same schema can have the same system name, even if their SQL names are different. You also cannot have two distinct types with the same name in the same schema.

The uniqueness rules for function and procedure names are a little more complex. SQL permits more than one function with the same name in the same schema as long as the functions have different *signatures*. A function's signature consists of its name and the number and type of its parameters. Similarly, no two procedures in the same schema can have the same name and number of parameters.

Each function and procedure in a schema must also have a unique *specific name*. The SPECIFIC clause can be used on the CREATE FUNCTION or CREATE PROCEDURE statement, as described earlier in this chapter, to specify a specific name. If no name is specified, SQL uses the function or procedure name, unless it is the same as the specific name of an existing function or procedure in the same schema, in which case SQL generates a name. The only time a specific name really needs to be specified is when creating a function or procedure implemented with SPL, in which case the specific name is used as the name of the generated service program (for a function) or program (for a procedure). If a service program or program with the same name already exists in the schema, SQL generates a unique system object name.

Another somewhat helpful use for specific names is when there is more than one function or procedure with the same name (and different signatures) in the same schema. By assigning a unique specific name, you can use a `DROP FUNCTION` or `DROP PROCEDURE` statement that identifies the function or procedure by its specific name rather than the full signature.

## END-OF-CHAPTER

### CHAPTER SUMMARY

1. The `INCLUDE` statement allows the specification of a source member to be incorporated into the source code that is processed during the SQL precompilation step. Using `INCLUDE` members can improve application consistency and increase productivity by reusing common source code.

2. Object and row locks are used to control the allocation of resources so that simultaneous object or row access by different jobs will not result in conflicting operations. Many automatic object and row locks are provided, but additional locks can also be placed explicitly. The `ALCOBJ` (Allocate Object) and `DLCOBJ` (Deallocate Object) commands, as well as SQL's `LOCK TABLE` statement, are used to place and remove object locks. There are five types of object locks that prevent conflicting types of locks from being obtained by different jobs. Row locks are placed automatically when a table is accessed for update or when commitment control is in effect. Transaction isolation levels, or commitment control lock levels, let the developer specify that the DBMS should place additional row locks beyond those normally placed without commitment control.

3. Commitment control provides an all-or-none facility for transactions that involve multiple database rows. Under commitment control, an application must execute a commit operation to make permanent those database changes performed since the last complete transaction. If the application or system fails before table changes are committed, the system subsequently backs out all uncommitted changes. An application can also explicitly execute a rollback operation to remove uncommitted changes. There are several transaction isolation levels, which provide different levels of isolation for transactions in different jobs. Each isolation level provides a unique combination of row lock types and duration, resulting in varying degrees of protection from conflicting updates.

4. SQL provides two naming options: system naming and SQL naming. The naming option determines the syntax for qualified names, the rules for implicit qualification of unqualified names, and the rules for which user profile a statement executes under. In general, SQL naming is recommended for greater consistency with the SQL standard and for increased application portability. Various command parameters and SQL options permit the specification of the default schema(s) for unqualified names used in static and dynamic statements. Additional parameters and options let the developer explicitly specify which user profile a statement executes under.

## KEY TERMS

| | |
|---|---|
| commitment control | qualified name |
| INCLUDE statement | row lock |
| isolation level | SQL naming |
| LOCK TABLE statement | system naming |
| logical unit of work | transaction |
| object lock | unqualified name |

# CHAPTER 17

## DATABASE SECURITY AND THE GRANT AND REVOKE STATEMENTS

## CHAPTER OBJECTIVES

Upon completion of this chapter, you should be able to

- Explain basic security
- Use the GRANT and REVOKE statements

## SECURITY BASICS

The system provides a wide variety of security mechanisms to control access to databases. This chapter introduces the way the system implements security and describes how user profiles and authorities can be set up to restrict the types of operations that can be performed. The SQL GRANT and REVOKE statements are covered, as well as commands to specify appropriate access to database objects. Other security-related topics covered include schemas, database tables and views, distinct types, stored procedures, user-defined functions, and SQL packages, the central SQL objects in database security.

Everything on the system is organized as an object, and SQL uses these objects for SQL-oriented database objects, as shown in Figure 17-1.

In general, SQL security builds directly on the operating system security; however, some aspects of database security can be controlled only using Control Language (CL). Accordingly, this chapter discusses objects and commands along with SQL objects and statements. It begins with an examination of the basic foundations of security and then looks at how to control security using both commands and SQL statements.

The core element of security is the **user profile** object, which, as the name implies, represents a user of the system. In SQL terminology, **authorization ID** refers to a particular user profile that is checked for appropriate authority when an SQL statement is executed. A user profile has a name, password, and set of values that control various aspects of security and the interactive and batch job environments. Typically, when a person who is not already authorized to use the system needs access to data in a database, the organization's security officer or authorized representative uses the CRTUSRPRF (Create User Profile) command to create a user profile object for the person.

| SQL object | System object | Special value (used in system commands) |
|---|---|---|
| Alias | Distributed Data Management (DDM) file | *File |
| Authorization ID | User profile | *UsrPrf |
| Schema | Library | *Lib |
| Distinct type | SQL user-defined type | *SqlUdt |
| Index | Logical file | *File |
| Package | SQL package | *SqlPkg |
| Procedure | Program | *Pgm |
| Table | Physical file | *File |
| User-defined function | Program or service program | *Pgm<br>*SrvPgm |
| View | Logical file | *File |

FIGURE 17-1   SQL and system object types

Each user profile is created with a unique password that the person uses to sign on to the system. The security officer or person in charge of the organization's applications then grants the user profile appropriate **authority** to various system objects so the person can work with application programs and data.

When a user signs on to the system, he or she must supply a valid combination of user profile name and password. After a user has signed on with a particular user profile, that user profile governs all access to other system objects, including schemas, database tables, and programs. When a user submits a batch job, the job normally runs under the submitter's user profile, and that user profile also governs data access in the batch environment. Because all SQL objects are system objects, this same principle applies to SQL operations. That is, user profiles govern all access.

In concept, security is simple: When an operation is attempted, the operating system checks to ensure that the job's user profile has adequate authority to perform the operation on the target object. For example, when a user tries to run a program to display employee data, the system first checks that the user profile with which the user signed on has authority to execute the program; then it verifies that the user profile has authority to access the EMPLOYEES table.

In practice, system security can become quite complex because a user profile might obtain authority to an object in many different ways. This chapter explores many details of security as it relates to a variety of database objects. Remember, every operation on the system, such as running a program or opening a table, requires appropriate authority to the target object. If a user needs to be able to perform a particular operation on an object, his or her user profile must have the required authority. If a user should be prevented from performing a particular operation on an object, that user profile must not possess the required authority.

## OBJECT OWNERSHIP

User profiles play another essential role: Every object is owned by a user profile. Thus, it is important to plan which user profiles will own application objects.

The owner of an object normally has all authorities to the object. For that reason, once application tables, views, programs, and so forth are put into production, the programmer who created them should not be left as the owner. Instead, one or more special-purpose user profiles should be created to own production versions of application objects. In small organizations, a single user profile, such as PrfAppOwn (application owner profile — application owner), may suffice. For larger organizations, there may be several user profiles, each owning objects of a particular application, such as PrfSaleOwn, PrfEmpOwn, and so on. An application's schema and most of the tables, views, programs, and other objects in the schema can be owned by one of the special-purpose user profiles. Later, we will examine a special case: programs that adopt the authority of the user profile that owns the program.

The CHGOBJOWN (Change Object Owner) command can be used to transfer ownership from one user profile to another, for example from a programmer's user profile to a special-purpose profile to own production objects. Another way to have production objects owned by a special-purpose profile is to delete the test version of the objects and then re-create them in a job that runs under the special-purpose user profile that should own production objects.

## AUTHORITIES

The system governs operations based on the authorities a user profile has. There are two major categories of authority: special authorities and specific authorities.

**Special authorities** are assigned to a user profile using the SPCAUT parameter of the CRTUSRPRF or CHGUSRPRF (Change User Profile) command. Figure 17-2 lists the special authorities, which generally have a system-wide scope and are not associated with individual objects.

| Special authority | Special value (used in commands) | Sample operations allowed |
|---|---|---|
| All object | *AllObj | • Access any object with all the specific authorities listed in Figure 17-3 |
| Audit | *Audit | • Change system auditing configuration |
| I/O system configuration | *IOSysCfg | • Change system I/O configuration |
| Job control | *JobCtl | • IPL the system<br>• Manage subsystems and jobs<br>• Manage queues, writers, and spooled files that are configured to allow operator control |
| Save system | *SavSys | • Save, restore, and free storage for all objects |
| Security administrator | *SecAdm | • Create, change, and delete user profiles |
| Service | *Service | • Start the system service tools<br>• Debug programs with only *Use special authorities (see Figure 17-4) |
| Spool control | *SplCtl | • Manage spooled files<br>• Manage job queues |

**FIGURE 17-2** Special authorities

In general, no user on the system should have *ALLOBJ or *SECADM special authorities unless he or she is responsible for system-wide security. In typical installations, trained and trusted system operators are usually given *SAVSYS authority so they can do regular backups. The user profiles for most end users have none of these special authorities and so need specific object authorities to work with the database.

**Specific authorities** are assigned to one or more user profiles to use one or more objects. Specific authorities are further subdivided into the three groups: **object authorities**, **data authorities**, and **field authorities**, as shown in Figure 17-3. The system also has several special values for specific authorities, shown in Figures 17-4 and 17-5.

The special values listed in Figure 17-4 are typically used for most system commands; those in Figure 17-5 provide Unix-like levels of access and are used with the WRKAUT (Work with Authority) and CHGAUT (Change Authority) commands, typically for non-database, integrated file system (IFS) files. Note that the special values, other than *EXCLUDE, are simply shorthand for various sets of values; they are *not* additional types of system specific authorities. The *EXCLUDE special value is not really a system authority but rather a way to explicitly *deny* authority.

| Type of authority | Special value (used in commands) | Operations allowed |
|---|---|---|
| *Object authorities* | | |
| Object operational | *ObjOpr | • Retrieve an object's description<br>• Use an object as determined by the user's data and field authorities to the object |
| Object management | *ObjMgt | • Grant and revoke authorities for an object<br>• Rename or move an object to another schema<br>• All *ObjAlter and *ObjRef operations |
| Object existence | *ObjExist | • Delete an object<br>• Free an object's storage on a save operation<br>• Transfer ownership of an object to another user profile |
| Object alter | *ObjAlter | • Add, clear, initialize, and reorganize member(s) of a database table (or SQL view; note that tables and views always have a single member)<br>• Alter and add attributes of a database table (or SQL view), including adding and removing trigger programs on tables<br>• Change the attributes of an SQL package object |
| Object reference | *ObjRef | • Specify a table as the parent table in a foreign key constraint |
| Authorization list management | *AutLMgt | • Add and remove user profiles and their authorities from an object's authorization list |
| *Data authorities* | | |
| Read | *Read | • Read the contents of an object (e.g., read rows from a table) |
| Add | *Add | • Add entries to an object (e.g., insert new rows into a table) |
| Update | *Upd | • Update the entries in an object (e.g., update rows in a table) |
| Delete | *Dlt | • Delete entries from an object (e.g., delete rows from a table) |
| Execute | *Execute | • Run a program or service program or execute statements in an SQL package<br>• Invoke an SQL stored procedure or user-defined function<br>• For schema objects, locate objects in the schema |
| *Field authorities* | | |
| Management | *Mgt | • Specify authority for a field (or column) |
| Alter | *Alter | • Change attributes for a field (or column) |
| Reference | *Ref | • Specify the field (or column) as part of the parent key in a foreign key constraint |
| Read | *Read | • Read the contents of a field (or column) |
| Add | *Add | • Add contents to a field (or column) |
| Update | *Update | • Update the contents of a field (or column) |

**FIGURE 17-3    Specific authorities**

| Special value | Equivalent specific authorities | Notes |
|---|---|---|
| *All | All object and data authorities listed in Figure 17-3 | — |
| *Change | *ObjOpr and all data authorities | Allows a user to have full read and update access to a database table or view, as well as execute a program |
| *Use | *ObjOpr, *Read, and *Execute authorities | Allows a user to execute a program or have read access to a database table or view |
| *Exclude | — | Explicitly denies all access to the object |

**FIGURE 17-4    Special values for sets of specific authorities (used by most commands)**

| Special value | Equivalent specific authorities | Notes |
|---|---|---|
| *RWX | *ObjOpr and all data authorities | Equivalent to *Change |
| *RW | *ObjOpr and all data authorities except *Execute | Read/write access |
| *RX | *ObjOpr, *Read, and *Execute authorities | Read/execute access |
| *R | *ObjOpr and *Read authorities | Read-only access |
| *WX | *ObjOpr and all data authorities except *Read | Write/execute access |
| *W | *ObjOpr, *Add, *Upd, and *Dlt authorities | Write-only access |
| *X | *ObjOpr and *Execute authorities | Execute-only access |
| *Exclude | — | Explicitly denies all access to the object |

**FIGURE 17-5    Special values for sets of specific authorities (used by the WRKAUT and CHGAUT commands)**

Authority can be granted to any object by using the GRTOBJAUT (Grant Object Authority) command or by using the EDTOBJAUT (Edit Object Authority) command to edit a displayed list of user profiles and their authorities to an object. To enable a user named Betty L. Smith with the user profile SmithBL to display CUSTOMERS rows, a command such as the following could be used:

```
GrtObjAut Obj( AppDta/customers )
          ObjType( *File )
          User( SmithBL )
          Aut( *Use )
```

If Betty should be able to read and add CUSTOMERS rows but not delete or update them, the following command could be used:

```
GrtObjAut Obj( AppDta/customers )
          ObjType( *File )
          User( SmithBL )
          Aut( *ObjOpr *Read *Add )
```

Authority can be revoked with the RVKOBJAUT (Revoke Object Authority) command or by using the EDTOBJAUT command. To revoke Betty's authority to add CUSTOMERS rows, a command such as the following could be used:

```
RvkObjAut Obj( AppDta/customers )
          ObjType( *File )
          User( SmithBL )
          Aut( *Add )
```

This command leaves intact any other authorities that the SmithBL user profile has to the CUSTOMERS table object.

To grant or revoke authority to an object, a user profile must satisfy one or more of the following conditions:

- Own the object, typically as a result of creating it
- Be the system security officer (QSECOFR)
- Have *ALLOBJ special authority
- Have *OBJMGT authority to the object

The *OBJMGT authority by itself lets a user profile grant and revoke only those authorities that the user profile has to the object; *OBJMGT authority does not let the user profile grant another user profile *OBJMGT authority.

The GRTOBJAUT, RVKOBJAUT, and EDTOBJAUT commands can use the *ALL, *CHANGE, *USE, and *EXCLUDE special values. The WRKAUT and CHGAUT commands, which use an IFS path to specify an object, can use *RWX, *RW, *RX, *R, *WX, *W, *X, and *EXCLUDE, as in this example:

```
ChgAut Obj( '\QSys.Lib\AppDta.Lib\customers.File' )
       User( SmithBL )
       DtaAut( *R )
```

## Public Authority

The system has two features, public authority and group profiles, that let authority be granted to more than one user profile at a time. Every object has public authority, which controls access by user profiles that are not otherwise authorized to the object. An object's **public authority** can include any of the object authorities listed in Figures 17-3 and 17-4, which can be granted and revoked using the *PUBLIC special value instead of a user profile name on the GRTOBJAUT and RVKOBJAUT commands. For example, to grant public authority to read data from the CUSTOMERS table, the following command could be used:

```
GrtObjAut Obj( AppDta/customers )
          ObjType( *File )
          User( *Public )
          Aut( *Use )
```

On the CRTLIB (Create Library), CRTPF (Create Physical File), CRTLF (Create Logical File), CRTPGM (Create Program), CRTSRVPGM (Create Service Program), and some other CRTxxx commands, it is possible to also specify one of the special values listed in Figure 17-4 for the command's AUT (Authority) parameter. The following command creates the CUSTOMERS table with public authority to read the table:

```
CrtPf File( AppDta/customers )
      SrcFile( AppSrc/QDdsSrc )
      Aut( *Use )
```

Although it is common practice in many installations to allow *USE public authority to most application objects, it is important to be sure it is desirable for everyone to be able to run a program or read data from a table before granting *USE public authority. A more cautious approach is to specify *EXCLUDE for schema, program, and database table objects' public authority unless a clear reason exists for allowing some higher level of access to everyone.

## DEFAULT PUBLIC AUTHORITY FOR NEW OBJECTS CREATED WITH A CRTxxx COMMAND

When an object is created with a CRTxxx command and the AUT parameter is not specified, the default is AUT(*LIBCRTAUT), which means that the object's public authority is set from a value associated with the schema in which the object is created. This value is specified on the CRTAUT parameter of the CRTLIB and CHGLIB (Change Library) commands. For example, if a schema is created with CRTAUT(*CHANGE), any new objects created with a CRTxxx command in the schema will have public authority *CHANGE, unless an AUT parameter value other than the default (*LIBCRTAUT) is specified on the CRTxxx command.

CRTAUT(*SYSVAL) is the default parameter for the CRTLIB command. The next section discusses libraries created with an SQL CREATE SCHEMA statement. This default specifies that a new schema's CRTAUT value is taken from the QCRTAUT system value. The operating system is shipped with QCRTAUT set to *CHANGE. As a result, if the default CRTAUT parameter is used for CRTLIB commands and the default AUT parameter is used for other CRTxxx commands, new objects will have *CHANGE as their public authority. This is generally not a good practice because it allows too much access.

This potential security risk cannot be avoided by simply changing the QCRTAUT system value to a more restrictive setting, such as *EXCLUDE, because doing so can cause other problems. Unfortunately, some system libraries, such as QSYS, are shipped with CRTAUT(*SYSVAL), so changing QCRTAUT may affect objects created in these system libraries. For example, workstation devices created in QSYS using a default AUT parameter might not be accessible by end users.

For most installations, schemas should be created with a CRTAUT value of *EXCLUDE or *USE. To simplify this practice, the CRTLIB command's default CRTAUT parameter value can be changed to something other than *SYSVAL, as in this example:

```
ChgCmdDft Cmd( CrtLib )
          NewDft( 'CrtAut(*Exclude)' )
```

This change will affect libraries subsequently created with the CRTLIB command, but it will *not* affect libraries created with the CREATE SCHEMA statement, which is covered below. The CHGLIB command can be used to change the CRTAUT attribute of existing libraries and schemas.

## Default Public Authority for New Objects Created with an SQL Create Statement

When an SQL Create statement is used to create a database object, the object's public authority is determined by the naming option in effect: *system naming* or *SQL naming*. The CREATE SCHEMA statement creates a schema with public authority set from the QCRTAUT system value and with the schema's CRTAUT value set to *SYSVAL. All other Create statements create objects with public authority determined by the containing schema's CRTAUT value.

With SQL naming, the public is generally excluded from access when an object is created. The CREATE SCHEMA statement creates a schema with *EXCLUDE public authority and with CRTAUT also set to *EXCLUDE. All other Create statements, except CREATE FUNCTION and CREATE PROCEDURE, also create objects with *EXCLUDE public authority, regardless of the schema's CRTAUT value. When a CREATE FUNCTION or CREATE PROCEDURE statement creates a new program or service program, the object's public authority is determined by the schema's CRTAUT value.

## SQL Privileges

In SQL terminology, a **privilege** is the authorization to use one of the following objects:

- Table or view
- Distinct type
- Stored procedure or user-defined function
- SQL package

If a user has the appropriate authority, the user can grant and revoke privileges using the SQL GRANT and REVOKE statements. Once a privilege is granted to a user profile object, that user profile has the corresponding authority that has been granted.

Table privileges correspond to operating system authorities. Figure 17-6 lists the privileges that can be granted to an SQL table and shows the corresponding authority that is granted to the database table. The WITH GRANT OPTION privilege is an optional clause on the SQL GRANT statement.

| SQL privilege | SQL statement privileges that are granted or revoked | Corresponding system authorities to table |
|---|---|---|
| All | All | *ObjAlter<br>*ObjMgt<br>*ObjOpr<br>*ObjRef<br>*Add<br>*Dlt<br>*Read<br>*Upd |
| Alter | Alter Table<br>Comment On<br>Label On | *ObjAlter |
| Delete | Delete | *ObjOpr<br>*Dlt |
| Index | Create Index | *ObjAlter |
| Insert | Insert | *ObjOpr<br>*Add |
| References | Add a foreign key constraint that references this table as parent | *ObjRef |
| Select | Select<br>Create View | *ObjOpr<br>*Read |
| Update | Update | *ObjOpr<br>*Upd |
| With Grant Option | Grant<br>Revoke<br>Alter Table<br>Comment On<br>Label On<br>Create Index<br>Add a foreign key constraint that references this table as parent | *ObjMgt |

FIGURE 17-6   SQL table privileges

View privileges correspond to operating system authorities to database logical and physical files. Figure 17-7 lists the privileges that can be granted to an SQL view and shows the corresponding authority granted to the database tables.

| SQL privilege | SQL statement privileges that are granted or revoked | Valid for views | Corresponding system authorities to logical file | Corresponding system authorities to referenced physical or logical files |
|---|---|---|---|---|
| All | All | All views | *ObjAlter<br>*ObjMgt<br>*ObjOpr<br>*ObjRef<br>*Add<br>*Dlt<br>*Read<br>*Upd | *Add<br>*Dlt<br>*Read<br>*Upd |
| Alter | Comment On<br>Label On | All views | *ObjAlter | None |
| Delete | Delete | If not read-only | *ObjOpr<br>*Dlt | *Dlt |
| Insert | Insert | If view is not read-only and allows inserts | *ObjOpr<br>*Add | *Add |
| References | — | Allowed, but not used for views | *ObjRef | None |
| Select | Select<br>Create View | All views | *ObjOpr<br>*Read | *Read |
| Update | Update | If not read-only | *ObjOpr<br>*Upd | *Upd |
| With Grant Option | Grant<br>Revoke<br>Comment On<br>Label On | All views | *ObjMgt | None |

**FIGURE 17-7** **SQL view privileges**

Distinct type privileges correspond to system authorities to an SQL user-defined type (*SQLUDT) object. Figure 17-8 lists the privileges that can be granted to a distinct type and shows the corresponding authority that is granted to the SQL user-defined type. The ALTER privilege permits the use of the SQL COMMENT ON statement, and the USAGE privilege lets the distinct type be used in table definitions, stored procedures, functions, and CREATE DISTINCT TYPE statements.

Stored procedure and user-defined function privileges correspond to system authorities to a program or service program object. Figure 17-9 lists the privileges that can be granted to an SQL procedure or function and shows the corresponding authority that is granted to the program or service program. The ALTER privilege permits use of the SQL COMMENT ON statement, and the EXECUTE privilege lets the procedure or function be invoked.

| SQL privilege | Corresponding system authorities to SQL user-defined type |
|---|---|
| All | *ObjAlter<br>*ObjOpr<br>*ObjMgt<br>*Execute |
| Alter | *ObjAlter |
| Usage | *ObjOpr<br>*Execute |
| With Grant Option | *ObjMgt |

**FIGURE 17-8** SQL distinct type privileges

| SQL privilege | Corresponding system authorities to program or service program |
|---|---|
| All | *ObjAlter<br>*ObjOpr<br>*ObjMgt<br>*Execute |
| Alter | *ObjAlter |
| Execute | *ObjOpr<br>*Execute |
| With Grant Option | *ObjMgt |

**FIGURE 17-9** SQL stored procedure and user-defined function privileges

Package privileges correspond to system authorities to an SQL package (*SQLPKG) object. Figure 17-10 lists the privileges that can be granted to an SQL package and shows the corresponding authority granted to the object. The ALTER privilege allows the SQL COMMENT ON and LABEL ON statements to be used, and the EXECUTE privilege lets statements be executed in the package.

| SQL privilege | Corresponding system authorities to SQL package |
|---|---|
| All | *ObjAlter<br>*ObjOpr<br>*ObjMgt<br>*Execute |
| Alter | *ObjAlter |
| Execute | *ObjOpr<br>*Execute |
| With Grant Option | *ObjMgt |

**FIGURE 17-10** SQL package privileges

## ACCESSING THE MAIN DATABASE OBJECTS

Next, we examine how the operating system authorities and the corresponding SQL privileges control user access to important database objects, including schemas, tables, views, distinct types, stored procedures, functions, packages, programs, and service programs.

### SCHEMAS

To access any object, a user profile must have *EXECUTE authority to the schema that contains the object. Without this authority, the user profile cannot do *anything* with objects that exist in the schema. The actual operations allowed on an object are, of course, also limited by the user profile's authorities for the specific object. To create most types of objects, a user profile must have at least *ADD authority to the schema that will contain the object. All of the SQL Create statements require both *EXECUTE and *ADD authority to the containing schema, and the CREATE ALIAS and CREATE DISTINCT TYPE statements also require *READ authority to the schema.

The CREATE SCHEMA statement creates a schema with either *EXCLUDE public authority (with SQL naming) or with the public authority specified by the QCRTAUT system value (with system naming). Generally, security can be increased by specifying *EXCLUDE for public authority to schemas. That way, only explicitly authorized users can access objects in the schema. Note that there is not an SQL statement to explicitly specify privileges for a schema; instead, CL commands must be used to grant and revoke authorities to the corresponding schema object.

To enable a user to access one or more of the objects in a schema, the person's user profile should normally be granted *USE authority, which includes the *EXECUTE and *READ authorities, to the schema. If any authorized application creates temporary or permanent objects in the schema, the user profile should also be granted *ADD authority, which is *not* included in *USE authority, to the schema.

### TABLES AND VIEWS

Application programs can access the data in a table either directly by accessing the table or indirectly by opening a view defined over the table. To access data in a table, a user profile must have SELECT, INSERT, UPDATE, or DELETE privileges to the table.

To access data in a table by way of a view, a user profile must have similar privileges (SELECT, INSERT, UPDATE, or DELETE) to the view. Notice from Figure 17-7 how each view privilege corresponds to system authorities both to the view's logical file and to the physical file(s) for the based-on table(s). For example, to read and update rows through a view, the user profile must have *OBJOPR, *READ, and *UPD authorities to the logical file and *READ and *UPD authorities to the physical file.

This dual check on data rights provides the basis for a column-level approach to database access. With a view, access can be limited to a subset of rows and columns. If a user profile is granted appropriate privileges to the view, but not to the underlying table, the user profile is limited to accessing only those columns and rows accessible through the view.

## DISTINCT TYPES

To use a distinct type in a CREATE TABLE statement's column definition or in other SQL statements, a user profile must have the USAGE privilege for the data type.

## STORED PROCEDURES, USER-DEFINED FUNCTIONS, AND PACKAGES

To invoke a stored procedure or user-defined function, or to execute statements in an SQL package, a user profile must have the EXECUTE privilege for the procedure, function, or package. The EXECUTE privilege corresponds to the *OBJOPR and *EXECUTE authorities to the corresponding program, service program, or SQL package object.

## PROGRAMS AND SERVICE PROGRAMS

Most applications also include system programs and service programs that are not SQL stored procedures or functions. To call a program or service program, the user profile requires *OBJOPR and *EXECUTE authorities to the object. These authorities must be granted or revoked with a CL command; even though SQL stored procedures are program objects and user-defined functions are system service programs, the SQL GRANT and REVOKE statements can reference only stored procedures and user-defined functions, not all programs and service programs.

Programs and service programs, including SQL stored procedures and functions, can provide an important means of controlling database access, so care must be taken to grant authority to these objects only to those users who should be allowed to run them.

## COLUMN-LEVEL PRIVILEGES

The authorities and privileges discussed thus far apply to the entire object. In the case of tables and views, this means that if a user profile has the UPDATE privilege to a table, for example, that user profile can update any column in any row in the table. For tables and views, SQL also supports control with column-level privileges.

When a user profile has column-level UPDATE privileges to a table or view, the user can modify only those specific columns for which the user profile has privileges. In other words, having column-level UPDATE privileges is more limited than having the UPDATE privilege to the entire table or view. The only way to grant or revoke column-level privileges is with the SQL GRANT and REVOKE statements; no comparable CL command exists. When a user profile has column-level REFERENCES privileges to a table, the user can specify the listed columns as the part of a parent key in a foreign key constraint. A column-level REFERENCES privilege can be granted for a view, but it is not used because foreign key constraints must reference a table, not a view.

## THE GRANT AND REVOKE STATEMENTS

The SQL GRANT statement grants privileges on database objects to user profiles or the public. The owner of an object, or a user who has been granted appropriate authority, can grant privileges on the object. There are several variations of the GRANT statement, depending on the type of object to which privileges are being granted. In general, all variations have the following form:

```
Grant privilege(s)
  On  object(s)
  To  user-profile(s)
  [With Grant Option]
```

Figures 17-5 through 17-9 provide the valid privileges for each type of object. The general form of the REVOKE statement is similar:

```
Revoke privilege(s)
  On  object(s)
  From user-profile(s)
```

## GRANTING TABLE AND VIEW PRIVILEGES

Suppose a CUSTOMERS table has been created, and the user profile SmithBL needs to be granted the ability to retrieve rows from this table. A statement such as the following could be entered:

```
Grant Select
  On  Customer
  To  SmithBL
```

The GRANT statement lists the privilege(s) being granted or specifies the ALL keyword, then specifies the ON keyword followed by one or more table and/or view names, and then specifies the TO keyword followed by one or more user profile names or the PUBLIC keyword. Here is a more comprehensive example:

```
Grant Select,
      Insert
  On  customers,
      customer_credit
  To  SmithBL,
      JonesRK
```

The ALL keyword can be used instead of a list of privileges, and the implicit list contains those privileges that the user profile executing the statement is authorized to grant and that are relevant to the type of SQL object; the INDEX privilege, for example, applies to base tables but not to views.

The PUBLIC keyword is an alternative to a user profile name; if used, it refers to the privileges that are available to all user profiles that have no other explicit authority, granted to their user profile by name, to the table or view.

The GRANT statement can optionally specify WITH GRANT OPTION after the list of user profiles. This clause permits the user profiles or PUBLIC listed on the GRANT statement to themselves grant the same privileges on the listed tables and views, as well as to perform operations allowed with the ALTER and REFERENCES privileges:

```
Grant Select
  On  customers
  To  SmithBL
  With Grant Option
```

For tables and views, column-level UPDATE and REFERENCES privileges can be granted by including a list of columns after the respective keyword. The following statement grants privileges to let the SmithBL user profile read all columns from the CUSTOMERS table but update only the CustStatus and CustCreditLimit columns:

```
Grant Select,
      Update( CustStatus,
              CustCreditLimit )
  On  Customer
  To  SmithBL
```

To limit which of a parent table's columns can be referenced in a foreign key constraint, a GRANT statement such as the following can be used:

```
Grant References( CustNo )
  On  customers
  To  SmithBL
```

Several additional considerations apply when granting privileges to views. The INSERT, UPDATE, and DELETE privileges can be granted only to views that allow those operations. A view can reference other views as well as tables. The rightmost column in Figure 17-7 shows the authorities that are granted to all the directly or indirectly referenced tables and views. Note, however, that the *ADD, *UPD, and *DLT authorities are granted only to objects that are not referenced by the view definition's WHERE clause. Only the *READ authority is granted to objects referenced by the WHERE clause.

Also, authorities are not granted to a referenced object if the object provides adequate public authority or if the user profile has adequate authority from an indirect source, such as by belonging to a group profile. This means, for example, that if the table referenced by a view already has *USE public authority, granting a user profile the SELECT privilege on the view will not grant explicit *READ authority to the referenced table.

## REVOKING TABLE AND VIEW PRIVILEGES

To revoke privileges, a REVOKE statement with a structure similar to the GRANT statement is used:

```
Revoke Select,
       Insert
  On   customers,
       CustCrd
  From SmithBL,
       JonesRK
```

When privileges to a table or view are revoked, the corresponding operating system authorities, as shown in Figures 17-5 and 17-6, are revoked from the underlying database table. However, when SELECT, INSERT, UPDATE, or DELETE privileges are revoked, the *OBJOPR authority to the database table is not revoked unless the user no longer has any data authorities (i.e., *READ, *ADD, *UPD, *DLT) to the object. A REVOKE statement does not revoke any privileges on tables and views referenced by a view because the user profile might be intended to have these authorities regardless of the authorities to the referencing view.

Granting a user profile the same privilege multiple times, whether done by the same user or different users, enables just one instance of the privilege. Thus, when a privilege is revoked, the privilege is removed completely, no matter how many times it has previously been granted.

If a user profile has previously been granted the WITH GRANT OPTION privilege for an object, the user profile has the system *OBJMGT authority. The only way in SQL to revoke the *OBJMGT authority is to use a REVOKE ALL statement. Of course, the RVKOBJAUT and EDTOBJAUT commands can always be used to manage authorities directly.

## GRANTING AND REVOKING PRIVILEGES ON OTHER DATABASE OBJECTS

To grant and revoke privileges to a distinct type, statements such as the following are used:

```
Grant Usage
  On   Distinct Type Dollar
  To   SmithBL

Revoke Usage
  On   Distinct Type Dollar
  From SmithBL
```

Figure 17-8 lists the possible privileges that can be granted and revoked on a distinct data type.

The GRANT and REVOKE statements for stored procedures and user-defined functions can have several forms. One of the following keywords is specified before the name of the object:

- FUNCTION
- PROCEDURE
- SPECIFIC FUNCTION
- SPECIFIC PROCEDURE

Following either the FUNCTION or the PROCEDURE keyword, use the same object name that was specified after the CREATE PROCEDURE or CREATE FUNCTION keywords when the object was created. This name can optionally be qualified by the schema that contains the function. The following example shows how the SmithBL user profile might be granted the privilege to invoke the EffectiveRate function.

```
Grant Execute
  On  Function EffectiveRate
  To  SmithBL
```

The same name can be used for different functions as long as the functions have different numbers or types of parameters. If multiple functions exist with the same name, a particular function can be identified by specifying a list of the target function's parameter types following its name:

```
Grant Execute
  On  Function EffectiveRate ( Int, Int )
  To  SmithBL
```

A final way to identify a function is to use the SPECIFIC FUNCTION keywords and specify the function's specific name. This name is typically a unique name specified on the SPECIFIC NAME clause of the CREATE FUNCTION statement:

```
Grant Execute
  On  Specific Function EffectiveRate2
  To  SmithBL
```

Note that a list of parameter types is never specified after a function's specific name.

The REVOKE statement for user-defined functions allows similar alternative ways to specify which function is the target. The GRANT and REVOKE statements for stored procedures are the same as for functions, except for the use of the PROCEDURE keyword instead of FUNCTION.

An SQL package is an object that lets an application on one system execute SQL statements on another system. To grant privileges to a package, use a statement such as this one:

```
Grant Execute
  On  Package GetItem
  To  SmithBL
```

The package must be on the same system as the job in which the GRANT statement is executed. The REVOKE statement follows the same pattern.

## GROUP PROFILES

**Group profiles** are a system feature that provides a way to identify an individual user profile as a member of one or more groups. Authority can then be granted to the group rather than to the individual user profiles. This approach can greatly simplify the administration of authority. SQL itself has no explicit statements to create group profiles or to assign individual, or non-group, user profiles to group profiles, but the GRANT and REVOKE statements can specify group profiles in the TO and FROM clauses.

To establish a group, the security officer or person with appropriate authority creates a user profile that serves as the group profile. This user profile should be created with no password, specifying the PASSWORD(*NONE) parameter on the CRTUSRPRF command, so no individual actually uses the profile to sign on.

To assign an individual user profile to a group, the group profile name is specified for the GRPPRF (Group profile) or SUPGRPPRF (Supplemental group profiles) parameter on the CRTUSRPRF or CHGUSRPRF command for the individual user profile. A user profile implicitly becomes a group profile when it is referenced as a group profile for any other user profile. A group profile cannot itself be a member of another group; that is, nothing other than GRPPRF(*NONE) and SUPGRPPRF(*NONE)—in other words, the defaults—can be specified for a group profile.

An individual user profile can be a member of up to 16 group profiles. The first group profile must be specified on the GRPPRF parameter, and up to 15 additional group profiles can be specified on the SUPGRPPRF parameter.

The following command assigns Betty L. Smith to the `GrpSales` and `GrpAccount` group profiles:

```
ChgUsrPrf UsrPrf( SmithBL )
          GrpPrf( GrpSales )
          SupGrpPrf( GrpAccount )
```

When the operating system checks for a user profile's authority to an object and the individual user profile has no explicit authority, including not having *EXCLUDE authority, to the object, it then checks the user profile's group profile(s), if any, to see whether group profiles provide any authorities to the object. If they do and the combination of authorities granted to the group profile(s) is adequate, the operating system permits the operation. If there are no group profiles or the group profile(s) provide no authorities to the object, the operating system next checks the object's public authority. If the group profile(s) have any authorities, including *EXCLUDE, to the object but the combination of authorities is not adequate for the operation, the operating system skips the check for public authority and continues with the check for program adopted authority, discussed later.

There are a couple of important aspects to the way the operating system checks authority. First, notice that the search for sufficient authorities stops with the individual user profile if the profile has any authority to the object. This means the *EXCLUDE authority or any other specific authority can be used to "short circuit" the authority an individual user profile derives from its group profiles and public authority because the operating system will not check either group profile authority or public authority if the individual user profile has any authority to the object. A similar principle applies for group profile authorities to an object; if there are any, the operating system does not check the object's public authority.

This approach means that the operating system does *not* add together the individual, group, and public authorities. Consider the following authorities:

- The `SmithBL` individual user profile has *OBJOPR authority to the CUSTOMERS table.
- The `GrpSales` group profile has *UPD authority to the CUSTOMERS table.
- The CUSTOMERS table has *READ public authority.

Even if the `GrpSales` profile is a group profile for `SmithBL`, a job running under `SmithBL` would not be able to open the CUSTOMERS table for read and update or any other operations. What is required is one of the following conditions:

- The SmithBL user profile has *OBJOPR, *READ, and *UPD authorities to the CUSTOMERS table.
- The SmithBL user profile has no authorities, not even *EXCLUDE, to the CUSTOMERS table, and the GrpSales user profile has *OBJOPR, *READ, and *UPD authorities to the CUSTOMERS table.
- Neither the SmithBL nor the GrpSales user profile has any authorities to the CUSTOMERS table, and the CUSTOMERS table has *OBJOPR, *READ, and *UPD public authorities.

The operating system does add together the group profile authorities when an individual user profile has more than one group profile with some authority to the target object. But this combination of authorities applies only for the group profile step of the authority check.

The CHGOBJPGP (Change Object Primary Group) command can be used to set or change an object's **primary group**. The following command sets the CUSTOMERS table's primary group profile to GrpSales:

```
ChgObjPgp Obj( AppDta/customers )
         ObjType( *File )
         NewPgp( GrpSales )
```

This command does not change the GrpSales group profile's or any other profile's authority to the CUSTOMERS table. All it does is store some information about the GrpSales profile's authority to the CUSTOMERS table in the table object itself, thus speeding up the operating system's authority checking in some cases. As a rule of thumb, performance may improve if group profiles are set up so that individual user profiles that frequently access an object have as their first group profile, as specified on the CRTUSRPRF command's GRPPRF parameter, a group profile that has also been made the primary group for the frequently accessed object. Obviously, there may be objects that are frequently accessed by user profiles that belong to different groups, and only one of the group profiles can be designated as an object's primary group.

## Authorization Lists

Group profiles provide a way to organize groups of individual user profiles so authorities can be granted to a single group profile and thus indirectly can be made available for the individual user profiles that belong to the group. **Authorization lists** provide a somewhat comparable feature that lets sets of objects for which identical authorities are granted be organized. SQL provides no statements to work with authorization lists, but the system authorization list commands can be used to work with the system objects, such as database tables, that are created by SQL statements.

An authorization list is a system object that represents a list of objects. If other objects are associated with an authorization list object, authority is indirectly granted to the objects associated with the authorization list when public authority or authority for a user profile is granted to the authorization list. To create an authorization list, use a CRTAUTL (Create Authorization List) command such as the following:

```
CrtAutL AutL( SalesObj )
        Aut( *Exclude )
        Text( 'Sales objects' )
```

This command creates the SalesObj authorization list and does not provide any public authority to the authorization list or the objects subsequently associated with it. All authorization lists are created in the QSYS library, so a qualified name cannot be specified on the AUTL parameter of any command.

To take advantage of an authorization list, one associates two lists with the authorization list:

- A list of objects that are in the scope of the authorization list
- An implicit list of individual user profiles and/or group profiles that are authorized to the authorization list

An object is put under the scope of an authorization list with a command such as this one:

```
GrtObjAut Obj( AppDta/Sale )
          ObjType( *File )
          AutL( SalesObj )
```

As an alternative, the EDTOBJAUT command can be used to edit a display of the authorities that exist for an object. This display contains an entry field for the object's associated authorization list, if any. An object can be associated with only one authorization list at a time, and authorization lists cannot be nested; in other words, OBJTYPE(*AUTL) cannot be specified along with the AUTL parameter on the GRTOBJAUT command.

To grant a user profile authority to an authorization list, and hence to the associated objects, a GRTOBJAUT command such as the following can be used:

```
GrtObjAut Obj( SalesObj )
          ObjType( *AutL )
          User( SmithBL )
          Aut( *Use )
```

The operating system has an ADDAUTLE (Add Authorization List Entry) command to slightly simplify granting a user profile authority to an authorization list. The next example is equivalent to the preceding GRTOBJAUT command:

```
AddAutLE AutL( SalesObj )
          User( SmithBL )
          Aut( *Use )
```

When a user profile is granted authority to an authorization list, the action effectively provides the specified authorities to the user profile for all the objects associated with the authorization list. Notice that each user profile has its own set of authorities, which are the same for all objects associated with the authorization list. Any of the values listed in Figures 17-3 and 17-4 can be specified for the AUT parameter on a GRTOBJAUT or ADDAUTLE command. A user profile can be granted authority to more than one authorization list.

If an object is associated with an authorization list, the operating system performs another round of authority checks when an operation is attempted. In simple terms, the operating system:

1. Checks the individual user profile's authority to the target object.
2. Checks the individual user profile's authority to the target object's associated authorization list object.
3. Checks the group profile, if any, authority to the target object or to the target object's associated authorization list object. If multiple group profiles exist, their authorities are added together for the test.

    Each group profile is first checked for authority to the target object. If the group has any authorities, including *EXCLUDE, to the target object, the group contributes these authorities to the combined total for all groups. If the group has no authority to the target object, the system checks the group's authority to the target object's associated authorization list object and, if any authorities exist, adds them to the combined total for all groups. Note that each group contributes either its authorities to the object or its authorities to the authorization list, but not both.

4.   Checks the public authority either for the target object or for the target object's associated authorization list object.

At the completion of each of these steps, if the operating system finds any authority to the target object, either directly or to its associated authorization list, it stops checking.

As step 4 implies, an object's public authority can also be controlled with an authorization list. To do this, the name of the authorization list is used as the value for the AUT parameter on the CRTxxx command, like this:

```
CrtPf File( AppDta/Sale )
      SrcFile( AppSrc/QDdsSrc )
      Aut( SalesObj )
```

After this command is executed, the public authority to the SALE table is defined by the SalesObj authorization list's public authority, which may be *EXCLUDE or any of the authorities in Figures 17-3 and 17-4.

Authorization lists can reduce the number of specific authorities that need to be granted to individual and group profiles. But because authorization lists add steps to the operating system authority checking, they may adversely affect performance. As a rule of thumb, if there are several objects for which the same set of authorities is frequently granted, consider an authorization list. It is not uncommon to have sets of application programs and tables for which *USE authority is frequently granted en masse (and public authority is *EXCLUDE). Such sets are good candidates for authorization lists.

## PROGRAM ADOPTED AUTHORITY

With all the different ways to specify authority, one might think every possible situation could be covered. In fact, there are many types of database-access rules that cannot be directly specified with the methods described so far. The problem stems from the broad meaning of the four kinds of data authorities: *READ, *ADD, *UPD, and *DLT. If a user profile has *OBJOPR and *UPD authorities to a table, any type of update to any column in any row is allowed. This level of access is not usually desirable. Instead, most applications are intended to let a user make only valid changes to some columns, often for only a subset of the rows in the table.

As discussed earlier, views can be used to limit access to a subset of a table's rows and columns. And column-level UPDATE privileges can be used to control update capabilities on a column-by-column basis. These column-level approaches to access are somewhat limited, however. The biggest problem is that they provide no way to control the *values* that are put in columns that can be updated. Thus, a payroll clerk authorized to update the salary column in EMPLOYEES rows can put in any value for the salary. Another problem is that the available row selection criteria on view definitions cannot express all application constraints.

Ultimately, application program logic must be used to control some access and to limit updates to valid values. The operating system provides an excellent tool for this purpose: **program adopted authority**.

Normally, when a program is created, any operations it performs, such as updating rows in a table, require the job's user profile to have adequate authority, either directly or via a group profile, public authority, or authorization list. However, a program can optionally be created that can perform any operation that the program's owner has authority to perform, in addition to operations that the job's user profile has authority to perform. Service program and SQL package objects can also adopt authority, and because SQL stored procedures and user-defined functions are actually system programs and service programs, these SQL objects can also adopt authority.

Let us look at a simple example. Suppose there is a user profile, created expressly for this purpose, named PrfChgEmp (profile — change employee). This user profile is made the owner of the ChgEmpSal (change employee salary) program; we will look at how this is done in a moment. The PrfChgEmp user profile is also granted *CHANGE authority to the EMPLOYEES table. Last, the ChgEmpSal program is designated as a program that adopts the authority of its owner when the program runs; again, we will look at how in a moment. With this arrangement, any user profile that has *EXECUTE authority to the ChgEmpSal program can run it. And, while that user profile is running the ChgEmpSal program, the program can perform any retrieval or update operations on the EMPLOYEES table, regardless of the authority of the user profile running the program.

What this setup lets us do is not grant individual user profiles full *CHANGE authority to the EMPLOYEES table. Instead, we can grant them *USE or no specific authority to the EMPLOYEES table and *EXECUTE authority to the ChgEmpSal program. Then, the only way they can update the EMPLOYEES table is through operations provided by the ChgEmpSal program, which, presumably, enforces the appropriate business rules for the application.

The user profiles that own programs that adopt authority do not represent end users, programmers, or security personnel. These user profiles should be created with names that reflect their purpose and with PASSWORD(*NONE) specified so no one can sign on with the user profile.

Using a command such as the following makes a special-purpose user profile the owner of a program:

```
ChgObjOwn Obj( AppExc/ChgEmpSal )
          ObjType( *Pgm )
          NewOwn( PrfChgEmp )
```

Then, the appropriate security person or application administrator changes the program so it adopts the authority of the program owner's user profile:

```
ChgPgm Pgm( AppExc/ChgEmpSal )
       UsrPrf( *Owner )
```

The PrfChgEmp special-purpose user profile can be granted authority, just like any other user profile:

```
GrtObjAut Obj( AppDta/customers )
          ObjType( *File )
          User( PrfChgEmp )
          Aut( *Change )
```

or, in SQL:

```
Grant Select,
      Update,
      Delete,
      Insert
  On  AppDta.customers
  To PrfChgEmp
```

With programs that adopt authority, a method is available to control access in precisely the way applications require.

Programs that adopt authority normally propagate their authority to programs they call. The operating system adds together all the adopted and propagated authority for programs in the job's program call stack when authority is checked. A program can be created with the USEADPAUT(*NO) parameter to prevent the program from inheriting any adopted authority from the program that calls it.

A user profile created to own a program that adopts authority should own only one program or a few programs that are closely related to the same application operations. The user profile should have the *minimum* authorities needed to perform the operations it implements. Do not use a user profile that owns all database tables and views as the owner of programs that adopt authority. This practice provides too much authority for a job while the program is executing. Although a full discussion of security risks and program adopted authority is beyond the scope of this chapter, it is important to ensure that if a user is able to circumvent constraints that are part of the program, the scope of the harm that the user can do is as limited as possible.

## DATABASE SECURITY PRINCIPLES AND GUIDELINES

Security is an important and extensive topic. The following points provide some principles and guidelines that can be used to help establish a solid foundation for database security:

- Security is a business function of protecting an organization's resources and operations; computer systems security should be designed within the context of the organization's overall security plan.
- Security rules cover different levels of threat. The more vital a security policy is to the organization's well-being, the more thoroughly it must enforce the policy.
- Assume that people who will intentionally try to breach security understand the technical aspects of the system as well as you do. Do not rely on an attacker's ignorance of the system to protect the system. What they should not know are the passwords.
- If the implementation of a security mechanism fails, the error should result in unintended restrictions on access rather than unintended additional access.
- Set the system's QSECURITY system value to 30 or higher. This setting enforces password protection and resource-level security. Level 40 is recommended and provides all the security enforcement of level 30 plus additional checks to see that various features of the operating system are not tampered with or used improperly to circumvent security.
- Assign a unique user profile and password to each individual who uses the system.
- Consider changing the CRTLIB command's CRTAUT parameter default to *EXCLUDE.
- Carefully consider how much public authority, if any, each database table and program should have.
- Use group profiles to organize user profiles into groups that can be granted identical authority for many objects.
- Use authorization lists to organize sets of objects for which identical authorities are frequently granted.
- Be aware of how the operating system's authority search works and the way granting any authority to an individual user profile short circuits

the search of group profile and public authorities. Avoid using this short-circuit technique unless it is necessary.

- Grant the minimum authority necessary for any operation. This principle applies for individual and group profiles, authorization lists entries, and adopted authority.

- Use program adopted authority to provide required authority under control of a program when you do not want to give the full capabilities of a specific authority, such as *UPD, to a user profile.

- For the user profile that owns a program that adopts authority, do not have a user profile that owns other application objects or that has more authority than the program needs for its operations.

- Have special-purpose user profiles, not programmer or end-user user profiles, own database objects.

- Be sure to consider remote PC and Web access to the system when setting up security and granting authorities.

## END-OF-CHAPTER

### CHAPTER SUMMARY

1. The operating system controls access to objects by checking the authority a user profile has to the target object.
2. A user profile is a system object with a name, password, and other attributes.
3. Each person that uses the system should have a unique user profile.
4. Each system object is owned by a user profile, and an object's owner normally has all authorities to the object.
5. SQL uses system authority to control access to SQL objects, including schemas, tables, views, distinct types, stored procedures, user-defined functions, and packages.
6. The two main categories of system authorities are:

   a. Special authorities
   b. Specific authorities

7. The *ALLOBJ special authority provides all access to all objects on the system and is usually assigned only to user profiles for people responsible for system-wide security.
8. The *SAVSYS special authority lets the user profile save and restore objects and is usually assigned to the user profiles for some members of the system operations staff.
9. Specific authorities are granted to a user profile or the public to provide various levels of access to a specific object.
10. Specific authorities are subdivided into object authorities, data authorities, and field authorities.
11. Object authorities control general use of the object, including basic access, changing object attributes, existence, and management operations, such as renaming. Data authorities control read, add, update, and delete operations on an object's contents, as well as the ability to find objects in a schema and to run a program. Field authorities control access to individual columns in a database table or view.
12. The GRTOBJAUT, RVKOBJAUT, and EDTOBJAUT commands can be used to grant and revoke specific authorities to system objects. SQL privileges correspond to system specific authorities.
13. An object's public authority governs access to the object when an individual user profile has no specific authorities to the object and the individual user profile's group profiles, if any, also have no specific authorities to the object.

14. The SQL GRANT and REVOKE statements:

    a.  Can be used to grant and revoke privileges to SQL objects, which results in the corresponding system authorities to the underlying system objects being granted or revoked.

    b.  Let column-level privileges be specified to update specific columns or to reference specific parent key columns in a foreign key constraint. Views can also be used as a means of limiting access to selected columns and/or a subset of rows in a table.

    c.  Grant and revoke one or more privileges to one or more specified user profiles to perform certain operations on one or more database objects.

    d.  The WITH GRANT OPTION clause can be used on a GRANT statement to let the specified user profile(s) also grant the same privileges to other user profiles.

15. To use an object in a schema, a user profile must have *EXECUTE authority to the schema.

16. To run a program or service program, a user profile must have *OBJOPR and *EXECUTE authorities to the program.

17. To access data in a database table, a user profile must have *OBJOPR authority and one or more of the *READ, *ADD, *UPD, and *DLT data authorities to the table. In SQL terms, the user profile must have the SELECT, UPDATE, DELETE, or INSERT privilege on a table or view to access the table or view data.

18. To use a distinct type requires the USE privilege.

19. To invoke a stored procedure or user-defined function or to execute statements in an SQL package, the user profile must have the EXECUTE privilege on the object.

20. Group profiles:

    a.  Provide a way to simplify authority management by organizing individual user profiles into groups and granting authority to the group profiles.

    b.  A user profile can have up to 16 group profiles.

    c.  Are just user profile objects referenced as the group profile by some individual, or non-group, user profile.

    d.  When an individual user profile has no authority to an object, the operating system checks the individual user profile's group profiles, if any, for sufficient authority. If the individual user profile has more than one group profile with any authority to the object, all of the group profiles' authorities are added together.

21. An authorization list object:

   a. Provides a way to organize objects for which the same set of system authorities is frequently granted.

   b. The `GRTOBJAUT` command, or the `AUT` parameter on a `CRTxxx` command, associates an object with an authorization list.

   c. All authorities granted to a user profile for an authorization list then apply to all objects that are associated with the authorization list.

22. Program adopted authority:

   a. Provides a way to control access under program logic, for example, to allow only certain types of updates to table.

   b. A program that has the `USRPRF(*OWNER)` attribute can perform any operation for which the user profile that owns the program has sufficient authority.

   c. A special-purpose user profile can be made the owner of a program that adopts authority and can be granted the required authorities to perform the program's functions. Subsequently, any user profile authorized to run the program can use it to perform the operations the program implements, regardless of the authority the job's user profile has for the target object.

   d. Special-purpose user profiles should be created to own application objects. One or more of these special-purpose user profiles can own tables and programs that do not adopt authority. Each program that adopts authority should be owned by a separate user profile that is not one of the user profiles that own other application objects. A user profile that owns a program that adopts authority should have no more than the necessary authorities to perform the operations the program implements.

## KEY TERMS

| | |
|---|---|
| authority | primary group |
| authorization ID | privilege |
| authorization list | program adopted authority |
| data authority | public authority |
| field authority | special authority |
| group profile | specific authority |
| object authority | user profile |

# INDEX

## A

access path, 75, 290, 294, 326
ADDAUTLE (Add Authorization List Entry)
    command, 465
ADDPFTRG (Add Physical File Trigger)
    command, 396–398
    ALWREPCHG (Allow repeated change)
      parameter, 398, 400
    RPLTRG (Replace trigger) parameter, 397
    TRGEVENT (Trigger event) parameter, 397,
      399
    TRGTIME (Trigger time) parameter, 397, 399
    TRGUPDCND (Trigger update condition)
      parameter, 398
%ADDR built-in function, 409
aggregate functions, 176–181, 187, 189, 190,
    191
AJAX, 336, 352
ALCOBJ (Allocate Object) command, 418, 419,
    421, 422, 425
    uses, 419
    WAIT parameter, 422
alias, 150–151, 171–172, 222–225, 239, 438
    column name, 222
    table name, 222, 284
ALIAS keyword, 311
ALL operator, 255–256, 257
ALLOCATE clause, 1-3–105
ALTER TABLE statement, 106, 119, 120, 197
ambiguous errors, 224–225
AND operator, 133, 160, 162, 324
ANY operator, 255, 256–257
apostrophe (single quote), 198, 392
application object, 72
arithmetic, 187
arithmetic operators, 154
array
    used for null indicator, 317
AS clause, 150, 151, 192, 223, 266, 274, 282
ASCII, 81
associative entity, 37–39
asterisk (*), 144, 240, 260, 262, 274
ATOMIC keyword, 385
attribute, 8, 15
    column, 116–117
    default value, 23
    derived, 23
    direct, 23
    documenting, 23–25
    entity, 19, 20–25

    multivalued, 38
    optional, 21–22
    representation in ERD, 21
    required/mandatory, 21
    time-dependent, 22
    volatile, 21
audit trail, 76
AUT parameter, 448, 449
authority, 443–450
    checks performed for an authorization list,
      465–466
    defined, 442
    public, 448–450
    special, 443–444
    specific, 443, 444–446
authorization ID, 441
authorization list, 463–466, 469
    guidelines, 466
AVG function, 177, 180, 187, 191, 264

## B

BASED keyword, 406
BEGIN/END delimiters, 377, 385
BETWEEN operator, 133, 162–163, 287
BIGINT data type, 84
blocking factor, 415
Boolean data type, 84, 89
    representing using a check constraint, 139–
      140
business model, 9
business rules/policies, 15, 70, 138

## C

CALL statement, 371, 377
candidate key, 25–27, 60, 61, 73–74, 117
carat (^) symbol, 79, 80
cardinality, 28–32
    categories, 28–29
    possible combinations, 29–30
    defined, 29
    many-to-many, 29
    one-to-many, 28, 29
    one-to-one, 28, 29
    rules, 29
    representation in ERD, 29
Cartesian product, 235
CASCADE option, 126–130, 211
cascading updates and deletes, 118
CASE function, 181–182